Relations between theatre and state were seldom more fraught in France than in the latter part of the eighteenth and during the nineteenth centuries. The unique attraction of the theatre, the sole source of mass entertainment over the period, accounts in part for this: successive governments could not ignore these large nightly gatherings, viewing them with distrust and attempting to control them by every kind of device, from the censorship of plays to the licensing of playhouses. In his illuminating study, F. W. J. Hemmings traces the vicissitudes of this perennial conflict, which began with the rise of the small independent boulevard theatres in the 1760s and eventually petered out in 1905 with the abandonment of censorship by the state. There are separate chapters on the provincial theatre and on amateur theatricals, while the French Revolution is given particularly detailed attention. Using a wide range of contemporary source material, Hemmings has produced a highly readable and absorbing account of this protracted campaign for the freedom of the stage. This work, complementing his earlier book, *The theatre industry in nineteenth-century France*, will be of interest to students of theatre history, French studies and European culture in general.

THEATRE AND STATE IN FRANCE, 1760–1905

THEATRE AND STATE IN FRANCE, 1760–1905

F. W. J. HEMMINGS

Emeritus Professor of French Literature, University of Leicester

CAMBRIDGE
UNIVERSITY PRESS

Published by the Press Syndicate of the University of Cambridge
The Pitt Building, Trumpington Street, Cambridge, CB2 1RP
40 West 20th Street, New York, NY 10011–4211, USA
10 Stamford Road, Oakleigh, Melbourne 3166, Australia

First published 1994

A catalogue record for this book is available from the British Library

Library of Congress cataloguing in publication data

Hemmings, F. W. J. (Frederic William John), 1920–
Theater and state in France, 1760–1905 / F. W. J. Hemmings.
p.   cm.
Includes bibliographical references and index.
ISBN 0 521 45088 8
1. Theater and state – France. 2. Theater – Censorship – France.
3. Theater – France – History – 19th century. 4. Theater – France –
History – 18th century. I. Title.
PN2055.F7H46   1994
792'.0944 – dc20   93–4418   CIP

ISBN 0 521 45088 8 hardback

CE

Contents

Chronology   *page* viii

Introduction   1

1 The royal theatres of the *ancien régime*   6

2 The rise of the commercial theatre   25

3 Dramatic censorship down to its abolition   44

4 The liberation of the theatres   55

5 The royal theatres under the Revolution   64

6 The theatre in the service of the Republic   92

7 Re-establishment of the state theatres   101

8 Curbs on the commercial sector   113

9 Politics and the pit   123

10 The theatre in the provinces   137

11 The licensing system, 1814–1864   160

12 The state-supported theatres in the nineteenth century   176

13 The theatre in crisis: competition from the *café-concert*   193

14 Dramatic censorship in the nineteenth century   204

15 The private sector   226

Notes   244
Bibliography   260
Guide to further reading   271
Index   274

Chronology

1761   (7 September) Comédie-Française granted letters patent.

1762   The fairground Opéra-Comique fuses with the Comédie-Italienne.

1764   Having earlier rented a booth on the Boulevard du Temple, Nicolet builds his own theatre there to house his company, Les Grands Danseurs du Roi

1769   Audinot opens the Ambigu-Comique on the Boulevard du Temple.

1774   Louis XV dies and is succeeded by Louis XVI.

1776   Inauguration of the Théâtre des Arts, Rouen.

1779   Variétés-Amusantes opens on the Boulevard du Temple.
(25 December) Comédie-Italienne authorized to abandon its repertory of plays in Italian.

1780   Comédie-Italienne granted letters patent.
Inauguration of the Grand-Théâtre, Bordeaux.

1781   Opening of the Porte-Saint-Martin, initially to house the Paris Opera.

1782   Opening of new building (on the site of the future Odéon) for the Comédie-Française.

1783   Comédie-Italienne move into their new theatre (the Salle Favart).

1784   Opera acquires control of all licences for minor theatres.
Petits-Beaujolais inaugurated in Palais-Royal gardens (closed 1790).
First performance of Beaumarchais's *Mariage de Figaro*.

1785   Variétés-Palais-Royal (renamed Théâtre de la République under the Revolution) gives its opening performance.

1786   Temporarily dispossessed, Audinot builds a new theatre, with the same name (the Ambigu-Comique) as the old one.

1787   (February) Opening of the Assembly of Notables.
Inauguration of Grand-Théâtre, Marseilles.

1788   Inauguration of Grand-Théâtre, Nantes.
Authorization given for opening of a fourth 'royal theatre', originally to be called the Théâtre de Monsieur, later known as the Théâtre Feydeau (inaugurated 1790).

1789   Summoning of Estates General, resulting in establishment of Constituent Assembly. The Bastille is stormed (14 July). Declaration of the Rights of Man (18 August).
M. J. Chénier, *Charles IX*, at the Théâtre-Français.
Théâtre-Français renamed Théâtre de la Nation.

1790   Mlle Montansier opens her theatre in the Palais-Royal.

1791   Decree of 13 January abolishing all restrictive licences for new theatres, all monopoly rights on repertoire, and establishing authors' copyright on plays. By clause 6, state censorship is abolished.
An important fraction of the Comédie-Française, led by Talma, leaves the company and joins that of the Théâtre de la Rue Richelieu (the subsequent Théâtre de la République).
(June) Arrest of royal family at Varennes.

1792   (10 August) Legislative Assembly assumes the powers of the monarchy; royal family imprisoned.
(20 September) Convention replaces Legislative Assembly.
(22 September) Proclamation of Republic.

1793   (21 January) Execution of Louis XVI.
Overthrow of Girondins (2 June), leading to start of Terror.
Closure of the Théâtre de la Nation by the Committee of Public Safety and arrest and imprisonment of most of the company (3–4 September)

1794   Censorship reintroduced by the Convention (*arrêté* of 14 May).
(27 July) Arrest and execution of Robespierre signals end of the Terror. Members of the Comédie-Française still imprisoned are released, but have no theatre to house them and accordingly disperse.

1795   Administrative power passes to the Directory.

1799   Bonaparte overthrows the Directory, replacing it by a
        Consulate with himself First Consul.
        The Comédie-Française regroups, using henceforth the
        theatre in the Rue Richelieu (formerly the Théâtre de la
        République), their previous building having burned
        down.
1802   Napoleon grants the Comédie-Française an annual sub-
        vention; state subsidies also allocated to the Opera and the
        Opéra-Comique.
        Peace of Amiens between France and Britain, lasting till
        May 1803.
1804   (2 December) Napoleon crowned Emperor.
1805   Napoleon abandons preparations to invade England but
        defeats combined Russian and Austrian armies at Austerlitz.
1806   By an imperial decree of 8 June, no theatre to be estab-
        lished in future without government authorization; the
        repertorial monopoly of the three state-supported theatres,
        ended by the decree of 13 January 1791, is reasserted.
1807   By the decree of 29 July, the number of theatres in Paris
        permitted to remain open is reduced to eight.
1808   (15 June) Odéon opened, as a fourth state-supported
        theatre, under the name Théâtre de l'Impératrice.
1810   Having divorced Joséphine, Napoleon marries (11 Feb-
        ruary) Marie-Louise of Austria.
1812   Closure of the Porte-Saint-Martin, which had reopened as
        the Jeux Gymniques in 1810.
        In June, Napoleon launches the Grande-Armée against
        Russia; 15 October, he signs the Moscow Decree, fixing the
        organization of the Comédie-Française.
1814   (30–31 March) Allies enter Paris. Napoleon abdicates and
        is banished to Elba. Louis XVIII restored to the throne.
        (26 December) Reopening of the Porte-Saint-Martin.
1815   Napoleon lands in France, retakes Paris, but is finally
        defeated at Waterloo and banished to St Helena.
1816   By an *ordonnance royale* of 14 December, Napoleon's earlier
        dispositions regarding the state-supported theatres are con-
        firmed with minor modifications.
        Permission given for the Funambules to open on the Boule-
        vard du Temple.
1819   First season of the Théâtre des Italiens (les Bouffes).

1820	Poirson obtains licence to open the Gymnase-Dramatique in Paris.
1821	Opening of the (short-lived) Théâtre du Panorama.
1822	Opening of the Théâtre de Belleville, first of a chain of theatres in the suburbs of Paris.
	(16 September) Death of Louis XVIII, succeeded by Charles X.
1824	(8 December) Decree on the theatres, urging municipalities in the provinces to subsidize local theatres.
1827	(1 March) Inaugural evening of the Théâtre des Nouveautés (closed 27 December 1831).
1829	(10 February) First performance of Dumas, *Henri III et sa cour*, at the Théâtre-Français.
1830	(25 February) First performance of Hugo, *Hernani*, at the Théâtre-Français.
	As result of July revolution, Charles X abdicates and is succeeded by Louis-Philippe. Suspension of the state censorship of plays.
1832	First outbreak of cholera in Paris empties the theatres.
1835	(28 July) Attempt on Louis-Philippe's life results in repressive measures (the September laws), one of which was the reimposition of dramatic censorship.
1847	Inauguration of Théâtre-Historique.
1848	February revolution in Paris: Louis-Philippe abdicates, a provisional government headed by Lamartine takes over.
	(6 March) Rescinding of September laws of 1835 incidentally abolishes dramatic censorship; but licensing system for theatres continues.
	(23 June–15 July) All Paris theatres close as fighting breaks out in working-class districts, but are subsequently compensated by the state for loss of business,
	(10 December) Louis-Napoleon elected president of the new republic.
1849	Arsène Houssaye imposed as government administrator on the Comédie-Française.
	Council of State circularizes playwrights as to whether all controls on theatrical repertoires should be lifted.
1850	(30 July) Dramatic censorship re-established.
1851	(2 December) Louis-Napoleon carries out *coup d'état* to change the constitution. Hugo and others go into exile.

1852   Dumas *fils*'s *La Dame aux camélias* has its first triumphant
        run at the Vaudeville.
        (2 December) Napoleon III proclaimed Emperor.

1862   Demolition of the theatres along the Boulevard du Temple
        as part of Haussmann's plans to modernize Paris.
        Erection of the Châtelet and the Théâtre-Lyrique (later
        the Théâtre Sarah-Bernhardt).

1864   (6 January) The so-called 'freedom of the theatres' is
        established by decree. The licensing system is abolished;
        there are to be no limits on the number of theatres oper-
        ating; any individual may open one and produce what
        plays he wishes – but the state retains the right to examine,
        modify or forbid the showing of any play.

1867   Record numbers of theatre-goers attracted to Paris by the
        World Exhibition that year.

1869   (May) Opening of the Folies-Bergère.

1870   (19 July) France declares war on Prussia. After French
        defeat at Sedan (1 September) Napoleon III abdicates and
        a republic is proclaimed in France (4 September).
        (19 September) Siege of Paris begins. Nearly all theatres
        close down, many being used as casualty stations.

1871   (28 January) Paris capitulates and armistice with
        Germany is signed.
        (26 March–28 May) Rule of Commune.
        Comédie-Française gives series of performances in London
        (1 May–8 July).

1879   Second visit of Comédie-Française to London, playing at
        the Gaiety; company includes Sarah Bernhardt, Sophie
        Croizette, Coquelin and Mounet-Sully.

1885   (29 October) Violent attack by Zola in *Le Figaro* on the
        whole principle of dramatic censorship, in connection with
        difficulties made over a stage adaptation of *Germinal*.

1887   (30 March) Antoine opens the Théâtre-Libre.
        A disastrous fire at the Opéra-Comique, causing the deaths
        of several hundreds of spectators, impels the government to
        impose better safety regulations at all theatres and hastens
        the replacement of gas by electric lighting.

1891   Parliamentary commission of inquiry into the working of
        the censorship: its recommendations not translated into
        law.

1894   (April) Antoine abandons directorship of Théâtre-Libre.
1905   After a long campaign inside and outside parliament, the
        Chamber finally refuses to vote the money necessary to pay
        the censors' salaries, and the censorship bureau is accord-
        ingly disbanded.

Introduction

Over the long period of time covered in this survey, the theatre represented for the French, to a greater degree probably than for any other nation, a unique focus of collective interest. Down to the end of the nineteenth century no other form of entertainment, engaging the attention of every class of people throughout the length and breadth of the land, had arisen to challenge its supremacy. The one and only purveyor of excitement, amusement and pathos that the mass of the population knew, the theatre was also the one and only escape from their usually laborious and lacklustre existence. Pierre Giffard, in the introductory chapter of an account published in 1888 of the social impact of the theatre in his day, reckoned that 500,000 Parisians attended playhouses once a week, while those who went once a month numbered between a million and 1,200,000. In other words, he concluded, 'the population of Paris lives at the theatre, of the theatre, and by the theatre'. And those domiciled in provincial towns were just as stagestruck, supporting their local theatre as well as travelling up to the capital in ever-increasing numbers to satisfy their craving for the glitter of the footlights and the excitement of a 'first night'.

Now the various governments on whom devolved the task of administering the country over this period could not have remained indifferent to the phenomenon. The theatre impinged on the national life at every level, from the highest to the lowest, and those who steered the ship of state could not afford to neglect it; these milling crowds, confined nightly in cramped buildings, required supervision and regulation, as did too the nature and content of the dramatic entertainment offered them. It was Louis XIV who had originally seen the three theatres he took under his protection, the Opéra, the Comédie-Française and the Comédie-Italienne, as conferring particular lustre on his reign. He granted them an absolute monopoly of the kind of dramatic, musical and terpsichorean works each of them specialized in, turning them into patent or 'privileged' theatres. The machinery of support and control set up by Louis XIV lasted down to the collapse of the *ancien régime*; but from 1760 onwards the system began to be duplicated and to a certain extent undermined by the advent of a new phenomenon, the commercial theatre. It was in 1760 that Jean-Baptiste Nicolet took over a ramshackle hall on the Boulevard du Temple, well away from the centre of affairs but near to where the artisan population of Paris was settled at the time, in which he proposed to provide all the year round the kind of dramatic entertainment sought by the poorer classes who until then had had to content themselves with fairground shows which, popular though they were, had the disadvantage of being open only at certain seasons of the year. Nicolet's pathfinding venture was so successful that it was not long before it found imitators, both along the Boulevard and, later, in the grounds of the Palais-Royal; these little theatres were collectively known as the 'théâtres forains', with reference to their distant origin in the fairs. Instead of forming a self-governing company like the Comédie-Française, the actors were hired, employed and fired by managers of a new species, men and women who built or rented their own theatres and engaged the services of occasionally talented but always prolific playwrights to provide them with a varied repertoire; and they prospered as long as they continued to offer their clientèle the kind of amusement that appealed to them. Although hardly anyone realized it at the time, the step taken by Nicolet in 1760 was destined to alter the whole trend of development over the next century and a half. All the theatres that attained prominence in the nineteenth century, the Gaîté, the Ambigu, the Variétés, the Vaudeville, the Gymnase, were modelled on the formula evolved by that mountebank of genius, Nicolet.

The organs of state, in the crumbling monarchy of the time, were divided as to the attitude to be adopted towards these commercial enterprises which, however trivial the entertainment they offered, were perceived as performing a useful function in providing harmless relaxation for the lower orders. The Revolution further enhanced their standing by cancelling the privileges – the monopoly on certain types of play and the financial aid granted by the Treasury – which the royal theatres had enjoyed; from 1791, by decree of the National Assembly, all theatres became purely commercial enterprises, the artificial restrictions on their number were abolished, and for a short period it seemed as though the state was renouncing all control over the theatres; even the censorship of plays intended for public performance was suspended.

Meanwhile, outside Paris, the situation had been developing a little differently. The representatives of royal authority governing the provinces under the *ancien régime* were impressed by the advantages that might accrue from promoting the growth of an organized theatrical life; with their encouragement, a network of new theatres sprang up in the latter half of the eighteenth century, particularly where troops were garrisoned or where there was a regular passage of visitors from abroad. In the course of the following century, admittedly, the provincial theatre declined steadily in importance. This decay was due to a number of factors, chief among them the political and cultural hegemony of Paris, and the reluctance of the central government to provide funding for these semi-commercial undertakings, which had therefore to rely on subsidies grudgingly accorded by the municipal authorities.

It is a matter of dispute whether the coming to power of Napoleon proved ultimately of net benefit to the theatres. True, he had a strong personal interest in raising their standards; but at the same time he was wary of the potential for subversion which in his view they might represent. He began by re-establishing the old system of state subsidies for a limited number of privileged theatres in the capital; later, he drastically restricted the proliferation of the commercial theatres by closing down the majority and insisting that none of the others should operate without a government licence. This reversion to pre-revolutionary controls was further reinforced by the appointment of certain court officials to supervise the state-supported theatres, as had been customary under the *ancien régime*, and by the reinstatement of preventive censorship whereby the state asserted its right to examine, modify or prohibit whatever plays it was proposed to enact on the public stage. The monarchy, when it was finally restored in 1815, made very little change in Napoleon's dispositions regarding the theatres: the state continued to subsidize the royal theatres, to issue licences, on a slightly more generous scale, to new commercial theatres and to keep a careful watch, via the censorship bureau, on what was permitted for public performance. The 1830 revolution tried to do away with preventive censorship and to revert to the practice which had grown up under the First Republic of forbidding only such plays as were seen to divide audiences and provoke dangerous excitement; this more liberal policy lasted only until Fieschi's attempt on the King's life in 1835 provided the excuse for reintroducing censorship in all its former rigour.

The licensing system, open to all kinds of abuse especially under the July Monarchy, was finally done away with by Napoleon III in 1864. Thereafter the state continued in France, as it does down to this day, to subsidize theatres considered to be of national importance, leaving the others to multiply, compete and experiment with different types of play as they wished. Various factors, notably a long trade depression together with competition from a cheaper form of entertainment, the *café-concert*, led to a so-called crisis in the theatres in the 1890s which was in fact little more than a levelling off in the expansion of the industry; but the theatre by and large retained its attraction as the one and only spectator art available to the masses as well as to the intelligentsia until the cinema eventually displaced it in the 1920s. Our survey ends in 1905, which was when the last weapon of control left in the hands of the state, the censorship of plays, was finally relinquished after a protracted struggle: in that year a majority in the Chamber voted against sanctioning the usual item in the budget to provide for the censors' salaries. Thus the long and chequered history of state intervention drew to its close.

It remains, however, to examine the one field of dramatic activity in which the state hardly ever meddled and consideration of which we have accordingly deferred until the end: this was amateur dramatics, which had attracted all classes of society at every period, providing an outlet for those who enjoyed acting in private but had neither the talent nor, perhaps, the ambition to appear in public. Marie-Antoinette could not resist the temptation to dress up and act on a private stage, and neither could the lady of fashion or the labouring man in the nineteenth century. Nothing shows more clearly how widely *théâtromanie* had permeated the French nation over this long period of time, for amateur theatricals were quite as popular in the provinces as in the capital. Since the state could hardly interfere in what was essentially a domestic activity, none of the repressive controls it exercised over the public stage could apply in this domain. Amateur theatres escaped, in particular, the attentions of the censorship bureau. Some took advantage of this to put on plays verging on the indecent, though more often in the eighteenth than in the nineteenth century; but the loophole did eventually permit André Antoine, when he founded the Théâtre-Libre in 1887, to produce plays with disturbing social implications which might never have been tolerated at any other theatre, for Antoine, who did not charge for admission 'at the door', could claim exemption from the rules governing public theatres, which included the obligation to submit the text of plays to the censorship bureau. His example was followed by others and led shortly to the formation of the experimental or avant-garde theatre which was so influential in the first half of the twentieth century. This fruitful development, however, owed nothing to state initiative, which did not re-emerge to any considerable extent until after the Second World War, with the generalization under the Fourth Republic of the notion of the theatre as a public service deserving of financial aid and encouragement from the state. But that is, as they say, another story and one that lies well outside the chronological parameters of the present study.

CHAPTER I

The royal theatres of the 'ancien régime'

In the course of his extensive peregrinations around France over the years between 1787 and 1790, Arthur Young found little to delight him and much to dismay him. Agriculture – his principal concern – was in a piteous state, and the constitution-mongering during the early years of the Revolution boded ill; nevertheless, he never had anything but good to say about the Comédie-Française and the new theatre into which the company had moved a few years before, which occupied the site of the present-day Odéon theatre. The circular shape of the auditorium struck him as ideal, both as regarded ability to see and to hear; after so splendid a building, he asked, 'how can anyone relish our ill-contrived oblong holes of London?' On 18 October 1787, having witnessed a performance of Piron's *Métromanie*, he declared:

the more I see it, the more I like the French theatre; and have no doubt in preferring it to our own. Writers, actors, buildings, scenes, decorations, music, dancing, take the whole in the mass, and it is unrivalled by London. We certainly have a few brilliants of the first water; but throw all in the scales, and that of England kicks the beam.[1]

True, great actors and actresses, 'brilliants of the first water', could be seen in London at the time Young was writing: notably of course Sarah Siddons and her brother John Philip Kemble; but the point Young is making here is that the Comédie-Française was much more than a chance grouping of talented players. Its customs and regulations ensured the permanence of a traditional style which, inherited from Molière and perfected by succeeding generations, had already lasted for more than a century. Supported, morally and financially, by the monarchy, it could be regarded as a theatre dependent on the state and reflecting the pomp and power of the state. It was, moreover, a patent theatre, whose exclusive right to perform what were considered at the time to be the finest exemplars of dramatic

6

literature was enshrined in law. As for the players, even Bachaumont, who in his annals habitually wrote of them contemptuously as *histrions* (mountebanks) and of their company as *le tripot comique* (the comedians' bawdy-house), nevertheless acknowledged that 'the Comédie-Française possesses the most accomplished actors in Europe'.[2] Its reputation in every continental capital as far afield as St Petersburg was indeed unassailable; and in the course of the eighteenth century the universality of French as the language of polite society owed as much, perhaps, to the lofty reputation of the Comédie-Française, attended devoutly by every educated visitor from abroad, as to the widely read works of the writers of the Enlightenment who, in a few cases, were also the authors of the tragedies and comedies it produced on its stage.

Its earliest beginnings can be traced back to October 1658, when Molière's company was granted permission by Louis XIV to produce plays in the Théâtre du Petit-Bourbon, part of the Palais du Louvre. After the death of their actor-manager in 1673, the group merged with another, and the joint company moved to the Théâtre Guénégaud in the street of that name. Then, in 1680, a further fusion was effected by royal command between this company and another playing at the Hôtel de Bourgogne, and from this ordinance of Louis XIV dates not merely the foundation of the Comédie-Française but also the launching of what had been a purely commercial, private-enterprise theatre on to the boundless sea of state patronage. The terms of the *lettre de cachet* of 22 October 1680, addressed to the Lieutenant-General of Police,[3] make it clear that Louis XIV, in organizing the merger between the two rival companies, intended to centralize theatrical activity in the capital instead of having it dispersed and impoverished by being spread too thinly; and, by an additional clause 'forbidding all other French actors to establish themselves in the city and suburbs of Paris without an express order from His Majesty', he tried to ensure that the company should never need to face competition in the future. It was to this fundamental act that the jurists representing the Comédie-Française implicitly or explicitly referred in the conflicts that arose from around 1770 onwards with the new private-enterprise theatrical establishments that had started to make their appearance in the capital over the previous decade.

In order to place the new royal theatre on a firm financial footing, Louis XIV further granted the company an annual subsidy of

12,000 *livres*. Even before 1680, his generosity towards the actors of Molière's company had been demonstrated by the allocation of smaller grants: 6,000 *livres* in 1665, raised to 7,000 in 1670. The increased subsidy continued to be paid, by him and his successors, with periodic adjustments to take account of the rise in prices, down to 1790. There were occasional delays, due to the depletion of the treasury, but the total sum always arrived eventually to replenish the coffers of the Comédie-Française and to be distributed, according to an agreed formula, to the actors and actresses of the company. Although they always depended far more on their box-office receipts than on this state subsidy, it was none the less a useful supplementary source of income and had the effect of turning them to a certain extent into servants of the royal household, Comédiens du Roi as they came to be called, that is, the King's Players.

For the next eighty years, the company continued to rely for its existence in law on the various edicts issued by Louis XIV. But in 1761 it was deemed desirable to give it the status of a legally established society, which was done by the granting of letters patent on 22 August, duly registered by parliament on 7 September. A little before this, in June 1757, Louis XV had approved a constitution consisting of forty statutes; this had the effect of codifying and in some cases improving on certain customs that had grown up in the course of time to regulate both the internal affairs of the society and its external relations with others, notably with the authors who wrote for it and the suppliers and contractors with whom it had business dealings.

The internal organization of the company, dating back in its essentials to Molière's time, was basically democratic, each member holding a share, that is, a financial stake in the enterprise. A resolution dated 3 April 1685 had fixed the number of these shares at twenty-three and this number remained unchanged over the years, though each share was subdivisible, and only a player of the first rank would be allocated, by general consent, a *part entière*, a full share. Normally the company needed about seventeen actors and twelve actresses to function adequately; junior members were awarded a half-share or some other fraction, so that the total of twenty-three shares remained constant.

In order to fill gaps due to retirement or death, the shareholders (*sociétaires*) occasionally needed to admit to trial membership a new actor or actress who, if after a year he or she proved satisfactory, could proceed to the status of probationary membership; they were then known (confusingly) as *pensionnaires*,[4] which implied no more than that they were hired by the company at a fixed annual rate (2,000 *livres*) for a limited period – two years maximum. At the end of this period they were either admitted to the ranks of the *sociétaires* or else turned away to seek their fortunes elsewhere. Such at any rate was the situation in the eighteenth century, though it was varied subsequently. In the 1760s the *pensionnaires* were few in number compared to the *sociétaires* – no more than five or six at any one time – though again the proportions were to alter quite considerably in later times.

Theoretically at least, the affairs of the society were in the hands of a small steering committee (*comité directeur*) of six or seven *sociétaires*, meeting weekly. The general assembly, consisting of the totality of the *sociétaires*, was a purely consultative body meeting once a month. The organizational framework might thus suggest that the Comédie-Française was at this period a self-governing body, a democracy functioning within an autocratic state which sponsored it. But if they ever enjoyed this paradoxical liberty, they had foregone it by 1764, when Charles Collé noted in his diary that the Comédiens du Roi had 'fallen under the cruellest of despotisms . . . Formerly, they did not labour under this servile subjection; they governed themselves, as in a republic; no one meddled in the business of the Company . . .'[5] And Collé, in the same breath, names the usurpers: the First Gentlemen of the Bedchamber.

These four powerful noblemen, appointed to their office simply on account of their high rank and standing at court, had little to do with any bedchamber except that of whichever actress they chose to favour for the nonce. Their functions in regard to the Comédie-Française were never defined; but as the actors were the King's servants, and as the King had many other preoccupations, it was perhaps thought necessary that he should delegate the business of supervising their activities to this quartet of lackadaisical and voluptuous aristocrats. They never, of course, attended the committees and assemblies of the *sociétaires*; that would have been beneath their dignity; but they delighted in drawing up regulations and laying down the law. Thus, in 1712 they ordered the actors to accept without argument whatever part they were assigned in a new play, and to present themselves on the dot for rehearsals; they forbade them to engage in personal quarrels with each other when in committee or to raise any business that was not on the agenda. No matter was too trivial to occupy their attention; one would have thought they were devising codes of conduct for mischievous school-children. It would indeed have been, as Collé called it, the cruellest of despotisms – except that these regulations largely remained a dead letter, since the Gentlemen were too indolent to oversee their enforcement. Nevertheless, their right to promulgate 'disciplinary regulations' was confirmed in one of the articles of the constitution of 1757.

Since members of the royal family only rarely came to Paris for an evening at the theatre, the Comédie-Française, together with the two other royal theatres, the Académie de Musique (the Opera) and the Comédie-Italienne, were expected to depute their best actors and singers at certain times in the year to entertain the court at Versailles or Fontainebleau. These visits took place during the hunting season in the autumn and winter, the three companies taking it in turn to perform: Tuesdays were devoted to tragedy, Wednesdays to the opera, Thursdays to comedy and Fridays to light opera. The duty of ensuring that no hitches occurred in these constant moves, which involved the transport of scenery as well as actors, dressers, etc., devolved on an official known as the Intendant des Menus: one might say, the Steward of the Minor Diversions of the King.[6] In the period we are concerned with, this functionary was a certain Denis-Pierre-Jean Papillon de la Ferté, and among his other duties was that of representing the Gentlemen of the Bed-chamber at the meetings of the committee of the Comédie-Française; he acted as a channel of communication between the two parties, conveying the grievances of the players to their superiors and endeavouring to present the superiors' decisions to the players in such a way as to cause as little offence as possible: no easy task, as many a passage in Papillon's journal shows. His entry for 5 May 1772 affords an exemplary instance of the Comédie's resentment at the petty interference of the Gentlemen. The dispute was, on the surface, quite futile; it arose from the actors' decision to dismiss a wig-maker in their service. Under the *ancien régime*, wigs were part of the normal stage costume for all plays, whether tragedy or comedy, and quite irrespective of the historical period in which the action was supposed to take place. Julius Caesar appeared with his head surmounted by an enormous powdered wig; as often as not, this wig would be crowned by a helmet or hat with plumes; at the Comédie-

Italienne, even peasant women would appear with three-tiered wigs adorned with ribbons. Hence the importance of the *perruquier*, whose business it was to provide close-fitting hairpieces which would not be dislodged by an inadvertent gesture by a fellow actor. The wig-maker at the Comédie-Française may not have reached the standards required in the confection of these important adjuncts to stage costume, and for this reason the players decided to replace him. However, the man owed his original appointment to the protection of one of the Gentlemen, the Maréchal Duc de Richelieu, who peremptorily demanded his reinstatement. In a stormy meeting, the actors said they found it quite extraordinary that they were being ordered to give the man back his job, seeing that they ought at least to have the final say in the choice of their own servants; after two hours' violent argument they flatly refused to give way. The following year there was a much more serious revolt in the committee, motivated by the widespread conviction that its work was futile. According to Papillon, the great tragic actor Lekain was insistent that 'one could not require of the committee that it should ensure the statutes be observed, when the Marshal [Richelieu] had no compunction in infringing them himself on the grounds that those who make the laws can also break them. Since the Marshal had only too often repeated this dictum in their presence', continues Papillon, 'I was somewhat at a loss to know how to answer them.' Brizard, another member of the committee, had declared earlier that he would no longer participate in the deliberations, 'saying it was enough for the committee to propose something for the Superiors to do the exact opposite'. In the end Papillon's diplomacy won the day; he got the members to see that if the committee ceased functioning, the Comédie-Française would lose all pretence of being a self-governing body, and they reluctantly agreed to continue to serve in office.[7]

One has the impression that in these disputes Papillon de la Ferté was privately on the side of the actors against their 'Superiors'. This was not, however, because he felt that the fault lay in the system, with its chain of command running from the monarch, via the Gentlemen of the Bedchamber, through the committee to the rest of the acting company; rather, it was that the particular courtiers chosen to represent the King in supervising the royal theatres (Richelieu and Duras sharing responsibility for them by an agreement apparently made in 1763[8]) were irresponsible, inconsistent, often at loggerheads with one another and given to favouritism. On the other hand, when it appeared to Papillon that the actors were overstepping the mark and arrogating to themselves rights and privileges that properly belonged to the Gentlemen, he was quick to show his displeasure. This occurred, for instance, in June 1762, in connection with a revival of Marc-Antoine Legrand's comedy *Le Triomphe du temps*. A certain Bonneval had been cast as a character not due to make his appearance until the third act; but after the first two, it became evident that neither he nor his understudy had remembered to come to the theatre that evening. The play had to be abandoned and the audience told that both actors had been suddenly taken ill; but after due inquiry the committee decided that the truants should be punished, that a fine did not suffice for such a blatant dereliction of duty and that they should both go to prison. Papillon disapproved strongly of this manner of proceeding, on the grounds that the actors were exceeding their rights; only the Gentlemen of the Bedchamber were empowered to commit an actor to prison and to order his release when they saw fit. When it was put to him that the audience might well have required condign punishment to be visited on Bonneval and his understudy for their inexcusable laxness, he reminded the actors tartly 'that they belonged to the King, that the Superiors were merely lending them to the public'.[9] Whether this theory commanded universal assent at this date may be doubted; certainly the actors, who had admittedly surrendered a measure of independence by accepting to be subsidized from the royal purse, never felt that they could disregard their Paris audiences and needed only to study to please their royal masters.

It is to be supposed that only rumours of these disputes between the Gentlemen and the players, and of the friction they generated, reached the ears of the general public; but it was otherwise with the public scandal provoked by the affair of *Le Siège de Calais* in 1764–5. This was a highly popular play, a verse tragedy with a strong patriotic appeal, the work of an author all but forgotten today, Pierre-Laurent de Belloy. At the centre of the fracas were the sexagenarian actor Dubois, who had a small part in the play, and his daughter Marie, a pretty 19-year-old who had been made *sociétaire* in 1760. Young as she was, she had already been in serious trouble: in December 1762, absent like Bonneval one evening when she was supposed to be acting, she was heavily fined and in addition sentenced to prison for a short spell. She submitted with a good grace however, and a little later succeeded in attracting the attention of Richelieu's son, the Duc de Fronsac; their liaison was well known, and played an important part in the subsequent *cause célèbre*.

It was, however, not she but her scapegrace old father who set in train the events that led to such a momentous outcome. Having contracted a minor venereal disorder, he had recourse to a surgeon who succeeded in effecting a cure but failed to extract his fee from his patient. The surgeon openly accused the actor of cheating him, whereupon the Comédie-Française, to hush up the scandal, took it on themselves to settle his claim, but decided that Dubois should be ignominiously expelled from the company. It seems that Richelieu was at first inclined to let the committee handle the question themselves, refusing to intervene in so unsavoury a business; but Marie Dubois, taking her father's threatened disgrace to heart, persuaded her lover to plead his cause. In consequence of the Duc de Fronsac's representations, Richelieu, overriding the unanimous decision of the players in a general assembly specially convoked, ruled that Dubois should be reinstated and, with extraordinary tactlessness, ordered the players to put on *Le Siège de Calais* with Dubois taking his original role. The company flatly refused; Lekain and Molé, who had leading parts in the play, left Paris precipitately; so it was decided on the night to substitute something different, using the actors who were to hand. But the audience, who included a number of Marie Dubois's sympathizers, raised a great clamour at being deprived of the tragedy they had come to see. The uproar lasted two hours, but in the end entrance money was refunded and the disappointed spectators made their way home in no very good mood.

But at any rate the company, by this unprecedented strike, had won, it seemed, the first round. Papillon de la Ferté says he attempted to dissuade Mlle Clairon, the great tragic actress, from joining the rebels, arguing that such insubordination amounted almost to treason, since it entailed disobeying a royal command. She replied that nothing would force her to act alongside Dubois; she was, she declared, 'determined to do anything rather than bring dishonour on herself', and she went on to tell the *intendant*

that she could not conceive why the First Gentlemen meddled in the affairs of the theatre in Paris; such matters concerned only the police, charged with maintaining order for a public service; that as far as their internal business was concerned, they were not children and could manage it themselves without anyone else butting in. She added that the actors were running a private concern [*que les comédiens étaient des entrepreneurs*], and that it was for them to judge what was most likely to advance its interests.[10]

There is no means of telling whether Papillon transcribed her remarks accurately, but he no doubt conveyed the sense of what she said, and the passage shows Mlle Clairon to be harking back nostalgically to a time before the granting of special privileges to Molière's heirs, when the company of actors that became the Comédie-Française had been a purely commercial concern; but state support implied, in the end, a measure of state control, and there was no going back so long as absolute monarchy remained the particular form in which state power manifested itself in France.

After this sensational act of disobedience on the part of the players, the Gentlemen, if they were not to admit defeat, had no other course open to them but to demand the arrest of all actors who had refused to participate with Dubois in the performance of *Le Siège de Calais*. Mlle Clairon made no attempt to absent herself, and Lekain and Molé, who were hiding outside Paris, on hearing that their fellow actress was locked up, immediately returned and constituted themselves prisoners. Before they did so, Lekain wrote a defiant letter to the Lieutenant of Police to justify his action and that of his colleagues.

You have no doubt learned of the violence done us to compel us to keep one of our number whom we had judged to be dishonest. The contempt with which Field-Marshal Duc de Richelieu treated our most respectful submissions revealed his want of delicacy or else his excess of pride. It affected me personally by that part of it which besmirched my good name. The line of conduct taken by the Comédie-Française in the present juncture deserves the approbation of all men of honour.[11]

Mlle Clairon was released after a week on the grounds of ill health, but had to submit to house arrest; Lekain, Molé and two other leading actors who had refused to obey the order to perform *Le Siège de Calais* alongside Dubois remained in prison for four weeks. The authorities were by now in a difficult position, having no wish to deprive the theatre indefinitely of the services of its star players. A compromise solution was finally reached: Dubois was persuaded, on promise of a golden handshake, to take immediate retirement, and the prisoners were released. The public, by now better informed of the details of the affair, gave them a warm welcome on their return. The players had certainly won a moral victory, but it had hardly advanced their cause; it had brought about no change in the system of state control, and the Gentlemen of the Bedchamber continued as before to interfere in the affairs of the Comédie, which had incidentally sustained a considerable financial loss due to the four-week absence of their best-loved actors. Mlle Clairon, realizing how matters stood, left the theatre and went down to Ferney to join her old friend and admirer Voltaire. After his death she took up residence in a small town in Germany, and when she finally returned to Paris, the whole world had changed. The storms of the Revolution swept away her fortune, and she was obliged, under the Directory, to plead for some small financial help from the controllers of the state's purse-strings, who had little idea who this elderly supplicant was, being too young to have seen her on stage. She struggled on in great poverty until 1803, when she died on 29 January, shortly after her eightieth birthday. Her refusal to compromise with an honourable principle had received no recognition, and her self-imposed banishment meant only that she had condemned herself to oblivion, 'out of sight, out of mind' being a saying even more applicable to actresses then than it is today.

The prison to which delinquent actors, not just those belonging to the Comédie-Française but to the two other royal theatres, were invariably confined down to 1782, was known as the For-l'Evêque. The punishment consisted only in the loss of liberty: they were free to entertain their friends there and, if their purse was long enough, to have wine and delicacies sent in. They were treated throughout with great courtesy, the men normally presenting themselves at the prison gates unaccompanied, their sword by their side, the women arriving in a coach. If their presence on the stage was considered indispensable, they would be conducted from the prison to the theatre and back again when the performance was concluded. In any case they rarely spent more than two or three days inside; the four weeks' confinement that Lekain and his fellow actors underwent was exceptional. An arrest could be ordered by any one of the Gentlemen of the Bedchamber, by means of a request to the Lieutenant of Police, who, having secured the prisoner, would then notify the minister; in due course the latter would sign a formal order for the arrest, to which the royal seal was attached. As often as not the order would arrive after the actor had been released. There seems to have been little more stigma attached to the procedure than was incurred by other officers of the royal household, who for some offence or other were 'invited by His Majesty' to take up residence, for a period, in the Bastille.

None the less, it was clear to the more advanced thinkers of the time that the premier theatre of the land was being kept under too tight a rein. Some direction had to be given to the players, but did it have to be that of the Gentlemen of the Bedchamber, who had no particular qualifications for the task and carried it out with scant regard for anything but their own convenience and pleasure? In a letter dated 12 July 1777 Métra, who although domiciled abroad seems to have been in close touch with currents of opinion in Paris, voiced this widespread feeling when he wrote that 'the remedy for all these disorders might be that the royal actors would cease to form a corporation or company, but should be a troupe of players under the exclusive orders of a director-manager who would answer only to the police authorities and solely for what concerns them' – that is, for maintaining order inside the theatre. 'For the rest, let him do with his troupe whatever the interests of his box-office receipts suggest; in this way the theatre-goers will be well served and the actors would cease complaining.' This solution, implying the abandonment of state control in favour of purely commercial arrangements, would have been, properly speaking, revolutionary, and even the coming revolution never tried to impose it; throughout, the actors of the former royal theatres continued to administer, as best they could, their own concerns, and never handed over control to a manager. But Métra was probably right in suggesting that the state was taking too much on itself. 'People', he wrote in conclusion, 'are for ever wanting the government to direct what it ought merely to protect.'[12]

Attempts on the part of the government to impose a strong directorial regime on the Opera were, on the other hand, constantly being made, for the Opera, unlike the Comédie-Française, had never had a self-governing constitution. It was in 1669 that Pierre Perrin – shortly to be supplanted by Lully – was granted the exclusive right to establish a theatre in which operas and other musical compositions sung in French should be performed. The idea was copied from similar institutions in Italy, and it was the Italian term *accademia* that was applied to the new foundation, of which the official title, Académie Royale (or Impériale or Nationale, depend-

ing on the political regime of the moment) de Musique, continued to
be used for the Opera from that time forth.

Under Lully's firm management, the Opera grew in importance
and reputation, but after his death in 1687 it fell on evil days, directed
by incompetents, chaotically administered, 'a hotbed of corruption
enjoyed by men of rank, power and wealth. What could be the
outcome? Only financial disaster. And who was there to come to the
rescue? Only the Crown.'[13] At the beginning of the eighteenth
century the debts of the Opera already amounted to 380,000 *livres*; by
1749, when Louis XV – at the instigation, it was said, of Mme de
Pompadour – finally shrugged off the burden and laid it on the broad
shoulders of the municipality of Paris, the city fathers found themselves obliged to service an accumulated deficit of 1,200,000 *livres*.
They managed eventually to find two competent musicians, Rebel
and Francœur, to run a reformed Opera for fourteen years until they
retired, loaded with honours from a grateful monarch, in 1767.

In expectation of this vacancy, the leading performers at the
Opera had agreed on a common approach to the government,
requesting they be treated in the same way as the Comédiens du Roi
and be allowed to administer their own affairs independently of the
state. But, notwithstanding the carefully detailed memorandum
which they submitted, the plan was turned down. The authorities
were far from convinced that self-government overseen by the
Gentlemen of the Bedchamber was a precedent to be extended; and
in any case the personnel of the Opera, consisting of singers, musicians and dancers, did not possess the homogeneity of the acting staff
of the Comédie-Française; their interests were too divergent, and it
was easy to foresee the endless infighting that would ensue if they
were granted autonomy. On the other hand it was far from satisfactory that the Opera, a state organization founded by the monarchy,
should become the responsibility of the municipality of Paris. The
compromise solution that had been adopted was to find someone to
run the business in the best interests of the paying public; this had
been achieved by the appointment of Rebel and Francœur in 1757
as administrators; but it was felt to be, at best, a provisional arrangement. As Bachaumont observed on 25 March 1775: 'This position of
general administrator of the Royal Academy of Music, established
like that of dictator in a republic which only a time of crisis could
justify, has become, as one can see, permanent: to such a degree does
power tend to enlarge and perpetuate itself.'[14]

For the next ten years, between 1767 and 1777, confusion reigned. The municipality continued to shoulder responsibility for the Opera since the Crown continued to shirk it, and a number of expedients were resorted to in rapid succession, with continual disputes between the city fathers, who were concerned above all to turn deficit into profit, and the relevant minister of the Crown, Malesherbes, who wanted the organization to be entrusted to a person possessed of at least a minimum of musical competence. The man eventually chosen, Jacques de Vismes, was in good standing at court (he was in particular a close friend of Campan, the Queen's secretary, who gave him financial backing) and acceptable to the municipality since he was prepared to put down half a million in surety money, requiring only payment of the interest together with the promise of an annual subsidy of 80,000 *livres*; but he had no previous operatic experience and lacked musical expertise.

This deficiency might not have mattered much, since he was known to be a competent administrator, but it did not endear him to his subordinates, who looked on him as 'an idle, haughty despot, incapable of performing an entrechat or of singing in tune'.[15] Idle he was not: he went about his task with a great deal of energy, but perhaps a little too autocratically. Since his overriding commitment was to cut costs, he needed to persuade the top opera singers and ballet dancers to accept, for a period, reduced salaries; but he imposed the cuts without any real consultation, riding roughshod over their susceptibilities. When the star dancer, Mlle Guimard, asked him for a new costume to appear in a new ballet, he told her this could not be managed on the revised budget, and she would have to wear her old dress; whereupon the dancer caused it to be cut to pieces and sent in a parcel to the director. De Vismes found himself obliged not only to have a new costume made, but to plead with the lady that she should be good enough to appear in it.

In September 1778 matters came to a head. The leading members of the Opera, determined to rid themselves of De Vismes, made an approach to the municipal authorities, offering to deposit 600,000 *livres* and to forgo all subvention, provided their director was dismissed; but the burgesses were wary of taking so radical a step without the prior agreement of the Crown. The struggle between De Vismes and his rebellious subjects – who openly compared themselves to the American colonists trying to throw off the tyranny of the British, and affected to call one another Washington, Franklin, etc. – was the talk of the town that autumn, and eventually the Secretary of State, Amelot, was obliged to show his hand. In a private audience with the King he reported the agitation and begged His Majesty to let him know if he had any orders on the subject. Louis XVI asked him what the Parisians in general thought of the various reforms De Vismes had tried to introduce. The minister replied that they had criticized certain changes at first but were now beginning to accept them, and thought they augured well for the future. 'Very well,' replied the King, 'let him stay in his post and let me hear no more of that scum [*qu'on ne me parle plus de cette canaille-là*]'.[16] Amelot had great pleasure in conveying the message to the beleaguered De Vismes.

It is true that impartial observers were already realizing that the Opera's fortunes were in better shape than they had been for years; playing night after night to full houses, its financial situation was beginning to recover from the years of dissipation and extravagance. All this was due to De Vismes; but he had proved a strict taskmaster, and his enemies inside the theatre were more determined than ever that he should go. It was the dancers who felt most indignant, partly because De Vismes, having realized the public wanted less ballet and more straight opera, allowed them fewer opportunities to display their talents. They took to planning their moves at nightly meetings in Mlle Guimard's house and, wrote La Harpe, 'were resolved on extreme measures rather than obey M. De Vismes. People talk of the "conspiracy of the Opera", and this quarrel which occupies all their thoughts and is a constant subject of discussion, appears more difficult to resolve than the wars in America and Germany.'[17] One evening two of the leading male dancers, Vestris and Dauberval, refused outright to go on stage and stalked the wings in mufti. After the performance, a police inspector presented himself at Mlle Guimard's address with an order for the arrest of Vestris, Dauberval and Vestris's son; they were given a short spell in the For-l'Evêque, and when they reappeared on stage were given a cool reception by the audience. Emboldened perhaps by this, the municipal authorities decided at last to back De Vismes a little more energetically. Dauberval was dismissed, along with two other dancers; Vestris and Mlle Guimard were warned against giving any more trouble in future. The whole company waited on the city fathers to make submission.

It seemed that the Opera had been brought to heel; but De

Vismes, probably fearing that the fires had been merely damped down and might roar up again at any time, preferred to hand in his resignation; and at the same time the city council begged the King to relieve them of this troublesome burden. Louis XVI consented, but insisted that the municipality remain responsible for the accumulated deficit; in return he promised the Opera a generous annual grant, conditional on performances being given twelve times a year at Versailles and Fontainebleau. Unlike the Comédie-Française, the Académie Royale de Musique had never been in receipt hitherto of a regular state subsidy; the usual procedure had been to allow it to go into debt, and for the Crown or the city treasurer to come to its rescue. Luckily, the Opera had certain other sources of revenue besides the sale of tickets and the rent from boxes: it had the right to demand payment from other theatres, including the Comédie-Italienne, in return for authorization to use vocal music at their performances; and it had enjoyed since 1716 exclusive permission to turn its building over to masked balls during the winter,[18] a custom which, discontinued during the Revolution but resumed in 1800, continued for much of the nineteenth century, providing a permanent and valuable source of profit. Originally held twice a week, from midnight till 6.0 a.m., in 1776 they were doubled in number, and in addition, on the days when there was no spectacle at the Opera, balls were held (known as *bals du jour*) from 5.0 p.m. to midnight. The price of a ticket was 5 *livres*, a sum cheerfully paid by happy crowds of carnival revellers, to the great relief and satisfaction of the hard-pressed treasurer of the Opera.

It should be said that, unlike the *sociétaires* in the two Comédies, whose shares fluctuated according to whether or not they were playing to full houses, the members of the operatic company could never suffer loss however precarious the finances of the Académie Royale, for they were employed on fixed salaries; and we have seen how indignantly they reacted when De Vismes attempted to tamper with these. They were at least partly mollified by his resignation and by their reversion to the Crown; for his successors did not enjoy the same absolute authority that had been allowed him. Although still called directors, their functions were more those of business managers and they had limited powers of initiative; decisions were taken, as at the Comédie-Française, in a small committee of six members which the director chaired and in which he had a casting vote. In 1782 even this shadowy presence disappeared, with the resignation of the last of the directors, Dauvergne, and the Opera became if not self-governing, at any rate accountable only to the King's minister. It could even be said to have achieved a greater measure of liberty than the other two royal theatres, since the Gentlemen of the Bedchamber had no say in the way it conducted its affairs.

The third royal theatre, the Comédie-Italienne, originated like the other two in the seventeenth century. It is known that a company of native Italian actors were sharing the Théâtre du Petit-Bourbon with Molière from 1658, and that in 1680, when the Comédie-Française was founded, they were left in sole occupation of the Hôtel de Bourgogne. Here they presented a repertory consisting basically of improvised comedies in Italian, a language at that time widely understood in court circles in France; commoners enjoyed the farcical business, without always understanding the remarks being made by the players. To make the action plainer, therefore, the actors began introducing phrases in French, later extending the practice to whole scenes; finally, despite the protests of the Comédie-Française, they even ventured on plays written for them in French by contemporary authors, permission to do this having been granted by Louis XIV in a famous judgement.[19] He took exception, however, to one of their comedies, thought to be a satire on his morganatic wife Mme de Maintenon, and expelled them in 1697.

Shortly after Louis XIV's death in 1715 the Italians deemed it safe to return to Paris and, thanks to the protection of the Regent, were able to reoccupy their former home in the Hôtel de Bourgogne. Louis XV took them under his protection on the Regent's death in 1723, conferring on them the title Comédiens Italiens du Roi and granting them an annual subsidy of 15,000 *livres*. They were organized internally on much the same lines as the Comédie-Française[20] and were subject in the same way to the overall supervision of the Gentlemen of the Bedchamber. They managed, however, to avoid the clashes with their superiors that were a source of such vexation for the Comédie-Française, and it was only exceptionally that the For-l'Evêque prison opened its gates to a member of the Comédie-Italienne. The main problem facing the company, in the earlier part of the eighteenth century, was that it lacked a 'reserved repertoire', one that it could exploit without fear of competition. The Comédie-Française had an absolute monopoly on tragedy and on most comedy, that of Molière and Regnard in particular. The Opera enjoyed the exclusive privilege of mounting musical spectacles: no other Paris stage could do so without their agreement, a concession for which they demanded suitable payment. The reserved repertoire of the Comédie-Italienne had been the *commedia dell'arte*, by now decidedly *vieux jeu*, at least for the more refined portion of the public. They held the copyright on certain French comedies, those by authors who had preferred to write for them rather than for the Comédie-Française; the most gifted of these, Marivaux, had however given up writing for them when he was elected to the Académie Française in 1742. Moreover, time had taken toll of the fabric of their playhouse, the Hôtel de Bourgogne, and they were at their wits' end to know how to pay for necessary structural work and renovations when their current liabilities already amounted to 400,000 *livres*. To refloat the enterprise, they decided to make a bid for the most successful of the fairground theatres, Jean Monnet's Opéra-Comique,[21] which was in a highly prosperous condition in spite of having to pay heavy dues to the Académie Royale de Musique for permission to operate. Accordingly they applied to the King to allow them to take over the fairground theatre, and the merger was eventually sanctioned on 3 February 1762.

The new acquisition proved invaluable. Favart, who had been the principal supplier of the now defunct Opéra-Comique, was delighted at the huge concourse at the Comédie-Italienne when it opened after the merger. 'From noon onwards, not a single ticket remained unsold. Several people were trampled underfoot; one would-be spectator gave up the ghost under pressure from the throng.'[22] Nor was this simply the attraction of novelty. The vogue held up, their creditors were satisfied and in 1767 the Italians were able to enlarge the seating room in their theatre, while in the same year the canny administrators of the Opera raised their demands from 22,000 to 40,000 *livres* per annum, which the Italians found no difficulty in paying out of their swollen profits. They were fortunate in finding two gifted composers to write a series of brilliant works for them between 1762 and 1771: Monsigny, remembered particularly for *Rose et Colas* and *Le Déserteur*, and Grétry, whose *Tableau parlant* and *Zémire et Azor* were still being played all over France until well into the next century. French comic opera took the provinces by storm, then spread over Europe and could be seen at all the princely courts in Germany and even in Italy, where, as Bachaumont proudly observed, 'the greatest musicians of Rome and Naples applaud the talents of our French composers'.[23]

Eventually comic opera displaced every other kind of entertainment at the Comédie-Italienne. In 1769 the French non-singing actors in the troupe were pensioned off, and the comedies in which they used to act were absorbed into the stock repertory of the Comédie-Française. Ten years later, the Italian actors were likewise sent packing. There was now nothing Italian about the Comédie-Italienne but the name; nevertheless, when in 1783 they erected a fine new building with its entry on the Rue Favart, they still had the words 'Théâtre Italien' inscribed above the portico in letters of gold. The fact that its façade did not face the much-frequented boulevard – still known even today as the Boulevard des Italiens – caused a good deal of amused comment at the time, including the following slightly ribald quatrain:

> Dès le premier coup d'œil on reconnaît très bien
> Que le nouveau théâtre est vraiment italien,
> Car il est disposé d'une telle manière
> Qu'on lui fait aux passants présenter le derrière.[24]

One cannot imagine so raffish a comment being made at the expense of the new buildings recently erected for the Opera and the Comédie-Française, but people did not treat the Comédie-Italienne with the same respect. The Italians were always regarded as the junior company, which in a sense they were, having been brought to Paris by the Regent as late as 1716; moreover, unlike the other two, the Comédie-Italienne had never received a royal warrant. People crowded into their theatre because they could count on being amused there; they were seldom greatly amused at the Comédie-Française, but there and at the Opera they had the impression of being given the best that the arts (of declamation, of ballet and of singing) could offer them. The Comédie-Italienne, it has been said, concentrated more on pleasing its audience than on upholding its own prestige; as a result, it had less prestige, but it was the more loved.

The book *Les Trois Théâtres*, published by Des Essarts in 1777, is concerned with the three royal foundations in Paris, these being evidently the only ones deemed worthy of the name of 'Theatres' in the author's view; any others were too marginal to deserve mention. Yet these three were already, at the time he wrote, facing serious competition from new establishments which owed nothing to royal favour and patronage. Owing their foundation and initial prosperity to the enterprise of private individuals who had previously been associated with the fairground booths, and whose playhouses were referred to for this reason disdainfully as the *théâtres forains*, they heralded a new departure in dramatic practice, both in the kind of productions they offered and in their reliance on winning the favour of the public by offering novelties rather than by seeking to maintain traditional standards under the cloak of state protection. Paris was no longer, over the last three decades of the *ancien régime*, served exclusively by the three theatres which Des Essarts felt worthy of attention; its needs were being met by a whole cluster of new establishments, before which the royal theatres found themselves increasingly on the defensive. The *forains* constituted a 'third estate' in the theatrical kingdom; and, like the Third Estate as Sieyès saw it, they were nothing to begin with, but destined, as the politician foretold, to become everything.

CHAPTER 2

The rise of the commercial theatre

If one defines commercial theatre as that which is totally independent of financial backing from the public purse, and free therefore
from the constraints and controls which such backing normally
involves, then in France at least it clearly antedates state intervention; one can trace the beginning of commercial theatre back to
when the earliest impresarios started journeying around the country
with a scratch company of actors, paying them wages from the
coppers extracted from their audiences, and pocketing what was
over as their personal profit. The only control to which these
itinerant companies were originally subject was the obligation,
before they set foot in a town, to obtain permission from the police
authorities to do so; this rule was enshrined in law by an edict dating
back to 1706, and was rigorously enforced down to 1790.[1]

Permission to put on performances was granted for short periods
only – rarely for longer than three months. Before a manager
embarked on a tour, he would normally take the precaution of
writing to the various localities he proposed to visit, asking for
permits to be delivered. Once he arrived in a particular town, he
found himself obliged to conform to all manner of occasionally
vexatious local regulations: performances had to start and finish at
stated times; he had to agree not to admit certain categories of
spectators – notably domestics in livery and even, in certain areas,
members of the Jewish confession – and to close the theatre altogether on Sundays and public holidays, which were precisely when
he might have expected the largest audiences.

If a town held an annual fair, the manager's chances of obtaining
a permit for its duration were that much better, since the presence of
an itinerant troupe usually formed an additional attraction and
increased the profitability of the fair. And this applied to Paris as
much as anywhere. A provincial company of entertainers was first

25

recorded in the capital in 1596, and within a few years, at the two great fairs that flourished there, showmen flocked from all parts of the country, setting up their booths and hustings, tempting the milling crowd with puppet plays, with caged bears and lions, with trained dogs and monkeys, with jugglers and rope-dancers. The first stage plays did not make their appearance until 1678; they tended to follow the Italian tradition of gross farce, and indeed after 1697, when the Italian company summoned earlier was expelled,[2] its repertory, together with the masks and costumes they had worn to identify the parts they played – Harlequin, Pantaloon, Columbine etc. – were taken over lock, stock and barrel by the fairground players.

The two principal fairs in Paris, Saint-Germain and Saint-Laurent, were of ancient foundation, dating back to the thirteenth century. The first, coinciding with the carnival season, opened six or eight weeks before Palm Sunday and closed then; the second lasted, in the eighteenth century, from the end of June to the end of September. There was a third, Saint-Ovide, which was supposed to last for a fortnight in August but could be extended (with the permission of the police authorities) for a third week or even longer. The police tended to look favourably on the fairground entertainers, as did the monks of Saint-Germain to whom the fairmen paid rent. From 1706 onwards the Lieutenant of Police was given the responsibility of supervising the fairground theatres and, being well aware that the actors provided the lower class with relatively harmless amusement, tended at all times to regard the humble buskers with indulgence and to take their side in the disputes that occasionally arose when the royal theatres objected that the *forains* were encroaching on their privileges.

However, it seems to have occurred to a few bold spirits that the way forward for a prosperous commercial theatre did not lie with the intermittent entertainment offered at the Paris fairs, which were in any case based on an older form of trading destined to dwindle and vanish even before the Revolution.[3] The disappearance in 1762 of that crowning achievement of the *forains*, the Opéra-Comique, swallowed up at one gulp by the Comédie-Italienne, coincided with the development of a new centre of popular amusement which was emerging along the northern boundary of the city. The earthworks thrown up in 1536 as part of its defences were in 1668 planted with four lines of trees and became a favourite walk for the citizens of

Paris, permitting a fine view of the surrounding countryside stretch-
ing away to the windmills of Montmartre. It ran from the Porte
Saint-Antoine to the Porte Saint-Martin, and owed the name Boulevard du Temple to the Knights Templars, who had established
themselves in this area until their order was suppressed under
Philippe le Bel in 1307.[4] It was some 30 metres wide, and there was
space for buildings along one side; in 1778 it was paved, so that
carriage folk as well as pedestrians could take the air, the people on
foot strolling along sanded sidewalks. Already in 1770 Goldoni,
during his stay in Paris, regarded the Boulevard as his favourite
place of recreation. It was, he wrote, 'an agreeable and salubrious
resort', in contrast to the airlessness of the narrow streets of Paris
flanked by tall buildings. At the same time there was plenty to
amuse the eye as one passed along under the shade of the trees:

crowds of people, an astonishing press of traffic, little boys darting among
the horses and carriage wheels to offer you all manner of wares, chairs on
the footpaths for the idler who wants to see the world go by and for ladies
who simply want to be seen, cafés all spruced up, with orchestras and
French and Italian singers, pastry-cooks, restaurateurs, puppet shows,
acrobats, barkers inviting you to come inside and see giants and dwarfs,
wild animals and sea-monsters, waxwork figures, robots and ventriloquists[5]

– all the fun of the fair, but with the difference that this fair was open
the whole year round. Mrs Thrale, staying in Paris in 1775, visited
the Boulevard which she described as 'a sort of Sadlers Wells where
rope-dancing, tumbling and pantomime preside – it was more
entertaining than a play'.[6] She returned on a number of occasions,
and it is clear, from the account she gives, that for her the great
attraction, though she never names it, was Nicolet's theatre, since
she describes several of the pantomimes and acrobatic displays
which from other sources we know to have been performed there.

Jean-Baptiste Nicolet was born in Paris on 16 April 1728; his
father had been a puppet-master working in the Saint-Germain and
Saint-Laurent fairs. Jean-Baptiste had a younger brother, François-
Paul, whom he left in charge of the puppet show in 1760, having
decided his own future lay on the Boulevard. Here he rented a
vacant hall where he started showing short plays taken from the
repertory of the Théâtre-Italien and the Opéra-Comique. Though
his original capital cannot have been large, before long he had put
aside enough to lease a plot of land further along the Boulevard and
erect a wooden theatre of his own on the side opposite the city. The

ground, boggy in the extreme, had to be drained and then levelled; once opened, however, the theatre proved amazingly popular. The inconvenience of making their way in winter across a rough path of sand and cinders appears not to have deterred his clients: on Sundays, it was by no means unusual to see a couple of thousand spectators besieging the doors. One reason was that for some years Nicolet had the Boulevard pretty well to himself; the few rivals he had at the start, who, like him, had moved from the fairgrounds, returned to them in disarray, for Nicolet's programmes were unbeatable. A certain Toussaint-Gaspard Taconet, formerly a joiner's apprentice, then stagehand and prompter at the Opéra-Comique, wrote a succession of lively playlets for the new theatre in which he occasionally acted himself, taking the part of a working man given to drink. In this he needed to do no more than follow his natural bent, for Taconet was more often to be found in his cups than not. It was probably drink that brought about his early demise; Bachaumont, recording this melancholy event on 21 January 1775, saluted him in a brief obituary as 'the soul of Nicolet's theatre'.

But Nicolet had many other attractions to fall back on. His repertoire ranged from 'pantomimes nationales' (patriotic pageants like *Le Siège de la Pucelle d'Orléans*, a re-enactment of a well-known episode in the life of Joan of Arc), to rustic comedies of a touching sentimentality and broad farces like *Les Ecosseuses* (The Pea-Shellers), written by Taconet and including a quarrel between two market-women exchanging vulgar insults, so successful that it was still being acted during the Revolution. Around 1767 everyone wanted to see the antics of the monkey Turco, in particular his killing imitation of the Comédie-Française actor Molé; Turco, to the delight of the ladies in the audience, would climb up and sit on the edge of their boxes in expectation of sweetmeats. At a later date, Nicolet imported a company of Spanish acrobats including one who, blindfolded, would perform the wildest dances, twirling like a dervish among a quantity of eggs he had previously distributed apparently at random over the stage: not a single one was smashed or even touched.[7]

After Taconet's disappearance, his coarse and rudimentary farces were replaced by the rather subtler and more polished comedies of the Abbé Robineau. His first great success, *L'Amour quêteur* (1777), full of licentious *sous-entendus*, aroused the indignation of the Archbishop of Paris, who caused this unworthy cleric to be defrocked.

Unperturbed, Robineau adopted the anagrammatic pseudonym Beaunoir under which he continued to write exclusively for Nicolet down to 1780. Every time *L'Amour quêteur* (Cupid Collecting for Charity) was announced, it was found necessary to double the police detachment keeping order outside and inside the theatre; at a later date, Nicolet's troupe had the signal honour of being summoned to Versailles to perform the play before Their Majesties. The fortunate impresario had the name of his company changed in consequence to that of Les Grands Danseurs du Roi.[8] Even as early as 1768 the *Calendrier historique et chronologique des théâtres* had been including details of Nicolet's productions; in January 1773 appeared the first issue of an *Almanach forain*, devoted entirely to the fairground and boulevard shows; and in 1779 Bachaumont, normally no great admirer of the popular theatre, was driven to admit that

it can scarcely be credited to what heights of industry this mountebank has ascended; his theatre today rivals the Opera itself and surpasses it in some respects: the stage machinery, admirably adjusted, functions very precisely, the scenery is magnificent, the costumes in the best of taste, the production not lacking in splendour, the actors numerous and excellently directed. The Opera, jealous of this success, has tried to have it suppressed; but the sagacious magistrate who presides over the police and has particular charge of the minor theatres has felt it only right to defend Nicolet against such unjust demands, all the more because this director has invested heavily in his theatre, and it is natural that he should get some return.[9]

The 'sagacious magistrate' to whom Bachaumont refers here was of course the Lieutenant-General of Police, at this time J. C. P. Lenoir. Having been appointed to keep order and deal with disturbances in the streets of Paris, his strategy, far from checking the development of the boulevard theatres, was rather to promote it, on the grounds that the expanding working-class population needed the relatively harmless diversion that a visit to the theatre represented. Being also responsible for the fairground theatres, it was in his interests to encourage them too, for the commerce of the fairs would have slackened considerably without the attraction of the theatrical establishments still operating there. So it remained obligatory for Nicolet and others on the Boulevard to keep these going: Nicolet's theatre at the Foire Saint-Ovide was particularly popular, and the crush to get in was made the subject of comment by Bachaumont in 1769.

Jean-Baptiste Nicolet counts as the first of the long and colourful

line of theatre directors on whose success depended not just their
own livelihood but that of their numerous employees and depend-
ants, from stagehands to playwrights. What little information of a
personal nature we have concerning the man suggests a certain
stinginess, compensated for by his undoubted intelligence and
energy. Mayeur de Saint-Paul, who worked for him, states that he
was totally illiterate; not above saving himself the expense of
employing a man to snuff the candles and sweep the auditorium at
the end of a performance by carrying out these menial tasks himself;
'for ever running from his theatre on to the Boulevard and back
again to his theatre; taking huge pinches of snuff every time: *ecce
homo*'.[10] He tried to cut his overheads by all kinds of petty tricks: he
would invite one of his actors to a game of draughts when a rehearsal
was shortly to begin, and then fine him for being late for the
rehearsal; or when another was on stage, he would run up to the
man's dressing room, light a candle there, and then fine him for
having forgotten to extinguish it. In earlier days he must have had a
hard struggle to make ends meet, which could account for his
legendary avarice; but he prospered where others had failed, at an
enterprise which no one had attempted before, and which went from
strength to strength[11] thanks to his acumen and resourcefulness.

If Nicolet was more a businessman than a man of the theatre
properly speaking, the reverse was true of his principal rival, Nicolas
Audinot. A native of Lorraine born in 1732, he was taught music by
his father and when qualified found employment as a professional
violinist in the town orchestra at Nancy and in the household of the
Duc de Gramont. Drawn to the stage, he joined a company of
strolling actors for a while; after that he came to Paris and in 1758
was taken on by the Opéra-Comique while that theatre was still
located in the Foire Saint-Laurent. In 1762 Audinot was one of the
half-dozen actors of the Opéra-Comique named by royal ordinance
as worthy to be transferred to the Comédie-Italienne at the time of
the merger of the two theatres. On the stage, he specialized in the
parts of comic servants; but he also found time to write a number of
plays, one of which, *Le Tonnelier* (The Cooper) was performed
regularly by the Comédie-Italienne down to the beginning of the
nineteenth century. At the Comédie-Italienne his position was that
of a *pensionnaire* only; it is said that he left, in 1764, when the
sociétaires refused to award him a rise in salary, or else because they
had declined to find an opening for his young daughter.

He took an unexpected and ingenious revenge on the Italiens for their refusal to meet his demands. After a brief engagement at the Théâtre de Versailles, he returned to the fairground and inaugurated a new type of marionette show. With the help of a former carpenter named Jean-François Mussot whom he took into partnership, he fashioned jointed figures to resemble his former colleagues at the Comédie-Italienne, and staged a puppet play, *Les Comédiens de bois* (The Wooden Actors), which delighted the crowds but infuriated the victims of this new type of satire; it was said he even guyed one of the Gentlemen of the Bedchamber, representing him as Punchinello and showing him distributing favours and punishments with grotesque impartiality. His success was such that, when the fair ended, Audinot transported the marionettes to the Boulevard du Temple where he opened a small theatre on 9 July 1769; he was joined by a couple of playwrights who similarly nursed a grievance against the royal theatre, and with their assistance he began showing short pieces which, in accordance with the traditional liberty allowed to puppet plays, included scenes and situations about as scabrous as could be imagined. This did not stop even ladies of fashion from attending, and in a short while Audinot, who had named his theatre the Ambigu-Comique,[13] was drawing bigger audiences than his neighbour Nicolet.

Within a year the marionettes were replaced by child actors, an even greater novelty, for most people had forgotten the occasion, forty years earlier, when spectators at the Opéra-Comique had been highly diverted by a performance of Fagan's *La Nièce vengée* played by children under the age of 13.[14] Audinot's original cast was aged probably about 10 or 11, and although he recruited a few younger girls in the following years, he also kept many of the original actors on his payroll, despite the fact that as time went on they could by no stretch of the imagination be called children any longer. As late as 1787 there were still child actors to be seen at the Ambigu-Comique, according to a guidebook to Paris of the time; they had special pieces written for them, we are told, 'in which sentiment, gaiety and decency go hand in hand'.[15] Such had not been the case earlier: part of the attraction of the show was the spectacle of underage, undersized actors speaking lines of the enormity of which, in their innocence, they were presumed to be unaware. The Archbishop of Paris protested to the Lieutenant-General of Police about this abominable profanation of the sacred rights of childhood; but there was another current of opinion according to which Audinot was performing a service to the dramatic art by establishing a seminary of young actors and actresses whose dispositions raised great hopes for the future. (This was a little disingenuous: none of the children[16] subsequently became ornaments of the French stage.) The argument was settled in Audinot's favour when, on 9 April 1772, Mme du Barry, in the hope of dissipating the ennui of the King, arranged for the company to give a command performance at Choisy-le-Roi. The royal favourite was highly diverted by the somewhat dubious nature of the comedies and ballet-pantomimes that made up the programme on that occasion; His Majesty, however, merely smiled politely from time to time, Louis XV being apparently as hard to amuse as Queen Victoria was later said to be.

The Ambigu-Comique reached the heyday of its popularity in the period between 1777 and 1784. Jean-François Mussot, now known as Arnould-Mussot, had undertaken to reform the repertoire, purging it of improprieties, and launched a series of pantomimes, that is, wordless spectacles, strictly the only kind of play the fairground and boulevard companies were allowed to perform. Pantomimes being in dumb show, the plots had to be fairly straightforward to be understood; recourse was occasionally had to an old device, that of displaying scrolls with a few words written on them to make explicit some otherwise incomprehensible development in the action. Music was pressed into service to evoke the appropriate emotion – pathos, excitement, terror – and increasingly speech was introduced to facilitate understanding. The pantomimes became *pantomimes dialoguées* and were so denoted in the programmes: a 'mongrel term for a mongrel genre' as it has been aptly described.[17] They were produced by Audinot with a wealth of decorative effects and stage machinery which put even the Opera into the shade: a version of the Sleeping Beauty legend proved such a draw in 1777 that the Opera forbade its performance on Tuesdays and Fridays, the two days in the week they could normally count on to fill their seats.

This was not the first time Audinot had had a brush with the Opera. In 1771 it had been notified to him that in future he was not to permit any singing or dancing on his stage, and that he was to reduce his orchestra to a maximum of four instrumentalists. The outrage caused by this measure, an outrage felt as much by Audinot's patrons as by the director himself, caused it to be withdrawn before long, but in return the Opera demanded from the Ambigu-Comique an annual payment of 12,000 *livres*; its chronic insolvency made a financial arrangement with the commercial theatres preferable to continuing interference with their repertoire. Nicolet did not escape this extortion: the phenomenal success of his production of *L'Enlèvement d'Europe* (The Rape of Europa) in 1773 led to similar pecuniary demands which had to be met, however grudgingly. Appetite increasing the more one eats, as the French proverb has it, these exactions, sanctioned by the state which saw in them an excellent method of financing a prestigious but poorly supported theatre by an impost laid on successful private enterprise, grew steadily through the years until, in August 1784, came the final bombshell: the Council of State announced that all licences hitherto granted to the managers of the minor theatres were revoked and would be transferred to the Opera, which would have the right to dispose of them at will to the highest bidder; this regardless of the fact that the Opera had had no part in founding them or in bringing them to their present state of prosperity.[18] They included, at this time, besides Nicolet's Grands Danseurs du Roi and Audinot's Ambigu-Comique, two others on the Boulevard du Temple that had sprung up alongside them more recently: the Théâtre des Associés in 1774, and Lécluse's theatre, later called the Variétés-Amusantes, in 1778.

The two men who ran the Théâtre des Associés in partnership were Nicolas Vienne and Louis-Gabriel Sallé. The former, named ironically Beauvisage because his face was covered with smallpox scars, was well known on the Boulevard for his skill as a mime: perched on a high stool, he imitated wordlessly every conceivable human emotion, and invariably collected round him an amused and attentive crowd. Having amassed in this manner a small fortune, he struck up a friendship with Sallé, who had been a member of Nicolet's troupe before leaving to work in a puppet show. Vienne offered to invest his savings in Sallé's small enterprise, on condition he be allowed to continue his grimacing act during the intervals. In 1774 the two associates decided to recruit a few down-at-heel actors[19] and start producing regular plays, including some from the protected repertory of the Comédie-Française. Peremptorily ordered to desist from this infringement of their copyright, Sallé invited the royal company to send observers to one of his forthcoming productions of *Zaïre*, adding that 'if you recognize Voltaire's tragedy, after seeing it performed by my actors, I shall accept your reprimand and promise never to play it again in my theatre'.[20] Lekain and Préville, among others, having witnessed this travesty or parody of a tragedy frequently performed on the stage of the Comédie-Française, were convulsed with laughter and the following day wrote Sallé a letter giving him full permission to make free of their repertory as often as he wished. So it came about that when, in 1791, copyright privileges were legally abolished, Sallé was the only theatre manager on the Boulevard to lose thereby.

As for Lécluse, he was already an old man (having been born in 1711) when in 1778 he was granted permission to open a small wooden theatre on the Boulevard Saint-Martin, adjacent to a popular amusement park known as the Vauxhall d'Eté. Lécluse had, at an earlier period, been an actor and had subsequently taken up dentistry; possibly it was the success of previous boulevard directors that prompted him to embark, at an age when most men are thinking of retirement, on this new and hazardous career. But his own savings proved insufficient to meet even the preliminary costs, and before the new theatre could be inaugurated, Lécluse had to go into hiding to escape his creditors. He succeeded, however, in disposing of the completed theatre building, together with the all-important *privilège* or licence granted by the police authorities, to a combine formed of three erstwhile members of the ballet at the Opéra, together with a coal merchant, one Lemercier, who agreed to put up the necessary finance. This seems to be the first recorded instance of a company consisting of men with theatrical experience to whom funds were entrusted by an outsider with disposable capital; it was to prove a model for future undertakings in the commercial theatre.

It would not seem that Lemercier had any cause to regret having invested in this way a portion of the profits of the coal trade; for a play, probably accepted for production by Lécluse before his creditors foreclosed,[21] proved one of the biggest popular successes of the later part of the eighteenth century. This was *Les Battus paient l'amende* (Those Who Are Beaten Get Fined) of which the hero, Janot, is an unfortunate who tries throughout to get his rights but is rebuffed at every turn and has finally to pay for his audacity by losing his little all. Janot is beaten by his boss, doused with the contents of a chamberpot by his girlfriend, cheated by the lawyer he tries to employ, arouses sympathy, perhaps, among the thoughtful and laughter among the majority – or certainly did in 1779: the farce opened at the newly named Variétés-Amusantes on 11 June and had 142 consecutive performances, a record to be surpassed in pre-revolutionary France only by *Le Mariage de Figaro* in 1784. At the 112th performance J.-H. Meister noted – without comment – that not even two boxes had been booked at the Comédie-Française for the first performance of Voltaire's *Rome sauvée*, while at the third, the royal theatre was deserted; everyone had flocked to see *Les Battus paient l'amende*. The ultimate accolade came with a command performance at Versailles on 23 September, though the august personages who deigned to attend were reportedly disappointed and wondered what the Parisians saw in this unseemly farce.

The play had been written by an actor recruited into the company from Nicolet's theatre, one Louis Dorvigny, reputedly a bastard son of Louis XV. The prodigious success of his farce was due, however, less to its own merits than to the brilliant comic who played the part of Janot. Applauded on the stage, fêted by people of rank who invited him to their homes to give private performances, Janot – or Volanges, to give him his real name – was modelled in porcelain by the factory at Sèvres and in wax by the celebrated Curtius, who placed his likeness beside the bust of Voltaire; and when the actor caught a chill, the street in which he lodged was blocked by the carriages of the great, anxious to hear how he was progressing. When he accepted an offer of employment at the Comédie-Italienne, the habitués of the Variétés-Amusantes descended on the old theatre in the Rue Mauconseil, at the best of times difficult of access owing to the narrowness of the neighbouring streets, to support their idol and, possibly, to protest at his defection; the tumultuous scenes, both outside the Théâtre-Italien before the performance began, and inside in the course of the evening, were of a kind seldom if ever witnessed before at a royal theatre. Volanges, returning subsequently to the Variétés-Amusantes, was almost as successful at later plays put on there, notably in Beaunoir's *Jérôme Pointu* which had its first performance on 13 June 1781. It enjoyed an uninterrupted run for the next eighteen months; Mme d'Oberkirch, visiting the theatre as late as 28 May 1782, found it 'full of people from the Court, all of them in fits of laughter'.[22]

Given the transfer of custom from the royal theatres to the Boulevard – for the phenomenal success of the Variétés-Amusantes also benefited the neighbouring houses, since spectators arriving late and disappointed in their hopes of a seat there would settle for Nicolet's show or Audinot's – it is not surprising that those responsible for keeping the Opera afloat financially started casting covetous eyes in the direction of the Boulevard du Temple, until in 1784, as we have seen, they persuaded the minister in charge to make over to the Académie Royale de Musique the overall *privilège* of the boulevard theatres. This did not mean, of course, that they would in future be run directly by the Opera; but the Opera was empowered to put in charge of them men of its own choice, to run them on its behalf. Effectively, this meant 'upping the ante'; the ransom money the commercial theatres had been paying to the Opera was enormously increased and, if they demurred, it was open to the state institution to hold an auction among prospective directors, if necessary ousting the original proprietors. Tenders were invited in September 1784. Nicolet, canny as ever, grumbled, but pretended to yield the point, consenting under protest to pay the Académie de Musique 24,000 *livres* a year for permission to continue managing the theatre he had built, literally, by the sweat of his brow; privately, he no doubt hoped to wriggle out of payment on the plea of reduced takings. Audinot tried to prevaricate, thought he could negotiate, but in the end was dispossessed. Two little-known newcomers from Bordeaux, Gaillard and Dorfeuille, had offered 60,000 *livres* annually for the next fifteen years for a package consisting of both the Ambigu-Comique and the Variétés-Amusantes; by the terms of the lease they signed with Jensen, inspector of the Opera, it was settled that they should 'direct and administer the said enterprises, either at their present location if MM. Gaillard and Dorfeuille reach agreement with their proprietors, or at any other location they prefer'.[23] What was important was clearly not to own or lease the theatre building, but to have a legal title to the *privilège* that went under the name of the theatre. The *privilège* for all the boulevard theatres had been transferred to the Opera by the royal edict of 18 July 1784: that portion of the *privilège* affecting the Ambigu-Comique and the Variétés-Amusantes was now transferred to Gaillard and Dorfeuille, capitalists of a new breed that was beginning to emerge on the eve of the Revolution.

They had no intention of taking over the two vacant theatres on the Boulevard; rather, their plan was to use their *privilège* to open a new theatre in a more fashionable centre than the Boulevard du Temple, namely the Palais-Royal. This palace, erected by Richelieu between 1629 and 1639, had been bequeathed at the Cardinal's death to Louis XIII; his successor, Louis XIV, had given it to his brother, Philip of Orléans, and it had remained the property of the Orléans family ever since; here the Regent had held his court and here his great-grandson, known under the Revolution as Philippe-Egalité, having inherited the palace decided to develop the gardens as a commercial centre. The Duc de Chartres, as he then was, needed to increase his income and reckoned that the rental he would derive from shops and gambling-houses would more than repay the expense of building them. In this he was initially disappointed, but in 1783 he decided to take the further step of setting up one or more theatres, correctly calculating that not only would they draw the crowds but that the turnover of the booksellers, jewellers and such-like would incidentally benefit, so allowing him to charge higher rents. In other words, the duke was proposing to turn the gardens into a permanent fairground, complete with places of theatrical entertainment, just about the time when the old fairs were disappearing for good.

A small puppet theatre had been set up in the north-west corner of the grounds as long ago as 1753, for the amusement of the children of the ducal family; it was enlarged and thrown open to the public on 26 October 1784. The director was one Jean-Nicolas Gardeur, credited with having invented the art of papier-mâché sculpture; he worked in partnership with his brother, a tailor who stitched costumes for the marionettes, and with a wood-turner who carved the figures. But puppet plays were no longer regarded as adult entertainment, and the new theatre did not begin to prosper until Gardeur decided to do exactly what Audinot had done some fifteen years before, and introduced a few child actors to play alongside the marionettes. This change proved so successful that in a short while the marionettes were relegated to an attic and all the parts entrusted to children.

However, the licence granted to the Théâtre des Beaujolais, as the new enterprise came to be called by the Parisians,[24] did not permit the appearance of speaking actors on stage. To circumvent the difficulty, the child actors were taught to mime silently while adults spoke or sang their parts behind the wings and backdrop; as the children moved about the stage, their unseen 'voices' were required to move about unheard in felt slippers so as to take up a new position behind the little ones who were mouthing the words. This called for careful rehearsal, but on the other hand there was no need for a prompter since the speeches could be read directly from copies of the play. The illusion was such that many members of the audience refused to believe that the children were merely acting in dumb show, or even that they were children at all, since the unusually low front friezes, the so-called sky borders, made them appear taller than they were. 'So perfect is the deception', wrote an English visitor, 'that it has given rise to considerable wagers whether the voices did not actually proceed from persons on the stage.'[25]

If the vogue of the Beaujolais was short-lived (it closed its doors finally, for want of custom, in 1790), the same cannot be said of Gaillard and Dorfeuille's Variétés-Amusantes, the second theatre to open in the Palais-Royal with the active support of the Duc de Chartres, and one destined to go from strength to strength and ultimately to replace the Comédie-Française in the course of the Revolution. A temporary wooden structure was put up in 1784, in the south-west part of the grounds, where the inaugural performance took place on 1 January 1785, the day after Audinot's Ambigu-Comique closed on the Boulevard. The directors made it clear from the start that they had no intention that the Variétés-Palais-Royal, as it was officially called, should be mistaken for yet another minor theatre: they pitched their prices quite high, hoping to attract the same kind of moneyed clientèle as was to be found in the royal theatres; they refused to open a booth in the fairground, as the boulevard theatres had been required to do; and in order to make sure of the goodwill of the Opera, they voluntarily increased their annual fee to this institution by an extra 10,000 *livres*. Most important of all, they succeeded in their petition to be relieved of the obligation to submit in advance, for the approval of the Comédie-Française and the Comédie-Italienne, the text of all new plays they proposed to produce. A special edict dispensing them from this requirement was signed by Louis XVI on 25 March 1786.

This preliminary inspection, commonly but incorrectly referred to as a second censorship above and beyond the police censorship to which all plays were subject at this time, had been instituted in 1769 in the hope of avoiding future arguments about the rights of Nicolet and Audinot to put on certain plays which might appear to infringe the monopoly of the Comédie-Française on straight drama and that of the Comédie-Italienne on comic opera. Two senior actors, Préville from the Comédie-Française and Dehesse from the Comédie-

Italienne, were nominated by Papillon de la Ferté to carry out these inspections. The manuscripts of all new plays had to be submitted to these two, or their successors, who had the right to make such alterations or deletions as they thought fit, or even to claim for their own companies works they deemed worthy of production on a royal stage. If the *sociétaires* entrusted with these supervisory functions

saw the play was well-constructed, they would not hesitate to strike out a few scenes in order to muddle the flow ... Often the actors from the privileged theatres would only admit disconnected scenes; occasionally they would reserve for their own theatres a play written for a minor theatre; but most frequently they would judge the play to be too good for the minor theatres but not good enough for theirs; in which case they would prohibit it entirely and it was never seen anywhere.[26]

This tyranny exercised by the royal theatres over the repertoire of the commercial theatres was primarily designed to maintain what the former saw as the proper distinction between the kind of plays they put on and the kind one went to see on the Boulevard. For this reason, a piece of gross pornography had a better chance of being approved than one that observed the proprieties. Louis-Sébastien Mercier, one of the most virulent critics of the Comédie-Française, in a chapter of his popular *Tableau de Paris* entitled 'The Hustings of the Boulevards', complained that

the King's players have made it a rule that the entertainments in the popular theatres should be either obscene or trivial, since their privileges are interpreted as forbidding any other company of players to enact moral and decent works. Thus, in accordance with these not only nonsensical but imaginary prerogatives, the common people are to be fed only poisonous filth: this is the strange theory they put into practice. Dirty plays are passed without comment; whatever has a tincture of morality is stopped; and that, in what passes for a policed society![27]

In fact, Mercier was overstating the low moral tone of many of the plays that were put on at the boulevard theatres in the last quarter of the eighteenth century. Contemporaries noted that Audinot, from 1776 onwards, followed by Nicolet a little later, started to show 'real comedies, so refined and delicate that they seemed *worthy of another place*'.[28] The plays that Robineau started writing for Nicolet about this time were a great improvement on Taconet's vulgar farces; as the author himself boasted, he had 'cleansed the Augean stables'.[29] At a later point he started writing for the Variétés-Amusantes where

– to cite but one example – *Le Danger des liaisons* (1783), no doubt inspired by the immense success the same year of Laclos's *Les Liaisons dangereuses*, was intended to warn society against the perils of promiscuity. Plays of this sort did not always avoid sentimentality, but they were also uplifting without being tiresomely didactic and were totally lacking in the coarseness associated with earlier boulevard productions. Prejudice against the minor theatres was still strong enough to prevent critical notice being taken of them in the public press – unless it was that, as Métra supposed, the Comédie-Française still retained enough credit to suppress the eulogies they might otherwise have earned.[30]

Interference by the major theatres in the repertories of the minors persisted down to the outbreak of the Revolution: a register of decisions taken over the years 1784–9[31] shows that they were particularly concerned with the protection of their property rights, which they interpreted with more than ordinary freedom. Not content with forbidding parodies of plays shown on their stage, they even claimed copyright on a character's name, so that for instance no boulevard play detailing the further adventures of Beaumarchais's Figaro had any chance of being staged. They also objected to the minor theatres producing any play that had appeared in print but had not been seen on the stage, on the grounds that – who knows? – they might want to produce it themselves one day. It goes without saying that any play exceeding the statutory three acts, or any play in verse, was automatically disqualified. What was more remarkable was that plays in which titled characters appeared were also barred, as being out of place in a theatre designed to amuse the dregs of society. The Comédie-Française affected to be unaware that the audiences of the more important commercial theatres were, by the 1780s, composed in a large measure of precisely those people of rank whose presence among the dramatis personae of a boulevard play would have been construed, so they claimed, as an impertinence.

Aware that the playwrights, with the exception of those who confined themselves to neoclassical tragedy, were tending increasingly to offer their products to the commercial theatres, the actors exercising supervisory rights did not scruple to use their powers to transfer to their own companies any play likely to prove successful. No inquiries were made, apparently, to discover whether the author desired this transfer; it was assumed the honour could not be declined. In 1780 the Comédie-Française, short of new material, decided to appropriate Dorvigny's *Les Noces houzardes*, which the author had originally offered to the Variétés-Amusantes; however, either because of the change of ambience, or because of inadequate casting, it did not do as well as expected. *Fanfan et Colas*, on the other hand, written by Robineau for the same theatre and similarly appropriated, was a useful permanent addition to the repertoire of the Comédie-Italienne, as too was Mercier's *La Brouette du vinaigrier* (The Vinegar Seller's Wheelbarrow), originally performed by the Associés; both these plays were put on within a month of each other in 1784. Writing of the new production of *La Brouette du vinaigrier*, J.-H. Meister observed sarcastically:

The actors of the Comédie-Italienne have had no qualms in laying their hands on this play, and their clients in the pit, almost as cultivated as those of the boulevard theatres, gave it a rapturous welcome; they welcomed it, one could say, as a tribute paid by the actors in receipt of a royal subvention to the noble school at which their taste was formed and cultivated.[32]

This remark, implying that the major theatres were actually beholden to the minor ones, is not untypical of the attitude of progressive-minded critics in the 1780s. The privileged position of the state theatres *vis-à-vis* the commercial sector seemed more and more difficult to justify as time went by. The former had, it was said, the best actors; this might have been true, but the boulevard companies were by no means short of talent. Thanks in part to royal largesse, the two Comédies undoubtedly possessed the finer theatres, but that they were in receipt of this bounty was yet another aspect of their special privileges, many of which were felt to be exorbitant and outdated. Gone were the days when the boulevard theatres were forbidden to perform anything but simple farces and knockabout shows; by now the situation had completely changed. The commercial sector, having grown in size and stature over a short space of time, could claim that it was meeting the current demands of the theatre-going public more effectively than the Comédie-Française, with its outmoded heroic tragedy. 'I, who will never go into mourning for Cleopatra or for Pompey', wrote a pamphleteer in 1786,

I, who believe I shed enough tears at the interments of today without shedding more at the funerals of antiquity – ah! do not deprive me of the resources of the fairground, and allow me my diversions at the theatres of the Boulevard! How many are there for whom the Comédie-Française is too fine! It would be a pity if a man could not find amusement unless he was a great wit or a great lord.[33]

Precisely because the commercial theatres had to comply with the requirements of the market, and because this market now included a great many more than the 'wits and great lords' that formerly made up a theatre audience, they were bound, in spite of being hampered by petty and vexatious regulations, to go from strength to strength.

Finally, it must be stressed that the three royal theatres did not present a united front when faced with the growing prestige of the theatres on the Boulevard and, more recently, in the grounds of the Palais-Royal. One of the three, the Académie Royale de Musique, had a vested interest in the continuing prosperity of the commercial sector. This was made crystal clear by Papillon de la Ferté in a memorandum to the administrative committee of the Opera, in which he wrote:

It is in maintaining and protecting these lesser theatres, it is in ensuring their success, that the Opera can count on the continuation of the payments that it requires of them. It cannot, therefore, neglect to place them under its wing. Its interests demand that it protect them vigorously against the renewed pestering to which the royal actors will subject them.[34]

An alternative way of looking at the question can be found in Métra's letter dated 7 October 1784, in which he deplores the plight of the managers of the minor theatres, subjected to a steep levy by the Opera, and at the same time losing their best plays to the two Comédies.

When one looks at the strangely contradictory way the directors of these theatres are treated by their arrogant rivals, one would never suppose that it is the same government that on the one hand causes them to be fleeced by the Opera, and on the other hand allows the actors of the two royal theatres to mutilate their plays.[35]

What exactly was the attitude of the government to this question? As far as the Opera was concerned, it was only too delighted, no doubt, that private enterprise was doing its bit towards keeping afloat this important, but ruinously expensive, cultural institution. In addition, it is likely that from time to time voices were raised in the council chamber in disdainful support of the minor theatres, for these fleapits were not to be despised: better lewd farces than rioting in the streets. When the Comédie-Française complained, the minister answered that some form of dramatic entertainment was necessary for the common people, and that 'the system of Louis XIV had changed'.[36] If occasionally he gave in, to the extent of promulgating severe edicts against the boulevard theatres, privately no doubt he winked at any infringement.

And so the old monarchy, in this matter as in many others, progressed cumbrously from expedient to expedient, trying to prop up the old system it had inherited, taking due note of new developments, hampering but not daring to suppress them outright, reacting sluggishly to circumstances which were pointing in one direction only, to the ultimate abolition of privileges and to what was called the 'liberation of the theatres', achieved by the National Assembly in 1791, destroyed by Napoleon I in 1807 and re-established finally by his nephew in 1864.

CHAPTER 3

Dramatic censorship down to its abolition

Throughout the entire stretch of time we are considering, there was no more contentious issue arising in state–theatre relations than that of the censorship of dramatic works, a duty which the various successive governments in France were on only rare occasions prepared to shrug off. Under the *ancien régime* the machinery of censorship was designed only for the control of dramatic works produced at the three royal theatres in Paris; the boulevard theatres escaped by and large the censor's attention, however coarse the theatrical fare they occasionally offered: this was presumably because there was general agreement that their repertoire was beneath notice. But the Comédie-Française in particular was regarded as the state theatre, bound to uphold the dignity of the monarchy and the inviolability of the Catholic Church. In addition it was at the Théâtre-Français, or as it came increasingly to be called by writers in the closing years of the *ancien régime*, the Théâtre de la Nation, that audiences, more quick-witted and better informed than elsewhere, were most liable to pick up references to matters of state. Before the outbreak of the Revolution, however, the existence of the dramatic censorship appears to have been regarded, even by progressives, as no more than a minor irritant. This was in part due to the fact that the main thrust of liberal resistance during the Enlightenment was directed against the censorship of books and pamphlets; in part also because the censors at this period, being for the most part playwrights themselves or at any rate men of letters, were not perceived as being closely implicated in the machinery of state authority.

The minister with overall responsibility for dramatic censorship was the Lieutenant-General of Police, but he normally delegated the task of actually reading the plays in manuscript to a 'censeur de la police', a post held in succession by some half-dozen men in the course of the eighteenth century. The Abbé Chérier was the first, followed by Crébillon the Elder, a dramatist of some repute in his day; Marin, another dramatist; Crébillon the Younger, a novelist remembered particularly for his work *Les Egarements du cœur et de l'esprit*; and finally Suard, a journalist and critic, appointed in 1777 and still in office when the Revolution broke out. In between the younger Crébillon and Suard, Sauvigny, another tragedian, held office briefly in 1776–7. Of them all, it was probably Jean-Baptiste Suard who was the least distrusted by the playwrights, if for no other reason than that he had no direct connection with the stage and could not therefore be suspected of partiality or self-interest, unlike, for instance, Crébillon senior, who invariably refused his visa to any play by Voltaire he was required to examine. (It needed the personal intervention of his superior to allow *Mahomet* to be shown in 1742.) Marin, on the other hand, was at first inclined to an inconceivable laxness, to which the government took grave exception, even going to the point of sending him to the Bastille for twenty-four hours for having allowed through untouched Dorat's *Théagène et Chariclée* (1763), in spite of a tirade it contained concerning the *rois fainéants* of Merovingian times, which the audience took to refer to Louis XV and roundly applauded. After this unfortunate incident Marin went to the opposite extreme, and works that came under his scrutiny risked being objected to on the slightest suspicion of subversiveness. In 1765 he even refused to admit Sedaine's brilliant comedy *Le Philosophe sans le savoir*, on the grounds that it constituted an apologia for duelling, a practice long forbidden by law. In fact, as Sedaine saw it, his play was primarily concerned with the prejudice in France against men of rank taking up a career in trade; the challenge to a duel arises from some slighting remarks about merchants made by an officer in the hearing of the merchant's son, and although the two young men meet to settle their differences in the time-honoured way, they discharge their pistols into the air and are reconciled. Sedaine appealed to Sartine, the then Lieutenant of Police, inviting him to attend a rehearsal, along with other highly placed officials – and their wives. The inclusion of a feminine contingent was a shrewd move, for *Le Philosophe sans le savoir* was an early example of the *comédie larmoyante*, and the women were, predictably, wiping their eyes before the end. The outcome of this private showing was that Sedaine was granted permission for its public performance on condition he agreed to a few minor changes.

One important difference between the functioning of the

censorship in the eighteenth century and its operation in the nineteenth was that in the latter period it was the manager's responsibility to obtain the censor's sanction for a particular play to be
produced, whereas in the pre-revolutionary period it was left to the
author of the play to obtain permission.[1] It was also open to the
author, if he disagreed with the official censor's verdict, to choose
some other well-known figure to vet his work (this happened notably
in the case of Beaumarchais's *Mariage de Figaro*): or else the censor
himself, in case of doubt, might refer the play to higher authority. In
some difficult cases the manuscript could pass through several
hands, being forwarded first by the censor to his immediate superior,
the Lieutenant of Police, by him to the Keeper of the Seals (i.e. the
Lord Chancellor), and by him to other high officers of state. 'A new
tragedy', as Grimm observed in 1783, 'is an affair of state and gives
rise to the trickiest negotiations; it is necessary to consult the King's
ministers and ambassadors of the foreign powers thought to be
involved, and it is only with the approval of these gentlemen that a
humble author at last obtains permission to expose his work to the
plaudits or the hisses of the pit.'[2] The tragedy Grimm alluded to
here was *Elisabeth de France et Don Carlos*, which dealt with the same
illicit passion of Philip II of Spain's son for his stepmother as was
later to furnish Schiller with the subject of his *Don Carlos, Infant von
Spanien*. The French foreign minister, asked for his opinion on the
propriety of permitting a dramatization of this historical passage,
passed the manuscript on to the Spanish ambassador, leaving it to
him to confirm that the play contained no objectionable matter.
The author, who had had two tragedies performed already by the
Comédie-Française, enjoyed the favour of the Duc d'Orléans whose
secretary he was; but in spite of this nobleman's pleas, the ambassador refused to commit himself one way or the other, and the play
was accordingly never staged.

Fear of giving offence to friendly powers was the reason why
several plays were refused a licence. La Harpe's tragedy *Menzicoff*
was forbidden when the Russian ambassador gave it as his opinion
that certain scenes might offend Catherine the Great. The ambassador of the Netherlands complained of the part given to the Prince of
Orange in Lemierre's *Barnevald*, which accordingly remained
unstaged until 1790. The British were just as susceptible. Sauvigny
had chosen as the subject of a new drama the adventure of Capt.
Asgill, captured at the surrender of York Town in 1781 and sen-

tenced to death by the insurgents in retaliation for the execution of an American prisoner of war. Even though Asgill had been reprieved, thanks to French intervention, it was thought necessary to suppress the drama based on this incident.

The censors were particularly cautious over authorizing plays tending to ridicule or slander persons in public life. In 1764, a comedy entitled *La Confiance trahie* (Trust Betrayed), which included several satirical portraits of well-known financiers, was disallowed for this reason. Grimm, for once, approved: 'the method of farming out taxes may be very defective, but that is no excuse for translating on to the stage individual tax-farmers, particularly in a country where personal affronts are so strongly resented'.[3] A similar case occurred in 1770, when a new play by Palissot, *L'Homme dangereux*, came before the censors for their approval. The author was well known for his earlier attacks on the *encyclopédistes*, and it might have been supposed that anything from his pen would be looked on indulgently by the authorities; nevertheless, when the manuscript of *L'Homme dangereux* was read by Suard, he pulled a long face and wrote to the Lieutenant of Police expressing the gravest doubts as to whether the play should be passed for public performance. It was full of transparent references to Palissot's enemies, who may also have been enemies of the state but, as Suard wrote,

this type of work should be forbidden, since it puts on stage men who are under our eyes and with whom we mingle in society; so that it would be impossible to stage such a play without allusions being made and without stirring up all kinds of evil passions and encouraging whispering and scandal-mongering apt to disturb the good order of a well-policed theatre.[4]

It is clear that the censorship, while always ready to pounce on plays covertly ridiculing the abuses and foibles of the current regime, did not necessarily put the stamp of approval on works attacking the critics of the established order. The guiding principle to which the censorship worked was apparently to make sure that audiences should on no occasion become overexcited or be given any opportunity to manifest political partisanship of one sort or another.

This tacit rule accounts for several other areas being regarded as 'off limits' for playwrights. Thus, dramatic works in any respect hostile to the state religion were automatically barred; the prohibition extended even to defunct pagan cults incorporating rites and ceremonies which could be regarded as versions of those practised by Catholics: the government had no intention of allowing the theatre to be used as a vehicle for the propagation of the views of the Enlightenment. When in 1762 Rousseau's *Emile* was published – including the defence of 'natural religion' contained in the *Profession de foi du vicaire savoyard* – not only was the author expelled from France, but the book itself was denounced as pernicious by the Archbishop of Paris and symbolically burned by the public executioner. Sauvigny saw here a golden opportunity to cash in on the affair and composed *La Mort de Socrate*, a tragedy in which those who could read between the lines could without difficulty equate Socrates with Rousseau, the high priest Anitus with the Archbishop Christophe de Beaumont, and the Areopagus of Athens with the Paris *parlement*. The censorship insisted on changes to eliminate all personal allusions, which Sauvigny, anxious to see his play performed, accepted, and it was duly put on the following year, though purged perforce of all the original attacks on the priesthood.

Marin had been the *censeur de la police* responsible for the delay in producing *La Mort de Socrate* and it was Marin, too, who refused to sanction the performance of Jean-Gaspard de Fontanelle's *Ericie*, billed for production in the winter of 1768. The tragedy was set in pre-Christian Rome; the heroine is a vestal virgin who, distraught at hearing that her lover has insinuated himself into the forbidden recesses of the temple, neglects to tend the altar flame and allows it to expire, for which sacrilegious act the only penalty can be death. It would have been possible, in Marin's view, to read this play as a covert denunciation of the practice in Catholic countries at this time of allowing fathers of undowered girls to have their daughters confined to religious houses for life, regardless of their personal wishes. The Lieutenant of Police, not altogether convinced by his subordinate's reasoning, sent a copy of the play to the archbishop, who nominated an *ad hoc* committee of priests of his diocese and doctors of theology to advise him. Knowing that the Comédie-Française had judged the play to be stageworthy, he was presumably anxious to cover himself in the event that the censor's verdict would have to be upheld; but anyone unacquainted with the French way of doing things must be astonished, observed Grimm, 'that a mediocre tragedy roughed out by a schoolboy should become an affair of state, and cause head-scratching in the highest places of the kingdom. The outcome of these deliberations', he went on to predict, 'will be that the play will not be produced and that the author will be forbidden to publish the text. He will laugh at the interdict and will arrange to have his play appear clandestinely. The public will not read it, and everyone will be satisfied.'[5] *Ericie* was, as Grimm foretold, accorded a decent burial, and not disinterred until August 1789, by which time the theatre-going public was ready for fresher meat and viewed the corpse with indifference.

The censorship did not, at this date, have judicial existence outside Paris, which meant that in theory it was open to the author of any dramatic work which had been forbidden in the capital to have it produced at some other regional centre; as indeed Fontanelle tried to do, taking his unlucky *Ericie* down to Lyons and offering it to the theatre there. But it was given only one performance; the credit of Mgr de Beaumont was sufficient to prevent a longer run. Voltaire, if he did not want to be embarrassed by having a new tragedy stopped in Paris, would arrange for it to be produced somewhere in the provinces. Collé's *Partie de chasse de Henri IV*, prohibited under Louis XV because of fears that disobliging comparisons might have been made between the present occupant of the throne and his popular predecessor, was performed at Bordeaux, Lyons and even at the civic theatre at Versailles before it was seen in Paris. At a time when the Comédie-Française was still forbidden to produce Beaumarchais's *Mariage de Figaro*, the players at Rouen had announced it in advance for a particular day and might indeed have scooped it, had not the local *parlement* slapped on an injunction. Normally, there being no organized system of censorship in the provinces, it was to the mayor or whatever magistrate besides had responsibility for policing a town that it fell to grant or withhold permission to enact a given play. Although the local director was required to submit his programme in advance, the authorities were not always alert enough to detect the presence of a forbidden work, particularly if its content was disguised by an alteration in the title. This happened notably with Fenouillot de Falbaire's *L'Honnête Criminel*, a play attacking the persecution of Protestants, which had been banned by the Paris censorship in 1768 but was occasionally shown in the provinces under its subtitle *L'Amour filial*.

Since it was principally at the Comédie-Française[6] that the censorship would make its authority felt on the rare occasions when it was called on to do so, it is hardly surprising that the campaign for its abolition at the start of the Revolution should have centred on what was still universally considered the premier theatre of the kingdom. The occasion for this campaign was a tragedy by an almost totally unknown young man, Marie-Joseph Chénier, which had been written between 1787 and 1788, accepted for production by the reading committee of the Comédie-Française on 2 September 1788, but refused by the censor on the grounds that it was violently anti-Catholic and that it portrayed a vacillating and bigoted monarch. It was entitled *Charles IX ou la Saint-Barthélémy*, its subject being the massacre of the Huguenots in Paris on 24 August 1572.

Chénier had, at this time, no strong body of support inside the Comédie-Française, but was not without political friends whom it is probable he met at the Café Procope, since he was lodging nearby. They were all men of advanced views: Fabre d'Eglantine, another playwright, remembered for having invented the poetic names by which the months of the republican calendar were later known; Camille Desmoulins, famous for having called on the Parisians to rise in defiance of the armies that were threatening them – an appeal made on 12 July 1789 that led directly to the storming of the Bastille; Danton, whose secretary Desmoulins became; and Collot d'Herbois, an actor and, until February 1789, director of the city theatre at Lyons. Of this quartet the first three perished during the Terror, while Collot d'Herbois was deported to Guyana, where the chances of survival were so small that it was known as the 'dry guillotine'; he died soon after his arrival. Only Marie-Joseph Chénier himself survived until the following century.

Encouraged no doubt by their inflammatory talk, and emboldened by the exciting events that marked the outbreak of the Revolution, Chénier made an appointment to see the *comité d'administration* of the Comédie-Française. Claiming that, with the advent of liberty, censorship had become a thing of the past, he demanded that they should put his tragedy into rehearsal. The committee, having deliberated, invited Chénier back into the council chamber to inform him that they had no option but to consider themselves bound by the old rules and regulations until such time as new ones had been promulgated. In this instance the rule was that they were forbidden to produce a play that had not received the authorization of the censor; so, much as they regretted the necessity, they were bound to decline, for the moment, to stage *Charles IX*.

Exactly a month later, a concerted effort was made by Chénier's friends to force the issue. On that day (19 August 1789) the walls of Paris were placarded with a stirring appeal to the public to demand the performance of *Charles IX*, 'a truly political, truly patriotic tragedy', in defiance, if need be, of the outdated authority of the Gentlemen of the Bedchamber. The same evening, a leaflet with a similar message was handed out to the audience in the theatre; it ended: 'The inquisition of thought still reigns in our drama; the time has come to throw off so odious a yoke! Let us unite in calling, in the name of liberty, for the speedy production of *Charles IX*.'[7] Then, in the course of the Molière comedy that was billed to round off the evening's entertainment, isolated shouts were heard from the pit; the players left the stage and a spokesman (the actor Fleury) came on to inquire what it was that had caused the commotion. It may have been Danton who thereupon, standing on a bench, claimed to be expressing the general wish in demanding that *Charles IX* should be shown without delay. Fleury replied that the company had not started to rehearse it, 'since up to now we have still not received permission to perform it'. 'Away with permission!' thundered the orator. 'It is time that the despotic power wielded by the dramatic censorship came to an end. We want to be free and to hear performed what works we will, in the same way as we are free to think what we will.' When Fleury objected that there were laws covering such cases, the other shouted 'these laws constitute an abuse, and as such they are invalid'. The argument was beginning to be drowned in the general hubbub, when another voice, shouting above the din, made the suggestion that the question be referred to the municipality of Paris, and that the outcome be announced from the stage the following day.[8]

Accordingly, on the morrow a deputation from the Comédie-Française waited on the mayor to report the incident and ask what instructions he had to give. Jean-Sylvain Bailly, the first to bear the title of mayor of Paris in modern times, had been appointed to his post the day after the fall of the Bastille; his particular responsibility was to preserve order in the city and to assure its provisioning. He was to serve in this office for two years, after which he sought the tranquillity of the countryside and there composed his memoirs, which include an account of the visit from the players on the morning of 20 August 1789. Bailly was not deceived by the report that the 'general public' was clamouring to see *Charles IX*; he realized perfectly well that the disturbance in the theatre had been orchestrated by a small group of agitators. As for the issue of principle raised, namely the question of dramatic censorship, Bailly remained far from convinced that these controls should be abandoned.

I believe that the freedom of the press is the basis of civil liberty, but that the same thing cannot apply to the theatre. I believe that in a theatre, attended by crowds of men who work each other up, one should ban anything that might tend to corrupt manners or undermine authority. The theatre is a branch of public education which should not be abandoned to all and sundry, and which ought to come under the surveillance of the government.[9]

The same distinction between the freedom of the press and the freedom of the stage had been made earlier by Suard, still theoretically exercising the functions of dramatic censor, in an article published in the *Journal de Paris* on 27 August 1789:

Freedom of the press is not attended by the same inconveniences as freedom of the stage. One reads a book on one's own, quietly, and communicates the impression it has made only in conversation with a few individuals. Theatrical performances, on the other hand, address themselves to the imagination and the senses; they can excite every passion, and the resulting impressions acquire an extraordinary energy by the simultaneous interaction of all the impressions received by a great multitude in concourse.[10]

Thus Suard makes it a question of public order; it is not the dissemination of dangerous ideas that he fears, but the stimulation of collective frenzy.

Bailly told the deputation of actors that he would refer the question to the National Assembly of which he was himself a member. The Assembly appointed a committee which made its report in due course, and authorization was given for production of the disputed tragedy. The delay before the play was finally put on was longer than would have been needed to rehearse it; it is possible that the Gentlemen of the Bedchamber, acting under instructions from Louis XVI, were making a last-ditch attempt to assert their powers over the activities of the Comédie-Française. The enforced return of the royal family from Versailles to Paris, on 5–6 October, made the question even more sensitive, for everyone knew that the play presented Charles IX in a far from flattering light; this was not the moment to fan the flames of anti-monarchic sentiment; and on 14 October the police department issued a statement to the effect that it had been decided the first performance should be 'provisionally suspended'. The inaugural performance finally took place on 4

November 1789. Earlier discussions about the advisability of authorizing it had had the predictable effect of providing Chénier with welcome publicity, and the audience was said to have been even larger than that at the first performance of *Le Mariage de Figaro*. But it was not, as had been feared, disorderly, perhaps because, before the curtain went up, an orator in the pit had proposed that the first man to interrupt the performance should be dealt with by 'popular justice' – a euphemism, well understood at the time, for stringing him up at the nearest lamp post.

The question whether dramatic censorship should continue or not, though raised by the affair of *Charles IX*, had not been settled by its authorization. The campaign for the abolition of the censorship was fuelled again in March 1790, when an anti-religious play by Bertin d'Antilly, *Les Religieuses danoises* (The Danish Nuns), which had been accepted by the Comédie-Italienne, was refused a licence by the censor. Exactly the same procedure was followed as for *Charles IX*. A friend of the author interrupted the evening's performance to demand the play be produced; the actor on stage replied they had not been authorized to perform it; voices from the pit were heard to fulminate against the censorship; whereupon the actor agreed to convey the wishes of the public to the mayor. Bailly on this occasion decided in favour of allowing performances, stipulating however that the author make various cuts and changes to render the play more seemly.

Finally, at the beginning of 1791, the whole question was debated in the Assembly in the context of a new law on the freedom of the theatres, and the vote went against the retention of the censorship. Clause 6 of the law of 13 January 1791 enacted that

> the managers or members of the different theatres, by reason of their status, will be subject to the inspection of the municipalities; they will receive orders only from municipal officers, who are not permitted to suspend or forbid the performance, saving the responsibility of the authors and actors, and who may require nothing of the actors but what is in conformity with police regulations.[11]

The vital phrase here was 'saving the responsibility of the authors and actors'.[12] The press at the time, or part of it at least, regarded this as constituting a dangerous loophole. 'Has it not been demonstrated,' wrote a contributor to the widely read *Révolutions de Paris*, 'and do we not have the proof daily, that the soundest ideas being by their very nature the strangest to a nation only just emerging from servitude, are precisely those which, when given publicity, cause the greatest effervescence?'[13] In other words, it is possible that a play putting forward very advanced but nevertheless tenable opinions might cause a considerable uproar in the theatre, for which 'the actors and authors' would be held responsible.

It is possible that the Constituent Assembly intended no more, by introducing this reservation, than to satisfy the objections raised during the debate by the Abbé Maury and others that if there were no laws against outraging morality and attacking religion and government, these things would be, as a matter of course, outraged and attacked in certain theatres. Nevertheless the loophole was a real one, and eventually, as we shall see, allowed the Jacobins, by referring to 'the responsibility of the authors and actors', to have the entire company of the erstwhile Comédie-Française arrested and imprisoned along with the author of the offending play, François de Neufchâteau.

CHAPTER 4

The liberation of the theatres

The law passed by the National Assembly on 13 January 1791 marks one of the two turning-points in relations between the theatres and the state (the other being Napoleon III's decree of 6 January 1864); it owes this distinction not just for the clause abolishing censorship which, as we shall see, proved short-lived. The decree on the theatres, as it came to be called, embodied two main provisions: first, that any citizen was henceforth free to open a theatre on a simple declaration to the municipality; secondly, that performing rights in any dramatic work were to be considered as vested in the author during his lifetime, and in his heirs for five years after his death; as soon as the five years had elapsed, the work became public property and could therefore be produced freely anywhere in the kingdom.[1]

It might be thought that the first to welcome a move to decontrol the theatres would have been the boulevard directors, who had suffered incessant harrying in times past when they were trying to establish themselves and attract sufficient custom to make their enterprises pay. But Nicolet, Audinot, the directors of the Théâtre des Associés etc. were none too anxious to see a mushroom growth of new theatres, on the Boulevard and elsewhere in Paris, leading to unwelcome competition. Even before the Revolution they had viewed with scant enthusiasm the founding, in June 1787, of the Bluettes-Comiques by Clément de Lornaizon; their complaints resulted in this upstart being confined to dumb show, with off-stage and unseen actors speaking or singing the parts. Another newcomer on the Boulevard had been Plancher-Valcour, whose diminutive theatre, called the Délassements-Comiques, had been very prosperous over its first two years, until in 1787 a mysterious fire destroyed it utterly. Plancher-Valcour was successful in raising the capital to rebuild it within a matter of months, but his jealous neighbours

55

managed to persuade the police authorities to impose draconian conditions on this struggling manager; like Lornaizon, he was limited to mime, and was in addition subjected to the humiliating obligation of keeping a gauze curtain drawn over the stage at all times, so that the audience saw the show as it were 'through a glass darkly'. The great comic actor Potier, one of the leading lights at the Variétés under the First Empire and the Restoration, learned his trade as a teenager at the Délassements-Comiques, and recalled later how, 'after the fall of the Bastille, one evening when we were putting on a patriotic piece, Valcour tore down the gauze curtain crying "Long live liberty!"'.[2]

Thus it was not to be expected that the existing private-enterprise theatre managers would feel moved, when the Revolution dawned, to start agitating for legislation that would have the effect of vastly increasing the number of Plancher-Valcours along the boulevards and side streets of Paris. The pressure group in favour of this reform consisted entirely of playwrights: Marie-Joseph Chénier and his two friends Collot d'Herbois and Fabre d'Eglantine, along with some older men, Beaumarchais, Sedaine and Louis-Sébastien Mercier. Their activities were fuelled by a rooted rancour towards the Comédie-Française; it was also the Comédie-Française that showed most persistence in defending the status quo, and in the end it was the Comédie-Française that suffered most grievously from the proposals that passed into law in 1791.

Complaints about the exorbitant privileges that the premier theatre enjoyed had been rife for a generation before this happened. As early as January 1769 Grimm passed a sombre judgement on the Comédie-Française, which he saw as travelling ever faster down the road to decadence and ruin; he finished with a denunciation of the whole system of entrenched monopoly in a passage constituting a remarkable forecast of what was actually to happen twenty-two years later.

I have the honour of wishing the King's players a happy New Year, and of advising them that on the morrow of the day when His Majesty appoints me first minister, I shall not fail to lay hands on all exclusive privileges affecting the theatres; that I shall give a free rein to all those who aim to make their fortunes by providing the public with decent entertainment; that I shall see nothing wrong in the plays of Molière and Voltaire being performed on the same day in two or three different districts of Paris; that I shall concern myself very little whether people grow rich or go bankrupt in these undertakings; but that I trust my government will ensure that the general public will be better served.[3]

The 'exclusive privileges' to which Grimm refers here were those granted to the Comédie-Française by Louis XIV when he decreed that his players alone, to be known henceforth as the Comédiens Ordinaires de Sa Majesté, should have sole rights of performing tragedy and comedy in Paris;[4] a privilege similar to, and possibly copied from, that which had been granted to the Drury Lane theatre in London by Charles II in 1660, by which that company (with the addition at a later date of Covent Garden and the Haymarket) became a 'patent theatre' with the sole right to perform Shakespeare's works and all other 'straight' drama, leaving only parodies and musicals to the minor theatres. But any special privilege, of whatever kind, and whether accorded by royal authority or by long custom, was looked on askance as a remnant of feudalism by those who were busy laying the foundations of the revolution which they trusted would lead to the regeneration of the French nation.

Argument at first centred on the question of the copyright enjoyed by the Comédie-Française on its own stock of plays, which included the complete works of Corneille, Racine, Molière, Regnard and Voltaire. As early as 1773, this entrenched monopoly was denounced by Mercier in writing of the Comédiens du Roi: 'It seems astonishing that they should judge themselves the rightful heirs of the masterpieces of the French stage; assuredly these immortal works that kings cannot pay for (their gold being too base a metal in comparison) belong as of right to the nation and cannot belong to any other but the nation.'[5] Perhaps more importantly, any new comedy or tragedy accepted for production by the Comédie-Française could not be legally withdrawn and offered for performance elsewhere even though, through the indolence of the players or the bottlenecks produced by their accepting too many, the author had often to endure inordinate delays in seeing it performed. It was to counter abuses of this kind that playwrights started agitating, particularly over the last two decades of the *ancien régime*, for the establishment of a second national theatre which might share the double burden the Comédie-Française could no longer shoulder unaided: that of continuing the tradition of performing the masterpieces of the *grand siècle* for the edification of later generations, and that of allowing new dramatists the opportunity to win their spurs.

Baron de Grimm (or possibly J.-H. Meister who succeeded him about this time as editor of the *Correspondance littéraire*) had already observed in 1773 that the Comédie-Française had a large enough company to provide two troupes of players of equal prowess who – if only their regulations permitted it – might perform simultaneously at different localities within the city; this fact was brought to public attention that year when the senior players were, exceptionally, detained at Fontainebleau, leaving their understudies to replace them in Paris. The latter acquitted themselves so well, putting on rarely seen works such as Marivaux's *La Surprise de l'amour* and Voltaire's comedy *Nanine*, that Grimm posed the question whether 'dramatic art would not benefit if we were no longer limited to a single company of actors'; and he pointed out that in Molière's day there had been two or three companies active in Paris, 'and the theatres were not nearly as frequented as they are now'.[6] The proposal to found a second Théâtre-Français was formulated and made explicit in 1779 in a pamphlet by Alexandre-Jacques du Coudray, who argued, a little optimistically, that its establishment would do away with all complaints at a stroke.

Dramatists would no longer have to wait ten years for a new work to have the honour of being produced, nor six months to be granted the quarter of an hour necessary to read it to the actors. Audiences would no longer be bored by the everlasting performances of tired old plays, but would at last have the chance to view those innumerable tragedies and comedies, perpetually announced as 'forthcoming' on the lists posted in the greenroom.[7]

It was, of course, a fact that not only the growth in size of potential audiences and what Lagrave calls the 'galloping theatromania'[8] of the Parisians, but also certain shifts in taste leading to an outpouring of new types of play, that made it materially impossible for the members of a single theatrical company, especially the 'fat cats' of the Comédie-Française, to rehearse, produce and perform all the interesting novelties that were offered them.

It was in the early 1780s that La Harpe, the vainglorious author of various tragedies that had been put on with indifferent success by the Comédie-Française, entered the fray. In his report on the 1780–1 season he contrasted the keenness of the Comédie-Italienne with the 'prideful indolence' of its sister theatre, which had, he claimed, produced only four or five new plays in the course of the twelvemonth, as against thirty-six undertaken by the Italians. Over the next ten years La Harpe emerged as spokesman of the group of dissatisfied dramatists; but by 1790, when he led a deputation to the Assembly demanding reform, his ideas had broadened beyond the simple one of a second 'national' theatre. What he wanted now was for a number of theatrical companies in the capital to compete among each other for audiences, each being free to produce any play of any type by any author living or dead. He demanded further that the copyright on all plays should no longer be vested in a particular theatre, but should revert to the author himself, who should be free to dispose of his property to any theatre director on mutually agreed terms. As for the works of playwrights no longer living, they should be treated as having entered the public domain; anyone who wished to perform them should be entirely at liberty to do so, irrespective of any claims to ownership or copyright that might be raised. This would, of course, effectively end the monopoly not only of the Comédie-Française but of the Comédie-Italienne as well.

La Harpe's speech at the bar of the Assembly (24 August 1790) was printed and, as was to be expected, its arguments were hotly contested in a number of brochures issued shortly by the jurists feed by the Comédie-Française and by senior actors in the company anxious to refute the playwrights' pretensions. Tacitly yielding the point about a 'second national theatre', they concentrated on defending Louis XIV's original policy in establishing the monopoly by repeating his own reasons for laying it down: the dramatic art is better served by a concentration of acting talents in one theatre than by their dispersal over several. But apart from this, there was the purely legal point that the Comédie-Française had acquired an inalienable right to the works in its repertory, by virtue of contracts freely entered into by both parties and payment duly made in times past. The National Assembly had declared that the Revolution would always respect the rights of property; how could it now strip a company of actors of property rightfully acquired by fair purchase earlier? To this it was easy for the authors to reply that these past contracts had by no means been freely entered into, since the very monopoly on straight drama unwisely conceded to the Comédie-Française had prevented authors in the past from seeking better conditions elsewhere.

The Assembly, when the matter came to them for decision, accepted the authors' case in entirety, as we have seen. One effect, of course, was to throw open the classical repertory to the generality of theatres, who resorted to it with abandon. Using a sample of theatre programmes over the years 1791–4, Michèle Root-Bernstein has been able to show[9] that, for instance, 25 per cent of plays performed at Mlle Montansier's new theatre in the Palais-Royal, and no less than 43 per cent at the Théâtre-Molière, were taken from the stock that had previously been an exclusive preserve of the royal theatres. One playhouse on the Boulevard, the Lycée-Dramatique, relied entirely on such plays. Over the revolutionary period, 30 per cent of productions at the Délassements-Comiques and nearly 50 per cent of those shown at the Théâtre-Patriotique were classical comedies and tragedies. Nicolet found the fortunes of his theatre, now known as the Gaîté, greatly improved by the immense vogue for Molière's plays, particularly *Georges Dandin* and *Le Médecin malgré lui*; his clientèle had never been able to afford the prices at the Théâtre-Français, and had so little knowledge of Molière that they assumed these comedies were new-minted, and when the curtain went down shouted vociferously for the author in order to express their appreciation in the customary way.[10]

Even more startling in its impact was the freedom now granted to every citizen to set up a theatre, hire actors and charge for admission. This was justified, as a corollary of the Declaration of the Rights of Man, in Millin de Grandmaison's pamphlet *Sur la liberté du théâtre*, published in 1790 as a contribution to the debate on the question. Grandmaison argued that 'all men have equal rights. Thus, any exclusive privilege is wrongful, since its existence would deprive the totality of citizens of rights conferred on a small number of them. If one man has the right to erect a theatre, all men must be given that right.'[11] To allow it was none the less revolutionary to a degree difficult to appreciate today. Ever since 1402, when Charles VI decided to call a halt to the proliferation of playhouses, permission to operate a theatre had been sparingly granted by the state; restrictions had thus lasted for nearly four centuries before 1791, and had come to be thought of as something unquestionable and quite indispensable.

In fact, since 1788 there had been some loosening of the strict controls set on the number of theatres licensed for public performances, allowing the total in Paris to rise from eleven to fifteen. A new royal theatre, known initially as the Théâtre de Monsieur, was authorized by Louis XVI on 23 July 1788; its subsequent chequered fortunes will be discussed in the following chapter. In the Palais-Royal complex, Gaillard and Dorfeuille's new permanent theatre, replacing the wooden one that had opened in 1785, was inaugurated on 15 May 1790, in a building facing the Rue de Richelieu and destined, nine years later, to become the permanent home of the Comédie-Française. The Petits-Beaujolais had been forced to move out to the Boulevard de Ménilmontant, but the lease of this company's theatre in the grounds of the Palais-Royal was acquired by Mlle Montansier, the ex-manageress of the Théâtre de Versailles, who wanted a foothold in the centre of Paris. Finally, at the start of the new season after Easter 1790, the Théâtre-Français Comique et Lyrique opened its doors in the Rue de Bondy, on the site of Lécluse's long since demolished Variétés-Amusantes;[12] in November of the same year it was performing to packed houses an innocuous fantasy by Beffroy de Reigny, *Nicodème dans la lune ou la Révolution pacifique*, in which a French peasant, having ballooned to the moon, brings the benefits of a 'pacific revolution' to that distant satellite. The play proved enormously popular and went through no fewer than 191 performances in the succeeding thirteen months.

As was only to be expected, the new decree, by taking the lid off the cauldron, resulted in a veritable eruption of new places of theatrical entertainment. *La Feuille du jour* asserted in November 1791 that no fewer than seventy-eight registrations had been notified to the police in the course of the year. The would-be directors included, naturally, a goodly proportion of over-optimistic speculators who, when it came to the point, were unable to find the necessary working capital; none the less, it has been established that by the end of the year twenty-one new theatres had opened, giving a total for Paris of thirty-six: twenty-five more than had existed in 1789; and yet already an estimated 65,000 families had emigrated, mostly well-to-do, educated and accustomed to attend the theatres regularly.[13] 'If this craze goes on', remarked Beffroy de Reigny, 'there will soon be one theatre in every street, one dramatist in every house, one musician in every cellar and one actor in every garret.'[14] But of course, as could have been foreseen, the ferment soon settled, and the number of theatres functioning in the capital levelled down to around twenty to twenty-three towards the end of the decade. Profits, it was discovered, could go down as well as up. There were a number of outright business failures: the Théâtre du Mont-Parnasse, the Théâtre de la Liberté, the Théâtre de la Concorde, which changed its name in vain to the Théâtre Jean-Jacques Rousseau. The Théâtre d'Emulation gave up after two months; like certain others, this had been a successful amateur group which had decided to go public in May 1791 but soon afterwards reverted to its former status. Some theatres found they could afford to open only on certain days of the week, some only on Sundays. The Théâtre des Variétés Comiques et Lyriques was founded by a certain Mme Dupré, who had been manager of a company of actors at Beauvais and who started it up in February 1791, using the hall that Audinot had built at the Foire Saint-Germain; it foundered after little more than a year. The Théâtre du Marais seemed destined for a better fate. Opening in the Rue Culture-Sainte-Catherine on 31 August 1791, it drew the nucleus of its troupe from actors formerly attached to the Comédie-Italienne; one of its wealthier backers was Beaumarchais, who seldom made mistakes in business matters; the district from which it drew its clientèle was settled by rich merchants and legal luminaries, and the theatre itself was spacious, comfortable and newly built. It did in fact prosper for the first twelve months or so; but as the political situation worsened, most of its wealthier habitués fled abroad; even Beaumarchais, whose last play, *La Mère coupable* (The Guilty Mother) had its first performance at the Marais, was forced to leave for England; and the theatre could not survive the desertion of its richer patrons.

Not all the new theatres became casualties of the Revolution, however, and those established before it did succeed in weathering the storm, with the single exception of the Comédie-Française which, as we shall see, constituted in many ways a special case. Gaillard and Dorfeuille's Variétés-Palais-Royal, under its new name, the Théâtre de la République, became the favoured resort of the revolutionaries; the Vaudeville, managed by two playwrights, Piis and Barré, was inaugurated on 12 January 1792 and, in spite of some unlucky brushes with the Jacobins, survived the rule of the Commune and, under the Directory, was one of the few theatres that prospered consistently; while the magnificent theatre erected by Mlle Montansier on a site in the Rue Richelieu facing the Bibliothèque Nationale would certainly have rivalled all others had not the lady's political enemies imprisoned her under trumped-up charges.[15] Another group of theatres, those that had established themselves on the Boulevard du Temple before the Revolution, survived intact, thanks perhaps to their predominantly *sans-culotte* audiences, or because their earlier experiences in baffling their opponents, the royal theatres, served them well in the changed circumstances. Nicolet's fortunes, which had been going downhill before the Revolution, made a spectacular recovery, and he was able to sell out at a good price in 1795 to a former member of his company, Louis-François Ribié. Audinot, after being dispossessed as we have seen by Gaillard and Dorfeuille in 1784, succeeded in regaining possession within a year, and relaunched the Ambigu-Comique, specializing in a new type of heroic melodrama. All the other minor theatres along the Boulevard survived intact: the Délassements-Comiques, the Théâtre des Associés, renamed in 1790 the Théâtre Patriotique, and a couple of others, the Bluettes (now called the Théâtre-Français Comique et Lyrique), and the Théâtre de Lazzari. The Boulevard du Temple, forsaken by the fashionable folk who used to enjoy sauntering there on an evening, may have gone downhill, as the Goncourts certainly judged it had: 'the Boulevard du Temple, the boulevard of Audinot, Nicolet, Sallé – what a sad decline! It is no more than an ignoble Palais-Royal for the debauchery of the working class, along which stroll, flirt and bawl at one another drunks and tarts, beardless mountebanks and eight-year-old Phrynes.'[16] But at least the Boulevard was still there, having outlasted the Revolution, as it was to brave Napoleon, defy the Bourbons that followed him and outlive even the starchy respectability of the July Monarchy.

CHAPTER 5

The royal theatres under the Revolution

Over the closing decade of the eighteenth century, the three privileged theatres that had formerly functioned under the protection of the monarchy were, as one might expect, subjected to every kind of pressure from the shifting currents of government policy during these ten years. They all suffered, though in different degrees: the Académie Royale de Musique and the Comédie-Italienne struggling through, the Comédie-Française torn asunder and temporarily disappearing under the waves. All three were still seen as state theatres, with the special responsibilities which that status involved; but, with the downfall of the monarchy, and the fluctuating fortunes of the administrations that succeeded one another for the rest of the century, they all felt tempest-tossed in the absence of a reliable sheet-anchor. Even the old names their houses had borne from time immemorial disappeared: the Théâtre-Français became the Théâtre de la Nation, the Théâtre-Italien was renamed the Théâtre de l'Opéra-Comique National, and the Opera was known initially as the Théâtre des Arts and later as the Théâtre de la République et des Arts.

The reputation of the Paris Opera in the first year of the Revolution stood high both in France and abroad. A German visitor in 1790 noted that 'the French are proud of their dancers, their Vestris, their Gardel, their Pérignon, and the whole world acknowledges that nowhere can one see finer ballets than in Paris. They are proud of their orchestra too; and in what other opera house will you find such unison in a group of eighty practised players, who all handle their instruments with such delicacy of touch?'[1] The squabbles and in-fighting that had caused such scandal a few years earlier had subsided; the quasi-autonomy they had been granted in 1782 was confirmed on 8 April 1790 when the municipality, resuming responsibility for the Opera, placed its management in the hands of a committee made up of representatives from the three constituent branches of the enterprise, the vocalists, the dancers and the musicians, with a trio of municipal commissioners (Hébert, Chaumette and Leroux) to represent the interests of the city. A note in the *Spectacles de Paris* for 1791, after announcing these new arrangements, added that the members of the company

give proof every day, by their zeal and their industry, how worthy they are of the trust they solicited. This was particularly noteworthy during the Fête de la Fédération; they kept the Opera open every day, an innovation which represented a complete break with tradition,[2] varying the programme so that the *fédérés*, if they had spent two years in Paris, would not have been able to witness as many complex operatic works as they did in the space of a fortnight.[3]

Later, with the performance in 1792 of Gossec's setting of the Marseillaise known as *L'Offrande à la Liberté*, the Opera gave positive proof of its loyalty to the new regime. The first performance, which took place on 2 October, was well timed, for on 20 September previously the Prussian invaders had been repulsed at Valmy, and on 22 September the Republic had been proclaimed in France; even before the oratorio began, the audience must have been keyed up to an extraordinary pitch of patriotic pride and fervour on that memorable first night.

When the curtain rose, a mountain was revealed centre-stage, round which were grouped warriors, some mounted, some on foot, together with women and children, while on the summit stood, motionless, the figure of Liberty, incarnated by a fair young member of the Opera company. (Nearly all the allegorical goddesses participating in the republican ceremonies were, like Mlle Maillard here, opera dancers.) As the Marseillaise was sung, at each verse the groups melted and changed. The last verse of all, beginning 'Amour sacré de la patrie', was sung slowly, in hushed tones, by the women alone, as though murmuring a prayer; and at the line 'Liberté, liberté chérie', the whole company knelt before the actress as she stood silent on the summit of the mountain, her eyes fixed on the distant horizon. Then a long silence supervened, followed not by the expected refrain, but by the sound of trumpets and a protracted drumroll; an army of extras rushed on to the stage carrying pikes, battle-axes, torches and standards, while the entire company took up the chorus: 'Aux armes, citoyens!', echoed spontaneously by the audience which at this culminating point, cheering and sobbing, were in a state of almost hysterical excitement.

The Opera at this time was working from the new timber structure run up for it in 1781 by the architect Lenoir to replace their former home adjoining the Palais-Royal, which had been almost completely burned out earlier that year. The new theatre, erected at top speed, was situated near the Porte Saint-Martin on the western end of the boulevard: it had been intended as a purely temporary edifice, to serve until the ending of hostilities between Britain, France and the United States, which came with the signing of the peace treaty at Versailles in 1783. Though not built of stone, in time it was seen that the new opera-house would stand up to hard wear; it was further agreed that its proportions were graceful and its acoustics excellent. Nevertheless, there were many who feared it would not attract audiences, stuck out there on the outskirts of the city. The Opera, said La Harpe, needs to have a central situation, since many people who are indifferent to music and bored by the ballet attend it only to meet each other, something they could do just as easily nearer home; moreover, the approach roads presented difficulties, particularly for pedestrians, in winter.[4] Since there seemed to be little chance that money could be found for the erection of a new and permanent opera house on the gutted ruins of the old one, questions began to be asked in the early years of the Revolution about the possibility of commandeering some other suitable building nearer the hub of affairs; and only one such, still in the course of construction, seemed to offer the desired qualities: this was Mlle Montansier's Théâtre National on the west side of the Rue Richelieu, recently renamed the Rue de la Loi.

The ex-manageress of the Théâtre de Versailles had already acquired a small theatre in the grounds of the Palais Royal: this was the erstwhile Théâtre des Beaujolais, from which its proprietors had been evicted in 1790.[5] But it was much too small to satisfy her large ambitions, which were to erect some commodious building where tragedy, comedy and musical drama could be played in turn. At last, on 7 December 1791, she acquired a suitable site, on the opposite side of the street from the Bibliothèque Nationale. There were initial difficulties in raising the capital necessary for a theatre of the dimensions and splendour she had in mind, but eventually, on 15 August 1793, the Théâtre National de la Rue de la Loi opened its doors, to the wonder of the Parisians who referred to it admiringly as the 'Théâtre des Trois Millions', this being the sum Mlle Montansier or her backers were rumoured to have spent on it.

It was a dangerous time to inaugurate a new theatre of such aristocratic pretensions. France was virtually controlled by the Committee of Public Safety, established in April that year and to which Robespierre had been elected in July. Himself a passionate music-lover, he had long been annoyed at having to trek out to the Porte Saint-Martin whenever he felt like a night at the opera, and it was his crony Hébert who launched the first public attack on Mlle Montansier in his scurrilous but widely read news-sheet *Père Duchesne*, suggesting that she derived her funds from highwaymen and the decorations of the new theatre from the shirts of army volunteers. These ridiculous libels were given a more dangerous turn by Chaumette, who denounced her to the Commune on 13 November 1793

for having built the theatre in the Rue de la Loi in order to set fire to the Bibliothèque Nationale; money from England has helped in no small measure towards the construction of this edifice, for which 50,000 crowns [150,000 francs] were contributed by the ex-queen Marie-Antoinette. I therefore demand that this theatre be closed, because of the danger it represents should it catch fire.[6]

The following day Mlle Montansier and her partner Nœuville were flung into prison, but the theatre remained open and functioning until 10 April 1794; on 16 April an order from the Committee of Public Safety, signed by Robespierre, Collot d'Herbois, Carnot etc. required the immediate transfer of the Opera to the Théâtre National. The operatic company did not, in fact, make the move until 7 August 1794, ten days after the execution of Robespierre. These new quarters, however, in spite of Mlle Montansier's strenuous efforts to recover her property, continued as the Paris Opera house throughout the Directory, the Consulate, the Empire and the reign of Louis XVIII, until on 13 February 1820 the Duc de Berry, heir to the throne, was assassinated on its steps as he was leaving at the end of a performance. Ecclesiastical pressure was sufficient to determine the Bourbons to demolish the theatre with the intention of erecting a chapel on its site; but only the first part of this programme was accomplished before the abdication of Charles X caused the work to be abandoned. Today, only a small park with a fountain in the centre, on the other side of the street from the Bibliothèque Nationale, remains to commemorate Mlle Montansier's vision; the library itself, happily, is still intact, despite Chaumette's sinister warnings.

Even after the fall of Robespierre and the closure of the Jacobin Club, the *ci-devant* Académie Royale de Musique continued to benefit from the encouragement and protection of the state. In 1795 it was granted a subsidy of 360,000 francs, which increased steadily until in 1801 it stood at 600,000 francs. Despite this assistance, it was in continual financial difficulties throughout this period. Rumours circulated that the government was helping itself to a portion of the takings at the door; these were hotly denied as an 'atrocious calumny', but – there is never smoke without fire. In 1797 a public loan was floated (240,000 francs in forty-eight shares) to enable the Opera to continue, but it remained in a thoroughly depressed state. The author of a brochure published in 1798 under the title *Melpomène et Thalie vengées* declared that the Opera

has never been so near collapse since it came into existence 120 years ago. For the last two years it has failed to produce a single new work – something unheard of in its whole history. Though this unforgivable torpor is one reason why the audience is so indifferent, it is not the main one. This is to be traced in the first instance to the poor administration of this theatre, which needs to be put on a completely new footing; and in the second place to the rivalry between singers and dancers, which has now reached an acutely critical phase.[7]

The two defects pointed out here were, in fact, complementary: a company which is divided into two branches with quite different interests and specialities cannot be expected to function as an autonomous body, and there was no real alternative but to revert to the system which had existed before 16 September 1793; it was then that the Commune had resolved that 'the artists of the Opera should provisionally administer this establishment', and at the same time ordered the arrest of the two men who had previously guided its fortunes, Cellérier and Francœur.[8] In 1799 the government decided to return to a system of directorship (the directors to be called 'commissaires du gouvernment'), and the first to be summoned to fill the post was another member of the Francœur family, Louis-Joseph.

Turning now to the Comédie-Italienne, the first point to be made is that in the years immediately preceding the Revolution this company had been enjoying a run of unprecedented prosperity. When the 1785–6 season closed, the dividend accruing to each share amounted to 21,000 francs; and the following season the decline to 19,300 francs was not so serious as to cause concern. Nevertheless the theatre was in a poor condition to face the approaching economic blizzards of the revolutionary years. The expense of the new building to which the actors had moved in 1783, and which – unlike the Théâtre-Français in 1782 – had not been built for them by the state, had left them in debt to the tune of nearly half a million.[9] Unless the season 1788–9 continued as profitable as the preceding ones, they risked being unable to meet their commitments; in fact it turned out to be disastrous, partly because of an exceptionally inclement winter when they were snowbound for much of the time, and partly because of the serious competition it was having to face from a new rival, the Théâtre de Monsieur.

This was, in one sense, the last of the royal theatres, hatched only a few years before the monarchy disappeared; in another sense it takes its place among the first generation of commercial theatres, since it was backed by a company of wealthy financiers. But the licence had been a personal gift by Marie-Antoinette to her hairdresser and wig-maker, one Léonard Autié; he, having no interest in the theatre, disposed of it to the Piedmontese violinist Giovanni Battista Viotti, who rapidly recruited a company of actors from the provinces and a well-grounded group of singers from Naples, Turin and elsewhere in Italy.

The title first given, by gracious permission of the young Louis XIV, to Molière's company shortly after their arrival in Paris had been 'Troupe de Monsieur, frère unique du Roi'. Establishing a distant though spurious ancestry, Viotti's new theatre was permitted by the Comte de Provence, the elder of Louis XVI's two brothers, to bear the same name, allowing it briefly to rank in popular estimation as the fourth of the royal theatres. Its foundation was officially sanctioned by the King on 23 July 1788, with the proviso that the new company should not use any play or comic opera taken from the repertoires of the Comédie-Française and the Comédie-Italienne. Viotti's rejoinder, when he was informed of this condition by the Comte de Provence, was typical of the man: 'Your Highness, one does not borrow from the poor.'[10] In fact, it seems likely that the impresario was originally counting on forming his own repertory chiefly from Italian opera – works by Cimarosa and Paesiello – with the addition of Goldoni's comedies; he had enlisted the help of Cherubini, a recent arrival in France, to select the players, and it was said at the time that the Théâtre de Monsieur had a better claim than the occupants of the building on the Rue Favart to call itself the Théâtre-Italien.

The Théâtre de Monsieur opened in a hall in the Tuileries Palace known as the Salle des Machines, which had served the Comédie-Française earlier while they were waiting for their new playhouse in the Faubourg Saint-Germain to be completed. The shareholders backing the new enterprise, who had taken the Salle des Machines on a 30-year lease, spent a quarter of a million on redecorating and refurbishing it. Their discomfiture may be imagined when, the royal family having been forced to return from Versailles to Paris on 6 October 1789 and requiring the Tuileries for their own accommodation, the actors were abruptly given notice to quit the premises by 24 December at the latest. They sought temporary refuge for a twelvemonth in a vacant hall at the Foire Saint-Germain, used earlier by Nicolet when the fair was open. Meanwhile a new permanent theatre, on a site approximately where the Paris Bourse now stands, and within a stone's throw of the Comédie-Italienne, was being made ready for them. Six months after its inauguration it dropped the name Théâtre de Monsieur; 'Monsieur' having fled the country to set up, with his brother the Comte d'Artois, the headquarters of the émigré troops at Coblenz, was not in particularly good odour among the Parisians in the summer of 1791. Thereafter its official title became the Théâtre Français et Italien de la rue Feydeau – Théâtre Feydeau for short.

For the remainder of the decade the two theatres, the Feydeau and the Comédie-Italienne, coexisted cheek by jowl in intense rivalry, since both were exploiting the same genre, the comic opera or *opera buffa*. As the political situation deteriorated, particularly after the invasion of the Tuileries by the mob on 10 August 1792, the Italian opera singers in the Théâtre Feydeau returned to their homeland and Viotti fled to England; Italian music was in consequence dropped from the repertoire. The few remaining Italian nationals in the Comédie-Italienne had similarly been repatriated, and on 5 February 1793 the society accepted the suggestion that their playhouse in the Rue Favart should henceforth be known as the Théâtre de l'Opéra-Comique National. As for the Feydeau, it came under strict surveillance by the Jacobins, well aware of its earlier connections with the court; Autié was actually sentenced to death by the revolutionary tribunal on the same day as André

Chénier but, more fortunate than the poet, he had escaped abroad some time before. After Thermidor the Feydeau actors reaped the reward of their anti-Jacobin stance in a way that the Opéra-Comique National, popularly known as the Favart, could not; and so the life-and-death struggle between the two theatres went on, each bidding against the other for the best singers, the most fashionable authors and the most talented composers. Finally the Favart was forced to close its building, which stood in need of urgent repairs, and beg hospitality from its neighbour and rival. Some of the refugee actors decided to stay on at the Feydeau rather than return to their old theatre once it had been refurbished, and so – after some arm-twisting on the part of the Minister of the Interior – the two theatres agreed to merge by a legal act of union dated 7 thermidor an ix (25 July 1800), and to adopt for a new joint enterprise the old name Opéra-Comique, having chosen as their venue the more modern theatre in the Rue Feydeau. Here the flood of foreigners that poured into Paris at the Peace of Amiens found it was the one theatre that counted. J. F. Reichardt, the musicologist from Halle, went straight to the Feydeau on his arrival in Paris in 1802; he described it as being 'of its kind the most perfect and, as best I can judge so far, the only theatre to have made progress over the past ten years'; while John Carr, barrister-at-law, for his part reported that 'the Feydeau theatre is very elegant and, on account of its excellent arrangements, good performers, and exquisite machinery, is much resorted to, and is in general preferred to the fourteen other dramatic spectacles which, in this dissipated city, almost nightly present their tribute of pleasure to the gay and delighted Parisians'.[11]

Of the three former royal theatres in France, it was unquestionably the Comédie-Française that suffered the most from the shift of political opinion that led to the downfall of the monarchy and the establishment of a republic. The reasons have much to do with the far stronger personal ties that had linked senior Comédie-Française actors and actresses with the monarchical establishment over the whole of the second half of the eighteenth century. When Mme de Pompadour inaugurated a private theatre at Versailles in 1747 to try and amuse Louis XV, it was Mlle Dumesnil, *sociétaire* since 1737, who was asked to take rehearsals and offer guidance to the titled actresses. Her colleague, Mme Drouin, fulfilled a similar function at the private theatricals of Mme de Montesson, the morganatic wife of the Duc d'Orléans, between 1770 and 1780. If Louis Michu, chosen as singing-master to Marie-Antoinette when the whim took her to act in comic opera at the Petit-Trianon, belonged to the Comédie-Italienne, it was a Comédie-Française actor, Dazincourt, who had the honour of tutoring the Queen in straight comedy; as late as 1785 he was advising her when she took the part of Rosine in a private performance of Beaumarchais's *Barbier de Séville*, in which her brother-in-law the Comte d'Artois played the key role of Figaro.

But apart from these particular instances where favoured individuals were called in to assist members of the royal family interested in amateur dramatics, it was by no means uncommon for the Comédie-Française to accept flattering invitations to perform at the houses of the great. Many of the nobles attached to the court had incorporated in their private mansions studio theatres of quite extraordinary splendour and luxury; they used them occasionally for private performances, but would also engage senior *sociétaires* to enact plays for the pleasure of their high-born guests. It was, as the actor Fleury wrote, 'a day to be looked forward to when our members could escape from the deserted halls of the Comédie-Française and take a bow on the boards of a theatre so elegantly furnished'[12] – not to mention the handsome honorarium that awaited them afterwards. On such occasions the parts normally taken by leading players at the Théâtre-Français would have to be entrusted to stand-ins; this sometimes led to violent protests from disappointed audiences who had paid good money to see their favourite actor or actress. To obviate such disgraceful scenes, Papillon de la Ferté records (4 November 1767) having added, at the request of the Gentlemen of the Bedchamber, a supplementary regulation for the Comédie-Française forbidding any *sociétaire* to appear at a private theatre during the hours normally devoted to public performances. But the prohibition, though it might have pleased the *parterre* of the Comédie-Française, was not to the liking of the titled gentlefolk who rarely occupied a box at the theatre, preferring to watch their favourite actors in private performances of works which the censor had banned. Five years later, on 3 December 1772, when the ballet dancer Guimard, a lady whose sexual talents quite as much as her terpsichorean expertise had won her notoriety and a large fortune, was inaugurating her new theatre in her town house on the Chaussée d'Antin, it was rumoured that the great attraction of the evening would be a performance by

members of the Comédie-Française of the prohibited comedy by
Collé, *La Partie de chasse de Henri IV*. The Duc de Richelieu and the
three other Gentlemen of the Bedchamber reiterated their previous
warning; but the Prince de Soubise, one of the dancer's many titled
lovers, had the ear of the King, and Louis XV benignly counter-
manded the order. Thereafter the actors of the Comédie-Française
regarded themselves as being at liberty to perform in the private
houses of the nobility whenever invited and no matter what their
professional obligations might be.

This past history goes a long way towards explaining why the
attitude of the Comédie-Française to the events of 1789 differed
notably from that of the Opera and the Comédie-Italienne, whose
members for the most part accommodated themselves fairly readily
to the political changes in the country. In the senior company,
which regarded itself in any case as forming a sort of aristocracy
among the others, several of the older actors and actresses continued
to think of themselves as bound by ties of gratitude and affection to
the old monarchy and so tended to side with the royalists: they
included Dazincourt who, as we have seen, had particularly close
teacher–pupil relations with the Queen; Fleury, who had made his
début in 1774; the tragic actress Raucourt, who had been a *sociétaire*
since 1773; and also two younger members, Louise Contat, who had
first sprung into prominence as Suzanne in *Le Mariage de Figaro*
(1784), and a lesser actor, Jean-Baptiste Naudet. In jocular reference to the two parties in the National Assembly, the blacks,
supporters of the clergy and the minor nobility, and the reds, who
set no limits to where the Revolution might carry the country, this
group was dubbed the black party, while others, notably Talma,
Dugazon, Grandmesnil, Mlles Vestris and Desgarcins, formed the
red faction. The greater number had no strong feelings either way
and switched their allegiance from one side to the other according to
the fluctuations in the political situation. Nevertheless the fact that
there were these divisions inside the company did not augur well for
the future.

The first clash between the conservative element in the Comédie-
Française and a leading statesman of the hour arose over the
attempt to have a revival of Chénier's *Charles IX* put on for the
benefit of the *fédérés*, provincial stalwarts who had travelled up to the
capital to join in celebrating the first anniversary of the fall of the
Bastille and to participate in the Fête de la Fédération held on the

same occasion. Their spokesman was Mirabeau, who called on the committee (17 July 1790) and demanded a fresh performance of the tragedy to coincide with these celebrations: after some acrimonious exchanges, one of the actors conceded that they might be willing to give a further performance if the public manifested a desire for this. Mirabeau then walked out, had a further consultation with the *fédérés*, and as a result wrote to the Comédie-Française reiterating his demand and ending on a slightly minatory note: 'Since a refusal on your part could give rise to suspicions that would not redound to the credit of the Comédie, I venture, in the interests of its cause, to counsel you not to compromise its reputation for patriotism.'[13]

This letter, dated 19 July, was left unanswered; but on 22 July, directly after the interval, a spectator in the pit stood up on one of the benches and read out a long petition from the *fédérés* to the effect that a revival of *Charles IX* should be given before they left for their homes. There were two actors on stage waiting to begin the comedy, Naudet and Talma, and an actress, Elisabeth Lange. Naudet answered the orator, explaining that it was materially impossible to accede to the request, since two of the original cast were ill: Mme Vestris, who had undertaken the part of Catherine de Medici, and Saint-Prix, who had that of the Cardinal de Lorraine. This brief speech provoked an uproar, and, seeing that Naudet, an irascible character at the best of times, was about to lose his temper, Talma stepped forward and suggested that, since Saint-Prix was indeed incapacitated by an erysipelas on the leg, his part might be read by a stand-in, and that Mme Vestris, whose indisposition was a minor one, could perhaps be persuaded to make an effort 'so as to prove her zeal and her patriotism'. Talma's intervention calmed the audience, and the comedy that they had been about to begin proceeded without further incident. The matter was, of course, referred to Bailly, who to avoid trouble told them to put on *Charles IX* the following evening. The actors had no alternative but to comply: Mme Vestris, rising from her sickbed, took her part, Grammont read the Cardinal's, and Talma was cheered for his performance. It is to be noted that all three belonged to the 'red' faction in the Comédie-Française.

The conservatives in the company did not take this setback quietly. A meeting chaired by Fleury was convened to discuss the situation; at the end of it nineteen *sociétaires* headed by Naudet, Mlle Raucourt and Mlle Contat signed a declaration expelling Talma from the Comédie-Française. This was an unwise step. The young tragedian had become the hero of the hour for the crowd, while the 'blacks' in the company, once the news broke, were roundly damned as aristocrats, traitors to the motherland and guilty of that novel crime, *incivisme*. For the next couple of the months the pit in the Théâtre de la Nation became the setting for regular noisy protests, sometimes drowning out the performance, with the 'patriots' in the audience shouting above the din for Talma and *Charles IX*. On 16 September matters reached a climax. No sooner had the curtain parted after the interval separating, as was traditional, the tragedy (on this occasion, Saurin's *Spartacus*) from the comedy that was to conclude the evening's entertainment, than the entire pit, rising as one man, began shouting in chorus: 'Talma! Talma!'. When silence was restored, Fleury stepped forward, saluted the audience as was customary, and made a brief statement intended to defuse the situation: 'Gentlemen, the Society to which I belong, being convinced that M. Talma has betrayed its interests and compromised the public peace, has resolved unanimously that it would henceforth have no further truck with him until higher authority has pronounced on the matter.'[14] By 'higher authority' Fleury was no doubt referring to the Gentlemen of the Bedchamber, but the allusion was vague enough to pass unchallenged on this occasion.

On the following evening the disturbance was even greater, since the Comédie-Française had taken the precaution of infiltrating its sympathizers into the *parterre*; the demonstration, which had been relatively good-humoured on 16 September, became quarrelsome, the women in the audience hurried to the exit doors, and the men in the pit started to break up the benches and fling the bits at the actors on stage; it ended with the militia being summoned to eject the crowd. The scene was apparently witnessed by several British visitors to the Théâtre de la Nation that evening, though it has not been possible to trace their accounts; but M.-J. Chénier, in an open letter to the press dated 18 September,[15] reported their astonishment at the actors' defiance of the general will, as though it were the audience who were expected to defer to the actors and not vice versa. They order things otherwise in London . . .

However, a riot had undoubtedly occurred in a public place, and the following day Bailly, as mayor of Paris, convened the leading members of the Comédie-Française to the Hôtel de Ville; a summons which they obeyed unwillingly, convinced as they still were that only the Gentlemen of the Bedchamber had the right to call them to account. Bailly began quietly enough, trying to persuade them that the reign of the Richelieus and the Duras was over, and that the authority they had exercised had now devolved on him;[16] and he warned them that the absurd quarrel with Talma must cease. Des Essarts, who had been chosen as the actors' spokesman, did not try to dispute the first point, but he claimed that in resolving on the expulsion of Talma they were only acting in accordance with their own statutes and were entirely within their rights; he reminded Bailly that in law they constituted an autonomous body and had every right to blackball a member who was not *persona grata* with their society. To this Bailly answered that the Comédie-Française was a national institution and that their internal regulations did not permit them to flout the wishes of the public, particularly when all the public was demanding was the reinstatement of a talented actor. Des Essarts replied hotly that they could not associate with a man who had broken their rules and earned their animosity. At this point the mayor rose to his feet, as did they all; and, without raising his voice, Bailly said to them: 'Take notice, gentlemen, that I am not asking you to love Talma, but to act alongside him. I am requiring of you nothing in the name of the gospel; my duty is to speak to you in the name of the law. For you especially, gentlemen, the wishes of the public must be sacred.' The audience was terminated.[17]

It marked a turning-point in the relations between the state and the theatre: admittedly the Comédie-Française was only one out of the dozen or so theatres in Paris, but it was still by general consent the main repository of dramatic talent. By insisting that it was a national institution ('un établissement national'), Bailly had given notice that it could no longer be regarded as autonomous under the King; what it did or refused to do was a matter of national concern, and the wishes of the nation were paramount. The *sociétaires* were not, as a body, converted by this argument; they continued to resist, but those who supported them were in a small minority. As the *Chronique de Paris*, a newspaper favouring at this time a constitutional monarchy, declared in its editorial of 25 September 1790: 'No good citizen can view such conduct [as that of the Comédie-Française] with equanimity; for if all the corporations in the kingdom were to defy the municipal authority and the elected magistrates, if they were to recognize no other power but that of the King, then the counter-revolution would have succeeded.'[18] In the end the *sociétaires* were faced with the choice between obeying Bailly's order or dissolving the society and going their several ways; for on 27 September, in face of their persistent obduracy, he had their theatre closed, and on 28 September, the actors having made submission, he allowed it to be re-opened, provided the first play to be put on was *Charles IX* and that Talma should take the part he had originally played. Bailly made a point of being present himself on this occasion, sitting in the royal box and surrounded by senior municipal officers. The Comédie-Française had been utterly humiliated, but the counter-revolution had not prevailed.

The deputation of actors that had waited on Bailly had presumably not included any women, but two of the senior actresses, Contat and Raucourt, were so incensed at Talma's return that they went into temporary retirement. Louise Contat wrote to the society on 31 October 1790, explaining why she had taken this step;[19] Mlle Raucourt apparently did not deign to, but shared her colleague's distaste at the idea of treading the boards with the detested Talma. However, the fit of sulks lasted only a couple of months, for they reappeared on 8 January 1791, and on the same occasion a forced reconciliation took place on stage between Talma, willing to let bygones by bygones, and Naudet, who consented to embrace Talma only in order to appease the evident fury of the pit when, following his first inclination, he had refused to.[20] But though harmony was restored on the surface, all was not well by any means. The Comédie-Française was faced with dwindling audiences and a disastrous drop in income, from over a million *livres* in 1787–8 to a little under 675,000 in 1790–1;[21] it was particularly their richer clients who had deserted them – the valuable advance booking of boxes had dropped by two-thirds. Only the turbulent pit could be relied on to be present in force, but paid only 48 *sous* a head as against 6 *livres* charged for the more expensive seats elsewhere. In addition the Revolution had forced on the company expenses which formerly had been borne by the Treasury or other public authorities.[22] Financial ruin was not far off. In an attempt to fill the empty boxes, La Rive, the tragedian who had retired from the Comédie-Française in a fit of pique in June 1788, was prevailed on to return in May 1790; he was welcomed back in a manner that satisfied even his vanity.

The loss of its monopoly consequent on the decree of 13 January

1791 was thus only an incident in the series of setbacks and disasters buffeting the old theatre in the first few years of the Revolution, and one that had probably long been discounted. It is true that there was now no legal prohibition against producing the masterpieces of Corneille and Racine on any Paris stage;[23] but classical tragedy, still regarded as the crowning glory of the dramatic art in France, required first-class performers, and the Comédie-Française still possessed an unsurpassable body of tragic actors and actresses. Now to outdo the senior theatre in what it was supposed to be best at had always been the secret ambition of the two interlopers from Bordeaux, Gaillard and Dorfeuille, who had already succeeded in enlisting the services of one gifted actor, Jacques-Marie Boutet de Monvel, a former member of the Comédie-Française and a playwright of talent if not distinction. Hounded by his creditors, and warned by the Lieutenant of Police that he could no longer protect him from arrest for the 'unnatural vice' to gratify which he had been caught soliciting a little too openly and a little too frequently,[24] Monvel had left France in 1781 and had found refuge in Sweden where the reigning monarch, Gustavus III, had offered him a well-paid job as director of the company of French players in Stockholm. Ten years later he returned to Paris, but decided to throw in his lot with Gaillard and Dorfeuille's company rather than seek readmission to the Comédie-Française. He then initiated undercover negotiations with Talma and a few other disaffected spirits, so that on 27 April 1791 the two directors were able to welcome six experienced recruits to their superb new theatre at the south end of the Rue de Richelieu. After the Easter break they opened with a performance of M.-J. Chénier's new tragedy, *Henri VIII et Anne de Boulen* (Henry VIII and Anne Boleyn); its success was contested (Chénier complained that a cabal had been mounted by the Théâtre de la Nation), but their next production, Corneille's *Le Cid*, was generally applauded, and it became clear that if tragedy was what you wanted to see, the Théâtre-Français de la rue de Richelieu was where you had to go.

On 30 September 1792, less than a week after the proclamation of the Republic, the upstart theatre changed its name to that of the Théâtre de la République, thereby signalling its total allegiance to the new regime and to the more radical elements in the Convention. The 'patriotism' of its members was above suspicion: 'every one of them strives to use his talents for the increase of enlightenment and the extension of the principles of our happy revolution'.[25] The Théâtre de la Nation, in contrast, down in the Saint-Germain district, with its well-to-do clientèle still royalist in sympathy and keeping a nervous eye on the trend of political events, seemed condemned to play second fiddle: its remaining actors, Molé, Fleury, Dazincourt, Mlle Contat and so forth, were best fitted for the elegant comedy that had delighted spectators throughout the eighteenth century but was now a perpetual reminder of an irrevocably vanished rococo past.

By the new year, tension between the moderates and the extremists in the country at large, and between the two opposing factions representing this division of opinion in the National Convention, had reached a new climax: Louis XVI had been put on trial for his life on 10 December 1792, and was to be executed on 21 January 1793. No one could foresee with confidence what would be the ultimate outcome of the trial of strength, and that by the summer the Jacobins would have the Girondins by the throat. The political context does not merely account for the extraordinary scenes to which Jean-Louis Laya's play *L'Ami des Lois* gave rise; it also, almost certainly, explains how it came to be written and why the Théâtre de la Nation agreed to produce it in the first place. Although by no means a dramatic masterpiece, it contained a clear ideological message, enshrined in its very title; it was meant as a plea for legality against expediency: the hero was the 'friend of the laws', the villain, unmasked at the dénouement in accordance with the basic principles of melodrama, was called Nomophage, which for the educated men in the audience was easily translated as Greek for 'eater of the laws'.[26] Thus the play was an early specimen of what the mid-twentieth century was to name *littérature engagée*; it was intended – and none of those who saw it at its first few performances could have been in any doubt about this – as a Girondist onslaught on Jacobin ideology.

For another reason, the short-lived 'affair' of *L'Ami des Lois* is interesting as being the first test case of clause 6 of the law of 13 January 1791 which, as we have seen, was supposed to have abolished dramatic censorship and to have left it to the theatres (meaning the management, or in the case of a self-governing body like the Comédie-Française, the society of actors) to decide on the fitness of any given play to be performed in public. Only if it gave rise to actual disturbances were the police permitted to intervene to preserve public order. Curiously enough, it is questionable whether, under the previous regime, the monarchical censorship would have permitted the showing of *L'Ami des Lois*, since one of its guiding rules was that recognizable personal applications in a play were strictly prohibited; and it was obvious to any spectator of the time that Laya had satirized Robespierre in the character of Nomophage and that other leading Jacobins were similarly pilloried (the journalist Duri-crâne was widely thought to be a portrait of Marat). Under the Republic there was – at least in 1793 – no preventive censorship, and no obvious redress for any individual who thought he might be recognized in an insulting caricature on the stage.

L'Ami des Lois opened at the Théâtre de la Nation on 2 January 1793. Rumours of the play's political implications had aroused considerable curiosity, and long before the doors opened a huge concourse had assembled outside the theatre, eager for admittance. Those who were unlucky spent the entire winter's night and most of the following day camped outside to make sure of seeing the second performance. The author was delighted at the readiness of the audience to seize every allusion he had written into the work, and willingly presented himself after each performance to take a bow (normally it was only on the first night that this little ceremony took place). Press reports of these disgraceful scenes enraged the Jaco-bins, naturally enough; Hébert's paper called on the *sans-culottes* to take along their cudgels and teach the effeminate actors a lesson they would not forget; and on 10 January the Commune, having received a deposition from one section which accused the Théâtre de la Nation of putting on unpatriotic and demoralizing plays, decided not to permit, allegedly for reasons of public order, any further performances of *L'Ami des Lois*.

The decision was duly posted on 12 January; whereupon the theatre was besieged by an angry crowd demanding to know the reasons for this veto. The mayor (Dr Chambon, who had replaced Bailly in this office) was sent for, but had the greatest difficulty in making his way through the milling throng and, once inside the theatre, in making himself heard. Silence was only restored when Fleury, who had the part of Forlis, the 'ami des lois' in the play, advanced to the front of the stage to propose the substitution of Demoustier's innocuous comedy *Le Conciliateur* – an apt choice – in place of Laya's contentious drama. But the audience was unani-mous: nothing would satisfy them but a fresh performance of *L'Ami des Lois*. Realizing that nothing could be done to calm the crowd short of a direct appeal to the supreme legislative body, Chambon consented to write a letter on the spot to the Convention asking them to pronounce on the issue; Laya, for his part, contributed a similar letter denouncing the tyranny of the Commune. The Convention at the time was engaged in debating the question of the King's guilt, but it broke off to consider and pronounce on Chambon's report and Laya's defence. The very suspension of *L'Ami des Lois* by the arbitrary action of the Commune, after four performances had passed off peaceably, was the cause, the playwright argued, of the ferment – not the play itself. Evidently the Convention accepted this interpretation of events. The terms in which it chose to overrule the Commune on this occasion were almost jocular: 'The National Assembly knows of no law permitting municipalities to exercise censorship over dramatic works. Apart from that, the Assembly has no reason for concern, seeing that the people have demonstrated that they are the *friends of the laws*.'[27] The message was taken back to the waiting audience, and although it was already 9.0 p.m., *L'Ami des Lois* was put on forthwith to general acclamation.

The Théâtre de la Nation would have liked to avoid trouble by taking off the wretched play after these six performances, but their public hotly demanded another, which they promised, one imagines a little reluctantly, for 14 January. Once more the Commune tried to block it, and once more the question came before the Convention. Pétion, a Girondin, accused the General Council of the Commune of trying to exercise preventive censorship, something explicitly forbidden since 1791; on the other hand another *conventionnel*, Dubois-Crancé, argued in favour of suppressing the theatre itself on the grounds that it provided a focal point for reactionaries and royalists – a momentous suggestion, which was to be acted on with the utmost savagery six months later. Danton impatiently wanted the debate cut short: to spend so much time arguing about whether to sanction performances of a mediocre comedy was not what the nation expected, but rather the final act of the tragedy that was to end with the beheading of a tyrant. The upshot of this wrangling was that the players, perhaps taking fright at Dubois-Crancé's intervention and not daring to defy the Commune at this dangerous political juncture, substituted for the promised performance of *L'Ami des Lois* an innocuous programme of Molière's comedies. The Commune, to make doubly sure, had the theatre surrounded by armed troops and cannon under the command of Santerre, a former brewer promoted to general in the National Guard. Despite these threatening preparations the audience, as numerous as ever, were vociferous in demanding to see *L'Ami des Lois*, and turned ugly when it became clear they were not to have their way. Thereupon Santerre marched in at the head of his detachment and, having obtained silence, announced that *L'Ami des Lois*, not having been advertised on the playbills, could not be shown that evening; then, incensed by the outrageous insults hurled at him from all quarters of the theatre, shouted back that he recognized no friends of the people in this gathering, only enemies of the Revolution. At this point an intrepid young man leapt on to the stage, holding in his hand a copy of the play from which, despite Santerre's attempts to silence him, he read out certain particularly stinging tirades, punctuated by rounds of applause. Finally the young man left the stage and was carried round the pit in triumph. After that the audience filed out, judging they had made their point, and the actors, who had been waiting idly in the wings, went up to their dressing-rooms to change out of their costumes.

In the Convention, voting on the King's guilt occupied the next few days; sentence was pronounced on 20 January. Thinking that political passions would by now have abated, the actors announced a further performance of Laya's comedy for 5 February, but the police sent for them and warned them that they would be held personally responsible for any disturbance. When their spokesman tried to protest, he was cut short and told: 'Your play is counter-revolutionary, contrary to true principles, and tends to excite disorder.'[28] This peremptory warning appears to have cowed the players, who took their leave after giving assurances that there would be no further attempt to stage *L'Ami des Lois*.

So ended this affair: a mediocre domestic drama had, over a critical fortnight, exacerbated the conflict between Girondins and Jacobins and occasioned a trial of strength between Convention and Commune, in which the Convention had twice repulsed the Commune and yet the latter had eventually succeeded in their object. The affair further demonstrated the fragility of the 'freedom of the theatres', established – or so it was thought – by the law of 13 January 1791. The proviso that the selection of dramatic works for public performance was to be made the responsibility of the theatres themselves had left unsettled what the procedure should be when a theatre was judged by one or other of the organs of state – in this instance, the police, controlled by the Commune – to have neglected to have discharged its responsibility. And, finally, the affair was important in the way it demonstrated to the leaders of the Revolution just how dangerous and defiant a theatre audience could become when influenced by a work of veiled ideological content.

It was not, however, until three months after the overthrow of the Girondins in the National Convention on 2 June 1793 that the Jacobins took the final drastic step of closing the Théâtre de la Nation for good and throwing the entire company of actors into prison. The pretext was François de Neufchâteau's *Paméla*, a play originally composed in 1788 according to the author, and given its first performance on 1 August 1793. It was based on Goldoni's *Pamela nubile*, which in turn had been inspired by Samuel Richardson's *Pamela*, with a significant modification of the dénouement: Goldoni had turned Richardson's Goodman Andrews into a Scottish laird, Count Oxpen, thus upsetting one of the incidental aims of Richardson's novel, which was to combat the prejudice against marriages between the social classes. Neufchâteau had followed Goldoni rather than Richardson in this respect.[29]

Paméla was performed eight times in the early part of August, but was withdrawn by the author in order that he might make certain changes in the text, as he explained in a letter to *Le Moniteur* published at the beginning of September. 'On Friday morning [30 August], the Committee [of Public Safety] inspected and approved my play. I had complied with the wishes of several patriots who appeared upset that Pamela was discovered to be of noble birth. She will therefore be a commoner and doubtless all the better for it.'[30] Accordingly the revised *Paméla* was given its ninth performance at the Théâtre de la Nation on 2 September. Fleury's description in his memoirs of the appearance and behaviour of the audience that evening is largely in conformity with the account given in the *Feuille du Salut public* at the time.[31] The ladies, present in considerable numbers, were not all wearing revolutionary headdress, and the majority of the men still wore powdered wigs, denoting a suspect adherence to the fashions of bygone times. The performance went off quietly enough until, towards the end, Fleury, as Pamela's father, had to deliver a tirade against religious intolerance with reference to the disputes between Catholics and Protestants, the tenor of his remarks being that differences in the form of worship were unimportant when the basic morality was the same. No objection had been raised to this Voltairian cliché by the Committee of Public Safety. But when it came to the last couplet:

> Ah! les persécuteurs sont les seuls condamnables
> Et les plus tolérants sont les plus raisonnables,

a prolonged burst of applause from the audience showed that the majority of the spectators took a different view of 'toleration' from that which Neufchâteau ostensibly had in mind when he wrote the lines. The implication did not escape a delegate from the Committee of Public Safety sitting in the dress circle; he rose to his feet, shouting: 'Down with political toleration, it's a crime!' and added – as may or may not have been true – 'You are reciting lines which have been deleted and which are forbidden.'[32] There were cries to expel him, whereupon the delegate, thumping the balcony rail, shouted: 'You are trying to justify the moderates. The play is counter-revolutionary!' and without attempting further argument, he hastened from the theatre straight to the Jacobin Club where he reported what had happened. Robespierre, who was present, moved the immediate closure of the theatre, this 'disgusting den of aristocrats of all kinds', and the arrest of the entire company of actors. Whether or not *Paméla* was monarchic in tendency was debatable; but the fact that it showed noblemen strutting about on the stage wearing their orders – even though they were supposed to be British, not French – was probably sufficient, given the current anglophobia, to damn the play. Since the Comédie-Française was still a society, not a troupe of actors under the orders of a director, it was necessary to make a mass arrest, which accordingly took place on the night of 3–4 September; but it is difficult to avoid the conclusion that the closure of the Théâtre de la Nation was the primary aim of the Committee of Public Safety. Theatres were among the few remaining places where dissidents could still forgather and, it was feared, conspire against the new order. As A. V. Arnault wrote, the actors were the whipping boys. 'The audience in the pit was chastised as legend has it were the heirs to the throne of France, on the posteriors of their fellow students: the actors suffered for this prince.'[33]

Not every member of the Comédie-Française was arrested and imprisoned. Three were passed over: Molé and Bellemont, who were in good standing with the Jacobins, and the overweight Des Essarts, who was taking the waters at Barèges on medical advice and was so shocked when the news was brought him that he succumbed there and then to an apoplectic fit. Of the remainder, the fifteen men in the company were taken to the Madelonnettes, and the fourteen actresses to the prison for women known as La Pélagie. Les Madelonnettes, as the name suggests, had been in pre-revolutionary times a religious house serving as a refuge for fallen women. It was reputed the least hygienic prison in the capital, being overcrowded and disease-ridden. The prisoners were confined to their cells and not even allowed into the yard to take exercise; the For-l'Evêque, by comparison, would have seemed a pleasure garden. But it must be said to their credit that the actors managed to keep up their spirits and to give heart to the other prisoners who were there awaiting trial. They may not have thought that their detention would last long: at the beginning of September 1793 the Terror had barely begun, and even the *Feuille du Salut public* had argued that no more drastic punishment should be visited on these 'shameless lackeys of the aristocracy' than that they should be kept under lock and key for the duration of the war, after which they should be escorted across the frontier to join the company of French actors at St Petersburg.

In fact, early in 1794 the men were transferred to a different and more salubrious prison, where they were permitted visitors, and the women sent to the 'couvent des Anglaises' in the Faubourg Saint-Victor. This was an Augustinian foundation of English nuns which had existed in Paris since the middle of the seventeenth century; the sisters had been permitted by the revolutionaries to remain, but the buildings had been commandeered as a supplementary prison from November 1793 when the regular ones became impossibly over-crowded. A few of the actresses, the Contat sisters, Elisabeth Lange (who had taken the part of Pamela in the offending play) and Joséphine Mézeray, were allowed house arrest: the Contats on health grounds (one had just given birth, the other was about to), the two others being entrusted to the care of Dr Belhomme, director of an asylum for the insane whose premises were occasionally used to house the less dangerous enemies of the state, provided they were in a position to pay his exorbitant charges. Thus the incarceration of the company continued, but in less rigorous conditions than before.

By a further act of leniency, it was decided in January 1794 to

release certain actors and actresses formerly belonging to the
Théâtre de la Nation on condition they signed on at the Théâtre de
la République: they included the Vanhoves (Talma's future wife
and future father-in-law), and Marie-Elisabeth Joly, who made her
first appearance after her captivity as Dorine, the impertinent
maidservant in *Tartuffe*, playing the part without her customary
verve however; the audience was painfully aware that her heart was
with her companions in misfortune.[34] As for the remaining members
of the Comédie-Française, they were kept in prison until after
Robespierre's fall from power signalled the end of the reign of
terror.[35] They were lucky to have escaped preceding him to the
scaffold, and owed their preservation, according to a story that
sounds like an invention of Baroness Orczy but is in fact well
vouched for, to the daring of a clerk in the record office, who made a
practice of abstracting incriminating documents from their files and
from those of perhaps a thousand other suspects, soaking the papers
in a bucket of water and throwing the sodden mass into the Seine
from the window of a bathhouse.

After their release from prison, the actors all appeared on the
stage of their old theatre, welcomed back by an exuberant audience;
the ovation given to Louise Contat was such that the actress, it is
said, collapsed in tears. But later, after the relief and congratula-
tions, disillusion supervened. Their theatre, renamed in their
absence the Théâtre de l'Egalité, had been so transformed as to be
barely recognizable. Gone were the tiers of boxes they had been used
to see crowded with ladies and gentlemen of quality: in their place, a
huge horseshoe amphitheatre swept around the auditorium, where
the spectators were henceforth to sit cheek by jowl in enforced
fraternity. The orchestra stalls had been suppressed: there was
nothing now on ground level but one vast pit, reaching from front to
back of the theatre, so aptly named the Theatre of Equality. The
internal decoration had been completely revolutionized: instead of
the light blue and white that had predominated, and indeed had
attracted some criticism in 1782, the whole of the inside, ceiling and
curtain included, was now painted in narrow strips of red, white and
blue. Scarcely less shocking was to find that their theatre had, in the
interval, been invaded by another theatrical company, that which
Mlle Montansier had recruited for her Théâtre National de la Rue
de la Loi and which had been forced to evacuate the building to
make room for the Opera; they had been glad enough to find refuge

in the fine hall that stood empty during the enforced idleness of its original tenants.

An arrangement was reached between the two disparate companies: the interlopers, forming a vastly inferior troupe, were to alternate with the released prisoners, the receipts going into a common pool to be shared out equally between them. But this arrangement worked to the disadvantage of the veterans of the Comédie-Française, who alone filled the house on the nights they played: so, one by one, they drifted away. Fleury was the first to leave, on 5 November 1794, the others followed his example, and by Christmas the Théâtre de l'Egalité, no longer financially viable, had been forced to close its doors once more. The unfortunate actors from the Théâtre National found themselves on the street, left to shift as best they could.

The next four and a half years constitute what could be called the diaspora of the Comédie-Française, during which what was left of the company wandered, homeless and disconsolate, from one temporary refuge to another. Four different playhouses offered them shelter from time to time: the Théâtre de la République, to which Talma and his fellow schismatics had emigrated in 1791; the Feydeau, offering comedy and comic opera, its new building known by the name of the street running off to the right as one goes up the Rue de Richelieu; the Louvois, a very fine theatre with excellent acoustics erected in 1791 by the directors of the Beaujolais, but which had suffered from its close proximity to Mlle Montansier's Théâtre National when that opened in 1793; and finally their original home, reoccupied for less than five months and then abandoned, which was situated at some distance from the others, on the left bank of the Seine.

Their first stopping-place was the Feydeau, which had become the rallying point of the gilded youth of the Directory. They opened here on 25 January 1795; but at the end of a twelvemonth the theatre was temporarily closed down in consequence of the scandal caused by one of Dorvigny's comedies, *Les Réclamations contre l'emprunt* (Objections to the Forced Loan, that of 10 December 1795 which was supposed to be levied on the wealthiest 25 per cent of the population). At this point Mlle Raucourt, by now the senior tragic actress in the Comédie-Française, took charge of some fifteen of her fellow actors in a move to the vacant Louvois theatre, which she hoped would prove a definitive asylum. At the same time she wrote to her ex-colleagues still at the Feydeau, and to those at the Théâtre de la République, inviting them all to join her at the Louvois so that the various sundered fragments of the old Comédie-Française could come together once more and face whatever the new century had in store. She even had certain dressing rooms in the Louvois labelled with the names of the missing *sociétaires*: Talma, Fleury, Dazincourt, Dugazon. But her ambitions were premature: none of them responded to her appeal.

Mlle Raucourt's tenure of the Louvois was terminated abruptly by an arbitrary act of authority on 7 September 1797. Her company had offered, as conclusion to the evening's entertainment, an innocuous one-act comedy, *Les Trois Frères rivaux*, which it never suspected could have any contemporary application, since it had been written by an obscure playwright, J. de La Fort, back in 1713. It contained, however, one scene in which a valet by the name of Merlin happened to incur the wrath of his master, who first called him a rascal, and then added: 'Friend Merlin, you will end on the gallows.' To the astonishment of the actors, this sally brought the house down; the laughter, the cheering, the stamping of feet lasted a full quarter of an hour. Only afterwards was it realized that the valet's name happened also to be that of the unpopular Minister of Justice, Merlin (de Douai). The comedy was withdrawn forthwith: but when some five weeks later, as a consequence of the *coup d'état* of 4 September 1797, Merlin was elected to the Directory, one of his first acts was to order the closure of the luckless theatre. Once more the power of the state was unleashed to punish the actors for an involuntary fault which could not be attributed to them, but only to the many-headed audience who had expressed a communal political judgement in a manner that was beyond the reach of affronted authority.

After various fruitless attempts to rent yet another hall, Mlle Raucourt and her depleted band found a last resting-place at their point of departure, the old theatre on the left bank which, when they had quitted it, bore the name of the Théâtre de l'Egalité and had since been renamed the Odéon. It had been used at first not for dramatic purposes at all but for concerts – hence the new name: the original Odeum had been a public building at Athens erected by Pericles for musical performances. However, it was at this point in their odyssey that an audacious outsider, one Sageret, formerly banker to the Court of Rome, began to make his presence felt.

Sageret had recently arrived in Paris hoping to profit from the fury for amusements of all kinds for which the Directory was noted; his ultimate ambition was to set himself up as supremo of the theatre industry in the city. He had gained a first foothold with the acquisition of the Théâtre de la rue Feydeau, where he organized the celebrated Concerts Feydeau which attracted all the music-lovers in Paris. Then he got in touch with Merlin, who suggested to him the idea of bringing together under one roof (that of the Théâtre de la République, whose fortunes had been wavering since the downfall of the Jacobins) all the dispersed segments of the Comédie-Française. The project appealed powerfully to Sageret's imagination, more particularly since it appeared to be backed by a vague promise of government assistance. Though this never materialized, Sageret went ahead, borrowing right and left, and in a short while managed to acquire the République (5 September 1798) and the Odéon (29 October 1798). With the Feydeau already under his thumb, he now had in his employ all the remaining members of the pre-revolutionary Comédie-Française. Instead of grouping them all under one roof, however, he arranged to have them play by turns in one or the other theatre and sometimes at two theatres on the same evening – in which case the unfortunate actors, having finished one performance, had to cross Paris and start all over again at a different playhouse. The theoretical advantages of this system (three lots of box-office takings instead of one) did not outweigh the considerable practical difficulties of transportation, to say nothing of the strain and fatigue imposed on the actors; and this Box and Cox game lasted a bare four months.

Sageret was by now in serious financial difficulties. An appeal to the two legislative assemblies, the Conseil des Cinq-Cents and the Conseil des Anciens, urging that it would be to their political advantage to take out subscription bookings to his various theatres, fell on deaf ears. The only possible way to economize was to impose cuts on the actors' salaries; this was, naturally, resented, and Talma and Mme Petit-Vanhove, who immediately took coach down to Bordeaux, set an example followed by others; it seemed that the Comédie-Française now risked being dispersed not just throughout Paris but over the whole of France. The final blow came when the Odéon went up in flames on the night of 17–18 March 1799. Sageret was arrested, accused of having set fire to the theatre in order to escape his commitments, and when at length he was released it was to find that the Théâtre de la République had also passed out of his hands.

By this time the government had at last been persuaded of the desirability of reuniting the two warring factions into which the Comédie-Française had split in 1791. Barras had already made one attempt to do this, inviting all the actors to a banquet in the hope that the convivial atmosphere would cause them to forget their differences; but having eaten and drunk their fill, the two sides fell to quarrelling and eventually left the room by different doors. So it was left finally to Jean-François-Régis Mahérault, a senior civil servant in the Ministry of the Interior, to bring about the reunion. The obstacles he had to overcome were endless. An influential group of playwrights, headed by Beaumarchais and including Ducis, Legouvé, Laya and Arnault, opposed the idea on the grounds that it would open the door to all the abuses they suffered from under the *ancien régime*.[36] However, the sudden death of Beaumarchais on 18 May 1799 cleared the way in this respect, though other difficulties remained: the absence of certain indispensable actors in the provinces, political divisions (Mlle Contat was heard to declare: 'I would as lief be guillotined from head to foot as appear on the stage alongside that Jacobin Dugazon'[37]), even financial considerations, since the salaries paid to some of the star actors by the commercial theatres in Paris had been considerably higher than what they could expect from a state organization. It needed all Mahérault's diplomacy and tact to work the miracle. As finally agreed, the membership of the reconstituted Comédie-Française included thirteen actors and ten actresses who had been *sociétaires* before 1791, together with a number of talented players who had been recruited to the Variétés-Palais-Royal before it changed its name to the Théâtre de la République.[38] There were also two new acquisitions, Monvel's promising daughter Hippolyte Mars and the lovely Marie-Thérèse Bourgoin, who made her début on 13 September 1799.

It had been a foregone conclusion, since the old theatre was now no more than a smoking ruin, that the Théâtre de la République, having changed its name to the honoured one of the Théâtre-Français, should serve henceforth as the home of the reconstituted Comédie-Française; and this building has lasted the society down to the present day. Once all the details had been settled, a banquet was organized by Dazincourt for all the prospective members; the occasion turned out to be considerably more peaceful than the dinner over which Barras had presided the previous year, and ended with the entire company linking hands round the bust of Molière and swearing an oath of fraternal unity.

CHAPTER 6

The theatre in the service of the Republic

The notion that the function of dramatic works was not primarily to move audiences or to entertain them, but rather to work for their moral improvement, was widespread among the adherents of the Enlightenment in eighteenth-century France; it underlay the thinking of Diderot, D'Alembert, Sedaine and Mercier whenever they wrote on the theatre. Mercier's complaint, already noted,[1] that the Comédie-Française, thanks to their 'not only nonsensical but imaginary prerogatives', were limiting the theatrical fare available to the common people to 'poisonous filth', was an extreme expression of this theory. It was an idea emphasized at the start of the Revolution by the playwrights rather than by the politicians. J.-L. Laya, the future author of *L'Ami des Lois*, declared in a pamphlet published in 1789 that actors were 'instruments in the hands of the moralists of a country';[2] and M.-J. Chénier, in the Easter address or *compliment* that Talma was to deliver from the stage in accordance with custom at the start of a new theatrical season (12 April 1790), stated that 'the theatre, this powerful agent of public education, can hasten the spread of truth'.[3] In their turn, the orators in the National Assembly lost no time in adopting and developing the idea. In the course of the debate on the liberalization of the theatre, at the beginning of 1791, Mirabeau declared: 'When the time comes for us to concern ourselves with the education of the masses, in which the theatre must play its part, it will be seen that drama can be transformed into a very active, very rigorous morality'; while on the same occasion Chapelier urged: 'The stage must purify morals, it must give lessons in good citizenship, it must form a school of patriotism, of virtue, and of all the affections that bind families together and contribute to their charm.'[4]

However much playwrights and legislators might pay lip-service to the idea that the theatre could, and should, subordinate its

properly artistic mission, or rise above its function as pure entertainment, in order to become a school of civic virtue guiding the
attentive audience towards a loftier morality, difficulties started to
manifest themselves as soon as theories had to be translated into
practice; such difficulties were noticeably exacerbated when the
happy harmony that had, by and large, prevailed in the first couple
of years of the Revolution was increasingly replaced by ideological
disputes of a more and more violent character. For who was to
decide whether a given play contributed to the purification of public
morality? and what was to be done when it fell short of achieving
this sublime purpose? The abolition of censorship at the beginning of
1791 had imposed on the state the obligation to tolerate whatever a
playwright chose to offer and a manager or company of actors
agreed to put on the stage; the most that could be done by those who
might view the work as politically retrograde or morally suspect was
to argue as much in the daily press. If it appeared to the police that
it was likely to lead to public disorder, they might be able to justify
the apparently illegal step of forbidding performances by reference
to their overriding duty to forestall civil commotion. Were this to
happen, it would amount to a form of censorship, but repressive
rather than preventive, in the terms of the useful distinction made
by Odile Krakovitch.[5] The difficulty was to draw a dividing line
between the normal sensation caused in an audience by a daring
play and the conflicts it would give rise to within the audience
between those who took offence at its tendencies and those who
welcomed them. At what point did such disagreement amount to
civil strife? And even before an actual performance, when the new
dramatic work still existed only in the form of a manuscript, was it
possible to foretell it would cause dissension of such violence as to
amount to a riot?

The first time these questions arose was in March 1792, when an
opera by Méhul on the Roman Emperor Hadrian was due to be
shown at the Théâtre des Arts. It was denounced as soon as its
forthcoming production was reported in the press as a dangerous
and highly demoralizing work, since it showed an autocrat victorious over his enemies. Hoffmann, who had written the libretto,
attempted to defend himself. Among those he asked to intervene was
Jacques-Louis David, who is said to have replied savagely: 'We will
burn the Opera to the ground rather than see monarchs triumphing
there.' It was pointless for Hoffmann to remind his opponents of the

recent law doing away with censorship; their reply was to cite articles 4, 5 and 10 of the Declaration of the Rights of Man which antedated this law: any citizen has the right to publish his opinions provided they do not give rise to civil strife in which others might come to harm. In a letter to Pétion, mayor of Paris, Hoffmann pointed out that if this argument were admitted, it would suffice, if anyone wished for whatever reason to interfere with a particular dramatic production, for him to hire a few rowdies to stir up a riot in the theatre. But his plea fell on deaf ears and *Adrien* was suppressed in advance of performance, a dangerous precedent which was to serve as an excuse ten months later for the suppression of *L'Ami des Lois*. The preamble to the blocking decree issued by the Commune on 10 January 1793 included the phrase: 'Whereas the police has at all times been invested with the right to halt such works and made use of this right notably in connection with the opera *Adrien* ...'.[6]

When the members of the Constituent Assembly voted the liberal law abolishing censorship at the beginning of 1791, they could hardly have foreseen that by August 1793 the Republic would be wrestling desperately with threats from every quarter. War was declared in February that year against the Dutch and the British, and initially went badly, with a defeat at Neerwinden and Dumouriez's desertion to the enemy. The Vendée rose in arms in March, and in the early summer the federalist challenge to the central power became a menace requiring more troops, particularly in the south. Consumer shortages in the capital itself caused disturbances, and in March the bad news from the fronts led to the setting up of a revolutionary tribunal to deal with those denounced for counter-revolutionary offences; the following month the Committee of Public Safety was established, with the power to pass decrees; on 27 July, Robespierre was voted on to it. It was on the initiative of this committee that on 2 August 1793 stiffer penalties were introduced to deter theatre directors who staged plays running counter to the prevailing ideology. The second of the two clauses of this decree ran: 'Every theatre in which plays are performed that tend to lower public morale and to revive the shameful superstition of monarchy shall be closed, and the directors arrested and punished in accordance with the full rigour of the law.' This clause was used against the Théâtre de la Nation the following month, and did not need to be invoked a second time: the one warning sufficed.

Preventive as opposed to repressive censorship was effectively introduced by a complementary law of 2 September 1793, in which the Commune was given the responsibility of overseeing the repertoire of every theatre to make sure that no hint of royalism or criticism of the new regime should be suffered on the stage. A document in the archives of the Préfecture of the Seine which was destroyed in the civil war of 1871 but, fortunately, had been published previously in Hallays-Dabot's history of the censorship, shows precisely how it worked at the time. It begins with a frank admission:

It does not appear that there is any law reinstating dramatic censorship; none the less, since the decree of 2 September which enjoins the Paris police to keep a closer eye on the theatres, censorship has to all intents and purposes been reintroduced. At the present time, the police administration exercises it in some fashion on all new plays and revivals, having regard as much to our new form of government as to the more austere way of life needed to maintain it. It is the actors in a company or the managers who bring along their plays in person, so as to avoid pointless expenditure in time and money. Two members of the police force have had to undertake the work in addition to their other duties, and since that time not a day passes without their having to examine several plays, because every day at one or the other of the twenty theatres in Paris some novelty is under preparation.[7]

Baudrais and Froidure were the names of the two overworked censors; both were arrested on 29 March 1794 in Robespierre's round-up of the *indulgents*, which suggests they might not have been discharging their duties with a sufficient sense of the heaviness of their responsibility. Their successors appear to have been more energetic. Over the last three months preceding the *coup* of 9 thermidor (May–July 1794), the censorship dealt with 151 plays, of which 33 were rejected outright and 25 others modified in one sense or another.[8] Alterations were made in the text of familiar classics, since the censors had to take into consideration 'revivals' as well as new plays; and nineteenth-century historians of the revolutionary theatre who, from the Goncourt brothers onwards, tended to judge developments from a reactionary standpoint, derived sour amusement from the kind of changes it was thought necessary to introduce in works as dissimilar as Molière's *Tartuffe* and Racine's *Britannicus*. Jules Janin claimed to have had in his possession a copy of *Le Misanthrope* containing the revisions made either by the police censor or, possibly, by Molé in anticipation of the censorship's objections.[9]

Every mention of royalty is carefully deleted, so that, for instance, changes are made in the folk-song Alceste sings for the edification of Oronte in the first act, 'Si le roi m'avait donné / Paris sa grand'ville' becoming 'Si l'on voulait me donner / Paris la grand'ville'. In the celebrated 'portrait scene' in the second act Célimène, poking fun at a pretentious snob known to the company, ends her little speech with the couplet:

> Il tutaye, en parlant, ceux du plus haut étage,
> Et le nom de Monsieur est, chez lui, hors d'usage.

Under the regime of universal equality and fraternity, it was obligatory to use the 'thou' form of address (*tutoiement*) which, before the Revolution, had been strictly confined to those with whom one was on terms of the utmost familiarity – small children and other domestic pets; as for 'monsieur' and 'madame', they had been replaced everywhere by the less deferential 'citoyen', 'citoyenne'. So the actress playing Célimène had to forget the lines Molière had provided her with and substitute:

> Le nom de citoyen est chez lui hors d'usage,
> Et d'être tutoyé lui paraît un outrage

– by no means a clumsy way of 'modernizing' the seventeenth-century author.

Several well-known plays of earlier times were, quite simply, dropped from the repertoire at this time – notably Voltaire's *Mérope*, which had been a favourite at the Théâtre du Marais, at Mlle Montansier's theatre in the Rue de la Loi (Rue de Richelieu), and at the Théâtre de la Nation between January and March 1793. It had been noticed that the plot of Voltaire's tragedy, involving a widowed queen calling on her brothers to avenge her husband's death, presented certain disturbing analogies with the plight of the imprisoned Marie-Antoinette; so for the time being, *Mérope* was forbidden on all Paris stages. The old repertoire would, it was thought, return once the political situation allowed. In an article, 'Réflexions sur les spectacles', published in the *Journal de la Montagne* on 7 September 1793, Aristide Valcour made this reassuring prediction.

It is not sufficient to have decreed that no more anti-revolutionary plays should be performed; we must be prepared to do without many of the masterpieces of French literature for ten years *at least*. When republican simplicity and decency have replaced the luxury and vices of the *ancien régime*, our children will laugh at the folly of our forebears. Let us bury monarchical plays in libraries and consign to the attic the gaudy costumes of our stage princelings ...[10]

Not all the old favourites were unsuitable for republican ears, however; plays such as Lemierre's *Guillaume Tell* (1766) and Voltaire's *La Mort de César* (1743) were endlessly applauded by *sans-culotte* audiences. There was also a constant stream of new plays designed to stimulate the patriotic ardour of the embattled nation, of which Sylvain Maréchal's *Jugement dernier des rois*, first performed at the Théâtre de la République in October 1793, was the most notorious: it showed all the crowned heads of Europe, together with the Pope and the Empress of Russia, being shipped off to a volcanic island and perishing in the final eruption. The actors had understandable qualms about accepting it when it was offered them, in case they were held to account at some future restoration of the monarchy; but they were asked if they preferred to be guillotined now rather than be hanged at some uncertain date in the future, and the argument proved irresistible.[11] It has been calculated[12] that of the 450 plays produced in Paris in the years 1793–4, some two-thirds carried a political message. But alongside these were others that can best be described as escapist, such as Mme Candeille's *Catherine ou la Belle Fermière*, first performed, with the actress who had written it taking the leading part, at the Théâtre de la République on 27 December 1793, and remaining wildly popular throughout the Terror; it was a sentimental pastoral play which at any other period might have been judged insipid, but which presumably formed a welcome contrast to the bloody drama being enacted day by day on the Place de la Révolution. Some theatres, notably Nicolet's on the Boulevard du Temple, appear to have been tacitly excused the need to toe the ideological line, and to have avoided all plays of a revolutionary or anticlerical complexion; the Gaîté, as it was now called, contented itself and no doubt pleased its audiences too with its stock line of farces, pantomimes and acrobatic displays, interspersed with the occasional comedy by Molière or Marivaux. The only pieces that sometimes got Nicolet or Audinot into trouble were those judged too broad by the prudish censors: a farce involving Harlequin disguised as a dog and cocking a leg against Pantaloon's cloak, another with a dubious sexual intrigue judged to be obscene, could cause the managers to be denounced and even imprisoned for a short while as a reminder that the era of liberty ushered in by the Revolution was never intended to be an era of licence.

The fall of Robespierre and the momentary disarray into which the Jacobins were plunged did not by any means lead to the dismantling of the censorship and a return to the relatively uninhibited days of 1791–2. After an interlude of confusion and uncertainty, an *arrêté directorial* dated 14 February 1796 reminded interested parties in its preamble that the theatres,

these public establishments to which, out of curiosity, love of the arts, and for other motives, citizens of both sexes and all ages are daily drawn in considerable numbers, having as their essential aim and purpose to contribute, by their very popularity, to the purifying of morals and the propagation of republican principles – these institutions are necessarily the object of particular solicitude on the part of the authorities.[13]

Such 'solicitude' bore, however, solely on the content of theatrical performances, and did not extend to indemnifying those who financed and ran the theatres and were finding it increasingly difficult to do so. Faced with brisk competition from other, newer forms of mass entertainment – the public balls that were so popular under the Directory, the numerous pleasure gardens, beginning with the Tivoli which opened in 1796 and had various imitators, among them the Jardin Biron which organized spectacular balloon ascensions and parachute jumps[14] – all these, together with the unregulated proliferation of the theatres themselves, made it more and more difficult for managers to make ends meet. But the state saw its only responsibility as being to clamp down on audacious playwrights, with the result that the latter were increasingly tempted to censor themselves in order to avoid trouble; consequently, what they had to offer the public lacked novelty and bite. As one of them remarked at the very end of the century,

whatever name one chooses to give to the meticulous inspection which dramatic works have to undergo before they are permitted on the stage, it is an undoubted fact that dramatists are more timid today than they were twelve years ago [i.e. before the Revolution] and that the censorship has become more rigorous. Any man of letters who, like myself, has pursued this career at both periods will bear me out in this.[15]

Evidence drawn from the censors' own reports on manuscripts submitted to them in 1798–9[16] show just how niggling and vexatious their objections could be. Anything that might remind an audience of what had been commonplace before the Revolution, even the gentlest criticism of reforms introduced since 1789, were unfailingly pounced on and alterations or deletions imposed. A character is called Louis: such a name should never be heard on the stage, except if applied to a villain; similarly the *louis d'or* should not be mentioned, even though gold coins with the effigy of former kings were still in circulation at the time. A play called *Minuit* was banned outright on the grounds that the whole plot turned on the question who was to be the first to wish the others a happy new year: 'it would be, to say the least, improper to remind an audience of a custom which the republican calendar has done away with'. Similarly, the author of *L'Homme sans façon* (The Rough-and-Ready Man) had to agree to the deletion of four lines about divorce. Divorce had been legalized on 20 September 1792 and, wrote the censor, 'to attack a new institution in its effects and to proclaim its abuses is to expose it too easily to its detractors and to slander the institution itself in its principle'. This line of reasoning was bound to discourage any but the most anodyne social comment in new dramatic works.

In a report dated 9 March 1798, objections were made to a play set in the United States: people make very little distinction nowadays, asserted the censor, between the English and the Americans, and France is at war with England; it follows that no American should be shown on the stage except in an odious light. Why, in any case, choose a foreign setting? The reason is clear enough: 'the authors, in order to avoid the title "citizen" or any other republican usage, have transported the scene overseas'. The point may well have had more to it than appears on the surface. The use of *citoyen* as a form of address rather than *monsieur* was continued after the end of Jacobin rule, but apologetically, with a half smile. The report of a police spy to the Minister of the Interior, dated 8 September 1794, shows that already the word was pronounced with marked irony from the stage.[17] Actors, often bolder than authors since they were not called upon to confront the censors directly, were not above adding sly remarks to their text, certain that such interpolations would delight their audiences however much the authorities might object – as happened at the Ambigu-Comique in 1796 when an actress, reaching the point where she had to say: 'he has just received 2,000 *écus*', added, after a significant pause: 'in specie'. This veiled allusion to the depreciation of the paper money put into circulation by the Republic caused much merriment and some applause among the audience. No action was taken against her, though the directors of the Ambigu-Comique received a letter of admonishment from the authorities.

Eventually, the discredit into which the Directory itself fell in its last stages extended even to the practice of repressive censorship. Nothing demonstrates this more strikingly than the well-authenticated story of Alphonse Martainville and his vaudeville *Les Assemblées primaires*, which included certain satirical comments on the electoral system introduced on 22 August 1795. The play, which went down very well with the audiences at the Théâtre des Jeunes-Artistes where it was produced on 17 March 1797, was banned by higher authority after the fourth performance. Martainville, informed of the decision by Limodin, secretary of the central police bureau, replied boldly that he would stir up trouble if they took his play off, and added: 'The general public wants to see it, and you have no right to deny it them'; to which Limodin retorted, glowering: 'What do I care about the general public? I don't give a damn whether it's pleased or not.' Martainville bowed himself out and proceeded to have posters stuck up in the principal thoroughfares of Paris, reporting this conversation in brief and adding:

The general public, for whom Limodin doesn't give a damn, doesn't, I imagine, give a damn for him, and yesterday protested vociferously at hearing the play was to be withdrawn. But I, who am not a member of the central police bureau, I have sent the play to the press in order to let the general public have the opportunity to decide for itself on its merits. It will be published by Barba, whose address is 27, rue Saint-André-des-Arts.

It would be difficult to find a clearer illustration of the contempt into which the efforts of the government to control theatrical productions and to suppress undesirable plays had fallen during the Directory. No playwright would have dared under the previous regime to do what Martainville did in 1797; and still less was anyone to risk cocking a snook at authority under the succeeding one.

CHAPTER 7

Re-establishment of the state theatres

The junketings, speechifying and fond embracing that marked the celebration dinner given by Dazincourt in 1799 denoted a natural feeling of relief that the fragmented company, the Maison de Molière, had after ten years of discord been reunited at last. The *sociétaires* supposed, short-sightedly, that they would take up where they had left off and would rapidly recover lost ground, regaining the high reputation they had enjoyed in the eyes of all those who appreciated good ensemble acting; and they probably looked no farther. Few of them could have reflected that the price to be paid for so glittering a future was yet to be determined. The Ministry of the Interior, which had worked to make possible this new beginning, had certain expectations that were not slow to surface; nor was it long before the actors realized that they were in future to obey the wishes of a stricter taskmaster than any of them could remember from pre-revolutionary times.

The first collision – and the last – between the actors and the government occurred in 1801 and settled matters once and for all: in future, the Comédie-Française was to give up all thoughts it might have entertained that it was to run its own affairs without inter-ference; quite a different political breeze was blowing now, and likely to continue blowing in the same direction for the foreseeable future. The company had been ill-advised enough to advertise one evening a vaudeville, that is, a light comedy interspersed with songs sung to well-known tunes, of the kind Piis and Barré had made popular on the eve of the Revolution. For this they were taken to task by Chaptal, Minister of the Interior, whom they told, none too politely, to mind his own business; they were running theirs, and it was part of this business of theirs to decide which plays were most likely to please their audiences. Chaptal's ensuing dressing-down put them right on a number of points:

The disobedience of the actors, their solemn conventicle, their stubborn resistance to the wishes of the government, all this is committed under cover of their antiquated statutes. The most bizarre of their arguments is drawn from the title they assume of *entrepreneurs*. They must never pursue an independent line of enterprise. The perfecting of dramatic art in France demands that the national theatre be exclusively devoted to the two forms that have enriched it by their masterpieces

– these two forms being, of course, tragedy and comedy, which the Comédie-Française was warned should be its exclusive province in future.[1]

It is, of course, not possible to know to what extent Napoleon inspired the terms of this rebuke, but his later decisions, in particular concerning the types of play to which each theatre in Paris was to be restricted, suggest he may have had a hand in its framing. The 'national theatre' was assured of the friendly interest of the state, but in return it was expected to follow in every respect the line laid down for it by the state. The question whether Napoleon, with his undoubted but possibly misguided interest in theatrical matters, had a beneficial influence on the development of the Comédie-Française during his reign, or whether he can be said more truly to have impeded its natural progress, is one that can be argued indefinitely. What is certain is that he knew what he wanted, and spared no pains to achieve his goal. In the next two years, while his own position as First Consul was rapidly evolving towards the ultimate end of absolute power, he took a series of steps designed to give every support to the home of tragedy and comedy and to provide it with a gilded cage, though a cage none the less.

The building it occupied on the Rue de Richelieu, originally erected for Gaillard and Dorfeuille on land belonging to the Orléans family, had been sold early in the Revolution by Philippe-Egalité to one we should now call a property developer; and it was to this individual that the Comédie-Française had to pay rent for the theatre and the ground it stood on. This was an undignified situation for a national institution to be placed in, but Napoleon's efforts to buy out the landlord, or alternatively to sequestrate his property, proved unavailing, and the society continued throughout his reign to remain leaseholders. Under the Restoration the Duc d'Orléans, the future King Louis-Philippe, did succeed in buying back the property, so that the rent for the Théâtre-Français was paid thereafter to him rather than to the propertied commoner who had previously owned it.

What Napoleon did in the circumstances was to make over to the society, in the form of an annual subvention, a sufficient sum to cover the rents and dues of the building. This was done as part of a general settlement, made on 2 July 1802, by which the First Consul assigned to the Minister of the Interior a very large sum (300,000 francs) to be used to put the enterprise on a sound financial footing. If the reconstituted Comédie-Française continued to be responsible for the debts accumulated earlier, particularly in the years 1792–3,[2] then their creditors needed to have their claims satisfied in case a successful action were brought which might lead to the company's bankruptcy and a fresh dissolution. In addition, there was a six-year backlog in the payment of pensions to retired *sociétaires* – eleven in all, including Mlles Clairon, Dumesnil and Sainval *aînée*, the last-named surviving until 1830: these pensions had formerly been a direct charge on the royal Treasury, but the obligation to pay them had been repudiated in 1790. And finally, there was the annual rental for the building itself, an obligation that the government was in honour bound to meet, since one of the promises made by Mahérault, in order to persuade the actors to agree to a reconstitution of the society, was that they would be provided with a playhouse free of charge. This item was to cost the Treasury a round sum of 100,000 francs a year, which continued to be paid so long as Napoleon remained in power.

All these financial arrangements were legalized in the so-called *acte de dotation* of 2 July 1802. This was followed by the signing at Saint-Cloud of a decree setting forth the definitive organization of the new national theatre (18 January 1803), and finally the drawing up, in a notary's office, of the articles of association, fifty-three of them in all, which had to be signed by all present *sociétaires*, with provision for further names to be added as and when an actor or actress was granted membership of the society. The collective signing of this instrument on 17 April 1804 marked the inauguration of the Comédie-Française as a legally constituted body, empowered to enter into commercial transactions, to pursue defaulters in courts of law, etc.[3] Finally, on 3 July 1804, the Empire having been proclaimed on 18 May previously, Mahérault headed the entire company in swearing, at the Hôtel de Ville, the oath of allegiance as prescribed by the Senate. The effect of this symbolic act was to raise the Comédie-Française to the position of a state institution, one which, of course, it still retains. On the same day, the formula

Comédiens ordinaires de l'Empereur replaced on the playbills that of *Comédiens-Français sociétaires* which had previously been used.

To ensure control of the Comédie-Française and of other theatrical enterprises that had been drawn into the ambit of the state, Napoleon revived the monarchical system of delegating supervisory powers to four Préfets du Palais, corresponding to the four Gentlemen of the Bedchamber of earlier days: the only difference was that, instead of owing their high position to the accident of birth, the Préfets du Palais were chosen from among the upper echelons of the judiciary and banking community. Thus, Auguste-Laurent de Rémusat, who was selected to supervise the Comédie-Française, was an eminent lawyer from Aix-en-Provence who also possessed considerable financial expertise. He was appointed to his post by an order dated 27 November 1802, and later promoted to the office of *surintendant général des spectacles*, with responsibilities not only for the Comédie-Française but for the Opéra-Comique and the Odéon as well.

His functions and duties, as set forth in the decree of 1 November 1807 which created this office,[4] were far-reaching and encroached in some respects on what had hitherto been regarded as the prerogatives of the administrative committee of the society. Thus, he had final say in whatever disputes might arise regarding the admission of new members, and he alone had the right to advise on the money payments to be awarded for special merit to senior actors. His agreement was required for all requests for retirement or for temporary leave of absence. The proposed weekly programme of plays had to be submitted to him for approval; and he alone was empowered to fine actors failing to notify in advance their inability to take part in a performance, 'or for any other act of insubordination of any kind towards their superiors'. The decree thus gave Rémusat far more than mere supervisory powers, and one unfortunate consequence was that the company, shorn of responsibility, was only too apt, during his occasional absences from Paris, to show itself incapable of effective self-government. In 1805, while Napoleon was away campaigning against the Austrians and Prussians, Rémusat accompanied him and, as his wife informed him, without his hand on the tiller the company started drifting on to the rocks. Fleury, now dean of the society, had visited her to pour forth a dismal story of the 'excessive disorder' into which it had fallen. 'Everyone does as he pleases; none of the regulations are being observed. The actors are all of them in the country, and in consequence their parts are taken by understudies and the box-office receipts have fallen to zero.'[5] In 1808 a major scandal occurred when Mlle George, one of the foremost tragic actresses in the Comédie-Française, failed to appear one evening to take her part in Delrieu's *Artaxerce* which was enjoying a highly successful run. It was not until some weeks later that it was discovered she had fled her creditors and was presently in Vienna, whence she made her way to St Petersburg. Here she was welcomed enthusiastically by the Francophile nobility[6] until the outbreak of hostilities between France and Russia obliged her to return to her native land. The Comédie-Française had, of course, expelled her as soon as her escapade was known, and cancelled her pension contributions; but Napoleon, perhaps in affectionate gratitude for past sexual favours on her part, caused her at a later stage to be reintegrated in the company and even to be paid arrears of salary for her five years' absence. The whims of the autocrat counted for more than any regulations he might promulgate.

The two other theatres that fell to Rémusat's responsibility in 1807 were, as has been seen, the Opéra-Comique and the Odéon; they gave him far less trouble than the Comédie-Française. It will be recalled that the Opéra-Comique had been formed from the fusion in 1800 of the remnants of the pre-revolutionary Comédie-Italienne with the company originally recruited for the Théâtre de Monsieur, later known as the Théâtre de la Rue Feydeau, and that the combined troupe agreed to perform in future at the Feydeau.[7] Presumably because its staple, light opera mixed with dialogue, was considered to be a type of dramatic entertainment in which the French excelled above all other nations, it was decided to include it among the theatres qualifying for a government subsidy: it was allocated 50,000 francs in 1801, an annual sum which rose to 96,000 francs under the Empire. It is true that its elaborate sets and stage machinery must have demanded constant expenditure for upkeep and renewal, like that of the Opera itself.

As for the Odéon, its building, the former Théâtre de la Nation, had been completely gutted by fire on 18 March 1799.[8] The actors, apart from the few who were given positions in the newly established Comédie-Française at its inception a couple of months later, led thereafter a nomadic existence, renting one vacant theatre after another on a temporary basis, and finally settling down in the Théâtre Louvois, near the Opera, on 5 May 1801. They constituted a talented company of players, however, and had they had premises of their own might well have formed the nucleus of that 'second national theatre' for which the playwrights had been agitating since long before the Revolution.

This permanent home came to them at last as a gift from the state. Various schemes had been floated over the years to rebuild a theatre on the site now occupied by a few smoke-blackened stones, all that remained of the Odéon. The government finally decided to make over the plot to the Senate, housed in the nearby Palais du Luxembourg, on condition the senators took it on themselves to finance the building of a new theatre. Work was started in 1807 and on 15 June 1808 the new playhouse, which was given the name Théâtre de l'Impératrice, although everyone continued to call it the Odéon, was inaugurated by the Louvois players. Regarded as an annexe to the Comédie-Française, it was not at first granted a separate subvention, though as from 1811 it was included in the budget for the state theatres.

By placing the Odéon under the tutelage of the Comédie-Française, Napoleon unfortunately started up afresh the old squabbles about privileged repertory which had caused so much hard feeling in pre-revolutionary times. The senior theatre had been repossessed of its monopoly on tragedy and on most of the great comedies of Molière, which the new theatre was therefore not allowed to include in its repertory. To circumvent the difficulty, the Odéon cleverly commissioned new verse transpositions of certain popular prose plays by Molière, including *L'Avare* and *Le Bourgeois gentilhomme*. But such outré devices hardly served to attract the crowds. What seems to have been overlooked by those who had been pressing for the reopening of a theatre adjoining the Luxembourg gardens was that it was situated at altogether too great a distance from the main theatre complex in the north of the city, and that the rich and lettered clientèle, which had supported the earlier Théâtre-Français before being dispersed to the four winds of heaven in the storms of the Revolution, had not returned in any great numbers to their old haunts. As an historian of the society of the First Empire later expressed it,

the free-spending, pleasure-loving, brilliant section of Paris society, confined to the area circumscribed by the Palais-Royal, the Chaussée d'Antin and the Faubourg Saint-Honoré, tempted by nearby places of entertainment, hesitated about making a long expedition through winding streets for the sake of a disappointing evening's outing. The legend took root at this time according to which the Odéon was considered a sort of suburban theatre situated outside the peopled world, if not beyond the known world.[9]

And this legend was to persist throughout the first half at least of the nineteenth century, until better communications and also a new generation of more talented directors put the Odéon on the map at last.

In view of the disappointing public response, the expedient was adopted of confining straight drama at the Odéon to four days a week, and opening the theatre on Mondays, Wednesdays and Saturdays to a company of singers specializing in Italian opera. They owed their presence in Paris to the undiminished energy of Mlle Montansier who, emerging from prison on 16 September 1794, had started a series of legal battles to obtain proper compensation for her arbitrary eviction, in favour of the Opera, from the theatre she had built in the Rue de la Loi.[10] Around 1800 this indomitable old lady, aware of Bonaparte's great fondness for *opera buffa*, had the idea of restoring her dilapidated fortunes by inaugurating an opera-house in the small but very elegant Salle Olympique, originally built for amateur theatricals by a stage-struck millionaire. She opened here on 31 May 1801 with a performance of Cimarosa's *Matrimonio segreto*, Stendhal's favourite Italian opera. As it happened, he was at Bergamo at the time and knew nothing of this new Parisian venture, which might well have excited him if he had; but the Duchesse d'Abrantès was in the audience which, she later wrote, consisted entirely of 'the flower of Parisian society at the time'. The front row of boxes was almost completely filled with young ladies dressed in the height of fashion. 'One other oddity', she added ingenuously, 'was that there were only two boxes not occupied by people we knew.'[11] However, the First Consul never put in an appearance. The Salle Olympique was situated in the Rue Chantereine, one of a warren of small, winding streets offering easy bolt-holes for terrorists, and the police could not guarantee his safety were he to attend: the attempt on his life by an 'infernal machine' detonated in the Rue Saint-Nicaise when he was on his way to the Opera had occurred less than six months earlier.

So, in the hope that she might yet attract Bonaparte's attention given a more favourable locale, Mlle Montansier moved her troupe of Italian singers to the presently vacant Salle Favart, the old theatre originally erected for the Comédie-Italienne in 1783, where she opened on 17 January 1802. But at the end of a twelvemonth the unfortunate directress found herself once more in prison, this time for debt. The company attempted for a while to run the theatre themselves, but by the spring of 1804, unable to make ends meet, they packed their bags and were on the point of returning to Italy. It was then that Napoleon, newly proclaimed emperor, came to their rescue, promising them a suitable subvention and appointing Picard their first director. Thus the Théâtre-Italien, as it was officially known though it had no connection at all with the Théâtre-Italien of the *ancien régime*, took its place alongside the other state theatres of the First Empire; it was, however, only later in the nineteenth century that, under the familiar appellation 'les Bouffes', it became celebrated as a centre for fine singing and a magnet for all music-lovers in Paris.

In this survey of Napoleon's efforts to reconstitute and expand the system of state-supported theatres as it had existed before the Revolution, we have left to the last the Opera, which in some respects represents a special case. From the very beginning of the Consulate it was clear that the government was determined to rescue it from the inertia and despondency into which it had fallen under the Directory. The reasons adduced then for buttressing the Opera were very similar to those that had motivated ministers in monarchic times: it was perceived as an important prop to national prestige, and there were in addition financial spin-offs, invisible earnings which, if they did not demonstrably benefit the country at large, were certainly of value to the capital city. It was a foreigner, Francis Blagdon, who after visiting Paris during the Peace of Amiens, summarized in his stiffly Frenchified English the reasons why it was thought vital to continue state support for the Opera and pointed out the catastrophic consequences if it were allowed to collapse:

This expensive establishment affords employ to a vast number of persons. The singers, dancers, musicians, machinists, painters, tailors, dressmakers, scene-shifters etc., attached to it would constitute a little nation. The richness and variety of the dresses give activity to several branches of trade, and its representations involve all the agreeable arts. These united attractions captivate foreigners and induce them to squander considerable sums of money in the country. Hence, were the opera-house shut up, commerce would suffer; there would be an absolute void in the pleasures of the Parisians; and, as experience proves, these volatile people would sooner resign everything most valuable than any portion of their amusements.[12]

But the costs of keeping the Opera afloat were enormous, and kept increasing. Under the Consulate the annual subvention allocated to it was 600,000 francs, though part of this was clawed back by the Treasury if the affairs of the Opera were prospering, as happened in the second half of 1802 when the influx of English tourists led to full houses night after night. Napoleon, on his coronation, raised the subsidy to 750,000 francs, but had to increase it again, by a decree of 1 November 1807, to 850,000, then a little later to 950,000 francs; even so, the Opera was running a deficit in 1810 amounting to 166,450 francs. As a wit was to remark under the subsequent regime: 'The Opera is, for the Treasury, the barrel of the Danaides; but for the administrator and contractors, it's the Garden of the Hesperides.'[13] Certainly, the Opera's accounts could have done with an independent audit.

In 1811 some brilliant mind in the Treasury, remembering perhaps how the finances of the Opera had been materially helped in 1784 by the simple procedure of allowing it to auction off to the highest bidder the right to operate all the minor theatres in the capital, proposed that a similar policy should be followed under the Empire; and this resulted in a decree promulgated on 13 August that year, requiring the payment to the Imperial Academy of Music (the Opera) of a certain proportion of their gross profits by all the secondary (i.e. commercial) theatres, and in addition by all circuses, concerts, public balls, waxwork shows, in fact every kind of entertainment for which the public had to pay an admission fee, not forgetting such new attractions as the panorama and the cosmorama. No one, of course, protested – save sotto voce – at the time; no one dared protest at a government decision, whatever it was, in 1811. It was left to later historians to stress the unfairness of this tax on individual enterprise, designed to support a theatre which could appeal only to a tiny minority of the population; none spoke out more fiercely than Albert de Lasalle:

The Vampire-Opera did not shrink from living at the expense of jugglers, bear-trainers, fairground giants from whom it exacted petty daily tribute. It was not just iniquitous, it was sordid! And yet these piles of ha'pennies represented for the Opera an annual sum of over 300,000 francs which, together with its subsidy from the state and its own takings at the box-office, provided it with the biggest income yet.[14]

So lucrative, indeed, was this extra subsidy that it continued to be exacted even after the Empire fell, and was not finally abolished until 1831.

Napoleon, it must be admitted, had scant respect for private-enterprise theatres, nor, probably, did he give a thought for the showmen who made a wretched enough living out of providing the poorer classes with the only kind of entertainment they could afford. But neither did he think all that highly of the pompous performances offered by the Grand Opera, his personal preferences in musical drama inclining rather to the old-fashioned Italian *opera buffa*: his intention was simply that the Opera should impress foreign visitors as the most brilliant to be found in all Europe. When Rémusat was urging one day the need for a further increase in the state subsidy for the Opera he referred to it as 'the glory of the nation'. The Emperor fired up at once. 'You are mistaken, Rémusat', he cried; 'it is the Comédie-Française that is the glory of the nation; the Grand Opera is no more than its vanity.'[15]

The last administrative act affecting his favourite theatre, the 'glory of the nation', was signed by Napoleon and dated from Moscow in 1812; it is accordingly always referred to as the *décret de Moscou*. The detailed work involved in composing and setting in order the lengthy document[16] had been undertaken beforehand in Paris by Bernard, Mahérault's successor after his retirement. Napoleon himself may have made minor textual emendations in the three days he allocated to the work in Moscow, and certainly the tenor of the decree bears the unmistakable imprint of his guiding spirit; but the choice of location for the signing was no doubt dictated more by transitory political considerations than anything else. Back in France, at that moment, few had any inkling of the disastrous situation into which he had led the Grande Armée, and he was no doubt hoping to allay public apprehension by providing positive evidence that he could find time, in the midst of his military preoccupations, to give thought to the reorganization of the Comédie-Française on a definitive basis.

Did it in fact represent a reorganization or did it do no more than record, in a convenient form, the detail of practices that had grown up over the years? The extreme view, that the decree in fact changed nothing in the essential power-structure of the Comédie-Française since its establishment by Louis XIV, was expressed by Jules Claretie, himself *administrateur-général* of the Comédie-Française, at the beginning of the twentieth century. 'People forget', he wrote,

that the celebrated Moscow Decree, drawn up in Paris by eminent legal experts, is nothing more, all said and done, than a codification of the customs, rights and duties of the members of the venerable Comédie; the Emperor was doing no more than ratify in a sense the charter that had been countersigned by a monarch, Louis XIV, after being drawn up by an actor, Molière.[17]

Claretie undoubtedly oversimplified the situation. Louis XIV had little to say about how the Comédie-Française should run itself; that was left to Louis XV, whose reign saw the drawing up of the constitution of 1757 and the granting of letters patent in 1761. It may well be that Napoleon altered little in the internal arrangements of the Comédie-Française; what he did, and what he had been doing consistently since the earliest decrees affecting it (those promulgated during the Consulate), was to ensure that the directing power of the state should emerge as supreme. The state had secured to the theatre its commodious building; the state subsidized its every performance; so the state, as was only right, had a large say, in fact the deciding voice, in all the most important aspects of its administration.

In her analysis of the Moscow Decree, in which she distinguishes what was merely reproduced from earlier enactments and what was new, Béatrix Dussane[18] draws particular attention to the powers attributed by Napoleon to the *surintendant des spectacles*, which were very clearly defined and went far beyond those of the *surintendant*'s predecessor under the monarchy, the *intendant des Menus*. The decree of 1803 had ruled that the steering committee of the Comédie-Française should consist of three members elected by the actors, and three nominated by the government; the Moscow Decree left it to the *surintendant* to nominate all six members of the committee (clauses 30–32). The *surintendant* had the final say in promotions to the *sociétariat* (clause 67); it was he who granted leave of absence to individual actors, and his permission was required before any actor who had taken retirement could appear on any public stage in Paris or in the provinces (clause 85). The net effect of the greatly increased powers given to the state, in the person of its representative the *surintendant des spectacles*, is summed up by Dussane in a lapidary formula: 'Contrary to what one might have imagined, it was before the Revolution, not after it, that the Comédiens were living under a republic.' It had been, of course, a republic always at the mercy of the arbitrary power of the Gentlemen of the Bedchamber; but during the Revolution, especially after 1791, the representatives of the state had no more say in the internal administration of the Comédie-Française than of any other theatre; they were solely

concerned, as Bailly's intervention in the 'affaire Talma' demonstrated, with ensuring that the theatre itself should not become an
arena for unseemly demonstrations. It needed the advent to power
of an autocrat who saw in the Comédie-Française an instrument for
conferring 'glory' on his reign, so to weaken its republican, or as we
should say today its democratic institutions, as to reduce it in time to
the same level as any other theatre controlled by a director whose
decisions could not be questioned. On occasion, in the course of the
nineteenth century, there were half-hearted revolts against some
new encroachment of state power, but they never came to anything,
for it is easier to accept a state of dependence than to try and recover
autonomy once a society has allowed it to slip away.

CHAPTER 8

Curbs on the commercial sector

The liberation of the theatres in 1791 had been justified, as we have seen, by the argument that the alternative, to allow only a few favoured individuals to engage in this particular form of the entertainment industry, would have been to perpetuate a system of privilege at variance with the basic ethos of the Revolution. But the immediate consequence had been more explosive than anyone had anticipated, and even though, after the first furious stampede, the number of new registrations dropped, the continuing eagerness to open new theatres caused concern even under the Convention. The question was referred to Anacharsis Clootz, the German radical writer who was granted honorary French citizenship in 1792 and elected to the National Assembly; in his report he discounted fears of a decline in the standards of the dramatic art, that 'more would mean worse', to use the modern catch-phrase, and argued in favour of allowing free play to the laws of supply and demand. 'Leave it all to private industry', he concluded; 'the theatres are in the same case as bakers' shops, the only concern of government must be to ensure that no poisonous stuff is offered for sale, whether for the mind or the body, nothing but sound nourishment.'[1] By 'poisonous stuff' Clootz clearly had in mind as much the ideologically dangerous as the indecent in stage offerings, and intended by this phrase a timely assertion of the state's duty to monitor the contents and tendencies of new plays.

But as time went on, it became more and more evident that private enterprise was drawing in a number of fast operators, concerned solely with personal profit, whose activities needed to be curbed; the only difficulty lay in seeing how this was to be done without tyrannous controls. Writing at the end of the century, Jean-Baptiste Pujoulx explained how these sharks went to work.[2]

The man who wants to open a theatre mentions to a few wire-pullers that he has his eye on a suitable building; immediately he is surrounded by a swarm of actors, prompters, musicians, scene-painters, playwrights. He signs up this man, drives a bargain with this other; within a month he has a complete theatrical troupe, he has absolutely all he wants ... except ready cash.

Nothing daunted, he opens his doors; spectators, always eager for anything new, crowd in, and healthy box-office receipts enable him to settle without difficulty the first month's bills. As interest falls off and audiences dwindle, he pays with promises, offers so much on account, or settles only the more pressing debts, and at the end of the fourth month, his starving actors being by now thoroughly dis-contented, he calls a meeting and explains that, because of unforeseen difficulties and the fierceness of competition, he is forced to put up shutters. From the wreckage of his fortunes, however, the cowboy manager has salted away enough to keep him in comfort for a year or two.

In the late 1790s there was a sufficient number of such scandals to attract the attention of the press. In a pamphlet entitled *Observations sur les spectacles* (1797) Amaury-Duval suggested that the 1791 law required revision; it had led to three unfortunate results, 'the decline of the dramatic art, the corruption of good taste and the ruin of theatrical managements'.[3] Much the same claims were made by M.-J. Chénier in the Council of the Five Hundred (16 November 1797); he put forward a proposal to allocate theatres on the basis of a population count. In the same chamber the following year there was a full-scale debate on the question (22 March 1798) which disclosed a variety of conflicting opinions about what action, if any, should be taken. Some speakers wanted a drastic reduction in the number of theatres; other felt that any restriction would amount to an infringe-ment of commercial rights and would be 'contrary to the freedom of every citizen to profit by his own enterprise; it would destroy the salutary effect of fair competition; it would put dramatists once more at the mercy of theatre managers, as they had been under the *ancien régime*'.[4] In the end, it was thought best to leave things as they were, and the decree of 1791 remained on the statute book.

But the problem persisted, and became even more acute when the state put itself firmly behind certain theatres, giving them financial assistance and promoting them to a privileged position; the old assumption, by which the others were relegated to the status of secondary or minor theatres, was a necessary corollary of this move, and it seemed inevitable that the state should take due note of the commercial sector, as it had under the *ancien régime*. The overthrow of the Directory gave an immediate impetus to this development, and a fresh inquiry was ordered on the desirability of halting by legal means any further expansion of the theatre industry. On 5 April 1800 the consuls instructed Lucien Bonaparte, then Minister of the Interior, 'to forward them, within the next ten days, a report on the measures to be taken to restrict the number of theatres, and on the statutes to be drawn up to ensure the surveillance of the public authority'.[5] Whether Napoleon's brother acted on this peremptory behest or not, no immediate steps were taken; but it became generally known that something of the kind was in the wind, and over the next year or two there was a good deal of talk about the impending closure of several of the minor theatres. Echoes of these speculations are to be found in the writings of two foreigners who travelled to Paris in 1802. The English journalist Francis Blagdon observed that

of late it has been rumoured that the stage is to be subjected to its former restrictions. The benefit resulting to the art itself and to the public, from a rivalship of theatres, is once more called in question: and some people even go so far as to assert that, with the exception of a few abuses, the direction of the Gentlemen of the Bedchamber was extremely good;

while J. F. Reichardt informed his readers that

they say that many of the small theatres will be suppressed. I am curious to see whether they will really dare to attempt such a measure; for whoever lays a finger on the Parisian and his theatres affects him spiritually, just as a rise in the price of bread affects him physically. Cheap bread, and plays aplenty![6]

So the glut of playhouses in Paris continued – twenty-three of them according to Blagdon – and the Abbé Geoffroy, who was to become the establishment critic under the Empire, commented on 4 October 1802 that 'the inhabitants of Paris see the sum-total of their pleasures increase pro rata with the number of their theatres, at the very moment when it is being noised abroad that a statesman wishes to make a holocaust of all these mountebank stages in honour of the god of taste'.[7]

It was no secret that Napoleon had scant respect for the 'mountebank stages' that continued to proliferate; but he was careful to take no action against them until he was sure of his ground. He undoubtedly listened to the complaints made by Talma and other members of the Comédie-Française invited to court receptions, and to Rémusat, *surintendant des spectacles*, who accompanied him during the campaigns of 1805 and whose worries about the situation in Paris were not allayed by the letters his wife was sending him. Fear that their hitherto invincible leader might be overwhelmed by the armies of the Third Coalition was filling the breasts of the people at home, who were more inclined to mull over the potentially disastrous situation in private than to seek distraction at the theatre – particularly a theatre specializing in tragedy. As a result, wrote Mme de Rémusat, the Comédie-Française was deserted and the actors were in despair. In these hectic months, those seeking entertainment preferred the frivolous or exciting novelties advertised by the 'minors'. 'These are for ever offering works that stimulate curiosity, too often unfortunately by their extravagance and, what is worse, their indecency, and Racine and Molière are forsaken for the crude farces of the Boulevard. I saw some of them myself last week with mother, and had the utmost difficult in finding seats' – both theatres, the Ambigu and the Jeunes-Artistes, being besieged by the fanatic followers of fashionable melodramas. This was in July 1805; people said it was too hot to go to the Comédie-Française; and in October they said it was too wet. 'The theatres', she wrote again, 'are absolutely deserted – except the minor ones. Your poor Comédie-Française struggles in vain'; at a recent performance of Molière's *Don Juan*, 'played beautifully by Dugazon and Fleury, there were not fifty people in the pit'.[8]

It was after Napoleon's return, crowned with the laurels of Austerlitz and Jena, that he finally made up his mind to take action against the pullulation of the minor theatres and in defence of those that enjoyed his favour. Even so, he moved cautiously at first. The decree of 8 June 1806 was relatively mild, as though the ground was being tested. It made no order for the closure of any existing theatre, merely reaffirming the principle, enunciated earlier by Louis XIV, that no new theatre could be opened within the capital without prior authorization; and that additionally, any manager wishing to start up a new theatrical enterprise would have to demonstrate that he had adequate financial resources. Here the intention was sound: an end was to be made of the fraudulent bankruptcies which had been so common under the Directory and possibly since then. There was provision for the drawing up of privileged repertoires for the Comédie-Française, the Opera and the Opéra-Comique; they alone would have the right to perform works in their stock, though other theatres might put them on, if given permission and after due payment. Effectively, this decree annulled the freedoms granted by the National Assembly on 13 January 1791. It further gave the Minister of the Interior the power to assign to each commercial theatre a particular type of entertainment from which it would not be allowed to diverge. Other clauses regulated similarly the situation in the provinces.[9]

Champigny, who had charge of the Ministry of the Interior at the time, issued his own order the following year (25 April 1807), naming five 'secondary' theatres still allowed to continue functioning: the Gaîté (the theatre founded by Nicolet in 1760 and the senior of the commercial houses on the Boulevard du Temple), the Porte-Saint-Martin (built as a temporary home for the Opera in 1781), the Variétés (located in the theatre opened by Mlle Montansier in the Palais-Royal, 1790), the Vaudeville (founded by Piis and Barré in 1792), and the Variétés-Etrangères. Each of them had to conform to various stipulations relating to the kind of play they could put on: pantomimes and farces at the Gaîté, melodrama at the Porte-Saint-Martin, and so forth. It was presumably because the rage for melodrama was at its height during the first decade of the new century that Champigny wished to confine it to one theatre; if the infection were to spread, every manager would be staging melodramas, much in the same way as, later in the century, nearly all the commercial theatres in Paris went over to the operetta. This was beginning to happen already: we have seen how Mme de Rémusat reported having watched two melodramas at two different boulevard theatres in the same week. By permitting only the Porte-Saint-Martin to stage them, Champigny no doubt hoped to limit the opportunities open to theatre-goers to indulge this dubious taste. But, for the moment, there was still no question of closing down theatres; those not among the five 'major-minor' theatres were allowed to remain open, provided they elected a particular type of entertainment in which to specialize. Thus, for a brief period, there was a three-tier hierarchy: the state theatres, in all their subsidized splendour; the tolerated popular houses, run without benefit of subvention; and at the bottom of the pile, a quantity of more or less shabby fleapits, catering in the main for

districts that would otherwise be deprived of dramatic entertainment.

The five theatres named in Champigny's order were all relatively
old foundations; even the Variétés-Etrangères was only a recent
name disguising the Théâtre-Molière which Boursault-Malherbe
had opened in 1791, a relatively commodious building with room
for close on a thousand spectators, situated in a populous district in
the east of Paris. Boursault had had to retire from the management,
which then passed through a variety of hands, changing its name
each time, but he remained the proprietor and in June 1806, having
resumed control of his theatre, he addressed a memorandum to the
Minister of the Interior advising him of his intention to use it to
mount foreign plays in translation: the works, in particular, of
dramatists of the second rank such as Sheridan, Garrick, Kotzebue,
Goldoni. It was an interesting and novel experiment and as such, no
doubt, merited the special treatment that Champigny gave it.

The careful arrangements the minister had made were, however,
rendered inoperative three months later by the Emperor in a further
decree dated 29 July 1807. Whereas Champigny had allowed the
existing theatres to survive, the smaller ones being subsumed as
'annexes' to the five more important ones, this subsequent act made
a clean sweep of the commercial sector. Clause 4 authorized only the
Ambigu-Comique (the theatre founded by Audinot in 1769, omitted
for some reason from the earlier list), the Gaîté, the Variétés and the
Vaudeville to continue in existence. Clause 5 stated baldly that

all theatres not authorized in the preceding clause will be closed before
August 15. In consequence, no theatre other than those designated above
will be permitted, under any circumstances whatever, to perform any play
in our fair city of Paris, under any pretext, nor to admit the public, even
non-paying, or to display any theatre bill or to distribute any printed or
handwritten tickets ...[10]

It will be noticed that a bare fortnight was allowed for the closure of
some fifteen theatres;[11] no compensation, financial or other, was
offered either to management or to the actors, stagehands, scene
painters, members of the orchestras etc., thrown suddenly out of
work. By this single, arbitrary stroke of naked power, the Emperor
had not merely decimated the theatre industry; he had all but
obliterated it, depriving whole areas of the city of any local dramatic
venue. The theatres left functioning in Paris in 1807 were actually
fewer in number than those permitted in 1788.

The proprietors of the buildings, who were seldom identical with the theatre managers, were of course left in possession; but the market value of their property was much reduced, since a theatre, being designed and built for a specific purpose, is not easily converted to any other use. Now property rights were as sacred to the imperial government as they had been to all previous ones – barring the special case of the property of the church and of *émigrés* – and in one instance the landlords did submit a claim against the government: this was in connection with the Théâtre de la Porte-Saint-Martin, which had been legally purchased by a group of financiers under the Directory when it was the policy to raise money for the state by selling off national property. Originally, as we have seen, the Porte-Saint-Martin had been built as an opera house, and by reason of its size and lay-out was not suited for any other purpose than to serve as a theatre; if the government now refused to allow it to be so used, and offered no compensation, did this not in fact constitute an infringement of property rights?

The argument was well founded. After 1794, when the Opera had moved out of it to occupy Mlle Montansier's new theatre in the Rue de Richelieu, the Porte Saint-Martin had stood empty for several years; but on 27 September 1802 it had opened up again, and by 1804 had become quite the most fashionable theatre on the Boulevard. This fact alone would not have troubled the authorities; but the petition, arguing that it was contrary to law and natural justice to dispossess property-owners without indemnification, put them in an awkward dilemma. They had no wish to undermine the credit of the state; on the other hand, to offer compensation would create a precedent and might open the floodgates to other claims. They prevaricated for three years and finally, by a letter dated 11 March 1809,[12] allowed the Porte-Saint-Martin to reopen for certain performances of a type that could not offer competition with the protected repertoire of the state theatres. Apart from prologues spoken by one of two actors at the most, of which the function was simply to explain the action of the principal entertainment, no dialogue was permitted, only old-fashioned rope-dancing, wrestling and 'military manoeuvres'. It was the latter that drew the crowds eventually. More by a decision of the manager, Augustin Hapdé, than by direction of the government, these 'military manoeuvres' consisted usually of stirring re-enactments of the famous battle triumphs of Napoleon's career, performed against lavish backdrops and involving a great number of extras. One such pageant, *The Passage of Mont-Saint-Bernard*, was so huge a success that it was even attended, incognito, by the Emperor himself – or so it was said ... Encouraged to believe their propaganda efforts were appreciated in high places, Hapdé ventured to introduce spoken parts, and was promptly ruled out of order. The theatre was once more closed down, on 4 June 1812, and remained an empty shell until the Restoration.

Even the four commercial theatres that had been spared by the decree were kept under close surveillance, and if it was thought they were interfering with the dignity and prosperity of the state theatres, which alone preoccupied Napoleon, appropriate steps were taken to abate the nuisance. There had been some question in the Council of State towards the end of 1806 of closing down the Variétés; its proximity to the Théâtre-Français was considered something of an affront. The Emperor expressed the view that it was undesirable to have theatres cheek by jowl with one another, and the Variétés, lodged in the grounds of the Palais-Royal and still owned by Mlle Montansier, was in this case; he wanted it suppressed, partly for that reason, partly because it was a notorious haunt of prostitutes. Cambacérès ventured to defend the cause of the Variétés-Montansier; it was well known that he posed as protector of a young actress in the company, one Henriette Cuisot; he was always to be seen in his box when she was on stage, particularly when she had a breeches part, Cambacérès reputedly preferring handsome youths to pretty girls. Napoleon, aware of the weakness of his former fellow consul, made a dry reference to it in the chamber: 'I am not surprised that the arch-chancellor is in favour of conserving the Variétés: it's what all the old bachelors in Paris want', at which the Privy Council, amazed to hear the Emperor crack a joke, could not restrain their laughter.[13]

Nevertheless, the management of the Variétés were told to move out of their premises and were forced to accept temporary accommodation in an empty hall known as the Théâtre de la Cité. This had been built as a speculative venture in 1790–2 by the same architect, Samson-Nicolas Lenoir, as had been responsible for the Porte-Saint-Martin opera house. Sited on the ruins of an ancient church named after St Bartholomew which had tumbled down in 1787, it was a handsome theatre, with room for up to 2,000 spectators. Lenoir's first idea had been to call it after the popular King

Henry IV; then, when kingship went out of fashion, he chose the name Théâtre du Palais-Variétés, since it was situated opposite the Palais de Justice. In 1793 even the word 'palace' had the wrong associations, and it was then that Lenoir hit on the innocuous name it bore thereafter. During the first years of the Republic the Théâtre de la Cité had prospered, thanks to Lenoir's astuteness in bowing to whatever political wind was blowing, but later it lost all popularity, situated as it was on the left bank of the Seine far from the usual haunts of theatre-goers at the time. It was taken over in turn by no fewer than thirteen different managers; the last, a resolute man called Beaulieu, decided to risk his luck and reopened it on 14 August 1805, declaring: 'If I don't make a success of it, I'll blow out my brains.' But he counted without Napoleon. Learning of the edict of 8 June 1806, he spent a few weeks putting his affairs in order and then, on 26 September, his friends heard that he had done just what he said he would do.

The company of the Variétés fortunately needed to spend only a few months at the ill-fated Théâtre de la Cité before a new one was built for them on the Boulevard Montmartre, 'a frightful location for a theatre', as Ludovic Halévy recorded being told much later by a veteran playwright called Dupin who remembered well the move. 'It was practically in the country; there was not one of those tall houses you see there now.' (Dupin, it should be said, was retailing these reminiscences in 1871). 'Nothing but little one-storey wooden shacks. No sidewalks, just an avenue of tall trees, not even paved, only a few old gigs and hackney cabs trundling by from time to time. In the depths of the country, I tell you.'[14] But there the Variétés pitched their camp, and there the theatre still stands to this day, though the built-up area now spreads many kilometres beyond. As for their original home, the playhouse in the Palais-Royal from which Napoleon had summarily evicted them, it was leased to rope-dancers, then to a puppet-master, then to a trainer of performing dogs. In 1810, denominated now the Jeux-Forains, it was used for short sketches or playlets, but this reversion to a quasi-theatrical status lasted only eighteen months, and it then became a café. The journalist John Scott, who visited it in 1814, mentioned that 'it still continued to be divided into galleries and pit – the stage is covered with a vast bouquet of flowers. Here the company is understood to be of a loose description; the men are chiefly military, the women prostitutes.'[15] The raffish reputation which the Palais-Royal gardens had acquired under the *ancien régime* persisted at least till the end of the Empire.

The remainder of the theatres condemned by the decree of 1807 were either pulled down, converted to other uses or else stood empty, awaiting better days. Boursault-Malherbe's Variétés-Etrangères was used as a ballroom, or occasionally for private theatricals, still tolerated provided they were given before invited audiences, with no money changing hands. Valcour's Délassements-Comiques, more recently revived as the Nouveaux-Troubadours, was demolished, though its entrance hall was still used to show trained dogs and monkeys doing their tricks. Prévost, the proprietor of the Théâtre sans Prétention, was ruined and died shortly after, cursing on his deathbed 'Bonaparte's second *coup d'état*'; the building was let to a seller of soft drinks and became the Café d'Apollon. The Théâtre des Jeunes-Artistes was turned into a factory producing spectacles and opera-glasses.

At the time, with a rigidly controlled press, the only arguments allowed to appear were those that justified the measure, or were at least apologetic in tone. Previously Paris had been, theatrically speaking, an overstocked pond in which no fish could grow to its proper size; much better to remove the smaller ones and give the others room to develop. The decree of 1806 had been clearly inadequate, at least in its immediate effect; the far more draconian one of 1807 did permit the state theatres to raise their heads again. Before that edict, the Variétés-Montansier, small though it was, had been making more money than the Opera, whereas in 1810 the same theatre had dropped to fourth place; its takings were still 613,673 francs, but the Opéra-Comique could boast an annual income of 950,172 francs, the Comédie-Française 867,393, and even the Opera had a larger paying audience than the Variétés. If his purpose had been to teach the Parisians to appreciate the best in the dramatic and operatic arts, it can be said that Napoleon had achieved it, at least superficially; but the methods he used were those of a martinet, violent rather than persuasive, forcing them through the portals of the Théâtre-Français since they could no longer pass through those of the Porte-Saint-Martin.

CHAPTER 9

Politics and the pit

During his stay in the French capital in 1779, John Moore, the Glasgow physician and friend of Tobias Smollett, did not miss the opportunity to attend a few performances at the Théâtre-Français, and in discussing the behaviour of the pit or *parterre*, he drew his readers' attention to the fact that in a society where free comment on public policy was not exactly encouraged, it served as a useful, though unattributable, source of popular opinion; for, 'by the emphatic applause they bestow on particular passages of the pieces represented at the theatre, they convey to the monarch the sentiments of the nation respecting the measures of his government'.[1] Moore gives no precise instances, but it is clear what he is referring to, and there were plenty of other contemporary observers to testify to the growing habit, among the young men standing or sitting jammed up together in the pit, of *making applications*, that is to say, seizing on a line or a couplet in a well-known play and drawing attention, by shouts and clapping, to its applicability to some current crisis. The guard in the theatre was powerless to prevent an unforeseen burst of applause coming to punctuate a maxim or simple phrase spoken from the stage which was perceived by the impertinent groundlings as being highly pertinent to some matter of burning public import; and all the authorities could do subsequently by way of reprisal was to ban future performances of the play or at the very least to insist on the removal of the dangerous words. Thus, under an absolute monarchy, the theatre auditorium became the ideal arena for the anonymous expression of subversive opinion, delivered in conditions that assured virtual impunity.

One of the most striking, though not the earliest of such incidents occurred a little later than Moore's visit. Jacques Necker's dismissal from the post of *directeur-général des finances* on 19 May 1781, news of which caused general consternation in Paris, happened to coincide with a dress rehearsal of Collé's *Partie de chasse de Henri IV* which the Comédie-Française had billed for performance the following day. Collé had written this comedy a long time previously, without much expectation that it would ever be shown on the public stage; for, as he noted in his diary as early as July 1763, 'such and such a play stands no chance of seeing the footlights, for fear it will lend itself to malicious applications, to odious allusions and to interpretations which the author could not have foreseen and which he even did his best to discourage'.[2] He had, however, published it in 1768, and it had occasionally been seen in private theatres where the writ of the censorship did not run. A comedy dealing with Henry IV, the founder of the Bourbon line, was unlikely to be permitted on the boards of the Théâtre-Français during the reign of Louis XV, if only because of the comparisons which the censorship foresaw would be made between the generous and tolerant earlier King and his idle and voluptuous descendant. However, in 1774 it was at last sanctioned, and frequent performances in succeeding years ensured that the play was familiar to habitués of the Comédie-Française. Nevertheless, when revived on the Sunday following Necker's fall from favour, it was heard with more than usual attention by a rapt audience. It was particularly in the first act, where the minister Sully is rumoured to be on the point of dismissal, that the analogies with the current situation struck everyone as particularly close. At one point, according to the *Mémoires secrets*, when, 'having pardoned him the king exclaims: "The wretches! They misled me!" a voice from the pit shouted "Yes, yes!" and the cry was immediately taken up by countless other voices. The same uproar started up afresh whenever there was mention of Henry.'[3] J.-H. Meister, Grimm's continuator, in the report he gave of the same scene, entered into greater detail concerning audience reactions:

Nothing of what could be effortlessly applied to public sympathy for M. Necker was overlooked; often the burst of applause interrupted the actor at the point when it could be foreseen that the rest of his speech would no longer be susceptible of so direct, flattering and natural an application. In short, we doubt whether there can have been many instances of so responsive, delicate and, if it can be so expressed, such an involuntarily unanimous expression of public opinion.[4]

For an understanding of the political background to this brouhaha, it is necessary to know that Necker's help had originally been enlisted by the monarchy to avert the risk of national bankruptcy, a task which could only be achieved in the long run by reforms in the notoriously inefficient and blatantly unfair taxation system. When it became clear that this policy must lead to curtailment of the exorbitant financial privileges enjoyed by prominent members of the first and second estates, support for Necker fell off, and those who had the King's ear were successful in engineering his removal. One can see how the pit, made up predominantly of members of the third estate, might have been electrified by an exchange between two officers at the beginning of the play, when they are discussing the rumour that Sully is to be exiled. One of them hopes the story may be true: 'I would much prefer it if he were banished already, there would be a stop to these unjust laws he draws up on the pretence they are economies needed by the royal treasury'; whereupon the other replies: 'True enough. Only recently he has had our rights suppressed.' Now Collé, when he introduced this bit of dialogue into *La Partie de chasse*, could not possibly have had Necker in mind, since he was writing long before the Genevan banker was summoned to Paris; chance alone gave it a peculiar appositeness in May 1781. The pit seized on the passage, and by their long and pointed applause gave expression to the widespread feeling of alarm, disappointment and anger that was in the air at the time.

The sequel to this stormy performance was that the actors, confounded by these unexpected and improper bursts of applause, guessed what had caused them and, in order to clear themselves of suspicion, despatched a delegation to remind the Lieutenant-General of Police that *La Partie de chasse* had been announced as forthcoming on the previous Tuesday, several days before the news of Necker's dismissal had become public property. The minister accepted this explanation and took no further action other than to satisfy himself that the play would be given no further performances in the immediate future. Clearly the audience alone was to blame for what the authorities saw as a disgraceful scene; but, equally clearly, they could hardly arrest the entire *parterre* at the Théâtre-Français.

As the fatal decade drew to its close, the pit grew bolder. At the beginning of 1787 there was talk everywhere of the impending opening of the Assembly of Notables, convened to ratify fresh financial reforms proposed by Calonne. A comic opera by Paesiello, *Il re Teodoro*, had been recently translated into French and was due to be shown at the municipal theatre in Versailles. In one scene, the king and his equerry, finding themselves short of ready cash, start wondering how to raise it. 'Why not send for the Notables?' shouted a wag in the pit. 'An immense roar of laughter greeted this sally, with its direct application to the difficulties the country was faced with at this juncture and to the ingenious means devised by Calonne to conjure them. The Queen [present at the performance] joined in the general mirth and forbade the guard to arrest the man responsible for this witty interjection.'[5] This was in January; in July of the same year, after the Assembly of Notables had dispersed without any agreement on the reform plans, a new version by Doigny du Ponceau of Sophocles' *Antigone* was put on by the Comédie-Française. It included a line spoken by Haemon in answer to Creon's argument that the death sentence on Antigone had been approved by the elders and that the common people had raised no objection: 'The nation is silent when it condemns its kings.' On its first performance at the Théâtre-Français this menacing remark was violently applauded by the pit; the police insisted that the words, whether or not they represented a line in Sophocles' tragedy, should be deleted in the French version; but the excision did no more than limit the damage.

Given the rapidly changing public mood at the time it was impossible for the censorship, no matter how meticulously a play was scrutinized for possible 'applications', to foresee where the pit would seize the opportunity to make a political point; it needed only a few attentive spectators to start the applause for the others to 'cotton on' and join in lustily. There can be little doubt that in the absence of any other way of expressing openly and with impunity views embarrassing to the government, this method was exploited to the full by pre-revolutionary theatre audiences and that they grew particularly adept in employing such guerilla tactics. The pit, especially at the Théâtre-Français, was intellectually more lively and therefore readier to 'make applications' in the 1780s than it was in the post-revolutionary period; a fact noted with regret by a German traveller in 1802–3 on his return to Paris during the brief lull that followed the Peace of Amiens. The passage in which J. F. Reichardt recalls nostalgically the far-off days when a visitor to the Théâtre-Français was surrounded by intelligent men capable of profiting by every opportunity offered them to express their political opinions in this way is worth quoting here:

In cases not covered by the laws and police regulations, it frequently used to happen that one line in a play, given emphasis by a general noisy outburst denoting either delight or disgust on the part of the pit, had an indescribable effect. But this presupposes not only a receptive, sensitive and even witty audience, but also a very cultured *parterre*, such as Paris formerly possessed to a greater degree than any other city in Europe, but which today it lacks entirely.[6]

At this point it would be convenient to draw a distinction, though the two words were often regarded as interchangeable at the time, between an *application* and an *allusion*. Plays like *Le Mariage de Figaro* and M.-J. Chénier's *Charles IX* admittedly delighted contemporary audiences by the unmistakable *allusions* to various abuses current at the time: to the gagging of the press, for instance, in Beaumarchais's comedy, or to the excesses of religious fanaticism in Chénier's tragedy. The spectators who applauded so enthusiastically such works needed no quickness of mind to work out what the playwright was getting at. But *applications* were something quite other. The difference is that *allusions* were inherent in the dramatic piece, placed there deliberately by the author who expected his audience to 'see' them and respond accordingly; while *applications* worked in the reverse direction – they were 'made' by the audience or rather by certain lively and subversive elements in the audience, and the enjoyment given had certainly not been intended by the author who, if he was still living, might well be dumbfounded at the sensation produced by even the most commonplace passages in his work.

During the early days of the revolutionary period, *applications* were made with particular bravado at theatres where the audiences were still largely monarchist. A couple of fairly pedestrian lines in Beaumarchais's opera *Tarare*, reminding the mutinous soldiers that their first duty is to the king, earned a hearty round of applause at its revival in 1790 which it would probably not have been given at its first performance in 1787, when it was still taken for granted that the army would always take its orders from the monarch. The Marquis de Ferrières, who as a representative of the nobles had come up to Paris to join in the deliberations of the Estates General, was present on this occasion and found himself seated next to an honest demo-crat who grumbled at this untimely demonstration of loyalty to the monarchy.

'What do you expect?' I replied. 'It's a remnant of the old-fashioned French character; it's good to see it hasn't completely changed.' My neighbour fell silent, meditating, but soon afterwards he got his own back.

Tidings are brought to Tarare that his new subjects are in revolt, where-upon the king in Beaumarchais's play exclaims that 'the people are never to blame, they have only been misled'. My sturdy democrat clapped so vigorously that he well-nigh deafened me,[7]

though it is probable that, the Opera at that time attracting few populists, he was alone in his applause. Similarly, at the Théâtre de la Nation (formerly the Théâtre-Français) the spectators, still in 1792 overwhelmingly anti-republican, clapped energetically certain lines in Lefranc de Pompignan's *Didon* (first performed in 1734) when the Comédiens dusted it down and presented it anew; lines such as 'The people and the soldiers alike adore the queen' (Dido here standing in for Marie-Antoinette who was not even born when the poet wrote the work); and even so dangerous a maxim, more applicable to an oriental despot than to the weak but well-meaning Louis XVI, as 'Kings, like the gods, are above the laws'. The obvious appreciation with which such sentiments were received would have delighted the worthy academician who composed the tragedy, could he have but heard the cheering that echoed through the auditorium, but he had departed this life eight years previously.

Those of Voltaire's tragedies based on the chronicles of republi-can Rome had been written originally for overwhelmingly royalist audiences, and in consequence, when revived during the Revo-lution, lent themselves to contrary applications, some speeches appealing to aristocrats in the boxes, other to the revolutionaries in the pit. *Brutus*, first performed in 1730, was revived on 17 November 1790 before an excited audience who knew the play well.

The curtain had scarcely gone up when the revolutionary maxims were frantically applauded; when a few isolated boos made themselves heard, the pit roared: 'Down with the aristocrats! Out, out!' The most remarkable moment in this performance occurred when the words 'still free, and in a Rome without kings' were uttered. The dead silence was broken only by a little shamefaced clapping; but then suddenly everyone in the boxes rose to his feet as one man, shouting 'Long live the King!' and the cry was immediately repeated in every quarter of the auditorium; hats and handkerchiefs were waved; in a word, public enthusiasm manifested itself in the most touching fashion.[8]

Twelve days later, at the same theatre (the Théâtre de la Nation) it was the turn of *La Mort de César*; on that occasion the pit made it very clear that their sympathies lay with the dictator's assassins, Brutus and Cassius, while Mark Antony's funeral oration – a rather poor imitation of Shakespeare's version on which Voltaire had probably based himself – was booed mercilessly. But when the same play was produced at the Théâtre Feydeau shortly after the Jacobins fell from power, Antony's eloquence was listened to with the greatest sympathy in every part of the house. The terms of the equation, by this time, had been altered to suit the new political climate: the murdered Caesar was Louis XVI, Brutus and Cassius, those 'honourable men', were the regicides in the Convention, while Antony represented, perhaps, the voice of posterity.

One of the most celebrated *applications* in the revolutionary period was occasioned by a line in a run-of-the-mill drama based on the Old Testament story of Susannah and the Elders: a line that roused the royalists still frequenting the Théâtre du Vaudeville to a dangerous demonstration of sympathy for Louis XVI, who was at that time on trial for his life. In the play Daniel, addressing the two elders, used the words: 'You are her accusers, you cannot be her judges.' The objection was suspiciously similar to one of the arguments used by Desèze, the advocate entrusted with the defence of the royal prisoner; this argument had been articulated in the Assembly on 26 December 1792 and would have been fresh in people's minds when *La Chaste Suzanne* had its first performance on 5 January 1793. It is possible, however, that the line had not been in the script – it is not to be found in the printed version – but was added by the actor playing Daniel in order to bring attention to the parallel. The authors of the play included Barré, at the time manager of the Vaudeville, who would certainly not have wanted to incur the wrath of the Jacobins for the sake of allowing his audience to demonstrate obliquely, by cheering and clapping, in favour of what was essentially a lost cause.

At the time the Consulate was set up in 1799, although the pit remained, as before, uncontrollable, it had changed its character as we have seen and was no longer politicized in the same sense as it had been before the Revolution. Realizing this, Napoleon – or more probably his henchman, the police minister Fouché – decided to canalize for his own purposes the old habit, not entirely forgotten in the *parterre*, of applauding lines or passages susceptible of some topical application. Earlier plays, due for revival at the Comédie-Française, were eagerly scanned for such *loci classici*. Thus we find Mme de Rémusat writing to her husband during one of his prolonged absences from Paris about the choice of plays to celebrate

Napoleon's return from his victorious campaign in 1805, and reporting the discussions on this important subject she had been having
with some of the senior actors of the Comédie-Française. They were
of a mind to stage a revival of De Belloy's *Gaston et Bayard*, first
produced in 1771. 'Having reread this work', she writes, 'I found
myself in total agreement with them. This play, mediocre though it
may be, is stuffed with the most splendid applications in almost
every line.' In the same letter she refers further to a new tragedy by
Legouvé on the death of Henry IV. 'What struck me as excellent
was a speech by the king in which he expounds the whole plan he
proposes to execute against the House of Austria, which is the
precise history of our last campaign ... It would be impossible,
applauding Henry IV, not to think instantly of the Emperor.'[9] Thus
the *application*, formerly a device whereby the theatre audience could
vent its disapproval of certain actions of the government, was now
being enlisted as a propaganda weapon in the service of the new
regime. In general, audiences were happy to cooperate and applaud
when they were expected to do so. At a performance of Racine's
Iphigénie on 24 October 1805, news of the capitulation of Ulm having
been announced from the stage before the start of the play, the
whole house burst into applause when, in the opening scene,
Agamemnon uttered the distich

> Mais qui peut dans sa course arrêter ce torrent?
> Achille va combattre et triomphe en courant

('But who can halt this torrent in its course? Achilles leaps into the
fray and triumphs as he runs'). A few months later, in a performance
of Voltaire's *Sémiramis*, the veteran actress Raucourt spoke with a
marked emphasis the lines:

> Ce qui fonde un Etat peut seul le conserver;
> Il vous faut un héros digne de cet empire

('He who founds a state has alone the power to conserve it; you need
a hero worthy of this empire'), and was rewarded by loud shouts of
approval from the pit, where it is not improbable that Fouché's
myrmidons were present in force, leading the applause. It was only
at the minor theatres that the pit, vaguely remembering its former
role as the unlicensed critic of the establishment, would pointedly
applaud a satirical sally against the profiteers who had bought up
nationalized property during the Revolution, or else a humorous

reference to the continental blockade which obliged the French to accustom themselves to drink their coffee unsugared. Needless to say, in such cases the police immediately pounced and forbade further performances.[10]

But at the state theatres, when a passage chanced to apply rather pointedly to some awkward turn in government policy, the audiences, overawed, were more likely to maintain a deathly silence. This is what happened during a performance of *Britannicus*, actually ordered by Napoleon on 9 April 1810 as part of the festivities at Compiègne to celebrate his marriage to Marie-Louise. It seems extraordinary that neither the Emperor himself, nor Rémusat who was responsible for the evening's programme, nor Talma who must have known Racine's play backwards, remembered the passage in act II which had a most painful application to the steps Napoleon had to take to free himself for this second union and to the overriding motive that caused him to take them, namely Joséphine's evident barrenness. Talma, in an agony of embarrassment, had necessarily to declaim, though without his customary clarity of enunciation, the fatal nine lines given to Néron, concluding: 'The Empire looks in vain for an heir'; to which the actor playing Narcisse falteringly rejoined: 'Why then delay, my lord, to repudiate her?' Napoleon in the imperial box pretended to have fallen asleep, and the rest of the audience heard it through soundlessly and with bated breath.

A couple of years later, shortly after his return from the disastrous Russian campaign, Napoleon, seeking distraction, had himself driven to the Opéra-Comique. The entertainment that evening happened to include *Le Tableau parlant* (The Talking Picture), composed by Anseaume in 1769 and set to music by Grétry, which incorporates a solo addressed by Colombine to an ageing beau who had been boasting about his former prowess in love. 'Ah, but you were what you no longer are, you were not then what you have become; you had what you no longer have, what is needed to make conquests. Those joyous days have passed, they have all passed and will never return!' Ludovic Halévy, who claimed to have heard the story from an old *habitué* of the Opéra-Comique with whom he fell into conversation many years later, goes on to relate how the girl playing Colombine

repeated five or six times, with improvisations and fioriture: 'They have passed, those joyous days, they have passed and will never return!' In the auditorium, a dead silence. No one dared to stare openly at the Emperor, but covertly, secretly, all were darting glances in his direction. As for Napoleon, he remained motionless, impassive, with no sign of having heard anything. No one dared to applaud, and the singer, distressed, realizing the reason for this great silence, began to tremble violently and stammered rather than sang the final refrain.[11]

In another two years, the Allies had overrun the frontiers of France and Napoleon was compelled to abdicate. In the Paris theatres, the 'great silence' ended abruptly, and audiences resumed their former privilege of expressing their political views by means of *applications*. An early occasion was offered by the first performance of a new melodrama by Paul de Kock who, long before he made his name as a writer of popular comic novels, had tried his hand with some success in the production of these fashionable stage works. *Madame de Valois* was put on at the Ambigu on 23 March 1814, eight days before the victorious Allies marched into Paris. The melo-drama ended with the traditional tirade addressed by the hero to the victim, who in this play was evidently the father of the villain: 'Good old man, I trust that you will make your home among us; we shall endeavour to make you forget, by the care we shall take of you and the friendship we shall extend to you, the misfortune that befell you in fathering such a monster as him of whom we are happily this day delivered.' Whereupon, as Paul de Kock relates in his auto-biography, 'it was not just applause that broke out in the audi-torium, but roars and howls of approval'. No one was more taken aback than the young author, who had no illusions about the literary value of his work, and who now heard the audience clam-ouring for him to come before the curtain to receive the ovation normally reserved for the creator of a new dramatic masterpiece. The actor who had spoken the closing lines rapidly explained to him what had happened: the audience had made an application of the words 'a monster such as him of whom we are happily this day delivered' – 'Don't you understand that the audience saw in this phrase an allusion to the *tyrant*, the *Corsican ogre*, beaten by the Allies and who, they hope, will never return to Paris?' – 'Ah! good heavens, such an allusion was never in my mind!' – 'I believe you; but it is enough that it is in the mind of the spectators for them to wish to express their gratitude to you.' But Paul de Kock, a con-vinced Bonapartist, could not so easily switch his allegiance, nor did he choose to accept a triumph he had not earned, and he left the theatre in a hurry, not even stopping to thank the actors and embrace the actresses, something he had been looking forward to with keen anticipation.[12]

Simultaneously, in the more sedate surroundings of the Théâtre-Français, the company was rehearsing a new tragedy by Pierre Lebrun, on the subject of Ulysses' return to Ithaca. It had been written some time before Napoleon's fall from power, and the author had certainly not intended the reference, which the first-night audience saw, to the execution of the Duc d'Enghien in the line: 'The gods of vengeance are seated near the tombs'; nor had he anticipated the *application* duly made to the old king's return from his long exile when Talma declared: 'All, with tears in their eyes, bless the happy day which, after twenty years, restores a father to their affection.' At the same theatre, a revival was staged a little later of Voltaire's *Mérope*, which had been banned during the Revolution and never shown, lest it encourage royalist sentiment, under the Consulate and Empire. In 1814, royalist sentiment being back in fashion, the audience at the Théâtre-Français expressed their appreciation noisily at the concluding scene where Euryclès begs the widowed queen, Mérope, to show herself to the people, who are all eager to welcome back the legitimate heir to the throne – in this case, her long-lost son, Egisthe. But a few years later, when the Bonapartists had succeeded in regrouping themselves, it was discovered that Voltaire had written *Mérope* as much in defence of their cause as of that of the legitimists, and members of the opposition party in the pit took to applauding vociferously the dictum of Polyphonte, the would-be usurper of the throne:

> Le premier qui fut roi fut un soldat heureux;
> Qui sert bien son pays n'a pas besoin d'aïeux

(The first to be made king was a victorious soldier; he who serves his country well has no need of ancestors).

In the earlier part of the Restoration period the search for *applications* was intense, a phenomenon attributable to the division of the country into two factions of approximately equal strength, the *ultras* and the Bonapartists, though it was primarily the latter, constituting the opposition, who seized every opportunity offered in the theatre to press their cause. Napoleon's death on St Helena afforded one such: the widespread belief that his life had been deliberately shortened by poison administered by his British captors led in August 1821 to an expression of emphatic assent at the line: 'Non, non,

Britannicus est mort empoisonné' when Racine's play was revived by the Comédie-Française. At the same theatre, also in 1821, Etienne de Jouy's *Sylla* aroused an interest not due solely to Talma's appearance on the first night, garbed in a toga but wearing a wig with the unmistakable Napoleonic lock of hair over his forehead, and imitating to perfection the look, the tone of voice, the gestures and habitual stance of the dead Emperor. The tragedy ended with a fine scene in which Sulla declared his intention to abdicate his powers and retire into private life; the one abdication could not but recall the other. There were no particular opportunities for applauding allusions in *Sylla*, the censors having made sure that no one line could be given a contemporary reference, but the play was so successful that they were initially very dubious about authorizing Arnault's *Régulus* later the same year. 'They feared *applications* to the King of Rome [i.e. the Duc de Reichstadt, Napoleon's son and heir] who had become a rallying-point for the opposition. In order to discourage *allusions* in this sense, they required Arnault to change the age of Regulus' son, making him a young man instead of a child.'[13] Napoleon's son, it will be remembered, was only a boy of ten when he lost his father.

But the censorship, however meticulously it went about its work, could neither foresee nor forestall every application that might be made by a politically hostile pit: something that was sensationally demonstrated by an incident a couple of years later. On 26 February 1823 the question of voting additional credits for the expedition to Spain came up for debate in the Chamber. One of the opposition leaders, Jacques-Antoine Manuel, made a speech attacking the military adventure on the grounds that, faced with foreign invasion, the Spaniards might well turn on Ferdinand VII, try him and execute him, exactly as the French had tried and executed Louis XVI thirty years earlier in similar circumstances. The right-wing majority, in great indignation, accused Manuel of equating patriotism with regicide, and succeeded in passing a motion for his exclusion from the Chamber. Manuel ignored this doubtfully legal decision, and the following day walked into the Chamber, escorted by his fellow liberals and refusing the Speaker's demand that he withdraw. Thereupon an unprecedented scene took place: a squad of gendarmes were ordered in, and when they hesitated to lay hands on the supposedly inviolable person of a deputy, their commander, the Vicomte de Foucauld, pointed at Manuel and barked the order:

'Empoignez-moi cet homme-là [collar that fellow]!', using words more appropriate to a suspected pickpocket than to an elected representative of the nation.

Within hours the incident was the talk of the town, and in the greenroom of the Panorama-Dramatique, where Bouffé was waiting his cue to go on as an alcalde in the evening's farce, the author, Ferdinand Laloue, took him aside and asked him to modify slightly a line in his part; instead of 'Emparez-vous de cet homme-là' (seize that man) he was to substitute the words: 'Empoignez-moi cet homme-là!' Bouffé, when the moment came, did as he had been bidden, and had hardly spoken the words when the whole house burst into furious applause, mingled with laughter. The actor now regretted having obeyed Laloue's instructions and regretted it even more when he found a police officer with two gendarmes waiting for him in the wings. After spending a sleepless night in a cell with some thirty or so thieves and vagabonds, he appeared before the magistrate the following morning. Having told his story, he was dismissed with a caution: 'Remember in future that an actor must never dabble in politics, particularly on the stage.'[14]

This could be regarded as the moral, not just of this particular incident, but of the whole history of the use of *applications* on the Parisian stage. The 'guilty party' under every regime, monarchist or republican, was the audience who could not resist the temptation to cock a snook at authority; but it was only too often the actors who got into trouble as a result. After the mid-1820s, however, the practice of making *applications* appears to have died out, except at the Odéon where the pit was notoriously turbulent.[15] The reasons for its demise were probably far from simple. In the first place, with the advent of romantic drama, literary rather than political quarrels tended to absorb the energies of the pit; and besides, if Hugo and his friends achieved little else of permanence, they did succeed in banishing the five-act verse tragedy of the seventeenth and eighteenth centuries from the French stage, at least until Rachel burst on the scene, to draw the crowds with her brilliant renderings of Camille in *Horace*, Emilie in *Cinna* and Hermione in *Andromaque*. Now, it will not have escaped the reader that it was above all classical and neoclassical tragedies that offered audiences the opportunity to make *applications*: they were so well known that troublemakers in the pit could without difficulty mark down in advance which line would lend itself to topical reference. Then again, it was in the late 1820s that claques succeeded in establishing themselves in every theatre in Paris. The claque would never have led the applause for political reasons; its sole concern was whether it had been paid to applaud, either by the author, the leading actor or the management, or preferably by all three. And thirdly, it should not be forgotten that *applications* were, in one sense, a means of making mock of dramatic censorship, primarily political in France rather than moral. If the censors had left a loophole somewhere in a play, the audience seldom failed to exploit it; so there is nothing very remarkable in the fact that when preventive censorship was suspended for five years after the July revolution, *applications* fell into abeyance likewise. Playwrights were now free to express themselves as they wished, and so audiences no longer felt it incumbent on them to emphasize, by applauding them, certain chance remarks in the text so as to make them relevant to the current political scandal.

Finally, it has to be admitted that under the July Monarchy and increasingly so later in the century, audiences were quieter than they had been, and in the pit in particular were content to sit mutely on their benches, hoping at least that the outlay on the evening's entertainment would not prove a waste of money. Moreover, as time went on, theatre-goers no longer consisted exclusively of Parisians, alert, impertinent, audacious; more and more, as the railways brought their trainloads from the provinces up to the capital and, later, when the same trains and steam-packets conveyed travellers from abroad, the pit lost its traditional homogeneity. The new-comers did not possess the inside knowledge that would have permitted them to make or to respond to *applications*, and besides, being strangers they were, as strangers tend to be in public places, on their best behaviour.

CHAPTER 10

The theatre in the provinces

Relations between the central government and the theatre under the *ancien régime* were not nearly so close in the provinces as in Paris, and depended to a greater degree on local conditions and circumstances than on the control and supervision of the court and the court magnates. Nevertheless a considerable, though apparently unconcerted, effort was made in the second half of the eighteenth century to endow most large centres of population with at least one major theatre, providing what a modern historian has called 'the infrastructure of French theatrical activity down to the Second Empire'.[1] The process was not entirely uniform: new theatres were erected chiefly at seaports and along the land frontiers, where the passage of travellers led to a heightened demand for entertainment; but they were also established at certain inland towns, Lyons, Toulouse, Montpellier, Caen. A theatre conferred a certain lustre on a town, and to possess one was a matter of local pride, held in check however by the grudging attitude of local taxpayers; for every theatrical enterprise demanded at some point, if only when a new building was under construction, financial assistance which the national Treasury was in no condition to provide.

Even before this building programme was embarked on, there is evidence that earlier strolling players were being, here and there, replaced by fixed and settled companies (*troupes sédentaires* rather than *ambulantes*), performing solely for the enjoyment of their fellow townsmen or occasionally shuttling to and fro between two neighbouring centres of population. The necessary initial financial backing was often provided not by the civic authorities but by a group of shareholders with money to invest. This happened at Bordeaux through the initiative of the Maréchal-Duc de Richelieu, the great-grandnephew of the famous Cardinal, who besides his responsibilities for the royal theatres in Paris was also governor of the province of Guyenne, of which Bordeaux was the chief city. The wealthier men of the neighbourhood were persuaded to form a joint-stock company with the Duke as chairman: the shareholders included gentlemen with manors in the vicinity, merchants trading from the port, influential members of the city council and even two foreign consuls. The capital raised permitted them to engage a company of performers under the management of a professional theatre director and also to renovate the building (a theatre in the Place Dauphine, built in 1756) in the interests of comfort and safety.

So successful did the organization at Bordeaux prove, both as a financial speculation and as a means of satisfying the demand for dramatic entertainment in the city, that it served as model for similar initiatives elsewhere, notably at Lyons and at Nantes. Properly speaking it was a commercial undertaking, but one that owed its stability and above all its sound credit to the fact that it had been formed under the patronage of a wealthy grandee who, with his court connections, possessed all the authority necessary to sweep away whatever difficulties might arise. But any citizen who could put up, singly or in association with others, the required capital, and could pull the necessary strings to obtain permission from the King in Council, could follow suit: the theatre later known as the Théâtre des Arts at Rouen, which opened in 1776, was built by a consortium of eight shareholders headed by a local architect, François Guéroult, while at Nantes the popular name of the Grand-Théâtre, the Théâtre Graslin, commemorates that of its principal promoter, a wealthy local philanthropist. At Bordeaux the company enjoyed a virtual monopoly, at least down to 1775;[2] returns mounted steadily, from 126,000 *livres* in 1761 to 213,000 in 1768;[3] but the shareholders' dividends were only one consideration, for they were also keenly interested in the prosperity of the enterprise as conferring distinction of a new kind on their city. This satisfactory state of affairs came to an end, paradoxically, when Richelieu, flushed with success, decided to have a new theatre built at Bordeaux which should outshine all others in splendour. The work of the architect Victor Louis, and possibly his finest achievement, the Grand-Théâtre was inaugurated on 7 April 1780. A visitor from the capital made a significant comment after the opening: 'One would look in vain, in Paris or in the rest of Europe, for a theatre even approaching this in beauty. It is really too magnificent for a provincial playhouse.'[4] Certainly the cost (two and a half million francs[5]) was a great deal more than the municipality, called on to foot the bill, could readily afford. To amortize this huge outlay, they raised the rental to 56,000 *livres*, as against the 6,000 *livres* that the old playhouse on the Place Dauphine had cost the original shareholders; the following year this conglomerate dropped out of sight, disposing of their interests to other financial bodies who, however, never succeeded in making the theatre pay. Richelieu, who had browbeaten the city fathers into commissioning a white elephant, died in 1788, having endowed Bordeaux with a monument, still standing to this day, of which he and they could be justly proud, but knowing also that the city, whose prosperity had been in decline for several years, had no hope of running it at a profit.

Altercations were not infrequent before the Revolution between the representatives of the royal government, as often as not members of the second estate, and the local worthies who belonged to the third estate and were required to find the money for these culturally valuable but none the less expensive ventures. In 1768 the Comte de l'Hospital, governor of Bayonne, was pressing for the establishment of a regular theatre in the town, arguing that the high rent required for hiring a building made it difficult for a theatre manager to break even, let alone make a reasonable profit. The Count's letter to the magistrates concluded, loftily and with just a hint of menace: 'I trust that by finding an equitable formula in the interests of the town, you will be ready to take proper measures for the general good.' At Grenoble the magistrates found themselves obliged to buy out the proprietors of the local theatre, while at Saint-Quentin the municipality, faced with insistent demands on the part of the authorities, were forced to yield in the end, though not without giving warning of the dangers, both moral and material, that they apprehended. Max Fuchs, who cites these instances, adds that more research by local historians needs to be done into the circumstances surrounding the commissioning of these civic theatres; the details, he observes, 'would be sometimes intriguing and always instructive'; but the general conclusion is likely to be that 'these edifices, the construction of which was often imposed by the central power for political or administrative reasons, represented an expense for the towns to which they were reluctant to agree'.[6] The thinking behind the far from gentle pressure exerted on the cautious husbandry of the burgesses was that the theatre, however reprehensible an institution in the eyes of the church, was a lesser evil than many others that tempted the idle young bloods of the town – gaming-houses, brothels and the like. Given this, the initial expense and the cost of upkeep of a theatre were as much the responsibility of the town council as were street-lighting, public sanitation, etc. The argument was difficult to refute; all that could be done was to ensure that the bills were not unmanageably heavy. Too often, this meant cheeseparing. At Rouen, for instance, the theatre viewed from outside was no doubt a fine one, while even inside it made a good impression; but behind the scenes it was a different story. Here it was necessary to negotiate a warren of constricted passages and steep, dark stairways down which the players tumbled at some risk to life and limb. Dressing rooms were provided for no more than half the company, there was no storage space for scenery and only a poky little room for hanging costumes.

Nevertheless, it has been calculated that at least twenty-three provincial towns were newly equipped with theatres between 1750 and 1773, at a time, incidentally, when the three royal theatres of the capital were having to make do with outdated and increasingly dilapidated premises, for it was not until the early 1780s that new buildings were erected for the Opera, the Comédie-Française and the Italiens. Between 1774 and 1789 construction slackened, probably for economic reasons: during this period only four more new theatres were built in the provinces, but several towns found the money to renovate older theatres that had fallen into disrepair and needed modernizing. This does not mean, certainly, that no provincial town of any size remained without a theatre at the end of this period; but travellers from abroad, like the Cradocks, a Leicestershire couple who in 1783–6 undertook a leisurely tour of the south and south-west of France, were impressed by the number of playhouses established everywhere, and in nearly every town Mrs Cradock, although a stringent critic, was agreeably surprised by the standards reached in the productions. Another British traveller, the Glasgow physician John Moore, reported on his return that 'in all the large trading and manufacturing towns, of which there are a great number in France, there are playhouses established. The same thing takes place in most of the frontier towns, and wherever there is a garrison of two or three regiments.'[7] The provision of theatrical establishments in such places was the direct result of demands from the War Ministry; regulations ensured that season tickets (*abonnements*) for all regimental officers were to be purchased by the local commander at a reduced rate, and the cost deducted from their pay.[8]

This policy was not dictated by any concern to elevate the minds of the military by forcing them to attend performances of the masterpieces of French dramatic genius; rather, it was a matter of providing them with a relatively harmless form of amusement in towns which otherwise, like Balzac's Issoudun in *La Rabouilleuse*, were completely lacking in recreational facilities and, once the shutters went up at sunset, offered nothing to high-spirited young men except what pleasure they could derive from engaging in dangerous horseplay. So Marshal de Castries, urging the need for a theatre at Dunkirk in 1770, finished his letter to the commandant by stressing 'from my personal knowledge of the life the officers are obliged to lead in Dunkirk, how essential a theatre is in the absence of any society'.[9] Arguments used in favour of establishing a theatre at Brest, where there was an important naval school, included not just the point that such entertainment took the young marines away from drinking parties which too often degenerated into brawls, but also that it allowed them to hear good French spoken from the stage, no doubt an important consideration when Breton would have been the mother-tongue of many of them. A theatre was accordingly erected at Brest in 1766, and others provided at other coastal stations, Toulon, La Rochelle, Le Havre and Abbeville; as also at important garrison towns along the land frontiers, at Arras, Douai, Metz, Strasbourg and Bayonne.

Strasbourg constituted a special case, since the theatre there found itself functioning in the midst of a largely non-French-speaking population. Since shortly after its annexation by France in 1681, there had always existed one theatre enacting French plays, alongside another for German-speakers, the latter always being better attended since it could rely on a far greater number of supporters. The French theatre could count on the garrison troops whose subscription was assured by army orders, and on the French colony which, however, was relatively small at the time.[10] This led to the occupying power obliging the German companies to sacrifice a quarter of their takings to help support the French theatre, which alone had the backing of the state. This exaction, together with the exclusive right the French theatre enjoyed to organize the traditional masked balls at certain periods of the year, caused some friction, though chiefly at the higher levels of administration: the mayor and the city magistrates tended to favour the German theatre, while the military commanders and their superiors outside Strasbourg used their powers and influence to secure the prosperity of the French company under its various directors. It was on 31 May 1800 that the French theatre had the misfortune, not at all uncommon in those days, to burn down; the tardiness of the municipal authorities in deciding on the site for a new one, the seventeen years that elapsed between the laying of the foundation stone and the completion of the building in 1821, may possibly have reflected their reluctance to find the money for a monument serving an art and culture which they still regarded as alien to their fellow citizens.

The habit of attending the theatre was deeply ingrained among provincial townsfolk under the *ancien régime*; and indeed it was more than a habit, it was a veritable passion affecting every class of society, and women – in spite of their confessors' warnings – quite as much as men. The second half of the eighteenth century saw a renewal of interest in dramatic productions at least as great as it had been in 1636 when Corneille described the theatre as

> L'entretien de Paris, le souhait des provinces,
> Le divertissement le plus doux de nos princes,
> Les délices du peuple, et le plaisir des grands.[11]

But now, with all these handsome, well-appointed new theatres everywhere, it was no longer just 'le souhait des provinces'; the provincials were able to satisfy their desires as easily as the Parisians. At Nantes, where the theatre, with its four tiers of boxes and the vast area reserved for the groundlings, could without difficulty accommodate two thousand spectators, the eagerness to 'see the show' was such that hundreds were turned away regularly and it was not unusual for two performances to be given on the same day, one in the afternoon and one in the evening. From Lyons, Grimod de la Reynière wrote to Mercier: 'Here the theatre is the principal and almost the sole amusement; it is the daily rendezvous of all businessmen; it is here they come to relax and to fix up to meet afterwards at some cheerful supper party.'[12]

At the same time one can hardly speak of an active dramatic tradition in the provinces at this period, any more than one could in the following century: the provincials were eager consumers, but rarely producers. Anyone born and bred in one of these industrious cities scattered throughout France who had any ambition to shine as a playwright would seize the earliest opportunity to make the journey to the capital and from that vantage-point sneer at the philistines in his native town. 'It is curious', commented Mercier, who himself had followed the trend and come up to Paris in his twenty-fifth year, 'that the dramatist has eyes only for the capital which occupies one point on the map, and forgets the rest of the kingdom as though it were nothing but a desert. There is at least as much good taste in the provinces as in Paris',[13] and in many ways it is sounder, he argues, less corrupted by the habits of disdain that encourage critics to find fault rather than admire, even when admiration is due.

It was not simply that Paris represented, for the provinces, a permanent 'brain drain', stealing all the potential playwrights who might otherwise have stayed at home and transformed a local reputation into a national one; the increasing circulation of journals at this period brought to the remotest parts of the kingdom news of all recent dramatic successes in the capital, and created a ready market for the importation of these novelties. It took time for the local theatre to acquire copies of the latest Paris 'hit', and more time for the local actors to rehearse and produce it; the Parisians were always several steps ahead of the provincials, and this was yet another factor tending to reinforce a cultural inferiority complex, to which the provincials themselves remained on the whole oddly indifferent. The emasculating effect of a centralized system of government on the intellectual life of the nation was something of which, even at the end of the eighteenth century, few thinkers, whether in Paris or the provinces, seem to have been fully aware, while those who recognized it saw it as perfectly natural and not in any way an evil to be overcome.

The turmoil into which the Paris theatres were flung during the Revolution was to a large extent mirrored in the provinces, though only Bordeaux has been made the subject of a detailed and documented inquiry.[14] The decision of the National Assembly on 13 January 1791 to do away with all restrictions on the setting up of new theatres had its effect in the provinces, enabling optimistic entrepreneurs to multiply the places of dramatic entertainment, just as in the capital. The scission within the Comédie-Française was duplicated in Bordeaux when on 29 April 1792 a fraction of the troupe at the Grand-Théâtre emigrated to a new theatre on the Rue du Mirail which called itself the Théâtre Molière and, from the start, advertised its anti-monarchical tendencies; in November it changed its name to the Théâtre de la République in obvious imitation of Gaillard and Dorfeuille's theatre of the same name in Paris. A little more than a year later, Mayeur de Saint-Paul, who had left Nicolet's company to come to Bordeaux, persuaded a group of discontented actors within the Théâtre de la République to split off and help him set up a new theatre, the Théâtre de la Montagne. Then, on 3–4 September 1793, less than four weeks after the mass arrest in Paris of the Comédiens-Français, the entire company of the Grand-Théâtre was thrown into gaol by the military commission headed by Lacombe, who justified his action in a brief message to the Minister of the Interior: 'It was a hotbed of aristocracy; we have extirpated it.' The same fate was also that of the company of Mayeur's Théâtre de la Montagne a month later. The Théâtre de la République, reputed politically sound, was ordered to take over the premises of the Grand-Théâtre until on 30 August 1794, shortly after Robespierre's fall from power, Mme Dorfeuille, director of the Théâtre de la Montagne, who had been imprisoned with the rest of her company, was set free and eventually put in control of the Grand-Théâtre. Thus, after these violent fluctuations, the status quo was more or less restored.

Although the imperial decree on the theatres of 8 June 1806 was principally inspired by a concern to regulate the situation in the capital, the provinces were not forgotten: clause 7 set strict limits on the number of playhouses to be permitted in future in the various towns, limits that were defined in detail by Champigny's subsequent 'règlement sur les théâtres' of 25 April 1807. Five cities in the Empire were to be allowed two theatres, namely, Bordeaux, Lyons, Marseilles, Nantes and Turin, the capital of Piedmont, a province annexed by Napoleon in 1802. A number of other towns were named as being permitted one only: they included Toulouse, Montpellier and Nice in the south, Rouen, Brest, Lille, Dunkirk and Strasbourg in the north. The number of closures consequent on this measure is difficult to estimate; proportionately, it might have been quite as high as in Paris. At Bordeaux, for instance, six theatres are known to have been opened to take advantage of the Convention's decree of 6 January 1791; after 1807, only the Grand-Théâtre and one other, known as the Théâtre-Français, were allowed to continue functioning.

In cities where two theatres were permitted, they tended not to compete directly with one another, but to offer different kinds of dramatic entertainment: at Lyons, for instance, the Célestins concentrated on straight plays, the Grand-Théâtre on musicals, mainly opera and comic opera; elsewhere there was one theatre that tended to draw on the more cultivated section of society, and a second one patronized mainly by the working classes. The latter was invariably a commercial undertaking, for which the city authorities accepted no financial responsibility; the former had a certain official standing which made it approximate to the state theatres of Paris. But the Ministry of the Interior had no direct control over it, state powers being delegated to the mayor and corporation. They would nominate a manager; their choice would be registered in Paris, but Paris scarcely ever queried their decision, nor did the prefect of the department concern himself greatly with the day-to-day running of the theatres in the area for which he was responsible. Even less frequently did the Minister of the Interior intervene in matters pertaining to the administration of the provincial theatres; though an ordinance issued on 8 December 1824 showed that Paris was not altogether unaware of the difficulties facing them. In its preamble, the ordinance recognized that 'a great number of towns have been struggling in vain to support these enterprises and that several theatre directors have compromised their personal fortune in the effort'.[15] The state, however, offered advice rather than support: theatrical companies should be granted lease of their premises free of charge, and a subvention should be paid the director where necessary. Possibly in pursuance of these recommendations, the city authorities at Lille agreed in 1824 to grant their theatre director free use of the building, together with a subsidy of 20,000 francs to cover the losses he necessarily incurred by remaining open during the summer months. At Rouen, where the building had been erected by a private consortium charging rent, Walter, manager of the theatre, wrote to the municipality requesting an annual subvention of 60,000 francs to cover the 'exorbitant' sums demanded as rental, pointing out at the same time that his theatre was too small, even when a particular play sold out, to allow him to meet his overheads out of receipts at the door. Eventually the town council admitted the justice of his claim and agreed to pay the rental, but not to subsidize him directly, for it was well known that as soon as a director was in receipt of a subvention, the landlords would find some reason to put up their charge.

Particularly in the earlier part of the century, subventions were a perpetual bone of contention both between theatre directors and municipalities and also within the council chamber itself, which was often divided on the issue. Some burgesses tended to regard the theatre as a commercial undertaking which it would be improper to subsidize out of local taxes; others felt it was a matter of local pride to ensure that their theatre was adequately funded. The managers themselves were always pleading special circumstances. Armand Verteuil, who was attempting to run the theatre at Marseilles in 1816, argued in vain for financial support, and in his motivated request enumerated all the other attractions with which he had to compete.

Since November, I have been the victim of lotto [an early form of bingo] in the cafés, which robs me of the custom of all the young men who would normally fill the pit; of a dance-hall which empties the 'gods' of sailors and their female companions. Amateur theatricals and private balls have reduced Sunday takings to nothing. It would be impossible for me to embark on another season under the same auspices and I implore your aid to relieve my miserable plight.

His successor complained about other diversions: writing in June 1819, he informed the mayor that 'last Sunday, at 7.0 p.m. when the theatre opened, 200 boats at least, full of working-class people, covered the surface of the harbour [the Vieux Port], and the quays and bar were likewise crowded; the theatre alone was empty'.[16] Similar difficulties were experienced at Bordeaux later in the century; here it was café life that competed, only too successfully, with the entertainment offered by the theatres. In 1860, there were roughly 150 cafés scattered throughout the town, frequented by

shopkeepers, small businessmen, people of the middle ranks of society. There is no need to dress up to go there – all that is necessary is that you should be reasonably clean and tidy. If it should come on to rain, you are only a few steps from home. Then it's so convenient, especially in the winter, not to have to cross the whole town. Those who make a habit of going to cafés are almost always to be found there of an evening on weekdays; only on Sundays does one see them occasionally making their way to the theatre, when they are in the mood for a change.[17]

In a café one can meet one's old friends, make new acquaintances, read the papers, discuss business, play a game of cards or dominoes; it is cool in the summer and better heated than the theatre in the winter.

Little wonder that in 1866 Bordeaux had to subsidize the Grand-Théâtre to the tune of 234,000 francs, almost as much as was allocated to the directors of the theatres at Marseilles and Lyons out of revenues twice as large.[18] The underlying injustice of the situation was patent: Paris, with revenues at this time of over 130 millions, provided not a centime to support the five subsidized theatres within its boundaries: their subventions came from contributions levied on every tax-payer in France. 'Why should not Paris,' it was asked, 'contribute, out of the resources of its vast budget, to the subvention of the theatres which are one of the most potent elements of its prosperity?'[19] The stock answer to this argument was that the Comédie-Française, the Opera, the Opéra-Comique etc. were national institutions, so that it was only right that they should be paid for, like the armed forces, the civil service and so forth, out of national taxes. But the objection remained, summed up in Fiorentino's caustic sally: 'Admirable distributive justice! Paris is entertained and Carcassonne pays the piper!'[20]

But Paris also had a large number of reasonably prosperous theatres that required no subsidy and were run as purely commercial enterprises; why did provincial theatres need to rely on the municipalities at all for even a portion of their running costs? Why, for instance, did Nantes, a wealthy trading city in a fertile area, boasting one of the prettiest theatres in France, which was let rent-free to the director who in addition enjoyed a subvention of 15,000 francs annually – why was it apparently incapable of balancing its books? Maurice Alhoy, who posed this question in 1824, blamed the state of affairs entirely on 'the parsimony of the inhabitants; they would all like to possess a theatre which did honour to the town, but few of them are disposed to make the necessary sacrifices to maintain it'.[21] Did this mean that they ought to insist that the town council increase the subsidy, even though this would involve in the last resort digging deeper into their own pockets to pay the higher prices of various commodities, since local revenue was largely raised from taxes on goods coming into the city? In 1828–9 the municipal council doubled the subvention to 30,000 francs, justifying this generosity with a rider to the effect that 'once it is admitted that Nantes cannot remain without a theatre, and that were it closed this would have the most serious effect on public order and on the peace of this mercantile city, then we cannot refuse the necessary support to the continued existence of theatrical

enterprise'[22] – from which it might be concluded that the city of
Nantes required a theatre not as a cultural centre but solely in order
to keep people off the streets and out of mischief. After the July
revolution, when the whole principle of state support for places of
public amusement was being called into question even in Paris, the
city authorities at Nantes reluctantly agreed to continue to fund the
theatre, though only at the earlier level of 15,000 francs. To those
members of the council who would have liked to abolish the subvention altogether, it was objected that the oil burned nightly at the
theatre afforded the town treasurer 2,000 francs a year in indirect
taxes; and that to allow the Théâtre Graslin to go out of business
would put some 150 jobs in jeopardy. Underlying these petty and
specious arguments, the real worry was no doubt that the town's
credit might be damaged if it were said that the municipality lacked
the resources to afford a decent theatre. The system of subsidizing
provincial theatres in France was by now so widespread and deep-
rooted that to dispense with it anywhere was almost unthinkable.

Over the next twenty years or so the subvention at Nantes
continued to rise inexorably, until in 1852 it had reached the figure
of 50,000 francs; even so it proved difficult to find any director
prepared to take on the task. In desperation, the town council
agreed to appoint an administrator whose function would be simply
to represent the municipality, which undertook to cover the
inevitable annual deficit. But it was soon realized that this was
tantamount to giving the director a blank cheque, and eventually,
in March 1880, the municipality reverted to subsidizing the theatre,
to the tune now of 120,000 francs.

Within certain limits, the story of the town council of Nantes,
fighting a rearguard action against everlasting demands for ever
higher subsidies, was that of every provincial town in France during
the nineteenth century; it so happens that the case of Nantes is
exceptionally well documented by an intelligent local historian.
Destranges concludes, after summing up the difficulties the Théâtre
Graslin had to contend with, that the system itself was fatally flawed
in that the playhouse remained the property of the town, but the
town could only keep it open by relying on a succession of managers
of dubious antecedents hired on short-term contracts. 'A theatre
director', he writes, 'is only a businessman. Once in a hundred times,
this businessman is also a man of artistic ability, but in the great
majority of cases the director, unless he is bound by an absolutely

watertight contract, will try and swindle the municipality and will succeed in so doing.'[23]

The enormous increases that the city councils were obliged to concede bore little relation to the general rise in prices over the years, and were clearly counterproductive, besides being altogether disproportionate to those that the state theatres in Paris were allowed. At Marseilles, for instance, between 1821, when the city council first set aside a sum of 6,000 francs to subsidize its theatrical concerns, and 1860, when this modest subvention had risen to 200,000 francs with no corresponding improvement, as far as can be judged, in the level of dramatic productions, the knowledge that the city fathers were prepared to disburse more and more money in subsidies appears merely to have stepped up the demands of actors, stagehands and others for higher wages and to have made the proprietors of the two theatres more and more rapacious in the rents they exacted – this being a matter for settlement between them and whichever director was in charge at the time. For Marseilles was one of the very few provincial cities that had not acquired the freehold of its theatres (the Beauvau and the Gymnase) by the mid-century. But even where the rent for the buildings did not enter into the financial equation, the subsidies still rose with alarming celerity. Lille bought its playhouse from the owners in 1821 at a price of 150,000 francs. But even so, managers appointed at Lille continued to encounter difficulties: there were no fewer than four of them between 1821 and 1830, all of whom had lost money and cancelled their contracts in spite of fairly generous financial support; it is true that a trade depression at the time may have thinned the audiences. In the 1860s the advent of the railways, cheapening as well as speeding up travel, turned the thoughts of theatre-goers at Lille to Paris and Brussels, and in order to counter the dangerous attractions of the new-fangled excursion trains – more aptly denominated *trains de plaisir* by the French – the city council had to agree reluctantly to an increased subsidy in order to bribe the management to keep the theatre open to smaller audiences. Once started on this path, it proved impossible to turn back or even to call a halt. The subvention was raised to 40,000 francs in 1862, increased to 66,000 in 1867, to 80,000 in 1889, to 110,000 in 1897 and to 140,000 in 1907.

The only alternatives to conceding these massive increases would have been either to throw in the sponge, pull down the theatres or allow them to stand as empty monuments to a glorious past; or else to suffer them to decay into establishments offering nothing but the cheapest and most mediocre of dramatic entertainment. Recourse was seldom, if ever, had to the first of these possible policies; as Baret wrote at the end of the period: 'a town without a theatre is a dead town ... One might even say that the disappearance of a permanent body of actors is the first knell that signifies a town's irretrievable decline.'[24] As to the second, the decay in dramatic interest by the end of the century of so important an establishment as the Grand-Théâtre at Lyons was admitted by no less a person than the city's chief magistrate, who wrote in a report dated 22 January 1902:

We see on our stage an endless series of antediluvian vaudevilles or prehistoric melodramas that offer no kind of interest whatsoever. While in Paris, at a number of theatres, bold attempts are being made to introduce contemporary audiences to foreign dramatic masterpieces and plays of social significance, we in Lyons are stuck with the outworn clichés of an old-fashioned dramatic tradition devoid of all interest.[25]

Yet the municipality of Lyons, at this time, was allotting a subvention of a quarter of a million to the Grand-Théâtre, the same as Bordeaux and rather more than Marseilles. The directors had no complaints, but the theatre had lost whatever pretensions it might once have had of offering its patrons the best in contemporary dramatic art. And the same was generally true of the provinces in the latter part of the century. Earlier, it was said that only light opera attracted the crowds, and that a director who had no ballet dancers in his troupe was in serious trouble; now, they seemed to want nothing but the old-fashioned melodrama which had been so popular under the First Empire, but by the 1880s was to be seen in Paris only at the Ambigu-Comique and in certain suburban houses. In the provinces the perennial theme of villainy punished and wrong finally righted in the last scene was still what drew eager theatre-goers, handkerchiefs at the ready. 'The manager of a provincial theatre well known to me', wrote Lhomme at this time, 'would never have put on, after Easter or Whitsun, some new comedy; the only money-spinner is the creaky old melodrama ... The primitive scenery, the childish acting never worries them; the audience is totally taken by the play.'[26]

If there was one exception to the hopeless decadence of the provincial theatre over this period, it was the Théâtre des Arts at Rouen. Ever since, in the eighteenth century, Mlle Montansier had assumed control of its fortunes, it had managed to preserve its reputation as an independent theatre of unimpeachable standards, due for the most part to its consistently discerning and exacting audiences. 'The citizens of Rouen', wrote Auger, 'pride themselves with some justification on being great music-lovers and excellent connoisseurs of dramatic art. To have succeeded at Rouen is, for any actor, a recommendation in itself, a guarantee of high ability.'[27] Towards the end of the nineteenth century, the renown of the Théâtre des Arts had spread far and wide: more than thirty new plays were given their first performance here from 1884 onwards, and it was to Rouen that opera fans flocked to witness the first production in France of Wagner's *Lohengrin* and Saint-Saëns's *Samson et Dalila* in 1891. But notwithstanding these sensational successes, over the period 1883–94 no fewer than four directors had to abandon their posts because of financial difficulties, and it proved so difficult to tempt a new man that the municipal council seriously debated whether it would be possible to continue maintaining the Théâtre des Arts as a going concern.

Grand opera, in the age bounded by Mozart at one end and Wagner at the other, emerged as the most sumptuous and enthralling of dramatic forms in the nineteenth century and drew steady attendances, particularly in the south of France, whose inhabitants are in any case credited with a strong innate appreciation for fine vocal music. The Théâtre du Capitole at Toulouse was noted for its excellent operatic company, and in the course of the century had virtually abandoned all other forms of theatrical entertainment in favour of serious opera, to the great satisfaction of its music-loving audiences. The Grand-Théâtre at Marseilles acquired a similar reputation towards the end of the century; it was here that Verdi's *Aida*, sung in French for the first time ever, was given a series of twenty-five performances between 31 January and 30 April 1877. But in 1897 the incoming radical council decided to do away with the city's subvention and appoint as manager of the Grand-Théâtre a man whose declared intention it was to economize by substituting comedy and melodrama for grand opera. The new regime was duly inaugurated with a revival of Auguste Maquet's hoary historical drama *La Maison du baigneur*. All the opera fans in Marseilles, furious at the niggardliness of the civic authorities, were present on this occasion; so too were some 150 police, posted here and there in the theatre in case of trouble. Trouble there was, soon enough.

Catcalls, whistles, booing arose on all sides, and the unfortunate players were obliged to act their parts in the midst of an indescribable tumult, while copper coins and other missiles were hurled on to the stage. In the auditorium, certain spectators unfurled huge banners bearing such inscriptions as: "We demand opera!", "Subsidize or resign!" Others started singing at the top of their voices well-known operatic airs.[28]

The police went into action, making arrests and dragging off the noisiest demonstrators to the cells. The curtain fell, the theatre emptied and remained officially closed for the rest of the year. But final victory remained with the melomaniacs: on 9 June 1898 the city council gave in, restored the subvention (though at a lower level than it had been), and appointed a new director.

The reason why the city fathers were so reluctant to continue allowing opera at Marseilles was purely economic. The very much higher salaries expected by first-class singers, the need too in the nineteenth century to maintain a company of dancers to perform the ballets always associated with opera, the larger orchestras and more impressive sets that were required to stage one effectively – all this meant that however great the demand for musical drama in a provincial city, it was rarely possible to offer it short of outrageously high subsidies. If provincial audiences everywhere had been content to watch their local company giving repeats of recent Paris stage successes, all might have been well; it was the desire to enjoy the supreme satisfaction open to any Parisian, to spend an occasional evening listening to the masterpieces of Auber, Meyerbeer, Donizetti and Verdi, that caused the difficulty. The monthly bill for the opera company at Bordeaux in 1864 was quoted as 622,500 francs; of the company playing straight drama, 186,000. At Lyons, about the same time, the enormous subvention of a quarter of a million francs paid to the Grand-Théâtre went nowhere towards meeting its expenses and obliged it constantly to plunder the profits made by the acting company in the same city, the Théâtre des Célestins.[29] In a large town, there might be enough keen followers of the opera to assure adequate attendances; in smaller ones, local pride insisted on occasional operatic productions even if the house remained three-quarters empty. Nantes disliked falling behind Bordeaux in this respect; and if Marseilles has an opera house, why cannot we? asked the inhabitants of Toulon. So the unfortunate director, faced with an almost certain financial loss if he put on opera, and with a mutinous clientèle if he did not, found himself between the devil and the deep blue sea.

The one sure and certain way of filling a provincial theatre to capacity was to entice down a famous or simply popular actor or actress from Paris. Few of the inhabitants knew of these paragons save by repute, or had any expectation, travelling being so time-consuming, laborious and expensive an undertaking in the pre-railway age, of ever seeing them in the flesh. This accounts to a large extent for the extravagant scenes witnessed when a wandering star took the trouble to shine on some remote city in the south or west, and the alacrity with which provincial theatre-goers paid up to three times the normal charge for the privilege of watching him or her act on their stage. Such visitations had started back in the 1770s, when the great tragedian Lekain had discovered, on his occasional trips to Ferney to stay with Voltaire, how lucrative guest appearances before a provincial audience could be, even though one found oneself too often backed by a supporting cast of hobbledehoys. His example was followed a little later by La Rive, his colleague at the Comédie-Française, who in 1779 was crowned with laurel wreaths by admirers at Aix-en-Provence and Marseilles; on the same trip, his appearance on the stage at Lyons caused a minor riot when a group of latecomers, having been detained by the irresistible spectacle of a public execution, overwhelmed the guard and burst into the already overcrowded pit in the middle of the play, determined to have a sight of the actor from Paris.

Members of the other two royal theatres were not slow in following suit. Mrs Cradock, at Toulouse, recorded having seen Mme Dugazon, a popular actress from the Comédie-Italienne, who 'in consideration of a 10-guinea fee, *condescended* to show herself on the stage ... They had doubled the price of tickets, but she created such a furore that the theatre was crammed; it was suffocatingly hot and the audience was so noisy that we could hardly hear the overture.'[30] Mme Dugazon had arrived from Lyons when after her final appearance she had been crowned on the stage to the acclamations of an enthusiastic audience. But these tributes were small beer compared to the rapturous welcome given to Mme de Saint-Huberty, the star of the opera in the 1780s, when she visited Marseilles in the course of a triumphal procession through France which took her besides to Toulouse, Lyons, Rouen and Strasbourg. Though the story that Napoleon Bonaparte composed a madrigal in her honour at this last-named city must be dismissed as apocryphal, since he was in Corsica and not at Strasbourg when she appeared there, it seems that at Rouen the custom of having the leading male singer crown her with a laurel wreath after the performance was judged too banal, and instead a dove was released bearing one in its beak which it deposited at her feet.[31] But at Marseilles the queen of song was given a civic welcome of a splendour normally reserved for genuine royalty. The cannon saluted her on her arrival; after each of her performances she was crowned on the stage, and on leaving the city she assured a witness[32] she had over a hundred of these trophies, some extremely valuable, stacked on the roof of her travelling coach. Besides that, she was entertained royally throughout her stay. The high spot of the festivities included a trip across the Vieux-Port in a gondola propelled by eight oarsmen; there was jousting on the water, which she watched reclining on a divan and receiving gracefully the tributes paid her by the city worthies; then she was conducted to a marquee, where a short allegorical play by a local poet was performed in her honour, and it all ended with a sumptuous banquet at which, one may be sure, numberless toasts were drunk in her honour.

Visits to the provinces by members of the royal theatres were supposed to take place only during their annual leave of absence; but in the past this leave (the *congé*) had often been anticipated, and even more often overrun. Under the Empire attempts were made to tighten up the regulations, but to little avail: the large fees the *sociétaires* commanded outside Paris, compared with the pittance they had often to make do with at home, made the offers almost irresistible; moreover, they were not indifferent to the extravagant adulation heaped on them by their admirers in the provinces. Clause 2 of Champigny's 'decree concerning the theatres' (29 July 1807) made it the responsibility of the prefects, sub-prefects and mayors 'to ensure that under no pretext should any actor belonging to one of the four major theatres in the capital, who has obtained leave to work in the provinces, be suffered to prolong his stay beyond the time when his leave expires'; failure to observe this rule would result in the provincial manager forfeiting the product of all performances that took place after the expiry date. Nevertheless, directors were eager to sign them up, and as for the *sociétaires*, they had nothing to fear but the fatigue and discomfort of long coach journeys over bumpy roads. For the citizens of the towns they visited, the arrival in their midst of these semi-fabulous creatures they knew of only by report through the local press was an event anticipated long in advance and discussed long afterwards; while over the duration of the visit itself the theatre, in spite of the higher prices invariably charged for admission, was always filled to overflowing.

In the more relaxed atmosphere of the Restoration, Talma in particular was eager to profit from this situation; not that he was by nature avaricious, but he was a notorious spendthrift; moreover he was not indifferent to the flattering reception he could generally count on outside Paris and away from its carping critics. If his first excursion, to Lille in 1816, resulted in a nasty brawl between those in the audience who acclaimed him and those who manifested their hostility, the reason was purely political: the royalist officers belonging to a regiment quartered on the town objected to the applause given to an actor suspected of Bonapartist sympathies, and tried to enforce their opinions at sabre-point. There were several casualties among the civilians, but the following day the entire regiment was marched out of Lille to barracks at Amiens.[33] Talma's presence at Bordeaux the following year also led to disorders, attributable in this case not to political quarrels but to the over-eagerness of the provincial audience to grasp at the chance of watching the greatest actor in Europe and to the recklessness of the management in 'double booking' the available seats in the Grand-Théâtre. In 1818 he descended on Toulouse, occasioning similar wild excitement. The doors of the theatre opened exceptionally at 7.0 a.m. and by noon the auditorium was filled to overflowing, as shops and offices in the town closed down for the day.

Dinner was served up in the boxes, and the orchestra played until the hour for which the performance was timed to begin. The desire or rather the frenzy to be there meant that a portion of the spectators were happy to be present even though they were placed where they could neither see nor hear. Quite apart from the three stepped rows of seats that had been erected on either side of the stage, obstructing the exits and entries of the players through the wings, a great number of holes had been cut in the backcloth through which protruded the heads of curious spectators. In such comical conditions it required all the actor's talent to maintain the tragic illusion.[34]

Down to the very end, Talma was still making guest appearances at provincial centres: on 27 April 1826, six months before he died, the *Journal de Calvados* reported his presence at Caen where he had agreed to give four performances; the same newspaper[35] also leaked details of the arguments beforehand between the manager and the actor, the latter objecting to the enormous surcharge for tickets and claiming that his name was being scandalously exploited. But the theatre was small, and every time Talma appeared it cost the director 1,000 francs; he not only had to balance his books, but make profit enough to see him through the lean months he knew would follow Talma's departure, when the inferior playing of the local actors came as a sad anticlimax.

From 1830 onwards, leading actors from the commercial theatres started to compete with those of the state-supported sector for the plaudits of the provincials. Frédérick Lemaître, fleeing the first, horrendous outbreak of cholera in Paris, performed in Normandy in 1832; the following year he embarked on a tour of the south of France, from Bordeaux to Marseilles, taking in Bayonne, Toulouse and Montpellier en route. Bouffé too, the comic actor who had made his name at the Théâtre du Gymnase, covered Normandy and Brittany in 1837 and the north-east (Nancy, Metz and Dieppe) in 1840. Celebrities of this kidney had always travelled on their own or with a single companion, and had relied on the resident companies to provide them with back-ups; only too often these proved quite inadequate, muffing their cues and forgetting their lines, so that the prodigy from Paris 'gave the impression of a rose bush in a field of turnips'.[36] After his departure the audience was left disillusioned and discontented, whereas before they had only half realized how mediocre their permanent company of actors had been. It was apparently Rachel who started the fashion of travelling with a rudimentary company of her own, composed of members of her talented family and *pensionnaires* from the Comédie-Française. This was in the grand tour she undertook between May and August 1848, extending from Perpignan in the south to the French-speaking islands of Jersey and Guernsey in the north. The route was, of course, carefully planned in advance and must have involved a great deal of preliminary correspondence (probably dealt with by her brother) with managers all over France to arrange bookings and terms. The tour was no doubt enormously profitable but, including as it did no fewer than thirty-five whistle-stops, also took severe toll of the actress's strength, for at this time the horse-drawn coach was still the norm for travellers, and Rachel and her party often had to snatch what sleep they could during night journeys.

However, in the 1860s the railway network was beginning to link up the major towns, and from that point on star actors or actresses rarely travelled singly; the practice grew up, after a play had enjoyed a pronounced success in Paris, for the original cast to tour the country with it. Thus Edmond Got, despite his earlier reservations about performing in the provinces,[37] decided in 1866 to take a large company on tour during the months of June and July with Augier's *La Contagion*, which had had a marked success at the Odéon earlier in the year. They played at all the important cities on the way (Rouen, Bordeaux, Marseilles, Toulon and Lyons) and also at some remote localities where he was quite taken aback at the primitive conditions: at Carcassonne, for instance, where the theatre had been established in a crumbling, secularized church, Got found himself assigned the former latrines of the sacristy as dressing-room. As leader and organizer of the expedition, it fell to him to cope with all manner of minor mishaps – the trunks containing the costumes sent to the wrong station, a dishonest theatre manager trying to cheat him, even the best hotels serving burnt cutlets, not to mention the risk, only too real, of bed-bugs. But the audiences everywhere were delighted to see them, and the Parisians played to full houses in spite of the rain in the north and the torrid heat in the south.

The success of this excursion may have prompted the decision to send an important fraction of the Comédie-Française to the south of France for a month in 1868 while their theatre in Paris was closed for essential renovation.[38] Once the itinerary was announced, every town on their route that boasted a theatre began agitating for the honour of their visit, but the actors were working to a tight schedule, and in the end they were forced to divide their time between five localities, Dijon, Lyons, Toulon, Nice and Marseilles. It had been hoped to include Bordeaux, but the Grand-Théâtre was discovered to have been booked by the Gaîté for sixty performances of the popular fairy-play *Peau d'âne* (The Donkey's Hide). Thus the competition between the Comédie-Française and the commercial theatres of Paris was now spreading to the provinces.

It will have been noticed that these tours took place only in the summer months, which in Paris tended to be a dead season for the theatres, many of which closed, for lack of audiences, from the end of June to the beginning of September; the obvious solution for actors temporarily unemployed was to band themselves together and try their luck in the provinces, or else place themselves under the orders of an impresario who would arrange an itinerary for them. The profitability of these summer excursions eventually suggested the idea of repeating them at other times in the year. If a particular Paris theatre struck gold, and embarked on a play which seemed certain to run for several months, one consequence was that a good half-dozen of the actors attached to that theatre, not being in the cast of the 'hit', would find themselves at a loose end. They would contact others in the same predicament, combine their forces, and form a temporary company to 'exploit the provinces' as the phrase was, playing as likely as not last year's great success. A chartered train, with special trucks for the scenery, would take them wherever they found a director willing to hire them for his theatre.[39] This development amounted to an invasion in force of the provinces by the Parisian theatres, and contributed as much as anything to the well-attested decline of the provincial stage in the nineteenth century, since local companies tended to be elbowed out in favour of the itinerant actors from Paris. Even if the strangers acted no better, at least they had new faces and curiosity alone was likely to draw in an audience.

The coming of the railways had a secondary effect, in that they made it easier in the latter part of the century for the well-to-do to travel up to the capital and crowd the theatres there. People of consequence were seldom to be seen in the audience of their home town – that was left to the country bumpkins. In towns within two or three hours' journey from Paris, the local newspapers reported only what was showing at the capital, without even bothering to inform their readers what was to be seen at the theatre on their doorstep: 'discreetly, they invite them to take the train and go and see a matinée performance of *Manon*, deliberately ignoring the fact that their municipal theatre is performing the same work on the same day'.[40] Those whom their trade, or the limitation of their means, did not allow to take this course, simply waited until their local theatre advertised another touring company from Paris, and were content to while away the interval listening to the singers in the *cafés-chantants*.

Everywhere in France the role of Paris as the *ville-lumière*, the unique focus of intellectual and artistic life, was tacitly admitted even in the cities which by their industrial and mercantile efforts were contributing far more to the prosperity of the nation. Mercier's worry, expressed in 1773, that as far as the output of dramatic work was concerned the provinces were virtually a desert, was echoed in 1825 by Etienne de Jouy, who argued that there could never be the same interest in the theatre in the provinces as there was in Paris, so long as the provinces were content to copy the capital.

In the theatre as in the world of letters, it is always Paris that furnishes them with objects of worship; it is always the theatres of the capital that supply our great provincial theatres with their watchwords, whereas they should be striving to attach to themselves poets and musicians and create a repertoire of their own.

The important playhouses at Lyons, Bordeaux, Rouen, Lille and Nantes, he goes on to say, should be providing openings for play-wrights instead of leaving it to Paris to offer the only market for their work. If that were to come about, the traveller would find a welcome variety as he went from one theatre to another, instead of the deadly monotony that now prevails: 'we should no longer be reduced to hearing the same songs on the stage from one end of France to the other, and to see actors striving to copy each other slavishly, raising their voices at the same hemistich, making the same gesture at the same exclamation'.[41]

By and large, and in spite of efforts at Rouen in particular to counteract the trend, Jouy's proposal for a number of active regional centres of drama was never translated into reality during his century. If, as occasionally happened, a play by a local dramatist was produced in his home town, it was dismissed witheringly as having no more than 'what distinguishes all productions of this type, namely an utter lack of distinction'.[42] The reason for this penury of new and original plays was not to be sought solely in the powerful pull of the artistic and intellectual prestige of Paris; it was also attributable to the constant fear dogging the provincial theatre manager that he would lose money if he were to put on a totally new play, whatever its merits. His company, small and overworked, could not be expected to devote much time to rehearsing an unknown work, and if a manuscript by a newcomer to the stage were offered him, as likely as not he would return it unread, with the well-meant and on the whole sound advice that he should get it produced in Paris first; if it succeeded there, the manager would be only too happy to have it performed subsequently in the author's home town.

CHAPTER 11

The licensing system, 1814–1864

One of the provisions of Napoleon's decree of 8 June 1806, as has been noted,[1] was that no new theatre might be opened in the capital unless specifically authorized by the sovereign, who would grant permission only if the applicant was known to be able to meet all likely financial contingencies. So rigorously was this clause enforced that throughout the Emperor's reign, no such applications were granted; quite possibly none were even submitted. But in the more benign atmosphere of the Restoration it became possible once more to think of reviving defunct theatres and even launching new dramatic enterprises: the first of Louis XVIII's ministers of the Interior, the Abbé de Montesquiou, sanctioned the reopening of the Théâtre de la Porte-Saint-Martin on 26 December 1814, and on 1 February 1820 a new theatre, known as the Gymnase-Dramatique, received official authorization and opened its doors for the first time on 23 December that year; it was to have a long and on the whole prosperous existence over the rest of the century and beyond.

Successive regimes over the next fifty years continued to pursue this slightly more relaxed policy, though always cautiously; and they retained the condition imposed by Napoleon, that a licence[2] would only be granted to an individual who could 'prove to the minister of the Interior that he has sufficient means to meet his obligations' (clause 2 of the decree of 8 June 1806). If satisfactory evidence of financial standing was lacking, he could be required to deposit caution-money, as had occasionally been done under the *ancien régime* in the case, particularly, of directors of the Opera. This precaution was rarely taken under the Restoration, though under the July Monarchy and the Second Empire it became more common, and varied in amount from 10,000 francs in the case of a modest establishment to 30,000 or even 50,000 francs for a theatre of larger size employing a considerable workforce. In case of financial failure, the caution-money deposited with the Treasury was in the first place applied in settlement of the claims of actors and employees and, if there was anything over, to pay the outstanding tradesmen's bills.[3] But though an unlucky director might fail commercially, in theory at least a theatre could not go bankrupt: the new incumbent, when taking over the licence, made himself responsible for the outstanding debts left by his predecessor and was expected to do his best to extinguish them before the period of the licence expired.

The duration of the licence was specified in the warrant (*brevet*) issued by the minister to the holder. In the provinces, it could not be extended beyond three years,[4] but exceptions were allowed in exceptional cases: Julien, director of the theatre at Caen, kept the job for twenty-eight years before retiring, to everyone's regret. In Paris it was variable, averaging nine years. A licensee could not, during his period of tenure, transmit his licence to another without the approval of higher authority, since the minister always had to be satisfied as to the financial standing of every incomer. This rule tended to be forgotten under the July Monarchy, when the licensing authority itself started to receive backhanders; all the same, when Crosnier, having been appointed director of the Opéra-Comique in May 1834, had his licence renewed in 1843 for a further ten years and then, in May 1845, surrendered it to Basset, the transaction caused scandalized comment in the press. It is true that Basset would have been quite acceptable to the government as the incoming director of a state theatre: himself a functionary in the Ministry of the Interior, he was also a member of the bureau of dramatic censorship and government representative (*commissaire royal*) guiding the fortunes of the Odéon, another state-supported theatre. But it was common knowledge that he had paid Crosnier a large sum, running into several hundreds of thousands of francs, for the remaining eight years of the licence. As Malliot, in the period immediately preceding the abolition of the licensing system, remarked with reference to this affair:

Is it true then that a licence awarded by the state, in the name of art, can be bartered away; that it becomes the private property of the man in whose name it is made out; that it can be converted into a cash sum and charged to whoever takes it over, at so heavy a cost sometimes that the successor succumbs under the weight of the repayments; and that, by such a transaction, the role of the state as protector of the arts is totally nullified? ... Alas yes, this has often been the case.[5]

The system, in effect, made the government ultimately responsible for all theatres through its appointed delegates, the directors, and could only be justified in terms of the theory, still current in the earlier part of the century, according to which the theatre was to be regarded primarily as an instrument of public instruction and as much the business of the state as any other form of education; theatre directors, like teachers in state universities, should therefore hold their appointments from the state, in accordance with its judgement of the varying capacities of the candidates to promote the interests of a supposedly didactic art.

Licences were always delivered to named individuals, never to associates, as had happened in the past when, for instance, Rebel and Francœur ran the Opera in tandem, or when Piis and Barré became co-directors of the Vaudeville. Another departure from eighteenth-century practice was that licences were invariably granted to men, never to women; this was not just common practice but was enshrined in law as clause 5 of the royal ordinance on the theatres dated 8 December 1824. This ruling is difficult to understand when one remembers the numerous highly successful women directors (Mlle Montansier being only the most prominent) who had managed theatrical companies in Paris and the provinces during the previous century. Even the most authoritative legal luminaries in the nineteenth century offer only lame explanations, lacking both clarity and cogency: 'this prohibition is founded on reasons of propriety; its purpose is to preserve the discipline of acting companies from the dangers it would incur if entrusted to women'.[6] In all probability it was simply an aspect of the widespread disinclination at this period to have any post of importance filled by a woman; it had very little to do with 'propriety' and much more to do with the current myth of the 'weaker sex'. The ordinance in question was abrogated by the decree on the freedom of the theatres of 1864. Thereafter, in law at any rate, any widow or any unmarried woman having attained her majority was at liberty to take over the management of a theatre; only married women needed their husbands' consent, which could be tacit.[7] Few took advantage of this new freedom. Sarah Bernhardt, who became sole director of the Théâtre de la Renaissance in 1893, and Réjane, who ran her own theatre on the Rue Blanche from 1906 onwards, were the only actress-managers of note before the Great War; Virginie Déjazet, who might have preceded them in this career, preferred to stick to acting where, she claimed, she could make twice as much money without having any of the worrying responsibilities that fell to a director's lot.

It was, then, always to a named individual of the male sex that a licence was issued. His application had to be accompanied by letters from referees 'guaranteeing his morals, his public-spiritedness and his loyalty to the regime', and once installed he was still subject to close police surveillance if there were any doubts about him on any score.[8] Preferably, of course, the successful applicant was one who, even if not known personally to the minister, came to him with recommendations from a trustworthy source. The story of how Anténor Joly, a former letterpress printer currently employed on the staff of a minor theatrical sheet called *Vert-Vert*, came to be designated a licensed theatre director may not be entirely typical but does show how strings were pulled in those days. Alexandre Dumas, who was a personal friend of the Duc d'Orléans, had mentioned in conversation with His Royal Highness that Hugo and he had no stage of their own on which their plays could be produced (this was around 1835–6). The Duke promised he would have a word with François Guizot, the minister concerned, and as a result Hugo was a little taken aback to receive a licence in due form to open a theatre. Protesting that he was a poet, not a business manager, Hugo was then asked in that case to name the man to whom the licence should be made out, and he bethought himself of Joly, who was not only a fanatic admirer of romantic literature but also had ambitions to direct a theatre. Accordingly, the former printer's name was substituted for the poet's, and in due course Hugo's new drama *Ruy Blas* was produced at the new theatre under Joly's direction.

Notwithstanding the rule that prospective licence-holders about whose solvency there were doubts should post a bond which would be held by the government in case of financial failure, an impecunious applicant whose credentials were otherwise impeccable was sometimes granted a period of grace to allow him to arrange his financial affairs and satisfy the authorities on this count. In the case of Joly, it took him fifteen months after the granting of the licence to scrape together enough money to engage a company of actors, hire a suitable building and have it fitted out and redecorated. But it was not unusual under the July Monarchy for a man of dedication but with scant resources to be chosen by the minister in preference to a rich but otherwise unqualified aspirant; the risk was always, of course, that the prospective licensee, eager to get his venture off the ground, would turn to money-lenders or else to wealthy society figures who, as a condition of their investment, would insist he accept as members of the new company actresses of limited talent to whom, for reasons of their own, they were anxious to do a good turn. Again, not all ministers took their responsibilities seriously; they were not above granting licences in return for political services, or simply as a means of pensioning off an underling who had outlived his usefulness. When the Théâtre du Panthéon was opened in 1832, in a deconsecrated church on the left bank, the licence was made over to Eric-Bernard 'as a reward for his patriotic activity during the three great days of July [1830]'.[9] Eric-Bernard, like Joly, had to hunt around for financial backing, for even if the church provided the outer framework of a theatre, there was still need for a clever architect to adapt the structure, and the employment of a considerable number of carpenters and joiners to erect the stage and fit out the auditorium with balconies, boxes and stalls.

If a theatre had to be built from scratch, it was even more necessary to resort to finance companies who reckoned to recoup their outlay by charging the director high rents. An early instance is provided by the brief history of the Panorama-Dramatique in 1820–3.[10] The licence had been given to a house-painter named Alaux, a friend of Baron Taylor who had doubtless recommended him to the minister. Unable to make use of it for lack of funds, Alaux contacted a couple of notaries, always looking for outlets for the funds deposited with them; together with two other associates from the banking community – still, in those days, very restricted compared to what it became later in the century – they purchased for 64,000 francs a suitable plot of land on the Boulevard du Temple, and then formed a limited-liability company (*société anonyme*) which contracted to build a theatre of which Alaux should be director. The company was formed on 22 October 1819, and by May 1820 had concluded arrangements with a firm of contractors prepared to erect the theatre within four months.

Alaux remained, of course, in possession of the all-important licence, which the state, as we have seen, invariably awarded to a named individual of its choice and consistently refused to entrust to an investment company of the type formed to fund the Panorama-Dramatique. As licence-holder, Alaux alone had the right to manage the theatre. In law, the shareholders owned both the site, which they had bought, and the building, having paid for its construction; but they had no control over who was to be director nor, should the director retire, become incapacitated or die, had they any say in who should succeed him; this was the privilege, jealously preserved, of the state. If a theatre, for any reason, were to lose its director, the proprietors could not refuse to accept the authorities' next nominee. If they tried to exclude him, the incoming director could obtain an order from a judge in chambers to authorize him to enter in possession of his office, and there were no legal steps the proprietors could take to prevent this happening. Equally, they could have no recourse to the courts to help them enforce the dismissal of an unsatisfactory director. In short, they had very little control over how the capital they had invested was being employed.

In fact, Alaux seems to have done his best; but at the end of the first year, he was only just breaking even. The costs of keeping the theatre heated and lit and paying the actors and employees their modest salaries amounted to 213,544 francs; his receipts from the sale of tickets, approximately 251,000 francs, would have covered these expenses comfortably had it not been for the various taxes for which he was liable, including the contribution (12,000 francs) exacted by the state on behalf of the Opera.[11] These reduced his net income from the enterprise to exactly 214,835 francs, leaving a net profit of a paltry 1,291 francs. On 21 July 1823 the shareholders decided to realize their assets by auctioning off land and building, as they were perfectly entitled to do; accordingly the Panorama-Dramatique was shortly after demolished and replaced by a six-storey tenement house.

Not all the new theatres inaugurated under the Restoration and July Monarchy came to so untimely an end, but none of them could have yielded great profits to the men who originally financed them and who could, presumably, have chosen less risky and more lucrative openings for their surplus capital. How then did it come about that hard-headed men of business, having made their pile in trade or in the exercise of a well-paid profession, were prepared to invest a portion of their savings in such unpromising ventures? In most cases not out of devotion to the dramatic art, certainly, though it may have tickled the vanity of some to be able to talk about 'our theatre' and to 'protect' the younger actresses in the company.[12] But shareholders were given, as of right, a certain number (proportionate to the number of shares they held) of free tickets to distribute among their friends and, in some theatres, the privilege of sitting on reading committees where the acceptance or rejection of a new play was decided. All this may have reconciled them to some extent to the minute or non-existent return on their investment, but even so, the cost to the management of providing these fringe benefits could tip the balance between the viability or insolvency of the enterprise. Thus, to return to the circumstances surrounding the launching of the Théâtre de la Renaissance under Joly's management, its financial structure was based on a share issue, undersubscribed, however, since only thirty-three of the ninety shares, at 5,000 francs each, were taken up. At a shareholders' meeting on 26 April 1839, it was decided to float a debenture issue to raise 60,000 francs at 1,000 francs each, bearing fixed interest at 4 per cent, and entitling every subscriber to free admission over the next six years to all stage performances and all balls held at the Renaissance. These masked balls had been started at the beginning of the year as a means of raising extra revenue; the dance music, composed by Musard, had proved wildly popular, with its furious quadrilles and frenzied galops, not to mention the ballets put on during the intervals and the raffles which were another feature of these occasions. But when the accounts were made up at the end of the 1839–40 season, it was discovered that in spite of box-office receipts of 715,000 francs and the additional product of the masked balls, the total takings had been so reduced by the free tickets and reserved boxes, which formed part of the perquisites of the shareholders, that the theatre, over the eighteen months during which it had been open, was in deficit to the tune of 280,000 francs.[13] In the circumstances Anténor Joly had no alternative but to abandon his licence, and the shareholders to agree to the liquidation of their company.

Difficulties in making theatres pay under the regime of licensed directors were attributable as much to the conditions embodied in the terms of the licences as to the system itself which, by restricting artificially the number of theatres in the capital, ought to have allowed each of them a sufficient share of that part of the population to whom theatre-going had become second nature. The most important of these conditions was that which regulated the type of play the licensee was permitted to produce. Napoleon, as we have seen, had imposed this restriction, and successive administrations had been content to continue his policy of predetermining the nature of the repertoire of each theatre. Thus, under the First Empire, two theatres only, the Variétés and the Vaudeville, were permitted to perform vaudevilles (light-hearted comedies which included numerous songs set to popular tunes); under the Restoration, the Gymnase too was for a while allowed them, as was the Palais-Royal, and there were audiences at all these theatres, for at this time the vaudeville, in one, two or three acts, was a form of dramatic entertainment on which the French unaccountably doted. The melodrama, so keenly followed under the Empire, was beginning to lose its hold on the upper classes of society, though the middle and lower classes still flocked to the three theatres which alone were permitted to show them, the Porte-Saint-Martin, the Gaîté and the Ambigu-Comique. For those who never troubled to consult the theatre bills, the arrangement had its advantage – one did at least know, when making one's way to the theatre of one's choice, what type of entertainment was on offer.

However, the system had drawbacks, especially for newly founded theatres struggling to attract audiences. One of the major reasons for the collapse of Alaux's Panorama-Dramatique in 1823 was widely held to be the excessive restrictions imposed on him with regard to the kind of theatrical fare he was permitted to offer his patrons. The licence he had been granted incorporated the provision that he might produce comedies, dramas and vaudevilles on condition there were never more than two actors on stage in any one scene: thus dialogue was allowable, not, however, a discussion between three or more persons. One imagines that this crippling restriction was imposed behind the scenes by Alaux's rivals, particularly those with whom he was in direct competition; it certainly must have imposed a great strain on the ingenuity of the authors who wrote for him, even though they included such clever playwrights as Taylor and Nodier. The government, in granting a licence, invariably attached to it a list of conditions, known as the *cahier des charges*, to which the director was obliged to adhere. In the case of the Panorama-Dramatique, these conditions were widely seen as tyrannous, and gave rise to fierce criticism in the contemporary press. It was acceptable that limits should be placed on the number of theatres in the capital, but once a new one was authorized it was absurd to put it in a straitjacket.

The system broke down eventually. Under the July Monarchy it became increasingly obvious that the old categories, valid under the

Empire, no longer corresponded to popular tastes: new types of play came into fashion, and the administration was driven to wink at infringements of the strict terms of a director's licence. The Théâtre du Vaudeville put on other plays than vaudevilles, and once Scribe, around 1830, gave up writing exclusively for the Gymnase, that theatre too began looking for other types of play. Gérard de Nerval, writing in Girardin's paper *La Presse* on 28 December 1837, noted 'the strangest muddle current in the dramatic world. The Gymnase has taken aboard Bocage and Mme Dorval' – two of the most popular stars of romantic drama. 'The Variétés are jettisoning saucy plays and turning to vaudeville seasoned with pathos, after the fashion started by the Gymnase. The Théâtre du Vaudeville itself, originally cradle to the genre, is abandoning itself with gusto to the melodrama popular on the Boulevard du Temple.'[14] Delphine de Girardin, in her column in the same paper (10 July 1840), repeated Nerval's observations, pointing out in addition that actors who had won celebrity for their performances in certain types of play were now moving from theatre to theatre, profiting from the readiness of directors to try any kind of play and from the reluctance of the authorities to insist on the old demarcation lines that used to confine a theatre to a given type. She deplored the tendency, which could only lead to a dangerous anarchy. The theatre world, from being so carefully regulated and partitioned as it had been in the past, was now given over to cut-throat competition. 'Ah! competition, what a deplorable thing it is, and how it reconciles one to monopoly! Competition, far from bringing about progress through emulation, produces nothing but impoverishment through struggle.'[15] But at least on paper the old rules remained valid, and even under the Second Empire an occasional genuflection in the direction of limitation by genre was required. Dumas *fils* recalled that when his *Dame aux camélias* was accepted for production at the Vaudeville, 'I had to keep the song in the first act, because the Vaudeville's licence permitted only "plays with dialogue interspersed with singing".'[16]

This was the official formula by which the vaudeville was designated; but it was also a description that could as easily apply to the comic opera. Ever since the Comédie-Italienne was granted the exclusive privilege of staging comic opera in 1762, it had been necessary to distinguish it from other musical entertainments in order to make sure that its monopoly was not being breached by the minor theatres, and so the dividing line was drawn between the comic opera, where the music (including the music for songs) was original, and the vaudeville, in which the songs were always set to well-known, traditional tunes.[17] This did not necessarily lead to monotony in the vaudeville, since established folk-airs numbered little short of a thousand;[18] but each one was known to the audience – only the words of the song differed from one vaudeville to another. It was of some importance to the state authorities to maintain this rule-of-thumb distinction, since the Théâtre de l'Opéra-Comique was a subsidized theatre and needed to be protected against competition. So any licence given to a director wishing to put on musicals of one sort or another usually incorporated somewhere a clause forbidding him to have music specially composed for the work.

Two major disputes arose at this period between the Opéra-Comique and certain newly established theatres which were felt to be encroaching on its monopoly. The first concerned the Théâtre des Nouveautés, which for its inaugural performance on 10 March 1827 boldly advertised a three-act 'opera' entitled *Le Coureur de veuves* (The Runner after Widows) with music by Blangini. But its licence did not encompass opera or indeed any kind of musical play for which a composer had written original music. The director of the Nouveautés, Bérard, was probably counting on his close relations with the then Minister of the Interior, Corbière, to obviate any difficulties that might arise; but the Duc d'Aumont, the court nobleman who had special responsibility for the Opéra-Comique, lodged an immediate complaint, calling on the minister to order the immediate closure of the theatre or at the very least to insist that the director pay greater attention in future to the conditions of his licence. Corbière had no alternative but to ask his friend to withdraw *Le Coureur de veuves* until Blangini's score had been replaced by music in the public domain. A few months later, however, the Duke overreached himself, taking exception to a musical version of *Faust* that had been put on at the Nouveautés: he demanded its immediate suppression on the same grounds as before. Corbière's reply did not lack tartness: the noble lord had been misinformed; the work contained no original music, and in the circumstances Bérard was perfectly within his rights in putting it on.

Undeterred, the Opéra-Comique continued its campaign against the Nouveautés until finally, in October 1829, the climax was reached when the upstart theatre achieved a considerable success with a three-act 'drama interspersed with songs' called *Isaure*, for which Adolphe Adam, a composer of distinction, had written a delightful score. The directors of the Opéra-Comique once more summoned their rival to substitute 'known airs' for Adam's music; but someone at the Nouveautés had a brilliant idea. Knowing that the music for *Jenny*, the work currently showing at the Opéra-Comique, was by common consent judged to be banal in the extreme, they issued a fake summons calling on the state theatre to take it off immediately, since the score, consisting entirely of 'known airs', was an infringement of the monopoly of the vaudeville theatres. This spoof, published in the *Figaro*, caused endless amusement at the expense of the Opéra-Comique, which did not dare press its claims regarding *Isaure* and for some time lay low, thus enabling the Nouveautés to grow bolder and bolder and to enter into direct competition with the state-supported theatre. For various other reasons, however, unconnected with these squabbles, the Nouveautés never prospered and was forced to close on 15 February 1832; by a stroke of irony, it was the Opéra-Comique which subsequently moved into the vacant building.

The second altercation between the Opéra-Comique and a new arrival on the dramatic scene occurred some ten years later, and involved once more Anténor Joly's Théâtre de la Renaissance. In between obtaining his licence and opening his theatre, Joly had struck up a friendship with Ferdinand de Villeneuve, a writer of vaudevilles with a keen interest in music and a number of contacts in musical circles. At this time, far more young men were graduating as composers from the prestigious state school, the Conservatoire de Musique, than the market for their talents could absorb. Aware of this, Villeneuve organized a petition to the minister signed by a number of outstanding musicians, including Berlioz, Cherubini, Auber and Meyerbeer, asking that the terms of Joly's licence should be enlarged to allow him to produce not just drama – as had been Hugo's original idea – but light opera as well. The petitioners reasoned that even the best of the young musicians from the school stood very little chance of having a new work produced at either the Opera or the Opéra-Comique, and could look forward to little better than careers as composers of dance music and drawing-room ballads.

The new minister, Montalivet, saw the force of the petitioners' arguments, more especially since the Conservatoire, as well as the

Opéra-Comique, were state-supported institutions. It was undeniable that young French composers found little demand for their works at the Opéra-Comique, and he felt that when the state had gone to the expense of educating them in their chosen profession, it was only right that the state should offer a helping hand in the first few years of their careers. But at the same time Montalivet shrank from breaking the monopoly enjoyed by the Opéra-Comique. So, in an attempt to satisfy both parties, when making out Joly's *cahier des charges* in 1837, he authorized him to put on at his theatre 'dramas, comedies, and vaudevilles set to newly composed music … not admitting the musical developments that characterize comic opera'.[19] But what was a 'vaudeville set to newly composed music', given that it had always been universally assumed that the songs in a vaudeville were invariably set to traditional tunes? The phrase involved a contradiction in terms and was bound to lead to acrimonious argument.

This started, indeed, even before the new theatre opened, with an exchange of letters between Anténor Joly and Crosnier, the director of the Opéra-Comique, as to what exactly were the 'musical developments' that might transform a vaudeville into a light opera; before long, the courts found themselves required to adjudicate on this conundrum. A new work, *Lady Melvil*, billed at the Renaissance as a 'comedy in three acts, interspersed with songs', touched off an absurd series of lawsuits; the Opera itself brought its guns to bear the following year when it objected to *La Chaste Suzanne*, a four-act opera with which the Renaissance was regaling its public in defiance of entrenched privileges. After hearing the legal arguments, the judges sensibly declared themselves incompetent to rule on the question, and the Renaissance was left free to ride roughshod over the monopolistic privileges of the two state theatres, to the greater profit of music-lovers in Paris; for it was at the Renaissance that Donizetti's masterpiece, *Lucia di Lammermoor*, was given its first performance in France, before moving on to Rouen to enthral Emma Bovary and utterly perplex her dim-witted husband.

The licensing system, introduced under Napoleon to defend the state-supported theatres and their monopolies, had proved incapable in the 1830s of fulfilling this task; in the 1840s people were beginning to ask themselves what possible purpose it served. The question surfaced in 1846 over discussion of Hippolyte Hostein's application for a licence to open a new theatre which would specialize in dramatizations of popular novels, particularly those of Alexandre Dumas *père*. Gautier wondered whether the time had not come

to abolish dramatic monopolies for good and to leave everyone free to open a theatre, under certain essential provisos, in the same way as anyone in possession of 100,000 francs is free to start up a newspaper and address the nation in its columns. Freedom for the theatres seems to us so just a demand and one so much in conformity with the needs of our time that the day surely cannot be far distant when our legislators will proclaim it, thereby satisfying the wishes of both artists and public.[20]

In the first flush of the 1848 revolution the matter came up for discussion in the State Council, along with the question of abolishing the censorship; but at the time there were more pressing issues claiming attention, and it was agreed to defer decision until the implications could be thrashed out by the prudent and time-honoured method of holding an inquiry. This was instituted in 1849; the views of thirty-two theatre managers, critics, actors, composers and dramatists were duly canvassed. Among the dramatists, Scribe showed himself the most reactionary, arguing that 'if absolutism is permissible anywhere, it is assuredly where the theatres are concerned'; Dumas the most anarchic; Hugo the most visionary (he was still in favour of the state organizing the theatres and dictating what kind of plays – improving and educative – they should put on). It was left to the minor novelist and playwright Emile Souvestre to suggest the most sensible policy. He drew a distinction between theatres concerned with the conservation and promotion of the dramatic art, and 'those that are purely an industrial enterprise, which like all industrial enterprises need to be allowed to compete with one another freely', and should be allowed to do so without being bound by their licences to stage a particular type of performance. In the end, however, the reformers' ideas were tacitly ignored, and the pre-revolutionary system was provisionally kept in place.[21]

However, the debate continued, though in the more repressive atmosphere that developed in the latter years of the Second Republic, talk of according new freedoms was not encouraged. The author of a treatise on the policing of theatres in Paris, published in 1850, advanced the antiquated theory that 'more means worse' where theatres were concerned and added that, in his view, 'a wise administration should not issue any new licences except in so far as it has come to the conclusion that the twenty-two theatres functioning in Paris today cannot suffice for the needs and pleasures of the population';[22] an opinion that some would regard as a recipe for stagnation, while others would take it to imply no more than a prudent consolidation. Meanwhile the pressure was building up. In an article dated 29 November 1859, Pier Fiorentino asserted that 'for every director's seat that falls vacant, there are a hundred candidates besieging ministerial offices and conducting savage campaigns to discredit their competitors'. Commonly, he went on to say, these licences were sold to the highest bidder, not to the man best qualified to fill the post; and he cited the case of one director 'who was not of the opinion he had driven a bad bargain in giving 600,000 francs for a licence which had only three years to run'.[23]

Gautier's prediction made in 1846 was eventually fulfilled, though at a rather later date than he had anticipated. In a speech from the throne on 5 November 1863, at the opening of a new parliamentary session, the Emperor announced his government's intention shortly to abolish the licensing system as it applied to theatres. Unlike his uncle, Napoleon III had no particular interest in matters dramatic; but the so-called 'liberation of the theatres' cost the state very little, and absolved it from its quasi-responsibility for the well-being of even commercial theatres.[24] It was also in tune with the ruler's well-publicized intention, in the latter part of his reign, to adopt more liberal policies, which would include the wholesale removal of antiquated restrictions on private enterprise.

The decree promulgated shortly afterwards, on 6 January 1864,[25] embodied two important principles, both of which were simply a reformulation of the main provisions of the decree of the Constituent Assembly of 13 January 1791, tacitly abrogated under the First Empire: that any individual was free to build a new theatre or rent an existing one and to manage it himself, with no other formal requirement than to notify the Ministry of Fine Arts and the prefect of police in Paris, or the prefect of the appropriate *département* outside Paris; and that, in the words of clause 4 of the decree, 'dramatic works of any type, including plays in the public domain, may be performed on any stage'. This last clause, of course, abolished at a stroke the copyright of the state theatres on plays 'belonging to their repertory', as well as putting an end to any future disputes such as had led to the unseemly squabbling between commercial theatres like the Nouveautés and the Renaissance and state-supported ones like the Opera and the Opéra-Comique. The news predictably evoked expressions of pleasure and gratitude in loyal addresses from the acting community, headed by Frédérick Lemaître, and from the Society of Composers. But there were – equally to be expected – dire forebodings among members of the Comédie-Française, as Got recorded in his diary, robustly dismissing them however as 'asinine'. 'When directors in Paris, profiting from the surprise effect of the novelty, have hastily put on *Tartuffe* or *Le Dépit amoureux* half a dozen times, is there any risk that they will revive for their uneducated audiences the old-fashioned plays which appeal to our more specialized clientèle on account of their quaintness alone? Of course not.' In the provinces directors had been free at all times to produce such plays, since copyright on them was confined to the capital, but had rarely ventured into this terrain, realizing that it was not what the public wanted. And Got concluded that 'freedom of the theatres in Paris is nothing but a catchword, mere ministerial claptrap. It will encourage speculation and the play of market forces, perhaps bring about a general decline in standards, but that's all.'[26]

In the event, Got was proved right in his first prediction, if not in his second. The decree of 6 January 1864 became effective on 1 July following, and there was a sudden rush to plunder the stock of the state theatres: *Tartuffe* and *L'Avare* were put on at the Porte-Saint-Martin, and some of Molière's other plays were tried out at the Gymnase; at the Vaudeville, the directors even ventured on a production of Jean-Jacques Rousseau's *Le Devin de village* (The Village Soothsayer). But it all proved a flash in the pan; as even the Comédie-Française was discovering at the time, there were more lucrative works waiting to be put on than the classics.

As for the other main clause in the decree, though the abolition of the requirement for a licence undoubtedly fuelled the expansion of the theatre industry, greater prosperity was not achieved without some suffering among the many thousands of subsidiary employees – stage painters, scene-shifters, not to mention the actors themselves – who had enjoyed considerable security of employment in the past under the old regulatory controls, since as we have seen the state had taken care that if a director failed and had to file a petition in bankruptcy, his successor was obliged to meet his liabilities; the licence was issued only on that understanding, and moneys owed to these people were to a large extent guaranteed by the state. Now, when a director became insolvent, his dependent employees did not merely lose their jobs, but lost also the wages they had agreed to forgo when he was struggling to keep the enterprise afloat; and there were a sensational number of bankruptcies in the late 1860s among long-established theatres, the Porte-Saint-Martin, the Gaîté, and some of the newer foundations, the Châtelet, the Théâtre-Lyrique. Thus, the withdrawal of state involvement in the theatres was not achieved without some unfortunate consequences; there were losers as well as gainers, and the losers came, as so often in similar circumstances, from those classes in society least able to support misfortune.

CHAPTER 12

The state-supported theatres in the nineteenth century

It was part of the mythology of the royalists under the Restoration that the hereditary monarchy had undergone no interruption – merely a temporary eclipse – during the unfortunate events of the Revolution, the Consulate and the Empire. Louis XVI had suffered a martyr's death in 1793; his rightful heir, the Dauphin, known to his loyal subjects as Louis XVII, had survived him for only two years and died in prison. The crown had then descended to Louis XVI's elder brother, the Comte de Provence, who re-entered Paris on 3 May 1814, hailed as Louis XVIII. In accordance with the fiction that his reign had begun when his brother was executed, and that he had been travelling abroad for his pleasure over the past couple of decades, he dated his first decree on the royal theatres (14 December 1816) from the 22nd year of his reign. This decree purported to reinstate the creaking machinery under which they had been governed during the *ancien régime*. The Comédie-Française and the Opéra-Comique (formerly the Comédie-Italienne) were once more placed under the supervision of the Gentlemen of the Bedchamber, represented on committees by the Intendant-Général de l'Argenterie et Menus Plaisirs, none other than Papillon de la Ferté. It was not, however, the same person as had played so important a part in the administration of the theatres before the Revolution (he had been guillotined in 1794), but his son, who claimed the office was hereditary; unfortunately he had not inherited his father's talents and before long was the laughing-stock of the actors and actresses nominally under his control.[1]

The Comédie-Française continued functioning under the general arrangements drawn up by Napoleon in the Moscow Decree of 1812, to which the only change of any significance was one affecting the composition of the *comité d'administration* (steering committee), which had been fixed by the Emperor at six senior actors (*sociétaires-*

176

hommes) and which the ordinance of 1816 altered to seven, to include one or two actresses. But the principle of state support, initiated by Louis XIV, continued by his successors down to the Revolution, and reinstated by Napoleon on an even grander scale, was maintained under the Restoration and has survived intact down to the present time. Though challenged on occasion, it was generally accepted by analogy with such other institutions as the State Printing Office (the Imprimerie Royale or Nationale, founded in 1640), and the Gobelins and Sèvres manufacturies. Although not necessarily viable as commercial undertakings, these had established throughout the centuries benchmarks in fine printing, tapestry and carpet-making, and the design and production of high-class porcelain respectively. Theatres and opera houses, founded and subsidized by the state, arguably fell into the same category, though there were differences, the most important being that the products of superb craftsmanship can be admired by future generations and form a treasure-house for all time, whereas the moments of high excellence in acting or singing remained only in the memory of those who had the good fortune to enjoy them at the time, at least until new methods of recording them for posterity had been invented.

What grumbling there might have been over the expense of subsidizing these musical and dramatic activities was moderated by the knowledge that the cash payments made to the theatres came not out of general taxes but from the revenue derived from gaming-houses. This system, initiated during the Napoleonic era, was continued under the Restoration, for gambling, as Balzac observed at the start of his novel *La Peau de chagrin* (*The Wild Ass's Skin*, of which the action is set in October 1829), can be characterized as 'an eminently taxable passion'; though only a portion (1,300,000 francs) was used to subsidize the theatres out of the five and a half millions raised by this impost.[2] A further 600,000 francs was added from the civil list, for Louis XVIII and Charles X spent money like water on the theatres: paying for a new building for the Odéon, completely gutted by a fire in 1818 which started on Good Friday and raged for a week; paying for an opera house in the Rue Lepeletier when the former one was pulled down after the Duc de Berry was assassinated on its steps on 13 February 1820;[3] paying for new quarters for the Opéra-Comique when the ruinous condition of their old theatre, the Salle Feydeau, had necessitated its replacement. The circumstances surrounding the erection of the new building into which the Opéra-

Comique moved in 1829 are worth examining in some detail, providing as they do an object lesson in the dangers inherent in negotiations between the Crown and a thrusting commercial concern, particularly when the Crown is represented by an incompetent aristocrat like the Duc de La Rochefoucauld, Minister of the Royal Household.

After thirty-five years the Théâtre Feydeau, which when completed in 1790 had been admired as the last word in the architect's art, had fallen into a dangerous state of dilapidation, and a major restructuring was considered essential to make it safe. At this point a financial consortium, the Compagnie Mallet, came forward with a proposal to transform the Rue Neuve Ventadour into a handsome square in the centre of which, they suggested, it would be possible to erect a graceful new theatre for the Opéra-Comique. Impressed by the boldness of the scheme, the government decided to underwrite it, and on 19 July 1826 an agreement was signed between the Compagnie Mallet and the Duc de La Rochefoucauld, providing initially for the sale of the plot to the Crown for 1,700,000 francs. In addition the company offered to advance a further 2,000,000 francs, repayable over eight years, for the construction of the theatre. This too was approved; the work was put in hand on 28 November 1826 and completed in the spring of 1829. Not content with having mulcted the state of these considerable sums of money, the shareholders of the Compagnie Mallet were able to secure various other extraordinary privileges for themselves and their heirs, such as free boxes in perpetuity at the new theatre: these were to prove in due course a crippling burden on the finances of the Opéra-Comique.

The next stage in this devious story was the appointment, on 14 August 1828, of an army officer, Lieutenant-Colonel Ducis, as the new director of the Opéra-Comique; his one qualification appears to have been that he was the nephew of Jean-François Ducis, whose versions or rather adaptations of *Hamlet, King Lear, Macbeth* and *Othello* had introduced Shakespeare to French theatre-goers between 1769 and 1792. Being unable to raise unaided the requisite finance, Ducis appealed to Boursault-Malherbe, himself formerly a theatre director,[4] who agreed to come to his assistance on certain draconian conditions. He obtained the freehold of the Salle Ventadour, still at this date only half finished, for 700,000 francs, considerably less than Ducis had pledged himself to pay. He demanded from the government, and secured, an increase in the state subvention from 120,000 to 150,000 francs, together with ministerial agreement that the government would subscribe to six boxes at 5,000 francs apiece for the thirty years of the duration of the licence. To raise the money he needed, Boursault-Malherbe formed a new commercial company, to the shareholders of which he relinquished his title to the Salle Ventadour. As for Ducis, no match for the financial sharks he was dealing with, his cash-flow problems persisted, and on 15 June 1830, the supply of gas having been cut off because of non-payment of bills, the theatre was forced to close. But Boursault had cannily included, in his contract with Ducis, a clause by which the latter agreed that his licence should pass to Boursault or Boursault's nominee in the event of his having to resign his directorship; and this clause now came into play. On 26 June 1830 Ducis was declared bankrupt, Boursault-Malherbe replaced him as director, but within less than a year had disposed of his rights to Lubbert, a former director of the Opera. The legal ownership of the Salle Ventadour remained firmly vested, for the next forty years or so, in the finance company that Boursault had founded, whatever theatrical company happened to be leasing the building.

This brief history of the wheeling and dealing needed to settle the Opéra-Comique in the Salle Ventadour illustrates, if nothing else, how difficult it was in the early nineteenth century for the state to avoid being worsted when it attempted to call on private money to finance what was essentially a public enterprise. The civil servants in the Royal Household were outwitted at every turn by the businessmen with whom they were negotiating; having agreed to pay for the site, they then had to pay in part for the building of the theatre, and in the end the state was left a simple leaseholder; and even then the company that owned it had incidentally secured for its shareholders rights and privileges which made it extremely difficult to ensure that the theatre could be run successfully, no matter how well attended its productions. Lubbert found that he could not even settle the salaries of his actors and musicians, in spite of the outstanding popular success of Hérold's *Zampa*, which was given its first performance there on 3 May 1831; the theatre closed once more, and Lubbert regretfully resigned on 8 December of the same year. The actors of the Opéra-Comique thereupon addressed an open letter to the newspapers, given wide publicity in the press,[5] in which they offered their own version of the reasons why the theatre was in constant trouble. 'How are we expected to pay a rent of 160,000 francs a year, with the additional obligation of keeping twenty to twenty-five boxes at the disposal of non-paying shareholders who besides have 300 names on the free list? How is one to cope with the enormous costs of every kind caused by the size of the building, a size not really suited to performances of light opera?' The letter concluded on a fairly desperate note. Unless the state ousted the Compagnie Mallet by making a compulsory purchase of the premises, and in addition allocated the Opéra-Comique an adequate subvention, then for purely economic reasons the company would have to disband; this would be disastrous not only for the musical reputation of Paris but also for the well-being of theatres in the provinces, whose audiences were clamouring for light opera and whose managers depended on the Opéra-Comique to keep up the supply. Finally they made a pathetic though no doubt fully justified plea for their employees, lacking all job security and forced now to opt between the two sorry alternatives of begging in the streets or throwing themselves into the Seine.

The shareholders relented to the extent of agreeing to reduce the annual rental on the Salle Ventadour to 100,000 francs, still insisting however on their rights to free entry which so cruelly diminished the potential revenue from the sale of tickets. The state subvention, reduced to 120,000 francs at the beginning of the July Monarchy, was gradually raised until in 1837 it stood at 240,000 francs, a figure that did not vary until 1870. Only the Opera received a bigger subvention. Even so, there were incessant grumbles. The Ventadour was too large, suited more for grand opera than for comic opera, and located in a district rarely visited by the ordinary theatre-goer; as a writer remarked in the *Journal des Comédiens*: 'the Odéon itself is better known and less truly isolated than the Salle Ventadour'.[6] Left without a government nominee as director, the company decided to revert to its earlier status as a self-governing corporation, and seized the first opportunity that presented itself to move out of the Ventadour; they took a lease on the Nouveautés which, situated on the Place de la Bourse, was much nearer the heart of the Paris theatreland and which had become vacant on 15 February 1832.[7] Here they remained until 1840, playing to audiences highly appreciative of the new works by Adam, Auber and Halévy which they were able to mount. Finally, a chance occurrence enabled them to return to the very location, if not the selfsame building, which they had first occupied in 1783 when they were still called the Comédie-

Italienne, and from which they had set out on their long odyssey at the beginning of the century. A fire having destroyed their old home, the Salle Favart, on the night of 13–14 January 1838, the Chamber of Deputies voted its reconstruction, and the new theatre, built on the site of the old one, was made over to the Opéra-Comique, which gave its inaugural performance there on 16 May 1840. It is worth noting that the job was not undertaken directly by the state in this instance, but was entrusted to a private builder who was to be reimbursed by annual repayments spread over the next forty years.

The same disaster caused the Italian Opera, which had been using the Salle Favart (it was in fact after a performance of Mozart's *Don Giovanni*, appropriately, that the theatre had been consumed by fire), to become the next occupants of the Salle Ventadour, where they opened on 31 January 1838; and although there were complaints (the approach road posed difficulties for carriages), the company, which included such singers as Rubini, Lablache, Tamburini and Mlle Grisi, together with the attractive works written for it by Bellini and Donizetti, were a sufficient magnet to draw music-lovers from all parts to this rather out-of-the-way quarter of Paris. Under the Second Empire the Théâtre-Italien, the Bouffes as it was commonly called, vied with the Opera as the most fashionable centre for musico-dramatic entertainment – Verdi's *Il trovatore* and *Rigoletto* were both given over 200 performances there. But its vogue did not survive the collapse of the Empire. When the Opera had to share the Ventadour with the Bouffes – a necessity caused by yet another fire – it was noticed that fashionable society visited it chiefly on the days reserved for the Opera. Five years later, in December 1878, the Italians departed, the boxes, stalls and balconies were all wrenched out to make room for counters and offices, and the trilling of sopranos was replaced by the ringing of gold napoleons: the Salle Ventadour had been converted into a banking house.

Despite initial doubts, the relative remoteness of the Salle Ventadour from the main axis of theatre activity in Paris at this time, which had caused so much recrimination on the part of the Opéra-Comique, does not seem to have been a factor affecting attendances at the Bouffes during its period of prosperity. The reason was probably that it relied not on passing trade but on a steady clientèle of faithful supporters, belonging either to the wealthier classes of society who subscribed to boxes, or to the young and relatively penurious music-lovers who could be relied on to fill the pit and the galleries. Neither group was much troubled by the need to spend the evening in a district considered to be well off the beaten track. It was quite other with the Odéon, situated on what visitors from London called the 'Middlesex side' of the river, in other words on the left bank, where its audience catchment area was on the whole restricted to the ordinary inhabitants of the Latin Quarter, the students, living on a shoestring, and their girl-friends, even more penurious. As the authors of a theatre directory published in 1824 remarked drily: 'if there is anything more extraordinary than the two fires that successively destroyed the Odéon [those of 1799 and 1818], it must be that the decision was twice taken to rebuild it on the same spot ... in a district so remote as to be practically cut off from the rest of the capital'.[8]

The reason why it was rebuilt so rapidly after the second of these two disasters may well have been that Louis XVIII, mindful of the large sums he had contributed, when he was still the Comte de Provence, towards the costs of the original building in the Faubourg Saint-Germain, felt that this monument to the splendour of the pre-revolutionary Comédie-Française should not be allowed to vanish permanently from the face of Paris. Whether or not this was so, a royal ordinance was promulgated on 21 July 1819 enacting that 'so long as it shall please Us to conserve for it the title and style of a royal theatre, it will occupy without charge the Odéon building'; and further that 'the licence for the royal theatre of the Odéon shall be granted to a company of actors, to exploit at their own risk, under the same conditions as those laid down for members of the Comédie-Française'.[9] The company, however, despite not ungenerous subventions (60,000 francs in 1823, raised to 100,000 francs the following year) was always in financial straits until finally, in March 1829, they gave up the struggle, explaining why in a letter to the newspapers: 'of the ten months, barely elapsed, of the current theatrical season, we are still owed our salaries for six' (it should be said that the company, although supposed to be 'exploiting the Odéon at their own risk', had long since, in despair, submitted to be managed by whatever outsiders were prepared to take the responsibility); 'if such a state of affairs places some of us in considerable embarrassment, it reduces the majority to utter destitution'. As for the small fry, choristers and stagehands, 'having suffered, without pay, all the frightfulness of an unusually hard winter, they have been

obliged to have recourse to charity' and to the product of a subscription opened for their benefit.[10] The letter did nothing to save
the situation: not only did the theatre close, but the state properties
were sold off at a public auction to satisfy the creditors.

Yet the company itself was an excellent one, including at different
times Mlle George after her expulsion from the Comédie-Française,
two of the rising stars of romantic drama, Frédérick Lemaître and
Bocage, and a whole series of future stalwarts of the Comédie-
Française, Joanny, Samson, Perrier, Provost, Suzanne Brohan, and
Pauline Anaïs Aubert, who acted at the Odéon for ten years and was
known (under her stage-name Mlle Anaïs) as 'the jewel of the left
bank'. But they all realized that the Odéon, though a good training
ground, did nothing for their careers in the long run, since it was
ignored by critics and fashionable audiences alike. David, a first-
rate tragic actor, having left the Comédie-Française of his own
accord to offer his services to the Odéon, had, professionally speaking, signed his own death-warrant. 'Anywhere else but in the Faubourg Saint-Germain, the name of David would draw the crowds;
but in this neighbourhood, where the most profound silence enve-
lops Melpomene's second temple [i.e. the Odéon: Melpomene was
the muse of tragedy], David is appreciated only by a handful of
students, from whom the tedium of an empty theatre is held at bay
by the pleasure of watching and applauding his acting.'[11]

After the July revolution, the Odéon at last secured the services of
a competent director, Auguste Lirieux, who, during the three years
he worked there, produced not only Ponsard's *Lucrèce* and Emile
Augier's *La Ciguë* (The Hemlock), but also Molière's *Don Juan*, that
strange work that had not been seen on the stage for fifty years. But
Lirieux had to contend with the dreadful reputation of the Odéon, a
theatre no sooner opened than it was closed, situated somewhere in
the antipodes. One evening, it was said, a group of young men
arrived carrying muskets, and begged the stupefied cloakroom
attendant to look after them during the performance, the theatre
being situated in such wild country that it might be dangerous to
venture out unarmed after dark. A caricature showed a gentleman
hailing a cab to take him to the Odéon, and the driver admonishing
him: 'Not so loud, mister, the 'oss might hear.' In a satirical skit, one
comedian declared that the Odéon was well worth a visit and –
don't forget – it's perfectly possible to get there and back in a day:
what's more, added his sidekick, you don't need a passport. But

Théophile Gautier, though he joined in the chorus with jests of his own,[12] also pointed out in more serious vein that 'the Odéon is an indispensable theatre; young poets, pioneers daring but hitherto unknown, everyone with vigour and ambition has need of this kind of trial arena in which to chance their hand at eccentric works, audacious novelties which would make the prudent senior theatre, the Comédie-Française, recoil in horror, reserved as it is in general for writers of proven reputation'.[13]

It is true that the Odéon was always readier to take risks than the Comédie-Française, which tended to fight shy of new developments in the drama unless put under the greatest pressure. Talma, who knew something of Shakespeare and the Elizabethans, having spent his youth in London where he had mixed in dramatic circles, was down to the end of his life always seeking some vital alternative to the lifeless monotony of current neoclassical tragedy; but even Talma could not persuade his colleagues to stray very far from the beaten track. 'When they decide to accept a new play,' observed a contemporary German visitor, 'there are always two unpleasant consequences involved: first, it has to be got by heart and rehearsed, and secondly, the author has to be paid royalties; so at least it is necessary that all the parts be good ones, and that there should be as little expenditure on scenery as possible.'[14] The result was that especially after Talma's death in 1826, people looked elsewhere for interesting new plays and stopped coming to the Théâtre-Français. The diary kept by the actor Joanny over the years 1827–8 is a revelation in this respect: time and again he deplores the thin audiences – for Guiraud's tragedy *Virginie* in April–May 1827, for Ancelot's adaptation of Schiller's *Fiesco* in September ('truth to tell', he writes, 'there wasn't a soul in the theatre, the pit was silent'), for Lucien Arnault's *Le Dernier Jour de Tibère* the following February ('How is it that so fine a work ... attracts so small an audience? What does the public want these days? It makes you despair'). What they wanted was precisely what the Comédie-Française could never give them. 'People go in droves to the Gaîté and the Porte-Saint-Martin, they submit to being crushed and suffocated to see *Le Bourreau* [The Executioner] at the Gaîté and *Faust* at the Porte-Saint-Martin.'[15] The *Faust* in question was Nodier's adaptation of Goethe's drama, with Marie Dorval in the part of Gretchen, a play that paid scant attention to Aristotle's venerable rules regarding the unities of time and place, so meticulously observed in every neoclassical tragedy.

Predictably, as at any time during the past forty or fifty years, the Comédie-Française and those responsible for its well-being saw the solution to their difficulties in a restriction of the activities of the commercial playhouses. A petition submitted to Charles X on 20 January 1826, signed by the Minister of Fine Arts, Vicomte Sosthène de La Rochefoucauld, trotted out all the old arguments; it was occasioned by rumours of the licence shortly to be granted to Bérard authorizing him to open a new theatre, the Nouveautés.[16]

The existence of the secondary theatres, more particularly those specializing in the vaudeville, is depriving the dramatic institutions entrusted with the priceless custody of our literary masterpieces, of the collaboration of the new generation of dramatists and of the services of actors, tempted away by the hope of easier and more lucrative successes ... In the interests of arts and letters, Sire, in the interests of the royal theatres and of the funds of the civil list, called on every year to make good the enormous deficits of these establishments, I beg Your Majesty to refuse to sanction the opening of a new theatre, the existence of which can only be disastrous for art and impose new charges on the privy purse of the King.

But the petition was rejected. Charles X was not, especially at this point, prepared to give a sympathetic hearing to the protests of cultural reactionaries, even when combined with specious economic arguments.

It was not, however, the vaudeville but a unique blend of melodrama with a heady draught of swashbuckling romanticism that was destined, shortly afterwards, to break the stranglehold of the five-act verse tragedy on the stage of the Comédie-Française and coax back, for a brief period, the enthusiastic audiences of former times. This happened in February 1829, when Alexandre Dumas's first major play, *Henri III et sa cour*, a historical prose drama full of tension and excitement and relying on action rather than tirades for its effects, was put on at the Théâtre-Français. Joanny's brief comments, night by night, testify to the wind of change that seemed to be blowing away the stagnant vapours of neoclassicism: the fact that he seems solely concerned with the play as a money-spinner is understandable when one remembers the short commons on which he and his companions had had to subsist for the previous three years. After the first performance, he noted: 'we have at last obtained a success which will be, I believe, lucrative'. On 12, 14 and 17 February he was delighted to find that the success was turning into a triumph, with full houses and soaring box-office receipts. On 19 February he wrote delightedly: 'It is one of those successes such as are rarely encountered. I doubt whether anything like it has been seen since *The Marriage of Figaro* and *The Sicilian Vespers*.'[17]

One windfall, however, could not set to rights a situation that had been steadily worsening for years, and for all the runaway success of *Henri III*, the Comédie-Française was still pulling in less money than its rivals in the commercial sector. Comparative figures for October and November 1829[18] show that three of the so-called 'secondary theatres', the Vaudeville, the Variétés and the Gymnase, although they charged less for admission, were all making much larger profits than the Théâtre-Français. Clearly, another product of the new-fangled 'romantic school' would be a godsend; it duly arrived the following year, when Hugo's hotly contested verse drama, *Hernani*, was given its first performance on 25 February 1830, a little more than a twelvemonth after Dumas's pathfinding *Henri III*. Once more, comparative figures demonstrate the extent to which audiences of the time had temporarily lost all interest in the classics and were only prepared to patronize the Théâtre-Français when it put on something entirely different. Even though many spectators came only to ridicule Hugo's play, still they came, they paid for their boxes, and with the shaky state of the society's finances this was what mattered above all. The first performance of *Hernani* netted over 5,000 francs, whereas on the previous evening *Phèdre* had yielded less than a tenth of that sum. Even at the tail end of its first, stormy run, on 21 November 1830, *Hernani* was still bringing in handsome receipts (1,476 fr. 45), while the following day, when the company reverted to Racine's *Andromaque*, takings fell to 405 fr. 90.[19]

It was, however, too good to last. Having enjoyed their hour of triumph, neither Dumas nor Hugo wanted to repeat the experiment of having further plays put on at a theatre where the actors were obviously – with a few exceptions, Joanny among them – so little in sympathy with romantic drama. Their next plays, Dumas's *Antony* and Hugo's *Marion de Lorme*, were both to be seen at the Porte-Saint-Martin, where the company could offer as fine a theatre and actors far more suited to the parts they had written; Dumas had indeed at first offered *Antony* to the Comédie-Française but, losing patience with the objections made during rehearsals to scenes the actors wanted altering, had withdrawn it in a huff. For the next two or three years, the Porte-Saint-Martin became the most popular theatre in Paris.

Police in great numbers could barely control the crowds that threatened to bear everything before them. It was only with the utmost difficulty that order was established. Queues, winding hither and thither for hundreds of metres, were organized as best they could be, and people waited there for hours in feverish impatience until the ticket offices opened – and then as often as not closed again shortly afterwards when the house was declared full. The disappointed spectators wandered off, only to return to the charge the following day.[20]

As for the Théâtre-Français, it might as well have closed down for all the interest its repertoire aroused. Morally as well as financially, the years 1831–3 represent the nadir of its fortunes in the nineteenth century. The most popular works of Molière and Marivaux, *Tartuffe* and *Le Legs* (The Legacy), superbly performed, were watched one evening by a mere handful of superannuated connoisseurs nodding in the galleries; the cashier reported afterwards that the total takings amounted to 68 francs and a few centimes, about £3 in the currency of the time. More recent plays, however successful they had been when first seen a few years back, did very little better: a double bill of Delavigne's *L'Ecole des vieillards* (School for Dotards) (1823) and Scribe's *Valérie* (1822) scraped together a meagre 226 francs. The drop in earnings was not due merely to the change in public taste which made the traditional fare seem so insipid. Consequent on the disappearance of the old dynasty, the Comédie-Française had at a stroke lost not only the 48,000 francs from the five boxes at the theatre subscribed to by the previous government, but in addition the large sum, amounting to something like 120,000 francs annually, which they had been able to count on from bookings made by the wealthy aristocratic families who had taken up residence nearby during the Restoration. After the July revolution these families had to a great extent forsaken the capital and were biding their time in their country estates; they constituted the so-called 'internal emigration', hoping for some political coup that would enable them to welcome back 'Henry V', Charles X's grandson, as the rightful heir to the throne. Moreover, the virtual certainty, which had previously sustained the *sociétaires*, that in the event of impending bankruptcy the monarchy would in the last resort come to their rescue, no longer existed; unlike the two previous kings, Louis-Philippe had no more than an adolescent's memory of the Comédie-Française as it had been before the 1789 Revolution and could not be expected to lend it his support for the sake of old times.

Samson later recalled this painful crisis in a significant passage of his memoirs. 'The new men in charge of the ministry,[21] violently prejudiced against the ancient administrative forms of our theatre, would have liked our [self-governing] society to be suppressed and replaced by an independent director, acting at his own risk.'[22] That this view was held in very high places indeed is suggested by the terms of a letter written by Perrier, a *sociétaire* of the Comédie-Française who had won his spurs at Rouen, to Morel, a retired director of the Théâtre des Arts in that town. Perrier explained that he had been granted an audience of the new King, whose words he claims to report verbatim: 'You have still some talented actors among you, and occasionally you work well together; but as a society, your system is absurd, it is out of touch with modern requirements. Your rules and regulations are worthless. You need a director.' Perrier, implying in his letter that the King's words had been reported back to the Comédie-Française and weighed in committee, went on to offer Morel, on behalf of the entire society, the position of director. 'I feel', he concluded, 'that if you were to consent to take up the reins of government, you would be in a better position than anyone else, as absolute master, morally speaking, of our administration, to give the Théâtre-Français a more fitting public image, and so facilitate the negotiations which will have to be conducted to fix our future destiny.'[23]

Morel, however, was not tempted to put his head into this hornet's nest, and the Comédie-Française continued to wallow rudderless through uncharted and dangerous seas. There was a time when it appeared to everyone to be breaking up under the strain. The best-paid *sociétaires* were drawing no more than 5,000 francs a year; some had to content themselves with a clerk's salary, 1,500 francs.[24] For these rates of pay it was hardly worth continuing. Michelot, doyen of the society, retired on 1 April 1831; Samson, who had a family to support, accepted a lucrative offer from the Palais-Royal in defiance of all the regulations; Mlle Mars, on the pretext of poor health, sent in her resignation, and when the committee refused to accept it, sought to obtain legally the dissolution of the society. She was finally allowed to retire, only to return by the back door, so to speak, and accept the position of *pensionnaire* at a basic salary of 30,000 francs, which was doubled by various additional provisions. The Comédie was constrained to make these sacrifices only because it calculated that it would lose more by letting her go.

Although turned 50, she had kept her youthful figure and was still a great draw in her major roles as Elvire in *Tartuffe* and Célimène in *Le Misanthrope*. Mrs Trollope, who saw her on the stage a year or two later, was totally enthralled. 'I would willingly consent to be dead for a few hours', she declared,

if I could meanwhile bring to life Molière and let him see Mars play one of his best-loved characters. How delicious would be his pleasure in beholding the creature of his own fancy thus exquisitely alive before him; and of marking, moreover, the thrill that makes itself heard along the closely packed rows of the *parterre* when his wit, conveyed by this charming conductor, runs round the house like the touch of electricity![25]

Owing to bunched retirements several other well-known faces disappeared at this time, and the clamour in favour of dissolving the society and selling off the Théâtre-Français to the highest bidder became even louder. This drastic solution, amounting to what would now be called the privatization of the national theatre, was, however, provisionally relegated to the back burner and it was agreed to petition the minister to relieve the *comité d'administration* of its duties and replace it by a manager (*directeur-gérant*) with similar responsibilities. A letter in this sense was signed by all the *sociétaires* in June 1833, and the name of Armand Jouslin de la Salle was suggested as the first to hold this office. In October it became known that Adolphe Thiers, one of the new politicians who had come to the fore during the July revolution, had secured a sizeable increase in the subvention and in addition had spruced up the dingy auditorium; a new mood of optimism was abroad. By May 1834 even the financial situation was beginning to look capable of resolution. But already new difficulties were emerging. Jouslin de la Salle, appointed by the minister but nominated by the *sociétaires*, was in an invidious position: was he, or was he not, a director with absolute authority, like those who ran despotically the highly successful theatres in the commercial sector? Did he have the right to decide which plays from the stock repertory should be revived? Could he cast them as he wished or were the senior actors and actresses to choose the parts in which they were to appear, as in the past? Was he within his rights in importing someone from outside, as he did when Vigny asked that Marie Dorval should be given the part of Kitty in his play *Chatterton* (first produced in February 1835), without securing first the consent of the society as a whole? All such questions provoked endless friction, and were usually settled as the actors wished; Jouslin de la Salle had been made responsible, but he was denied any right to discipline the actors and consequently lacked any real authority over them. Behind the scenes, disputes and quarrels continued as before, acrimonious and interminable.

In the end he was forced to resign. He was replaced by the long-serving cashier of the theatre, Védel, who himself resigned in 1840, and for the next few years the government contented itself with having the affairs of the Comédie-Française supervised by the royal commissioner (François Buloz) who had no power to interfere directly in its administration. At the end of 1846 Got commented dolefully:

For two years now, no outstanding success, and few on the horizon, all playwrights of any distinction having deserted us – the theatre understaffed or staffed inadequately, and in spite of a few actors of real talent, only one – Rachel – capable of filling the house. Administration slack, a mood of despondency, the entire press hostile, the public lethargic. These are the evils besetting our ancient corporation which have finally forced Duchâtel's rather philistine ministry to nominate a commission of inquiry to advise on energetic remedies.[26]

This royal commission duly met early the following year and as a result of the report it submitted, an ordinance was issued on 29 August 1847[27] which effectively abolished one of the main planks of the Moscow Decree, handing over to an administrator the powers of control and direction that had, ever since the society was founded, been vested in the *comité d'administration* of the Comédie-Française. The administrator would in future be a government appointee: the *sociétaires* were stripped of the right to nominate him when the post fell vacant, or to dismiss him when they were displeased with his administration as they had dismissed Jouslin de la Salle.

They were, however, granted a surcease when revolution broke out in February 1848, sweeping away the July Monarchy and placing a question-mark against all decrees and ordinances it had initiated. The provisional government of the Second Republic had more pressing matters to attend to than the reorganization of the Comédie-Française, which was left to blunder along for a few more months. But once the new presidential regime had been installed, swift action was taken. By a decree promulgated on 15 November 1849, the company was placed under the control of a *commissaire-administrateur*; a further decree, defining the powers and duties of this new official, appeared on 27 April 1850.[28] Though the *comité d'admi-*

nistration was allowed to continue in existence, effectively the government's administrator was empowered to take what decisions he chose, which were merely rubber-stamped by the committee; it was he who decided on the admission of new members to the society, on the promotion of those already admitted as *pensionnaires*, on the casting of new plays – in fact, there was little difference henceforth between his powers and those of the director of any other theatre at the time.

The *sociétaires* made one feeble attempt to prevent the first holder of this post, Arsène Houssaye, from entering on his duties. He was served with a writ contesting his rights on his arrival at the Théâtre-Français, but when an application was made to obtain an injunction through the courts, the judges declared themselves incompetent to interfere with a government order. But before this happened, Houssaye had a trying time in spite of his aplomb. He found the director's office at the theatre already occupied – by Edmond Seveste, whom the society had nominated as their administrator in December 1848 – and only got rid of him by threatening to have him ejected by armed force. He was threatened in his turn by a mass walk-out by the senior actors, starting with Provost who announced he had been offered a salary of 25,000 francs by the management of the Palais-Royal. Houssaye riposted by telling them they were free to leave if they wished: he could count on Rachel, who had been delighted to hear of his appointment and may have had some hand in engineering it, and on the *pensionnaires*, talented actors such as Got, Monrose, Delaunay, who had been waiting far too long for their promotion to the *sociétariat*; and he even spoke of recruiting players from outside the Comédie-Française, such as Frédérick Lemaître, Bocage, Rouvière, Mélingue. This was a bluff: Houssaye knew very well that he could never prise such men from their well-paid jobs, but the *sociétaires* were too flustered to call his bluff and in the end gave in.

Arsène Houssaye continued to occupy the director's chair down to 1856, and his successors, Empis, Edouard Thierry, Emile Perrin and Jules Claretie, reigned undisturbed thereafter down to 1913. Appointed invariably by the government and paid their princely salaries out of state funds, they stayed by and large on the best of terms with the rulers of the country both under the Second Empire and the Third Republic. Brander Matthews, writing in 1880, described the Comédie-Française as forming 'a commonwealth – an association of actors governing itself, with a Lord Protector, as the manager may be called, appointed by the national authorities'.[29] In reality, the Comédie-Française was no more self-governing than England had been under the Protectorate of the Cromwells. Francisque Sarcey, who called the administrator 'a kind of constitutional monarch', was nearer the truth; and he was not far wrong either in arguing that it depended on the personal qualities of the administrator how wide his powers were: 'when he is strong-minded, he acts more or less as he wishes, provided he conforms to certain honoured traditions rendered respectable by their antiquity, and provided above all that he is justified by success when he ventures on some innovation'.[30] There were fortunately very few occasions, over those sixty years, when any of the innovations these five men introduced were not crowned by success.

CHAPTER 13

The theatre in crisis: competition from the 'café-concert'

In 1889, looking back nostalgically at what appeared to him the golden age of the July Monarchy, the theatre critic Jean-Jacques Weiss painted a glowing picture of that distant age when, whatever the quality of the theatrical entertainment on offer in Paris, there could be no argument about its quantity. Apart from the five state-supported theatres, 'eight dramatic blast-furnaces were constantly alight and kept stoked up under King Louis-Philippe': the Porte-Saint-Martin, the Ambigu and the Gaîté, specializing in melodrama; the Gymnase, the Vaudeville and the Palais-Royal whose repertoire stretched from vaudeville to farce and appealed primarily to the lower middle classes; the Funambules, where Deburau reigned supreme in the pantomime; and last and least, the tiny Petit-Lazari, favoured resort of the prentice boys, a fleapit of the basest sort but always well attended. 'None of these stood idle for a single day ... It was a furious seething, the pot boiling over with plays of every description, comic, dramatic, farcical, lugubrious, nonsensical, realistic, warlike, pacific, familiar, epic, the effect of which was still felt during the succeeding period even though it was more sterile, the fizz having gone out of it.'[1] An evening at the theatre commonly lasted from five in the afternoon to ten or eleven at night, each programme including three or four different plays all of which had the shortest of runs; the fifteen theatres open in Paris, not including the suburban houses, offered in 1832 no fewer than 257 new plays. Plunkett, who gives these statistics,[2] adds that, as one might expect, most of them were worthless; but at least they demonstrated the furious activity among playwrights and the hardworking actors who were obliged to commit all these ephemera to memory.

With the advent of the Second Empire, in spite of the declining effervescence that Weiss spoke of, a count shows that there was very little diminution in activity: in 1862 the busy dramatists turned out 258 new plays, in 1865 and 1867, 262, in 1869, 284. However, a better indication of the growing prosperity of the theatre industry during the Second Empire is provided by the annual gross receipts of the Paris theatres over this period which can be calculated from the published figures of the 10 per cent entertainment tax. These show that over the fifteen-year period from 1850 to 1864 a rapid expansion took place, gross receipts almost doubling from 8,206,818 francs to 16,023,665 francs. But it took another twenty-five years for them to double again, to 32,138,998 francs; this, however, was the figure for 1889, a World Exhibition year, when receipts were abnormally high on account of the great influx of visitors to Paris. Christophe Charle, who has reproduced these statistics from an article in *L'Economiste français* of 23 March 1901, characterizes the process as 'a phase of strong growth during the Second Empire which lasted down to the early 1880s: the highest figure for box-office receipts is recorded in 1883 ... After 1883 there begins a second phase of decreasing rate of expansion until 1892, then of levelling off until 1900.'[3] This flattening of the curve is what was known, at the time, as the 'crisis in the theatres' though, as Charle adds, it might have been better described as a fairly lengthy depression, coinciding with, though not entirely attributable to, the slump of the 1890s which in France appears to have been exacerbated by the crisis of confidence resulting from the collapse of the Panama Canal Company in 1892. In a pamphlet entitled *La Crise théâtrale*, published in 1895, Jean Dubois argued that

the theatre is inevitably affected by the commercial and industrial crisis which for several years has been paralysing business activity. Tradesmen, faced with declining profits, are reducing year by year that part of their personal budget set aside for unnecessary expenditure, and instead of visiting the theatre once or twice a week as they used to, they scarcely go once a month; what began as a measure of economy soon turns into indifference and bit by bit the habit of theatre-going is lost.[4]

Dubois adds – though without giving any corroborative evidence – that it is particularly small businessmen, shopkeepers and their families, whose absence from the theatres is felt in this way.

There were, it was suspected, other contributory factors. The old argument, first heard under the Directory, that too many theatres were in direct competition with one another, was trotted out anew. 'The Porte-Saint-Martin duplicates what is being done at the

Ambigu', wrote Antoine. 'When one of these houses prospers, the other goes into a decline.'[5] Sardou wanted to go back to 1807, when the problem was solved by state intervention. 'There were far too many theatres about ... For myself, I can only see one remedy, a radical one, that which the First Consul tried: with a stroke of the pen he suppressed, I believe, eighteen theatres. The public immediatcly flocked to those that remained.'[6] (Sardou, of course, could be reasonably confident that however few theatres were left after the decimation he proposed, any one of them would be glad to put on his next play.) In fact, the economic crisis had already, by 1889, wiped out twenty of the forty-nine theatres struggling for survival in 1885.[7] Others put the blame on the inflated expectations of actors and actresses, which, together with the more elaborate stage sets which were now commonplace, were inevitably reflected in higher admission charges; these had risen to the point when an evening at the theatre could not be contemplated by couples on small salaries, for to the cost of a couple of stalls had to be added the tip to the usherette, the price of a programme, the charge for hiring opera-glasses, buying drinks in the interval and paying for a modest supper afterwards, not to mention the cab fare to and from the theatre.

And then there were the newer sources of amusement which competed directly with the theatres for the spare cash of their former clientèle. Bicycling had become all the rage; suitable for both sexes, it was healthy exercise and, once the machine had been purchased, cost virtually nothing. Horse-racing, a spectator sport since the First Empire, had come to absorb a larger proportion of disposable personal income with the growth of betting and the inauguration in 1891 of the Pari-Mutuel, the French equivalent of the 'tote'. But neither of these amusements posed the same threat to the prosperity of the theatres as did the *café-concert*, that peculiarly French institution which had been going from strength to strength for a generation at least. In 1894 there were as many *cafés-concerts* in Paris as there were theatres; in 1900 one of the larger ones, the Olympia, netted 2 million francs, more than the Comédie-Française in the same year. The vogue owed nothing, or very little, to the relative quality of the entertainment found in these institutions; what counted was that it was markedly cheaper, to a degree where the theatres could never hope to compete. Our imaginary couple, who found that an evening at the theatre ran away with 30 francs at the very least, were able to pass the time almost as agreeably at a *café-concert* for 6 francs, including the obligatory *bock* or *mazagran* (beer or glass of coffee)

Cafés at which musical entertainment was provided for customers had existed in Paris for well over a century. The *Almanach forain*, in 1773, made mention of several establishments called 'musicas', defined as 'boulevard cafés where music is provided'.[8] Mayeur de Saint-Paul, writing a little later, names a number of cafés on the Boulevard du Temple where the drinkers could sit and listen to music of a 'detestable' quality, played as accompaniment to 'yelping vocalists of both sexes singing out of tune and bruising your eardrums with their cacophony; that is what attracts the riff-raff', he adds, 'and holds them in thrall in these dens where they stupefy themselves with punch and spirituous liquors'.[9] Mayeur, however, affected a marked disdain for all boulevard establishments; a rather less derogatory account is given by Métra, who refers to the cafés as possessing, each of them, 'quite good orchestras accompanying young girls, the indispensable ornament of our public places, who sing solos', though they were occasionally the cause of rivalry between their hot-blooded suitors which could lead to outbreaks of violence: Métra goes on to report a stand-up fight, with artisans pitted against soldiers, which resulted in four deaths besides considerable bloodshed.[10]

A German traveller to France at the start of the Revolution offered his countrymen a somewhat daunting description of what the visitor might expect to encounter in a *café-concert* of this period.

Imagine a long hall, at one end of which is installed a regular orchestra for vocal and instrumental music. Imagine fifty little tables with marble tops, surrounded by chairs without arms on which sit old and young, fat and thin side by side, laughing, weeping, quarrelling and flirting; imagine the strange howling, whining, joking and chattering of two hundred customers of all ages, and then in the midst of it let military drums thunder, trumpets blare, ill-tuned fiddles croak, flutes squeak and double-basses grunt, while in between bark or mew the singers; let this whole chaotic concert, the bellowing, the shrieking and the thundering, reverberate from the low ceiling of the room and burst on you in a roar as you enter: in this way you have a graphic, audible description of this peculiar hall and you will rest content with perusing it. That is a *café à concert*.[11]

The most celebrated, and possibly the most respectable of these establishments was the Café Yon or Café Young as Mayeur calls it.

Founded shortly before the Revolution, it was the first to add to its orchestra a proper stage, diminutive but equipped with wings and a back-cloth, 'in which are performed complete comic operas which cost no more to see than what one pays for one's drink. They show a few really pretty pieces, with actors not altogether devoid of talent, some of whom have performed successfully in the provinces.'[12] Others of note were the Café Goddet, frequented it was said by people of the best society, and the Café des Aveugles in the Palais-Royal, famed under the Directory for its star singer Rosalba who, 'when she made her rounds caused the silver pieces – even though specie was rare at the time – to rain into her begging bowl';[13] for artistes were not paid at this period by the café proprietor but had to rely on the generosity of the customers.

Gradually, it seemed, the *café-concert* was shedding the scruffy reputation it had when seen by Mayeur de Saint-Paul and Friedrich Schulz in the 1780s. But its development was abruptly cut short by an *arrêté* dated 12 November 1807 which forbade cafés to engage in musical or dramatic entertainment; this was part of Napoleon's drive to enhance standards in the theatres and to dragoon the Parisians into them. *Cafés-concerts* reappeared after his abdication and were, assures one memoir-writer, 'very much *à la mode* in 1816. If a stage was lacking, the artiste stood on a table and while he or she charmed the company, the ladies of the troupe walked round making a collection.'[14] Very occasionally a *café-concert* would succeed in wresting from the authorities a licence to transform itself into a theatre. One curious instance of an establishment which had started existence as a playhouse, was ordered to close by imperial decree, reopened as a café and, after the collapse of the Empire, was allowed once more to convert itself into a theatre with a box-office, is afforded by the history of the former Théâtre sans Prétention, one of the many axed in 1807. When it started up business again around 1809 it called itself the Café d'Apollon: tables were set up in the pit and lower gallery, while the stage remained unaltered and was used in a small way – the police having evidently been squared – for performances of a dramatic nature. 'For the price of a bottle of beer and a small glass of cassis', wrote Brazier, 'you could sit and listen to an arietta. The management even put on short scenes, harlequin-pantomimes involving three actors only.'[15] The Café d'Apollon was acquired at some point by Marguerite Lelanne, the celebrated acrobat better known under her married name, Madame Saqui: her most famous exploit was to have a rope attached at one end to the back of the stage and at the other to the topmost gallery, along which she would walk above the heads of the drinkers, trundling a child in a wheelbarrow in front of her, after which she would retrace her steps, walking backwards. In 1816 she obtained a licence under her husband's name to convert the café into a regular theatre charging for admission; the licence permitted her to put on melodramas as well as acrobatic shows. The Théâtre Saqui, as the Café d'Apollon was henceforth called, lasted till 1833 when financial difficulties forced the resourceful lady to dispose of it.

Successive administrations under the Restoration did their best to discourage the spread of *cafés-concerts*: they may have been tolerated here and there, but only one is well documented – the Café Montansier, formerly the Théâtre des Variétés-Palais-Royal,[16] and transformed after 1807 into an ordinary coffee-house known as the Café de la Paix. This was closed down by the police in 1816 because of a reputation for rowdiness belying its name. However, in time the authorities relented and 'permitted it to reopen as a *café-spectacle*, authorizing exceptionally the performance of short pieces limited to two characters and subject to certain restrictive conditions. People entering this public place paid by ordering their refreshments and for several years it proved highly popular, frequented however not precisely by the cream of society.'[17] In 1831 the Café Montansier was granted a licence to open as a regular playhouse and, under the name of the Théâtre du Palais-Royal, became one of the more popular Parisian places of entertainment, kept supplied later in the century by such well-known writers of comedy and farce as Eugène Labiche, Gondinet, Ludovic Halévy and Théodore Barrière.

The strict application of the licensing laws for theatres is probably responsible for the restrictions placed on *cafés-concerts* in the first half of the century: it would have been illogical to restrict the number of theatres permitted in the capital if no limits were set to the proliferation of minor establishments in which dramatic performances, however amateurish, were to be seen. Under the July Monarchy only one *café-spectacle* is referred to by contemporary writers on the stage; this was situated on the Boulevard Bonne-Nouvelle, and was managed by a certain Captain Legras, whose troupe was 'composed of actors who could find no better engagement elsewhere, his orchestra, of two blind men, and his repertoire, of pieces refused by every other theatre and purchased by him at the rate of 10 francs apiece'.[18] Théodore de Banville remembers visiting it around 1841, and speaks well of the interior decoration and the forestage curtain of white satin. Legras seems to have been a somewhat simple-minded soul, however acute a man of business. Having been told by some straight-faced joker that during the Revolution the Théâtre de la Porte-Saint-Martin had attracted a huge audience to *La Chaste Suzanne* by getting the actress representing Susannah to take her bath – in the scene depicted by so many great artists over the centuries – completely naked on the stage, he conceived the idea of repeating the feat. Though the police constantly denied him permission, he never gave up hope, and so as not to be caught unprepared if and when nudity on the stage was eventually authorized, he recruited to his company all the most shapely young ladies he could find. This had the result of drawing to his *café-spectacle* a small group of connoisseurs of feminine beauty, but the majority of his clients, says Banville, 'were none too appreciative of a diet of uninteresting sketches put on by actresses who resembled goddesses but were innocent of the first elements of their profession'.[19]

The *café-spectacle* of the Restoration and July Monarchy, which resembled a theatre in most respects except that there were no admission charges, appears to have given way to the *café-chantant* around the middle of the century, with the foundation of the Estaminet Lyrique shortly after the February revolution. This was a sort of halfway-house between a club and a theatre, wrote Audebrand, and appears to have been not dissimilar from the 'Temple of the Muses' described in Benjamin Disraeli's *Sybil* (book 1, chapter 10), though the setting for the novel is a Yorkshire mill-town at a slightly earlier date, around the time of the Chartist agitation of 1839.

Imagine an enormous hall. Every evening you could see, furiously puffing away, some two or three hundred tobacco pipes, while at one end, hidden behind the clouds of fragrant smoke, six or seven singers of either sex, devotees of the drawing-room ballad – still, in those unsophisticated days, greatly in demand – were trying to make themselves heard to the accompaniment of a tinkling piano. Nobody paid them much attention; the noise of people talking drowned their singing; how could they find the strength to battle against the clatter of coffee cups and spoons? But around half past nine, when the hall was crammed to capacity and the atmosphere was at its thickest, if one's eyesight was good enough it was possible to discern a strange figure making its appearance. At the sight of this newcomer, a sudden silence fell; the busiest pipes went out; the waiter, like Sisyphus forgetting to push his rock uphill, stood motionless, holding his tray of drinks aloft in his hand. The matron presiding at the counter uttered an injunction and those on their way back to their seats stood stock still. 'Here is Darcier, gentlemen!'[20]

Darcier, by his real name Joseph Lemaire, had started taking singing lessons at the age of 12, but had ignored his teacher's advice to interrupt his studies while his voice was breaking; he had then turned to acting and gone on tour in the provinces. Returning to Paris in 1848, he threw himself into the revolutionary turmoil and incidentally made the fortune of the Estaminet Lyrique, the proto-type of all the *cafés-concerts* of the latter half of the century. His career was as brief as his popularity was extraordinary; he disappeared from sight after the *coup d'état* of 1851, but is known to have survived until 1884. Darcier was the first of the *café-concert* idols; he was succeeded by Thérésa (Thérèse Valadon) who had begun life as an apprentice needlewoman and took Paris by storm in the 1860s, singing at the Eldorado and the Alcazar and in demand at every chic upper-class *soirée*; and by Paulus (Jean-Paul Hubens) with his hair flattened over his skull, his blue coat with gold buttons, his top hat and his cane, and a voice which, for all his meridional accent, was so clear that he attracted huge crowds along the Champs-Elysées who, though they could not see him, joined in the applause of the customers inside the café.

The *café-chantant* or *café-concert* – the latter term eventually pre-vailed – was a peculiarly Parisian institution; attempts to popularize it in the provinces never seem to have come to anything, though there was a strong tradition at the Café Vivaux in Marseilles, which opened in 1863.[21] The *café-concert* differed from the Anglo-American music hall or variety show in not taking place in a recognizable theatre, though the entertainment – songs, recitations, sometimes dancing of a sensational nature, juggling or acrobatics – was not unlike what awaited visitors to the Empire Theatre of Varieties, the Royal Holborn or the Tivoli. Brander Matthews described it as

a concert hall with a shallow stage at one end. At the rear of this stage, in a semi-circle, sits a row of fair vocalists in full evening toilet, arranged much like the negro minstrels of our native land when the trouble is about to begin. These are the stock company, and from time to time one of them advances to the footlights and sings a song, sentimental or humorous, or of that more wearying variety known as 'serio-comic'. The star singers do not sit on the platform, but emerge from the side screens when their turn comes, which is always towards the end of the evening ... The great peculiarity of these café-concerts is that the admission is free, but the spectator must give an order to one of the many waiters in attendance. You must either eat or drink for the good of the house. A cup of coffee or chocolate, an ice-cream, or a glass of beer – that will suffice. Of course the prices are higher than at an establishment where there is no music. You 'consume' something, for as the sign reads: 'the consumption is obligatory'.[22]

This was one reason why the management postponed till as late in the evening as they dared the eagerly awaited appearance of the star entertainer. Customers arriving early – and there were plenty of these, wanting to make sure of a seat – were constantly urged to drink up, and when their glasses were empty it was difficult to shrug off the waiter with his persistent inquiry: 'Monsieur renouvelle?'

Partly in consequence, no doubt, of these 'renewed potations', the *café-concert* tended to grow very noisy as the evening wore on: there was none of the religious hush one found in a theatre audience. The efforts of the singers and the funny men were acknowledged not just by shouts and clapping, but in addition by the deafening noise of 'canes hitting the tops of tables, the rattling of saucers and hundreds of coffee spoons hammering the glasses. Incessant explosions, in short, presided over by the waiter, his apron tied tightly round his middle, as in a drawing in *Le Charivari* [the French equivalent of *Punch*], his little tray with its liqueurs and the blue soda-water siphon held high above his head.'[23] In 1865 the brothers Goncourt visited the Eldorado, one of the more palatial of the new *cafés-concerts*, and consigned to their journal an interestingly impressionistic description of the place, seen from above. They found themselves, they wrote, in a

large circular hall with two tiers of boxes, gilded and painted to resemble marble; dazzlingly lit by chandeliers, with a café in the middle, the men's black hats, working-class women in their bonnets, soldiers, schoolboys with peaked caps; a few hats worn by tarts accompanying shopmen, a few pink ribbons adorning the women in the boxes; the visible breath of all this crowd, a dusty cloud of tobacco smoke. At the back of the hall, a stage with footlights; on it, a comic in evening dress. He sang disjointed fragments, interrupted by clucking, the cackling of poultry in a farmyard, and epileptic gesticulations – the St Vitus dance of an idiot. In the hall, delirious enthusiasm ...[24]

The two brothers, in the statistical introduction to their *Mystères des théâtres* of 1851, had reckoned that at that date there were thirteen *cafés-chantants* (as they were still called) in Paris alongside twenty theatres; but their numbers were swelled immensely in the course of the Second Empire, thanks in part to the destruction of the little theatres on the Boulevard du Temple, whose former audiences sought their quota of amusement for preference in the cafés, but chiefly owing to the decree of 1864 which resulted in an immense expansion of the *café-concert* industry. It was reckoned that there were more than 60 of them in 1867, and around 150 by 1875.[25] By the 1880s they were beginning to attract the intellectual élite of Paris: after a dinner party with Banville on 8 January 1887 Edmond de Goncourt noted that Daudet was humming the latest hit song and that François Coppée confessed he doted on Paulus and preferred the *café-concert* to any other form of amusement. And by 1894, almost at the end of his life, Edmond admitted taking great pleasure himself in listening to the star singer at the Ambassadeurs, Yvette Guilbert, whose swan-like neck and tentacular arms ending in black gloves live for posterity in the posters of Toulouse-Lautrec. His one reservation was that the songs she sang were so paltry; he would have liked to hear her recite some of Baudelaire's verses . . .

In the 1880s, too, the sense of superiority that actors in theatrical companies still felt in relation to café artistes – sometimes compared to the disdain of cavalrymen for privates in the infantry – was beginning to be eroded. The traditional distinction had been badly undermined when, towards the end of the Second Empire, a former tragedy actress at the Comédie-Française, Mlle Cornélie, made an unexpected appearance at the Eldorado to declaim a celebrated passage from Racine's *Athalie*, where the infidel queen relates a fearsome and prophetic dream that had troubled her sleep the previous night: a doom-laden passage, which was not on the face of it likely to appeal to the light-hearted revellers crowding a *café-concert*. But this improbable recitation had been furiously applauded. However, journalists present on the occasion commented on the absurdity of the rule that required the actress to appear in evening dress instead of the traditional robe of a tragedy queen, and as a direct result of the incident, a new regulation drawn up in 1867 by Camille Doucet, head of the Fine Arts division of the ministry, authorized artistes at *cafés-concerts* to wear the stage costume hitherto reserved for performers at regular theatres. It was a first step towards a gradual merging of the two forms of entertainment, and thereafter it was not unheard of for a *café-concert* star to be engaged to sing a favourite piece at a theatre during an interval; *chansonniers* were as much in demand at private functions as were actors and actresses, and commanded similar fees to appear at dances and evening parties.[26]

Financially, too, the *cafés-concerts* represented big business for those who wrote for them, just as much as did the theatres. In 1851 the cafés had paid out in authors' royalties less than 15,000 francs; in 1891 this item accounted for the fabulous sum of 1,383,000 francs. Such disbursements narrowed the gap between the *cafés-concerts* and the theatres, but was also responsible in part for the steady increase in the prices they had to charge; henceforth, the *café-concert* could no longer be regarded as an inexpensive form of entertainment. A seat at the Eldorado, the so-called 'Comédie-Française of the *cafés-concerts*', which in the early 1880s cost 2 francs 50, including the price of a cherry brandy, had by 1902 climbed to 6 francs and by 1911 to 10 francs. The more successful of the *cafés-concerts*, like the Scala, had by this date effectively transformed themselves into theatres; and in this simple way, by moving 'up-market', had finally resolved the slightly bogus and in any case short-lived 'crisis of the theatres'.

CHAPTER 14

Dramatic censorship in the nineteenth century

With relatively brief intermissions, the system of preventive censorship as set up by Napoleon shortly after the *coup d'état* of 18 brumaire
(9 November 1799) lasted all through the nineteenth century. The
speed with which action was taken after the collapse of the Directory
is some indication of the authorities' sensitivity to the importance of
the stage as a possible focus of political dissent; less than a month
after the new regime had been installed, a letter was despatched to
all theatre managers informing them that the Ministry of Police
required them to suspend performances of any play 'which might
become a source of disaffection', and that in consequence all new
plays accepted for production and 'all dramatic works composed
since 14 July 1789 relative to the Revolution, of which it was desired
to stage revivals' should undergo examination or re-examination.[1]
These provisions were confirmed and given even wider extension in
a letter addressed by the three consuls to Lucien Bonaparte, then
Minister of the Interior, by which he was enjoined to circularize all
Paris theatre managers advising them that no new dramatic work
was to be staged without his permission. 'The head of the department of public instruction in your ministry is to be personally
responsible for anything which, in the plays produced, could be
construed as contrary to morality or to the principles of the social
pact.' Every provincial prefect was to be advised in a circular that
no play he had not personally authorized was to be shown at any
theatre within his zone of jurisdiction.[2]

The official whose unenviable job it was to peruse all plays, old
and new, proposed for performance in the capital was a certain Félix
Nogaret, a man of advanced years and nervous disposition who
scrutinized them with painful seriousness and was capable, so the
scoffers said, of tearing his hair if he could find nothing to strike out
or change in a manuscript submitted to him. He was replaced in

1804 by a board of four censors, directly answerable to Fouché, chief of police; these men remained in office for the rest of Napoleon's reign. The most notorious of the four was Joseph-Alphonse Esménard, whose earlier royalist persuasions did not stand in the way of his becoming an ardent Bonapartist after the *coup d'état*. He was rewarded first with the post of consul in Martinique and later given a situation on the all-powerful *Journal de l'Empire*, combining this with his duties at the censorship bureau. Having gained a certain reputation as a poet (he put to use his experiences of overseas travel during the emigration to compose a didactic poem, *La Navigation*, after the fashion of the period), he was entrusted with the ticklish task of 'correcting' the works of Corneille, Racine and Voltaire intended for revival. This involved excising whatever passages might lend themselves to awkward topical allusions; but, as Mme de Rémusat remarked in her memoirs, 'with all deference to the precautions taken by an overzealous police authority, the lines struck out, like the statues of Brutus and Cassius, were all the more noticeable by their absence'.[3] He occasionally felt obliged, as another observant lady reported, to substitute new material for the passages he had deleted. 'A performance of *Héraclius* [a late play by Corneille, dealing with an episode in the history of the Empire of the East], was curious to watch: a score of men in the pit had brought along copies of the play and were noting the passages suppressed and those intercalated. I mentioned it to Fouché one day. "You have to agree," he replied with that assurance of tone that would never admit a doubt, "that Esménard's lines are a lot better than Corneille's."'[4]

It is hardly surprising that in these conditions no dramatist of any distinction came to the fore during Napoleon's reign. The Emperor himself was always eager to read or have read to him any new tragedy that it was rumoured might prove a masterpiece, but his critical comments and suggestions were seldom well taken by the authors, who thereafter became marked men. A case in point was Népomucène Lemercier, regarded as an up-and-coming young man after the outstanding success of his *Agamemnon* in 1797. A second play, *Ophis* (first performed 24 December 1799), was intended as an act of homage to the modern conqueror of Egypt, who was present on the first night to applaud the work of the playwright he considered his friend at the time. Unfortunately *Ophis* did not enjoy the same success as *Agamemnon*, but Lemercier remained on terms of some intimacy with the First Consul and was made welcome at Malmaison, where he gave a reading of his next play, *Charlemagne*. This was in 1804, shortly before the Senate was due to proclaim Napoleon Emperor; having listened to the new work, he asked the author to intercalate a scene in which a deputation would arrive from Rome to offer Charlemagne the title of Emperor of the West. Lemercier, a convinced republican who disapproved strongly of Napoleon's autocratic ambitions, refused flatly to do any such thing; he was not prepared to allow his tragedy to be used as a vehicle for Napoleon's political programme, even though this would have undoubtedly ensured its success. *Charlemagne* was withdrawn and not seen at the Comédie-Française until the Restoration; and Lemercier compounded his fault by turning in his order of the Legion of Honour at the coronation. Thereafter the censorship refused all his plays, except for *Christophe Colomb* (1809) which was shouted down at the Odéon, nominally because it violated the sacrosanct unities, more probably thanks to the lungs of Fouché's henchmen posted in the pit. Realizing that he stood no chance of a fair hearing, Lemercier abandoned the attempt to soften the hostility of the imperial censorship. Seeing him at a meeting of members of the Institut in the Tuileries Palace, one day in January 1812, Napoleon sauntered up to him and asked him: 'Well, Lemercier, when are you going to give us a fine new tragedy?' Lemercier looked the Emperor straight in the eye and answered: 'Soon. I am waiting.' Victor Hugo, who related this anecdote in the course of a eulogy of Lemercier pronounced after the tragedian's death, characterized this laconic reply as both terrible and prophetic: 'spoken as it was at the beginning of 1812, it contained within itself Moscow, Waterloo and St Helena'.[5]

Another distinguished playwright who fell foul of Napoleon was François Raynouard, remembered today more for his pioneering work on Provençal language and literature than for the three plays he wrote under the Empire, the first of which, *Les Templiers*, was produced at the Théâtre-Français, while the second and third were not. *Les Templiers* was a historical drama turning on the destruction of the order of the Knights Templars in Paris in the fourteenth century; this event was presented by Raynouard as an arbitrary act by a covetous king (Philippe le Bel) in which the Templars played the part of innocent victims. Raynouard had not departed greatly from the historical record; but Napoleon, who had arranged to have the play read to him by Fontanes before he left for Milan to be crowned King of Italy, had misgivings about the tragedy, in particular about the odious role given to the French monarch and his counsellors. He was further disturbed by the news of the wild success the play was having in May and June 1805; after the first five performances, people were still fighting to get into the theatre, and there was talk of taking it on tour in the provinces. The Emperor, having returned to Paris on 11 July, ordered the Comédie-Française to put on a special performance for him at Saint-Cloud on 25 July. According to one not altogether trustworthy source,[6] he asked to see Raynouard subsequently at the Tuileries and made certain overtures to him, offering him in particular a seat on the Senate, to see whether he could attach the dramatist to his interests. He found, however, that Raynouard was without ambitions of this sort and, in confiding the gist of their conversation to Fontanes afterwards, Napoleon reported that Raynouard had indicated that he preferred to keep his literary independence. 'Yes, the independence necessary to foment opposition! Well, let him have his independence, but we will keep an eye on him. Let's see what he will write next.'

It turned out that Raynouard's next tragedy dealt with Charles I of England. Imagining that the great popular success of *Les Templiers*, acclaimed as the one dramatic masterpiece to have emerged during Napoleon's reign, gave him special privileges, he decided to bypass the censorship and sound out Fouché directly. The Minister of· Police consulted his master. 'Don't do anything,' answered Napoleon; 'send Raynouard to me.' When the playwright presented himself, Napoleon greeted him affably enough. 'Come, sir, you want to set all Paris by the ears? Your play is an absolute firebrand. Withdraw it; incendiary works have no place in my reign. I have been sent to damp down passions, not to let them flare up again.'[7] Raynouard tried once more. In 1810 he offered the Comédie-Française a new tragedy, *Les Etats de Blois*. The actors were delighted to accept it, and it was duly sent for approval to the censorship bureau. Napoleon was once more consulted, had the play privately performed at Saint-Cloud, but could find nothing overtly subversive in it; his one reservation was, as he is alleged to have said immediately afterwards: 'I am not such a simpleton as to permit Henry IV, a Bourbon, the founder of a dynasty, to preach peace for five acts before me, Napoleon, whose element is war.'[8] Fouché was ordered to suppress the play and to halt all attempts to have it published – though manuscript copies were later discovered to be circulating inside Paris, eagerly snapped up and passed from hand to hand by the royalist opposition.

Napoleon would no doubt have preferred it if his reign could have been illustrated, like Louis XIV's, by the emergence of dramatists of genius; but he chose to ignore the elementary truth that writers need to breathe the air of freedom, and never take kindly to men of authority meddling with their works. Above all, he was acutely aware of the dangers presented by a theatre audience which inevitably included a small element of disaffected spirits, chiefly royalists who regarded him as having usurped the throne and who would seize on any passage in a play that could be construed as a veiled attack on some aspect of his regime; and he looked to the machinery of dramatic censorship to ensure that no such opportunities were given them.

Although on his return from Elba Napoleon signed a decree (24 March 1815) abolishing the censorship of plays and printed matter, he retained power for too short a period for it to be possible to guess whether these measures would have had any permanent effect. The old system of requiring all new dramatic works to receive the prior approval of the censorship bureau before being shown in public was reinstated almost immediately by the new government and was not generally felt to be in conflict with article VIII of the Charter signed by Louis XVIII, which gave every French citizen the right to 'publish and cause to be printed his opinions, while conforming to the laws that limit the abuses of this freedom'. From the point of view of the dramatist, this did mean some slight improvement on the conditions under which he had operated during the Empire: if a play were banned, it could at least be legally printed and published. Realizing this, the censors concentrated on 'cleaning up' the text of new plays instead of prohibiting performances outright: an extreme sanction used against at most a score of plays during the Restoration period.[9] Those that incurred it were often historical dramas dealing with former kings of France, particularly those whose conduct reflected scant credit on the institution of monarchy; thus Népomucène Lemercier, decidedly the censorship's predestined victim both under the Empire and the Restoration, ran into trouble with a drama on the mad King Charles VI, due to have its first performance at the Odéon on 25 September 1820 and forbidden at the last moment by a decision of the State Council.[10] At the more popular places of entertainment, melodramas involving royal personages of the past, even those of foreign countries, were frowned on; as the censors commented at the time, 'the monarchy has already lost too much of its remote magic without playwrights stripping it of the remnants of its dignity'.[11] Even the slightest reference to historical events occurring between 1789 and 1815 were rigorously expunged; Napoleon was as though he had never existed, though, curiously, military pageants involving episodes from the wars of the Empire, such as *The Death of Kléber* or *The Siege of Saragossa*, were still permitted at the Cirque Olympique; the exception was presumably made with the idea of sustaining the patriotic fervour of the unthinking masses.

The censors were just as solicitous of the clergy as of the monarchy and the servants of the Crown. No minister of religion, not even the worthy village priest, was allowed a part in a comedy. Etienne de Jouy's *Julien dans les Gaules* ran into trouble because of the passages in which the apostate emperor inveighed against Christianity; and Antoine Arnault's *Les Vénitiens*, written in 1798 and revived by the Odéon in 1826, could not be shown until the author had agreed to forgo the representation on stage of a wedding mass in the fourth act. Curiously, the same scene had been objected to by the censorship at its first performance: a marriage ceremony performed by a Catholic priest in a chapel before an altar – intolerable! exclaimed the freethinkers of pre-Concordat days; what a profanation! cried the self-appointed defenders of religion in the reign of Charles X. Even a play in a foreign language needed to be carefully examined in case it should offend a Catholic audience. When a company of players from London gave a highly successful series of renderings of the English classics at the Odéon in 1827, certain of Shakespeare's audacities were felt to require deletion. Ophelia, in *Hamlet*, was not allowed to adjure her brother to eschew the example of 'some ungracious pastors' who practise not what they preach, since anyone in holy orders was *ipso facto* irreproachable; and the discussion between the two grave-diggers about class distinctions in the burial of suicides was likewise excised.[12]

Safeguarding, in this way, throne and altar, the censorship under the Restoration could be described broadly as political; censorship on the grounds of morality was hardly needed, since dramatists were well aware that certain subjects, adultery, for instance, would not be tolerated on the stage by any audience. All the censors were required to do was to watch for any improprieties of language or even faintly shady sexual innuendoes. In Carmouche's *Le Marchand d'amour* (The Love Merchant, 1823) they struck out the remark 'on the eve of one's wedding, one needs to avoid strenuous exercise', presumably for fear it might give rise to questions in the mind of any unmarried girls in the audience; and in another piece, in which a bride was depicted as something of a shrew the day preceding her wedding, but lively and cheerful the day after, the censor demanded that 'the alteration in the woman should be justified in a decent way', such as that beforehand she had not been given the opportunity 'to talk with her husband and get to know his character and tastes'.[13]

Towards the end of Charles X's reign, particularly under the liberal ministry of Martignac, a greater laxity crept into the functioning of the censorship. Plays and operas centring on popular heroes and national uprisings, such as Delavigne's *Marino Falieri* (1829) which so impressed Stendhal's Julien Sorel, and Auber's *La Muette de Portici*, more commonly known in this country as *Masaniello*, were allowed with some misgivings and shown with great success. Dramatic works dealing with events during the French Revolution were now permitted; other plays previously banned, like Jouy's *Julien dans les Gaules* and his *Intrigues de cour* (Court Intrigues) were produced at the Théâtre-Français in 1827 and 1828; while at the same theatre, a violent attack on political gerrymandering, La Ville de Mirmont's *Une journée d'élection* (Election Day), was allowed with only minor modifications. There remained only two subjects still considered strictly taboo: plays evoking the memory of the Napoleonic era, and plays portraying a former monarch. It was supposedly for introducing Louis XIII into *Marion de Lorme* that this verse drama of Hugo's was refused its visa in 1829. As for Napoleon, though the great man had died, his son survived him and the government remained alive to the possibility of a Bonapartist coup even yet; the censorship was accordingly under instructions to ensure that not the slightest reference should be made on the stage to his reign or his achievements. One line in a play put on at the Ambigu-Comique in 1829 was cut by the censor: an old sergeant, drilling an awkward squad, told them they would have had to smarten up if they had been parading before the Emperor ('l'ancien', as he called him; but everyone knew who that meant). The actor, however, remembered the line from rehearsals, and re-introduced it at the first performance. This daring act of defiance was hissed by some in the audience, applauded by others; the play disappeared from the repertoire for a few days and then reappeared, with due precautions taken against any repetition of the incendiary remark.

It was widely assumed at the time that the July revolution had delivered the theatres once and for all from the bondage of the censorship. As Dumas *père* later expressed it, the three days' fighting in July 1830, 'while overthrowing not a few other things, overthrew the censorship too without noticing the fact'.[14] This flippant remark did contain a grain of truth: article VII of the Charter of 7 August 1830 not only confirmed that censorship had no further legal existence in France, but went so far as to add that 'it could never be re-established'. But there was no specific mention of dramatic censorship in the Charter; in reality, its framers were probably thinking only of the freedom of the press, the suppression of which by one of Charles X's ordinances of 26 July 1830 had led directly to the revolution and to his enforced abdication. Thus, Dumas was not far wrong in implying that dramatic censorship had been abolished as it were in a fit of absence of mind; or, as a more recent writer has expressed it, the men who drew up the new Charter 'accorded the freedom of the spoken as well as of the written word, unconsciously and probably against their better judgement'.[15]

Certainly the system of preventive censorship as operated under the Restoration was provisionally suspended. Theatre managers were no longer obliged to submit the text of a new play to have its public performance authorized, and the immediate consequence was seen in two areas in particular which had, under Charles X, been strictly off limits: anti-clerical plays (particularly those attacking the Jesuits), and plays celebrating the career and exploits of Napoleon Bonaparte. Previously, even the gesture of an actor in a mime, taking a pinch of snuff in the way characteristic of the dead Emperor, was enough for him to be jailed for a month and heavily fined besides.[16] Now, there was hardly a theatre in which Napoleon was not impersonated by some actor or other, both on the stage and off it, for they strutted along the boulevard copying the Emperor's gait and mannerisms, stared at in awe by urchins far too young ever to have seen the great man in real life. For the Napoleonic legend had struck deep roots in the imagination particularly of the uneducated classes for whom the epic story, kept alive by Béranger's songs as well as in the memory of army veterans, had acquired the power to arouse the deepest emotions. Heine, who came to Paris in April 1831 and remained there for the rest of his life, was greatly struck by the response of working-class audiences to any reference to that time of derring-do and martial glory.

If, in the insignificant vaudevilles of the boulevard theatres, some scene from the imperial past is presented, or if the Emperor in person makes his appearance, then however bad the play, there is no want of wild applause; for the souls of the spectators join in, and they cheer their own feelings and memories. There are verses containing key words (the eagle, the sun of Austerlitz, the Grande Armée, the old guard) which smite the brain of a Frenchman like clubs, others that work on his lachrymal glands like onions ...[17]

It was one of this series of plays dealing with recent history which, as early as October 1831, first raised in an acute form the question of the censorship under the July Monarchy. Entitled *Le Procès d'un maréchal de France* (The Trial of a French Field-Marshal), it was announced as forthcoming at the Théâtre des Nouveautés which was at that time on its last legs; the manager, Langlois, was hoping for a hit – if not a *succès de scandale*, at least *de curiosité* – which might enable him to tide over his financial difficulties. The play concerned Marshal Ney, one of Napoleon's bravest commanders, who after his leader's abdication in 1814 had sworn allegiance to the new monarchy and was accordingly despatched with an army to halt the ex-Emperor's triumphant march up to Paris in 1815. Instead, Ney placed his forces at Napoleon's disposal, fought alongside him at Waterloo and was afterwards arrested for high treason and tried by the Chamber of Peers. He was executed by firing squad on 7 December 1815.

In 1831, some of the peers who had voted in favour of the death sentence on Ney were still alive and would have been seriously embarrassed if their actions on this occasion had been made the subject of public discussion; moreover, the play cast grave aspersions on the entire Chamber of Peers, which was an integral part of the legislative system introduced under Louis-Philippe, and in the uncertain temper of the times the authorities considered it too dangerous to allow the performance to go ahead. Accordingly, a police inspector visited Langlois on the morning before the opening night (22 November 1831) to notify him of the ban; not having received satisfactory assurances from the manager, the officer reappeared at five that evening and posted policemen at the doors of the theatre to stop any spectators entering. On the following day the same scene was repeated, and this time Langlois, bowing to the inevitable, agreed under protest to mount an alternative entertainment that evening. The public was admitted, the change of programme was announced from the stage, but noisy protests from the audience prevented the substitute plays (which included one entitled, by an unintentional irony, *Le Voyage de la liberté*) from being given a hearing, and the police entered the hall to evacuate the theatre at bayonet point. The two authors of the play, Fontan and Dupeuty, brought a suit against Langlois, who however successfully pleaded *force majeure*. Their intention had not been, in any case, to claim an indemnity from the director whom they recognized as blameless, but to give wider publicity to what they saw as an infringement of the liberties conferred by the Charter.

The authorities had cause to regret having had recourse to armed force to prevent *Le Procès d'un maréchal de France* being seen. They claimed to have been acting in accordance with an earlier law, predating the abolition of preventive censorship, which permitted the police to clear a theatre if a play gave rise to a disturbance of the peace.[18] But for this to happen it was necessary for at least one performance to take place; Fontan and Dupeuty had not had even that satisfaction. In 1832 Hugo's new verse drama, *Le Roi s'amuse* (The King's Diversions), was forbidden further performances after the first two, though it was generally admitted that the play had caused a good deal less disorder than had *Hernani* when produced under the Restoration; but it did include certain scabrous scenes and, more to the point, shed a poor light on the private life of an earlier King of France, François I. Hugo thereupon had the play printed, organized a press campaign and finally brought an action against the Comédie-Française for withdrawing the play without his consent. In fact, like the Nouveautés the year before, the Comédie-Française had only bowed to *force majeure* – the actors would have much preferred to continue with *Le Roi s'amuse* which was drawing large crowds. But Hugo could not sue a minister of the Crown: by the terms of a law which had been on the statute book since 24 August 1791, the courts were forbidden to hear any case involving the legality or otherwise of an administrative action. So Hugo lost his case, which had aroused intense public interest, and from this point on the authorities were able, in theory, to stop any play which for any reason displeased them, though only after it had been given at least one public performance.

This form of repressive censorship was far less to the liking of theatre managers than had been the preventive censorship to which they had grown used since the beginning of the century. To produce a new play might require expenditure on new scenery and invariably put the cast to the trouble of learning and rehearsing their parts; if the play risked being halted after the first couple of performances, the director was liable to financial loss as well as having to pacify a disgruntled cast. So the custom grew up, over the next few years, for a theatre director to 'consult' the minister over certain passages in a new play that he feared might be construed as dangerous. Often the difficulty was turned by eliminating the odd subversive remark; the director would raise no difficulty about this and in most cases he got the author, however grudgingly, to agree. Only rarely did a seditious play slip through, as when in 1832 the left-wing playwright Félix Pyat offered the Odéon a seemingly innocuous recapitulation of the circumstances leading to the succession of Claudius to the Roman Empire after the assassination of Caligula. This play was entitled *Une Révolution d'autrefois* (A Revolution of Former Times) and included a scene in which a member of the pretorian guard suggested Claudius should become the new emperor; he would be 'the best sort of emperor, an utter fool from head to foot; he will be the cream of emperors – big, fat and stupid'. These three epithets, *gros, gras et bête*, were taken by the audience, as Pyat probably had hoped, to be an allusion to the new King of France, and provoked roars and stamping of feet. Applause also greeted the contribution of another speaker in the debate: when Caligula was out of the way, he said, 'we should set up a new form of government: the old and well-tried republic. It's hardly worth killing Caligula to make room for Claudius.' Given the disappointment of so many republicans at the turn of events after the July Revolution, Pyat's intentions were all too plain – to make clear the parallelism between the raising to the purple of Claudius in AD 41 and the accession to the throne of Louis-Philippe in 1830. Harel, director of the Odéon at this time, insisted on certain cuts before the second performance; but the spectators, all agog for the celebrated *gros, gras et bête*, raised the roof when the words remained unspoken. This constituted 'civil disorder' within the meaning of the act, and Pyat's play was not allowed a third performance.

Occurrences such as these appear to have convinced Louis-Philippe that the hitherto ramshackle controls needed tidying up,

and accordingly he asked a member of the cabinet, Camille Montalivet, to prepare a draft law to put a curb on seditious plays.
Montalivet's proposals were relatively mild: the criminal courts
were to be empowered to take cognizance of direct attacks on the
person of the monarch, on the Charter, on the legitimacy of the
bicameral government; misdemeanours, heard by the lower courts,
were to include insults to religion and attacks on the civil authorities. But the bill, intended to conciliate those who on ideological
grounds opposed the idea of re-introducing the censorship and
others who felt that the time had come to set up the old machinery
again, never actually came to the vote. The uneasy truce continued
until an event entirely foreign to the theatre, the attempted assassination of the King and his sons by Giuseppe Fieschi on 28 July 1835,
led to the implementation the following September of a series of
emergency measures, which included the re-establishment of preventive censorship. In future no play could be publicly performed
without prior authorization; the state additionally re-asserted its
right to suspend the performance of any play and to order the
closure of any theatre. The new powers remained in force until the
monarchy itself crumbled in 1848.

Over this twelve-year period, half the plays submitted for authorization were passed without difficulty; most of the remainder underwent minor modifications. The number of plays rejected outright, as
unsuitable for performance on the stage, was a little over 300. In
general, the July Monarchy showed greater leniency in operating
the censorship than had the previous regime.[19] Groups enjoying
special protection were fewer than they had been, and confined to
members of the two chambers, high government officials and
electors (a limited number of property-owners at this period).
Foreign policy was another preserved area. When in 1841 Eugène
Sue, in collaboration with Goubaux, wanted to put on a play
dealing with the inhuman treatment of French prisoners by the
British during the wars of the Republic and the Empire, the censorship insisted that the title, originally *Les Pontons anglais* (The English
Prison-Ships), should be abridged to *Les Pontons* and that all allusions to the ferocity of the islanders should be expunged – even
place-names like Devonport and Plymouth had to disappear. Louis-
Philippe's policy of seeking a *rapprochement* with Britain was not
popular among his subjects: the two countries had been mortal foes
within the memory of most Frenchmen, and they were still keen

commercial rivals. It needed all Talleyrand's well-tried diplomacy to promote the new *entente*, and the French government did not intend their efforts to be frustrated by any dramatic work that harked back to old grievances or could be interpreted as insulting by the British. A musical by Léon Gozlan, so inoffensive that the censorship had found nothing to change in it, was ordered to be withdrawn at the last moment (this was also in 1841). It had been entitled *Il était une fois un roi et une reine* (Once Upon a Time, a King and a Queen ...); the purely imaginary events were supposed to take place in England under the Protectorate. But ... it concerned a young princess and her betrothal to a German prince, and Queen Victoria's ambassador to France thought it could lead to the drawing of improper parallels with his sovereign's recent marriage to Prince Albert of Saxe-Coburg. The first performance of Gozlan's play was due at the Théâtre de la Renaissance on 9 January 1841, and the last-minute interdict created an enormous scandal, with deputies demanding explanations of the minister who, naturally, denied having yielded to pressure from the British Embassy. The incident was very similar to that of 1783, when Lefèvre's tragedy *Elisabeth de France et Don Carlos* was forbidden public performance for fear it might give offence to the King of Spain.[20] One of the drawbacks of an official censorship is that the government is forced to take responsibility for any work considered objectionable by a foreign power, and if it bows to complaints, will then run the risk of being thought pusillanimous by its own nationals. In this instance, the sticker placed over the theatre bill: *Relâche par ordre* (withdrawn by order) was quickly transformed by some patriot in the opposition who scratched out the first two letters, so that the notice read: *lâche par ordre* (cowardly by order).

When it came to deciding how the censorship office should function, the administration simply reactivated the machinery that had served under the previous regime, though the personnel staffing it did not have the same intellectual status as those that had been recruited under the Restoration. These earlier censors, some of whom had performed the same duties during the Empire, had been on the whole men of discretion and even of distinction, who had made their mark in their various professions. Quatremère de Quincy, who served in the censorship bureau between 1822 and 1827, is still remembered for his monumental *Dictionnaire d'architecture*, published in three volumes between 1795 and 1825, and for his later work, *Monuments et ouvrages d'art antique*; he had been appointed by Napoleon to a chair in archaeology which he kept until his death in 1850. Jean de Lacretelle held a professorship of history at the Faculty of Letters in Paris and had been elected a member of the Académie Française in 1814. Like many other liberal thinkers of the period, he saw no contradiction in giving his time to the censorship of plays while simultaneously defending tooth and nail the freedom of the press. It was perfectly possible, at the time, to hold this paradoxical viewpoint in all honesty. The press under the Restoration was a forum for serious, well-informed debate, read primarily by those interested in such arguments; the theatres appealed in contrast to a more frivolous and less well-educated section of the population, who expected to be entertained rather than confronted with matter for reflection.

Under the July Monarchy, the ministry saw no need to seek out men of high intellectual calibre for the routine job of censoring plays; it was content to leave it to minor civil servants, of a class the French call slightingly *ronds-de-cuir*, with reference to the round leather cushions designed to ease long sessions at their desks. Their post was one envied by their colleagues, however, since it carried with it various fringe benefits – tickets for dress rehearsals and free seats at the theatre for their friends and relations, not to mention, it was whispered, the occasional kindnesses bestowed by certain actresses ... Their activities with the red pencil were supplemented by those of the inspectorate, whose special responsibility it was to check on the propriety of costumes, dances, etc. Charles Hervey mentions a certain actress at the Vaudeville, 'profoundly versed in the mysteries of that elegant series of evolutions familiarly known by the name of the *can-can*' which she danced in 'a carnival farce called *Les Gamins de Paris* with such vigour and precision that the authorities became alarmed and the piece, being voted immoral, was suppressed'.[21] The action was no doubt taken on the advice of the inspector attached to the censorship bureau.

At the head of this bureau was a certain Hygen-Auguste Cavé, director of the Fine Arts division of the Ministry of the Interior. He was suspected – as indeed were his four subordinates – of taking bribes from theatre managers or playwrights in consideration of lenient treatment, but nothing was ever proved against him. Cavé was responsible not only for running the censorship bureau but also for recommending or blocking the granting of theatre licences, which again may have been a useful supplementary source of income. Corruption was widespread under the July Monarchy in the lower echelons of government, and Cavé, a forceful but generally detested public figure, may not always have resisted the temptation of discreet backhanders; at all events he appears to have accumulated rather mysteriously a not inconsiderable fortune. He remained in office undisturbed until the 1848 revolution.

One of the first acts of the provisional government set up after the fall of the monarchy was to abrogate (6 March 1848) the harshly repressive laws of September 1835, so that once more the theatres were free to show whatever they chose, at least in theory. Hostein relates how he and Védel, respectively manager and proprietor of the Théâtre-Historique, were summoned by the then prefect of police, Caussidière, who addressed them as follows: 'Citizens, you are free to do and say what you will on your stage. But watch out! If your plays don't suit me, I'll chuck you in prison and throw away the key.'[22] In fact the Théâtre-Historique, like every other theatre in Paris, did lamentably little business in the first few months of the revolution, and after the bloody suppression of the working-class rising in June 1848, the terrified middle-class audiences, wanting only to be reassured, found greatest satisfaction in various crude right-wing satires put on notably at the Vaudeville: a piece, denoted a *folie socialiste*, caricaturing the ideas of Proudhon and entitled *La Propriété, c'est le vol* (28 November 1848), followed in the course of 1849 by a constantly changing series of political sketches called *La Foire aux idées*, in which the new Republic, and the National Assembly which directed its fortunes, were subjected to outspoken attacks so entertainingly presented that they were said to amuse even the staunch socialists in the audience. Any other government would have taken action to stop this running fire; but the idealistic 'men of February' had tied their own hands by abolishing the censorship, and though they may have resented the travesty of their policies performed nightly before a predominantly hostile audience, there was nothing they could do to stop the performances.

The work that finally irritated the authorities beyond endurance, and played the same part in the history of the Second Republic as had *Le Procès d'un maréchal de France* in that of the July Monarchy, was not a piece of political satire but a slanted dramatization of very recent events: the French expedition to Rome in April 1849 to come to the rescue of Pope Pius IX, ousted from the Eternal City by

Mazzini the previous month. Opinion in France on the military intervention was sharply divided, and these divisions were reflected in the violent reactions of the audience at the first night of Ferdinand Laloue's *Rome* on 29 September 1849. Théodore Muret, who was present at the Porte-Saint-Martin on this occasion, claimed[23] that the majority of the spectators showed greater sympathy for the heroic defenders of Rome led by Garibaldi than for the French troops assailing the barricades; but the fact that the play had provoked violent scenes gave the authorities the excuse they needed to forbid further performances. After Laloue had agreed to certain cuts, it was in fact allowed a second and third performance, but powerful voices were raised – those of the papal nuncio and of General Changarnier commanding the army in Paris, who claimed that the uniform had been insulted by the catcalls on the first night – in favour of suppressing the drama. The minister gave in, and *Rome* disappeared from the stage for good.

In the course of the debate on the budget in April 1849 Jules Favre had argued against the re-establishment of the censorship (which would have required separate financial provision) and was seconded by Victor Hugo in a well-reasoned speech which, for the moment at any rate, swung over the waverers. Hugo distinguished between two censorships: that exercised by the good sense and instinct for what is decent that one always finds in a mature nation; and that imposed by the authority of the state. 'When you destroy the freedom of the theatre, are you aware what you are doing? You are removing the first of these censorships and handing over to the second', with the result that the public will covertly side with a playwright whom, were it not for the existence of an official censorship, that same public would condemn. 'The censorship, by denying the public its natural jurisdiction over the theatre, is denying it the sense of its own authority and responsibility; once it ceases to be judge, it becomes an accomplice ... ending up by adopting what it would have rejected, and by protecting what it would have condemned.'[24] There was undoubtedly much truth in the argument, provided one subscribed to Hugo's optimistic faith in human nature; but he was referring only to immorality on the stage, whereas over the first half of the nineteenth century the censorship had, in nine cases out of ten, been employed against what were considered as subversive and seditious works rather than those offending against the proprieties. There was nothing indecent, though there was much that was impolitic, in Laloue's *Rome* when it was put on five months later.

The following year, on 30 July 1850, Baroche introduced a bill to put the censorship once more on the statute book, provisionally to begin with; it was made permanent after the establishment of the Second Empire. It was as comprehensive a law as any of those that had preceded it. A circular sent to all theatre managers in France ordered them to submit within five days details of their current repertoires so that these could receive ministerial approval. No new plays could be performed without express authorization.

Odile Krakovitch, who has contributed as much as anyone to archival research into the functioning of dramatic censorship in the nineteenth century, has discovered a memorandum preserved in the papers of the Ministry of the Interior which records that during 1852, out of 682 plays examined by the censors, 59 were forbidden outright, 323 underwent modifications of greater or lesser importance, and 54 were awaiting consideration: this leaves only 246 (36%) authorized without further discussion.[25] She further notes that every time preventive censorship was reintroduced after a period of relative laxity, in 1800, 1835, 1850 and 1874, there was an immediate rise in the number of plays suppressed. One imagines that the officials entrusted with the task were anxious to demonstrate their competence and reliability;[26] as time went on – and also, it must be admitted, as the regime itself became rather more self-confident – so they took up a more and more relaxed attitude. This hypothesis is borne out by the fact that complaints about the stiffness of the censors when interviewing playwrights were far more marked in the earlier part of the Second Empire. 'The dramatist bidden to appear before this commission, as pretentious as it was offensive, was made to feel exactly like a prisoner facing his judges. Théodore Barrière, on several occasions, had violent arguments with these portly gentlemen in white ties who had an inflated opinion of themselves and omitted even to show due deference to a talented writer.'[27] His *Filles de marbre* (1853), an early attempt to portray the courtesan realistically, underwent such mutilation that Barrière felt obliged to take the matter up with the minister, always a last resort provided an author had sufficient standing to gain access to him. Another playwright, Brisebarre, was so exasperated by their footling objections and inept observations that he threatened to cane them all on the spot and had to be forcibly removed. Léon Gozlan had no fewer than five meetings with the censorship commission before he agreed the various changes and cuts they demanded in his play *Le Gâteau des rois* (The Twelfth-Night Cake), finally produced by the Comédie-Française in 1855.[28] But by 1867 the censorship, as Hostein admits, had become 'much more obliging, dispensing advice rather than obstinately sticking to the letter of the law'. The officials one encountered were 'affable and enlightened, with no set prejudices, prepared to engage in friendly discussion with authors and managers' – something one does not find, he adds, in England, 'where the theatre is subjected to a totally arbitrary and autocratic censorship'.[29]

At the same time, particularly for a young dramatist, the knowledge that his best efforts had to be submitted to this official body must have been present in his mind from the very moment he settled down to write, giving him doubts about his choice of subject, his presentation of the characters, the fine line to be drawn between formal and colloquial speech in the dialogue.[30] He could never be rid of the feeling that the censor, with pursed lips, was reading over his shoulder the lines he was tracing on the paper. 'How many plays have miscarried and been abandoned', exclaimed Claretie, 'at the mere thought that it would never be possible for them to be produced! If you deprive an author of the dream that sustains him, the hope that warms him, the prospect of a battle to win over an audience, he will drop his subject and forget all about it.'[31] If, in spite of the undoubted talent of a handful of Second Empire dramatists, all their more serious plays seem so dull and lifeless today, the existence of the censorship – objecting to a new translation of *King Lear* on the grounds that it showed a monarch in his dotage, to Sardou's dramatization of *Candide* on the grounds that it was based on a tale by that revolutionary Voltaire, to Musset's *On ne badine pas avec l'amour* (There's no trifling with love) on the grounds that the hero shows himself disrespectful towards nuns in closed orders[32] – must bear a large part of the responsibility.

Predictably, the apparatus of preventive censorship was dismantled by a decree dated 30 September 1870, less than a month after the proclamation of the Third Republic. The restoration of their freedom hardly impinged on playwrights at the time, since over the duration of the Franco-Prussian war the majority of theatres in Paris either stayed closed or else opened only for the occasional patriotic programme. Only the Ambigu-Comique and

the Théâtre Beaumarchais are known to have remained active
during the siege and to have mounted the occasional new drama.[33]
During the immediate post-war years the principle of state control of
the theatres was hardly challenged; only the machinery by which it
was administered – the so-called 'commission d'examen des ouvrages dramatiques', in other words the censorship bureau – had not
been re-established. This deficiency was made good by a decree
dated 1 February 1874, ratified the following June by a vote of
credits to the Ministry of Public Instruction and the Fine Arts to
enable the bureau to be set up again. It consisted of a body of censors
similar to that which had functioned under the Second Empire,
named now 'inspectors' rather than 'examiners', since they were less
concerned with vetting manuscripts than with judging the possible
effect of a production on the eventual audience. For this reason the
custom grew up of holding a 'censors' rehearsal' three days before
the dress rehearsal; it was only after this that final authorization was
given. The censors' rehearsal took place in the presence of three
'grave, austere, impassive' gentlemen sitting in the orchestra stalls,
charged with the duty of

pronouncing anathema on any play containing allusions or ambiguous
remarks by which the author had hoped to make his meaning understood
by the public and the critics. Guardians of morality and of government
policies, these three censors do not take their functions lightly and order the
immediate deletion of all sentences which appear to them to be subversive
or immoral.

Little attention was, however, paid to these cuts. 'However massa-
cred it may be at the "censors' rehearsal", the actors usually restore
the original text on the opening night.'[34] The censorship was clearly
beginning to lose its teeth.

New plays were still required to be submitted in advance, but
over the first two decades of the Third Republic only eight were
banned as a result of these preliminary readings; in general, a much
greater latitude was allowed than had been customary under the
Second Empire. Whereas before 1870 any play casting aspersions on
ministers of state, criticizing parliamentarians or satirizing magistrates would have been pitilessly banned, it became possible now to
do all these things: Courteline in particular can be said to have
specialized in making fun of professional groups – lawyers, policemen, officials of all kinds – formerly regarded as 'protected
species'.[35] The banning of such plays as Albert Guinon's *Décadence*,

published in 1901, on the grounds that it dealt with the problem of anti-Semitism when, as a consequence of the passions aroused by the Dreyfus Affair, this was a peculiarly sensitive area, and of Georges Ancey's *Ces Messieurs* (The Reverends), which dealt with clerical influence in education, again a contentious issue in view of Emile Combes's proposals for purely lay control of the schools, was attributable to the desire to keep off the stage any 'problem plays' liable to divide an audience. As Guinon observed drily at the time:[36] 'if I interpret rightly the functioning of the censorship ... its role is to forbid any work of social satire which might be of a nature to arouse passions among the spectators and thus provoke a certain effervescence judged to be dangerous'. Thus, only innocuous plays were, in the last resort, allowable, such as disturbed no one's digestion. A writer with fire in his belly would think twice before venturing to compose for the stage; there were, after all, other outlets for what he wanted to say. It was a consequence pointed out earlier by Zola, when he wrote of the

certainty every beginner has that his play will not be authorized if he raises one of the more serious questions of our time. Should not politics be our area of study – politics which contains the germ of all the comedy of our age? Does not the real source of tears lie in social questions, which we are brutally forbidden to raise? This is why young writers are turning their backs on the theatre.[37]

Zola was speaking from personal experience: the dramatized version of his novel *Germinal*, with its denunciation of the brutal methods used to break strikes, had but recently been forbidden by the censorship.

From 1881 onwards, scarcely a year passed without some radical or socialist deputy, at the time of the budget debate, getting on his legs to propose withholding the moneys allocated to pay the salaries of the officials employed to inspect new dramatic works, this being the simplest way to abolish the censorship. Finally, in 1891, as the result of a motion proposed in the Chamber by Antonin Proust and Charles Le Senne, it was agreed to set up a parliamentary commission of inquiry on the model of that of 1849. It concluded, after hearing evidence from fifteen experts in the field, by proposing that the censorship be suspended for three years on a trial basis, except for plays that might have international repercussions; these were to be referred to the Minister for Foreign Affairs. However, the report was discussed at the butt-end of a parliamentary session and a vote was never taken.

By the end of the century it was clear that the censorship bureau was beginning to seize up under the sheer weight of the number of theatrical performances on which it was required to adjudicate (9,000, including the vocal repertoires of *cafés-concerts*, in the year 1900 alone). There were serious infractions of its operating rules, notably when on 23 January 1900 the manager of the Athénée was given permission by one of the censors to put on a play (Wiener's *L'Homme à l'oreille coupée*) which the director of the Fine Arts division, Roujon, had forbidden as pornographic. Oscar Méténier's *La Brême*, a play dealing with prostitution, was shown at the Grand-Guignol in 1897 in spite of having been refused authorization by the censors; no action was taken against him. But the affair which did as much as anything to tip the scales against the censorship was that associated with Eugène Brieux's *Les Avariés* (Damaged Goods), when Antoine wanted to produce it in 1901. He was sent for by Roujon and told that unless he withdrew it, the government would be asked to forbid it as 'odious and insane'.[38] Brieux's play concerned a victim of syphilis who, believing himself cured, contracts marriage with a girl who, naturally, has been left in ignorance of her husband's medical history. The truth emerges when she gives birth to an unhealthy child. Her father, an influential deputy, asks her husband's doctor to testify that his patient had been a syphilitic, in order that he may take immediate steps to have his daughter's marriage dissolved. The doctor refuses on the grounds that practically every man frequents prostitutes before marriage and risks contracting a venereal disease; his son-in-law has been unlucky and deserves compassion rather than the additional shame of having the circumstances made public in the divorce courts.

Brieux, on learning that *Les Avariés* was to be suppressed, organized a private reading of the play at the Théâtre-Antoine, inviting leading lights in the medical profession as well as fellow dramatists and theatre critics to attend. As a result, a petition in favour of the suppression of the censorship was submitted and the affair was given wide publicity in the press. The matter was raised in the Chamber, but no immediate action was taken. The Mary Whitehouse of the time, René Béranger, nicknamed Père-la-Pudeur by his opponents, kept the flag flying for the next few years, until at last, on 17 November 1904, a vote was taken in the Chamber of Deputies to deduct 4,000 francs – the salary of one of the censors – from the following year's budget for the Fine Arts; this time there was a majority of over a hundred in favour. The year after, the remaining censors lost their salaries and as a result quit their jobs. Except for periods of national emergency, notably during the two world wars, censorship of the theatres had passed into history, in France at least; it was to need another sixty-three years before Great Britain followed suit.

CHAPTER 15

The private sector

Lurking on the fringes of the theatre industry, occasionally quiescent but never entirely dormant over the whole of the period considered here, testifying above all to the intense interest in the stage among all classes of society in every part of the country, amateur dramatics or private theatricals constituted an activity apart, with which the state rarely meddled except to keep a careful watch in case its devotees overstepped the legal limits it imposed on their activities. Since France was never, even under the First Empire, a totalitarian state as the word came to be understood in the mid-twentieth century, rehearsing and acting plays in private was always suffered to flourish unimpeded. In law, the line was normally drawn between theatres charging for admittance (these being regarded as public enterprises) and those that waived all payment and simply issued private invitations to interested parties who would provide the audience.

One function of the state which the private sector was able to sidestep at all times was its power to halt performances that the censorship had forbidden. A notable case in point was the production of *Le Mariage de Figaro* at the private theatre belonging to the Duc de Fronsac at a time when Beaumarchais was still fighting for permission to have his comedy produced on the public stage. The difficulties he had been encountering could be broadly described as political; the same was true of Collé's *Partie de chasse de Henri IV*, constantly proscribed by the censorship down to 1781, when at last the Comédie-Française was allowed to stage it. But Collé's play had been regularly seen at private performances, notably at Mlle Guimard's mansion at Passy (7 December 1768) and to inaugurate her town house in the Chaussée d'Antin (8 December 1772). In the aristocratic but unprincipled high society of the *ancien régime* it was, however, particularly those plays and sketches which on moral grounds would never have been permitted on the public stage that constituted the principal attraction, escaping the attentions of the police less on account of the high rank of those in whose châteaux they were performed than because they were not regarded as public performances. The Duc de Chartres, before he inherited the title of Duc d'Orléans and came under the reforming influence of Mme de Montesson, was much given to these indecent farces, some of which were specially composed for him by Collé; so too was Louis XVI's younger brother, the Comte d'Artois (the future Charles X) at his private theatre in the Château de Brunoy. Mme d'Oberkirch recalled, in 1784, being told about the broadness of the entertainment given there a few years earlier. 'The King was weak enough to attend on one occasion out of friendship for his brother, but regretted it heartily; it is difficult to conceive of such licentiousness. There were only two women in the audience, and they were obliged to withdraw.'[1] At the theatre in her country house at Passy, Mlle Guimard, the opera ballerina and mistress of a succession of wealthy and highly placed noblemen, was notorious for the pornographic displays she was in the habit of putting on; her audience included 'women who do not wish to sacrifice their reputation and at the same time want to be amused; they attend incognito and take their seats in boxes fitted with gratings; but that is just for form's sake, for they are soon identified'.[2] The texts of these farces have mostly disappeared or, if preserved (as in the case of Collé's *Théâtre de société*), give only an approximate idea of what they must have been like when performed, since it was necessary to expunge most of the smut before they could be granted a licence to appear in print.

They accounted, however, for only a small proportion of the repertoires of private theatres in the eighteenth century; for the most part such groupings of amateur enthusiasts preferred to draw on the current stock of the Comédie-Française and the Comédie-Italienne. Thus Marie-Antoinette, whose choice of plays in which to act was always above reproach, inaugurated the theatre built for her at Trianon with two comedies regularly to be seen at one or other of the royal theatres. The advantage for amateur actors was that they were able, after studying the plays in private, to watch the productions in Paris and do their best to copy the performances of the professional actors. In addition, they could count on expert tuition from reputable players: Caillet, formerly a distinguished member of the Comédie-Italienne, and Dazincourt of the Comédie-Française were co-opted to advise the palace troupe during rehearsals. Occasionally too the *sociétaires* were invited to put on performances to entertain the company at other private houses, mostly of plays of too free a nature to obtain the censor's visa for public viewing, and we have seen already the unavailing attempt made at the end of 1767 to put a stop to this practice.[3] By encouraging in this way the rage for private theatricals among the court aristocracy, it has to be admitted that the Comédie-Française was to a certain degree acting against its own interests, as Fleury, one of the leading members of the company, pointed out in his recollections of the 1780s.

Dangerous or illustrious rivals, they [the titled amateurs] deprived us of the best portion of our audience, that occupying the most expensive seats. We were reduced to playing to the pit, and our boxes were empty as the quality abandoned us to occupy those in the private theatres of rich and powerful amateurs. The mania for private theatricals inflicted grave damage on the Théâtre-Français; this fashion, which had spread through all sections of society, made acting almost an essential accomplishment of every young fop or dandy. There was no daughter of a noble house, no court lady or wealthy banker's wife who failed to greet in the street the Lisette or the Célimène of a rival company; one heard titled noblemen address one another by the name of the character they most often impersonated – Duke so and so was Crispin, the Marquis of what have you was Dorante, such and such a respected magistrate was Damis, this or that officer, Purgon or Sganarelle[4]

– after the names, of course, borne by characters in the comedies of Molière or Lesage.

To dress up and act before an indulgent audience of one's social equals was regarded not just as an amusement, but was looked on as part of the continuing education of young men of rank, most of whom had absorbed the 'terpsichorean virus' at school, for it was an integral part of the educational system of the Jesuits to get their pupils to rehearse and act plays written specially for them in Latin and excluding, of course, any feminine roles; these would be performed, on solemn occasions, before audiences consisting of members of their families. Admittedly the Jesuits were expelled from France in 1762 and thereafter this element of the school syllabus fell into abeyance; but it had already marked the generation which came to maturity in the 1770s. In the best society, play-acting was much more than a frivolous pastime, wrote the Belgian nobleman Charles-Joseph de Ligne: 'it gives a man self-assurance, a good bearing, and teaches him how to speak in public and to the public'; and it saves a lady of fashion from being embarrassed when she is 'at the centre of a large circle before going in to supper'.[5] Nor was it merely among people of rank that acting in front of an audience on a private stage was considered useful in banishing shyness and inculcating self-assurance. Mercier recommended every young man to attempt it: 'it fortifies the power of memory, teaches one deportment and clarity of enunciation', and as a pastime is much to be preferred to 'sitting in cafés playing cards or giving oneself up to complete idleness'.[6] Mercier further confirms that the taste for amateur acting had spread from the highest classes to the lowest. The number of private theatres in Paris in pre-revolutionary years can only be estimated: there were certainly well over a hundred.[7] The craze extended to the provinces too. 'There is no attorney in his country farm', wrote Bachaumont, 'who is satisfied unless he has a stage on trestles and a company of actors.'[8] In the ducal château at Aiguillon, Arthur Young was impressed to discover 'an elegant and spacious theatre' filling one entire wing. This was not at all uncommon in France, or indeed elsewhere in Europe, he reflected; but it is rare in England, 'the possessors of great estates here preferring horses and dogs very much before any entertainment that a theatre can yield'.[9] Readers of Jane Austen will recall how sharply Sir Thomas Bertram reacted when he returned from his travels to discover his children had erected a stage in his billiard room during his absence.

It would not have been necessary, strictly speaking, for the house party in *Mansfield Park* to go to the trouble of getting the estate carpenter to assemble a proper stage. Drawing-room dramatics, *théâtres de salon* as they were called in France, required no great outlay and were consistently popular from the latter part of the eighteenth century to the beginning of the twentieth; it was enough to isolate one part of a reception room from the rest and to perform a harmless playlet with perhaps a screen to figure the wings and a chaise-longue and a couple of armchairs for stage furniture. Simone de Caillavet Maurois recalls such occasions at her grandmother's house in the Avenue Hoche during the *belle époque*, with her mother taking the principal feminine lead, Robert de Flers alternating with Georges Feydeau as *jeune premier* and Marcel Proust intermittently obliging as prompter.[10] Slightly more elaborate versions of the *théâtre de salon* involved procuring assembly kits that could be fitted together, say in a ballroom, and afterwards dismantled and stored away for when they were next required – or else returned to the shop from which they had been hired.[11] These were strictly for the richer members of the upper middle classes, having at their disposal at least one room large enough to accommodate a select audience as well as a small stage. But amateur acting was an activity just as keenly pursued by enthusiasts lower in the social scale. Too poorly lodged to put on a production at home, they formed drama clubs, known as *sociétés bourgeoises*, each acting member being required to subscribe a small sum, the product of which would be put aside for hiring a suitable hall for the occasional performance. Contributions from members of the audience were, strictly speaking, not in order, since this would have altered the status of the club, turning it into a profit-taking organization. Various devices are known to have been resorted to in order to charge the public without 'going public', a step which would have necessitated making a declaration to the municipal authorities; for instance, tickets of admission were not on sale at the theatre itself but could be procured under the counter at the corner grocery shop or in a neighbouring café.

Some of these clubs were used by young people looking for a professional engagement and needing to practise their art before an audience; thus there came into being the *théâtre d'application*, where would-be actors and actresses could try out what they had learnt before taking the plunge at some provincial centre. The best-known of these *théâtres d'application* before the Revolution and in the years immediately following it was undoubtedly Doyen's, founded by an interior decorator who started acting in a *société bourgeoise* and, some time in the 1770s, opened a private establishment known as the Boule Rouge in the Marais district of Paris. This soon came to be patronized by some of the leading lights in the Comédie-Française. Charles Maurice tells how the tragedian Lekain, arriving there on foot in pouring rain one evening, exclaimed on seeing the proprietor: 'Ah! my dear Doyen, what really *disastrous* weather!' This banal remark, delivered by Lekain in a voice 'harmonious and vibrant with the emotion appropriate to the situation, gave these simple words an unexpected dramatic power, and those who heard him fell involuntarily silent in order to hear him speak more'.[12] Lekain's presence at the Boule Rouge was no doubt attributable to the desire to act as talent-spotter for the Comédie-Française; he was sometimes joined there by other senior actors, Molé, Fleury, Vanhove. It is related that Talma, when he was hesitating between continuing his career as a dentist and adopting the profession he was later to illustrate, invited a few friends to see him perform at Doyen's theatre; they were not as impressed as he would have wished, and Talma was only persuaded to persevere by the vehement encouragement of a junior *sociétaire* of the Comédie-Française, the younger of the two Sainval sisters, who chanced to be there that evening.

During the Revolution Doyen let his establishment, transferred since 1790 to the Rue Notre-Dame de Nazareth, to three speculators, who opened it in May 1791 under the name of the Théâtre d'Emulation; but like so many others at this period, the enterprise did not prosper and Doyen, having regained possession, decided it should revert to its original function as a *théâtre d'application*. Many of the promising amateurs who first took their bow there – Talma, Samson, Bocage, Beauvallet, Suzanne Brohan – subsequently attained celebrity, and in his later years, whenever Doyen heard of a new actor arriving in Paris from the provinces, he would habitually raise himself on his toes, saying: 'I remember him; he used to come here in the old days when he hadn't learned how to speak or walk.' It was not until 1824 that Doyen's private theatre, now in the Rue Transnonain, was closed by administrative action and pulled down, after a virtually uninterrupted existence of some fifty years. For the most part, however, amateur theatricals went into temporary eclipse during the Revolution, when there was real drama on the streets and in the political clubs, though they re-emerged under the Directory when, according to Brazier, Paris alone boasted more than two hundred private theatres of one sort or another.

Play-acting was going on in wineshops, cafés, cellars, garrets, stables, sheds. All the humbler classes of society were stage-struck: it was a raging epidemic ... From the lower middle class it percolated down to the working class. Locksmith journeymen, butchers, ironmongers, coopers quitted their forges, their shops, their tools to dance attendance on the owner of a theatre or the costumier; they often lost a day or two's wages a week, not counting what they spent on the mortifying pleasure of making fools of themselves in public.[13]

It may well have been this unauthorized shortening of the working week that impelled Napoleon to include, in his decree affecting the commercial theatres in 1807, all those in which 'the public was admitted free of charge', in other words the *sociétés bourgeoises*. Even the powerful imperial police, however, found it difficult to enforce this prohibition, since little publicity was given to amateur performances, which took place at irregular intervals and of which the venue was constantly changing. Reviewing in 1811 a play at the Variétés subtitled *la Comédie bourgeoise*, which appears to have been a satire on the craze, the Abbé Geoffroy drew attention to the fact that such activities, although illegal, were still as popular as ever. 'The mania for acting', he wrote, 'has seeped down to the lowest classes of society; it is highly detrimental not just to the art of drama, but to those who neglect their duties in order to exercise, without having the talent to do so, an art uniquely fitted to make them discontented with their lot and dissatisfied with their trade'.[14] A strange complaint, considering that it was overwhelmingly from the lower classes that the great actors and actresses of nineteenth-century France were drawn.

Never completely suppressed under the Empire, the *théâtres de société* or *théâtres bourgeois* sprang into new life under the Restoration. Bouffé reckoned that in 1817 at least one flourished in every district of Paris, though no more than four counted in his eyes as authentic theatres, with all the normal adjuncts: a reasonably sized stage, with curtain, backdrop and wings, and an auditorium, handsomely decorated and with comfortable seating. He names them as Doyen's theatre in the rue Transnonain; that built by Gromer, former chief machinist at the Opera, in the Rue Chantereine; the Théâtre Mareux in the Rue Saint-Antoine, a foundation dating back to 1791; and the Marais, in the Rue du Paradis, owned by a house-painter called Thierry who let it out by the hour, and rang down the curtain pitilessly as soon as the allotted time was up, whether the performance was over or not. Audiences, admitted free of charge, consisted mainly of neighbourhood cronies happy to spend a couple of hours there, usually on a Sunday afternoon. Bouffé records the odd scrap of conversation he overheard after an ambitious performance of Delavigne's tragedy *Les Vêpres siciliennes*: 'Ah! how beautifully M. Lambert acted!' – 'What about your son then? There's one who would do well in the profession; there are plenty of players in the theatres that charge who are a lot worse than him.'[15]

Some of the private theatres were suspected, as time went on, of breaking the rule against extracting payment from their invited audiences and thereby entering into competition with theatres licensed for public performance. This was, at any rate, the pretext for the *arrêté ministériel* dated 2 April 1824 which, once again, ordered them all to be closed down. But it was, legally speaking, a grey area: domestic activities were not regarded as something with which the state had the right to interfere; it was not only the Englishman's home that was his castle. Anyone could give private piano lessons at home, so why not private acting lessons? A certain Beunier, who entitled himself 'professor of declamation', persisted in keeping open his private theatre, was arraigned before the courts and won his case. This was in June 1828; in October 1829 Doyen similarly established his right in law to continue his theatrical activities, 'given that they are never publicized in the press or by means of advertisements, and that it has not been proved that tickets were distributed to spectators to enable them to attend M. Doyen's performances'.[16] At the end of the Restoration period there still remained at least three *théâtres de société* in full activity: Doyen's, on the fourth floor of his house; Ducrocq's, down in a cellar; and the Théâtre Carlotti, 'hidden in a courtyard at the end of a cul-de-sac.'[17] Neither the July Monarchy nor the Second Empire was able to suppress amateur performances by working-class enthusiasts: the worst that could be done by their 'betters' was to hold up their efforts to ridicule. If you want to attend one of these picturesque gatherings, wrote Bernier de Maligny, you must be prepared to endure being

crushed between friends and relations who turn up to applaud noisily these young devotees of the theatrical art who, often lacking the indispensable qualities needed to succeed, disfigure imperturbably all the masterpieces of our great dramatists. That is where you must go if you want to see one of these neophytes leaning over to where the prompter sits – and whom he has not heard as distinctly as the audience did – and anxiously inquiring: 'Eh? what did you say?' That is where you can hear these beggarly imitators of the most remarkable of our actors in the Paris theatres struggle to offer pitiable caricatures of them to their awe-struck audiences.[18]

The writer might have done better to bear in mind Theseus' remark in palliation of Bottom and company's efforts: 'the best of this kind are but shadows, and the worst are no worse if imagination amend them'.

In the provinces, particularly where a town did not possess a permanent theatre of its own – as at Clermont, where Etienne de Jouy arrived in the course of his peregrinations on 30 June 1818 – the *comédie bourgeoise* was all the rage, performances being given, as he discovered, 'with an ardour which has often led to funnier scenes than those they purported to enact'.[19] Even in towns where a public theatre existed, audiences were sometimes found to be disappointingly thin because of the keenness of the local inhabitants to put on and watch amateur theatricals. Then there were the titled landowners, many of whom, having returned to their châteaux in the wake of the Bourbons, had reopened their private theatres, and others who followed their example. Paul de Kock, having made a fortune writing humorous novels, acquired a country estate where he constructed an open-air theatre in the glade of a wood. 'The audience sat on the grass under the trees; ladies only were provided with chairs. The cast consisted of my children and their friends; the orchestra was my humble self, playing the fiddle when we were showing melodrama, the piano when it was comedy or vaudeville.'[20] Even though such initiatives were private and non-profit-making, they remained strictly speaking off-limits under the July Monarchy as they had been under previous regimes. A circular of 1832 signed by the Prefect of Police drew the attention of all police commissioners to the multiplicity of these clandestine establishments, enjoining them to take appropriate action: 'they exist in defiance of the law and distract artisans and young people from a sound line of conduct by encouraging dissipation'.[21] The specific reference in this warning to 'artisans and young people' suggests that the outlawing of amateur theatricals was primarily directed against the working-class clubs that had proliferated under the Directory and continued to flourish under the Empire in spite of Napoleon's efforts to stamp them out; they were still perceived as a social danger, drawing apprentices and idle workmen away from their proper occupations. Middle-class amateur dramatics were tolerated provided due application was made for their authorization and provided the *préfet* of the department was satisfied that the amateur company included no paid professionals and that the profits, if any, went to a good cause; if these conditions were satisfied, permission was rarely withheld, and they continued to function here, there and everywhere in the provinces in growing numbers.[22]

Sometimes these private theatricals had their source in some innocent domestic pastime, such as that which George Sand records as having provided amusement at her ancestral home in the province of Berry during the winter of 1846–7, when heavy snow made outdoor excursions impractical. It was decided to experiment with a largely improvised dramatic text, the scenario of which, seldom strictly adhered to, was read out at the dinner table by George Sand herself and converted into dialogue by the five young people staying with her, who were all either close relatives or their friends. Performances took place in the drawing-room, from which the servants were strictly excluded; there was no audience other than 'a great mirror which reflected us weakly and confusedly and a small dog who whined lamentably at our outlandish costumes'.[23] In succeeding years these performances at the Château de Nohant became something of a tradition; professional actors were now and then invited to take part and several of George Sand's plays were given their first performance there before being put on in Paris on the regular stage; thus Nohant served her in much the same way as Ferney had served Voltaire a century earlier.

In Paris itself, it was particularly after 1835, when the new monarchy appeared to be firmly in the saddle, that the wealthier classes began to take up this amusement. Count Jules de Castellane, a middle-aged millionaire, formerly one of the Gentlemen of the Bedchamber at the court of Charles X, was the undisputed leader here. The private theatre he built in the garden of his mansion in the Rue Saint-Honoré was apparently the last attempt to rival the sumptuous eighteenth-century establishments of Mlle Guimard, Mme de Montesson and the Verrières sisters, Marie and Geneviève Rinteau. Invitations to the dramatic performances put on by Castellane's company of amateurs were eagerly angled after but hard to come by: mostly, one had to content oneself with the glowing accounts of them that appeared in the press over the signature of one of the more fortunate guests. The theatre was not large, though it seated 400 comfortably, but in other respects it vied with any of the state-supported or commercial houses for the splendour of its decoration and surpassed them all by the glitter of its audiences, particularly under the Second Empire when, as Arsène Houssaye observed, 'the cream of Parisian society attended, beginning with the Faubourg Saint-Germain. After the performance, after the contests of wit and beauty, the guests withdrew to sup cheerfully if a little constrainedly, for the countess was at pains to recreate the ceremonious atmosphere of Louis XIV's court.'[24] It was not uncommon for plays to be put on here in advance of production at one or the other of the public theatres of the capital. Michelot, who had retired from the Comédie-Française in 1831, was the unofficial stage manager, and other acting members of the senior theatre were occasionally called on to participate.

Castellane's private theatre was acknowledged to be the most

brilliant of the period, but it was by no means the only one: the rage
for amateur theatricals extended from court circles[25] down to the
middle classes. Daumier executed a series of caricatures on the
subject in *Le Charivari* during 1859 and the journalist Villemot
satirized it in an article of around the same time:

Men and women take an excessive pleasure in these theatrical pastimes – or
should one call them rather theatrical toys? You can find here in miniature,
behind the scenes in these amateur productions, every variant of every
intrigue of a subsidized theatre: the parts of young girls grabbed by mature
matrons, those of elderly eccentrics finding no takers unless by youthful
aspirants. The actors burden their memories with the lines of plays seen
scores of times at the Théâtre-Français or the Gymnase; there are rehearsals, costumes are tried on, and so the idle hours are beguiled, so hard to fill,
aren't they? when one owns a house and carriage-horses and has no serious
function in society.[26]

Even humbler families sacrificed to the craze. The Goncourt
brothers were invited, on 31 August 1862, to a birthday celebration
in honour of Théophile Gautier at his house at Neuilly.

Almost as soon as we arrived, after greeting some twenty-five or thirty
other guests forgathered in the drawing-room of the Rue de Longchamp,
we were led up a narrow staircase to the room made over to the daughters
of the house which had been transformed into a theatre, with a curtain and
footlights. All the chairs in the house had been crammed in here; the
mantelpiece served as balcony, with people perched on top of it. Beside the
door, above which was a painting of a nymph in anacreontic pose stretch-
ing her arms, the poster
                THEATRE DE NEUILLY – PIERROT THE POSTHUMOUS
was stuck on the wall together with the names of the actors. The curtain
went up to disclose the stage for which Puvis de Chavannes, the historical
painter, had provided some rather comical scenery – a stage on which there
was just room enough for Pierrot to receive a box on the ear or a kick in the
behind.[27]

Pierrot was played by Gautier's son; his two daughters had the parts
of Harlequin and Esmeralda, and Gautier himself was superb as
Pantaloon. Afterwards there was supper followed by fireworks in the
garden and dancing indoors.

     After the Franco-Prussian war certain gentlemen's clubs, which
had sprung up in Paris in imitation of the London ones, started to
put on a special form of entertainment, namely a *revue*. *Revues* (called
originally *revues de fin d'année*) were sketches in which the various

notable events of the past year, scandals, literary sensations, even scientific discoveries and technical achievements, were presented in an amusingly irreverent way. They had had a long history in France, going back to the Directory,[28] but the period of their greatest popularity dates from 1841, when the Cogniard brothers achieved a major success with one purporting to juxtapose the present year with an imaginary scene in the Paris of 1941 (the reality would no doubt have startled the audiences of the time even more). Thereafter *revues* became a regular feature of the theatrical year and were even put on at the end of 1871, though recent events were of a kind, it might have been thought, that the Parisians would have preferred to forget. As it developed, the *revue* came to consist of a series of disconnected scenes; they were usually written by a number of playwrights, each inventing one episode, and this circumstance may have commended them to certain clubs, like the Club des Mirlitons in the Place Vendôme, where 'a dozen or so witty men, dramatists, poets, novelists, journalists, musicians both amateur and professional, all contribute their quota of jokes, puns, humorous scenes and neatly turned lyrics'.[29] They drafted in actresses from the professional sector, but all the male parts were taken by the clubmen: in the programmes the women figured by name, the men invariably by an 'x'. Another club that ventured on dramatics was the Gardénia, founded jointly in 1887 by Paul Fabre, a secretary at the Canadian legation, and Duplay, an actor at the Variétés; their productions were patronized principally by the Canadian colony in Paris. Like the Mirliton their cast was a mixed one, actresses from commercial companies playing alongside the male members of the club. The aim here was to put on performances of hitherto unacted plays, but of a strictly traditional kind: they were not out to break new ground.

The ancestor of all such amateur dramatic societies of the latter part of the century, differing from the earlier *sociétés bourgeoises* in that the participants had no intention of turning professional, was undoubtedly the Cercle Pigalle; founded as early as December 1850 by a group of musicians, scene painters, playwrights and amateur actors, it was originally known simply as 'la Société dramatique'. In 1855 the members decided to move to a vacant warehouse on the Boulevard de Clichy, where they set up a rudimentary theatre consisting of a fair-sized stage with, in front, rows of hard benches covered in grey linen. Initially, their activities attracted little interest in the press, although in 1867 Gautier devoted a few paragraphs of his theatre column to one of their productions. He had difficulty, it appears, in locating the theatre, situated in a district populated mainly by monumental masons and manufacturers of funeral wreaths, whose presence was explained by the proximity of the Montmartre cemetery. It was run, he reported, by

a group of respectable young writers, musicians, and artists. They compose their own plays, they paint their own scenery and play their own music; they spend their evenings in these agreeably intelligent pursuits, much to be preferred to sitting in a brasserie drinking pints in an atmosphere thick with smoke. Audiences consist of friends and relations and members of the circle not included in the cast that evening.[30]

All expenses were met out of subscriptions from the members of the Cercle Pigalle, who came from every station of society but were valued only for their contribution to the evening's success: a humble clerk, with a gift for comic parts, was treated with the greatest respect by a rich banker who could perform only such subordinate tasks as making sure that all the necessary stage accessories were to hand. No sleeping partners were admitted; a member not otherwise employed joined the team of scene-shifters, and fell into this part so well that while an act was in progress, like his real-life counterparts he resorted to the local wineshop where as often as not he would be rooted out by someone from the audience offering him a tip to go and fetch a cab. All this appealed strongly to Henri Duvernois when, as a teenager, having written a one-act comedy he took it to the Cercle to ask them if they would put it on. He describes the atmosphere as cordial and completely democratic: a band of brothers linked together by nothing more than a fervent love of the boards. Not a single new Parisian production, advertised at any theatre big or small, was missed: some saw it from the gods, others from the front boxes, but they all greeted one another on the way out and agreed that they would have done it much better themselves. The scratch theatre they had first run up was rebuilt for them by the architect Charles Garnier, by way of recreation from his work of designing the new opera house at the end of the Boulevard des Italiens. With little space at his disposal, he managed to fit in two galleries with boxes, dressing rooms in the basement not much bigger than large cupboards, and a greenroom complete with mirrors. There was, however, no foyer, so the public were obliged to saunter up and down the street during intervals, sheltering under umbrellas if it was wet. All the same they were glad to escape from the stuffy auditorium where the rows of seats were jammed together so tightly one behind the other that unless you were abnormally short in the leg you had to sit slightly sideways. But as Jules Lemaître, who gave these details in 1893, observed: 'the Cercle Pigalle, founded forty-three years ago, gives us the best *revue* it is possible to find in Paris, I mean the liveliest . . .'[31]

It was particularly over the last two decades of the century that such groupings of amateurs sprang into being, flourished and after a few years withered away. Most of them, unlike the Cercle Pigalle, had no theatre of their own but moved from place to place, renting whatever suitable hall became available. Thus the Cercle des arts intimes, better known as les Castagnettes, moved from the Rue Cadet to the Tour d'Auvergne, then to the Folies-Marigny, finishing in the Salle Duprez where, over the last five years of its existence (1881–4) it attracted some attention. It tended to put on little-known plays by well-known authors, such as Musset's *La Coupe et les lèvres* (Between Cup and Lip) and Mérimée's *Les Mécontents* (The Discontented). Like other societies of the same sort, notably Paul Fort's Théâtre d'Art of 1890, les Castagnettes was founded by a schoolboy, a pupil at the Collège Sainte-Barbe. In like fashion Les Escholiers owed its existence to an initiative taken by a group of pupils at the Lycée Condorcet in November 1886; they followed the example of older men's clubs in inviting professional actresses to play the women's parts. The first clause of the articles of association stated that the society had been formed 'with the purpose, notably, of performing unpublished works, bringing to light dramatic and musical talents, and helping young playwrights to gain a footing in regular theatres by getting their works known'.[32] This worthy objective, which was never lost sight of and was eventually crowned with success when Les Escholiers gave the first performance in France of Ibsen's *Lady from the Sea*, distinguished them from similar dramatic circles, including the Pigalle, which had no such literary pretensions and were content, on the whole, with revues and run-of-the-mill comedies, entertaining but not in any way revolutionary.

At about this time the same idea as had inspired the Escholiers occurred to an ill-paid clerk in the Paris Gas Company, André Antoine, who had been persuaded by a colleague in 1886 to join the Cercle Gaulois, an amateur group organized on the same lines as the Cercle Pigalle, but of more recent foundation. Like the Pigalle, the

Gaulois had its own theatre, built by his own hands and with loving care by a certain Krauss, a retired army officer. Here it had been customary for the members to practise their art by mounting private performances of the classics. Antoine saw little future in this; his ambition was to put on hitherto unacted plays by newcomers to the dramatic scene, and to invite the press to the performances. The first of these productions, for which the Cercle Gaulois refused to take responsibility, took place on 30 March 1887; Antoine had sent out invitations to the dress rehearsal the previous day to some 300 guests, including Zola, Daudet, Henry Céard and the art critic Théodore Duret. They were all adherents of the recent naturalist movement, and the main attraction of the evening was a dramatization by a disciple of Zola's, Léon Hennique, of one of the master's short stories, *Jacques Damour*. In taking their bow, Antoine's group, who by now had adopted as a distinctive name, the Théâtre-Libre, posed ostensibly as the dramatic wing of the naturalist school.

The second performance, consisting of Oscar Méténier's *En famille* and Emile Bergerat's *Nuit bergamasque*, to some extent corrected this impression by having a more eclectic programme. Méténier was a novelist specializing in studies of the Paris underworld, who later founded and directed, between 1895 and 1899, the theatre of horrors, the Grand-Guignol; Bergerat, on the other hand, Gautier's son-in-law, was primarily a poet, acquainted with Zola but not particularly sympathetic to his aesthetic. *La Nuit bergamasque* was a considerable success and, even more important from Antoine's point of view, the audience included many of the leading critics of the day, Francisque Sarcey, Auguste Vitu, etc. It took place on 30 May 1887, though Antoine had wanted it postponed until October; he was completely broke and heavily in debt, and it was only Bergerat's furious insistence that had persuaded him to risk this second venture so soon after the first.

On 8 June 1887 Antoine noted in his diary his ambition to 'create a solid, permanent organization for the Théâtre-Libre', to be financed from contributions by 'honorary members, theatre lovers'.[33] This implied a departure from the normal arrangements for such amateur groups, whereby costs were met from subscriptions paid by the participants. The acting group Antoine had assembled were all amateur performers, but he saw no reason why they should be expected to meet from their own often meagre resources the expenses of the Théâtre-Libre. Instead, he decided on a system of annual subscriptions (*abonnements*) from well-wishers, giving them the right to attend performances. In this way he remained firmly in charge, a director like any other, but one relying not on box-office takings or on a group of financiers in the background, but on advance payments made by sympathizers. These subscriptions flowed in readily and rapidly enough, but even so Antoine found himself constantly struggling with a troublesome financial situation. He relinquished his job at the Gas Company on 25 July 1887, and so could devote all his time to the Théâtre-Libre, from the resources of which it was, however, necessary to pay himself at least a living wage. Moreover, it was now urgent to find a different locale for future productions. Old Krauss, fearful of the threat to the delicate fabric of his theatre represented by the thunderous applause at the second of Antoine's two productions, refused to consider letting it to him again. Fortunately, Antoine was able to negotiate an agreement with the manager of the Théâtre-Montparnasse for the use of his premises on Fridays, when it was normally closed. There was one drawback: the Théâtre-Montparnasse was on the less popular side of the river, the left bank, but in spite of this the first season there proved completely successful, and included (10 February 1888) one major triumph, the first production in France of Tolstoy's *Power of Darkness*, repeated the following Friday no longer as a private but as a public performance, which netted a welcome 4,000 francs.

The following season (1888–9) Antoine was able to find a more favourable site for his company in the Théâtre des Menus-Plaisirs on the Boulevard de Strasbourg, near the heart of the Parisian theatre world. His original policy of looking for new dramatists had not been forgotten; by the summer of 1889 he had shown the works of thirty-eight different playwrights, of whom twenty-seven could count as 'unknown', never having had more than one work accepted for public performance.[34] Even if few of the indigenous playwrights he revealed to the public subsequently achieved prominence, Antoine did at least have the merit of introducing French audiences to the Scandinavian masters, with his productions of Ibsen's *Ghosts* and *Wild Duck* and Strindberg's *Miss Julie*. Some of his experiments in the direction of realism on the stage met with a hostile reception; the proportion of adaptations of contemporary works of fiction was perhaps unduly high; and, as Bernheim observed a little peevishly, 'the spectator was expected to go the theatre to instruct himself, whereas previously he went solely to be amused'.[35] But this was precisely what Antoine wanted, to rescue the dramatic art from its slide into pure entertainment, and make it something rather more challenging, more thought-provoking and more worthy of serious study.

The decision to raise the necessary finance for the Théâtre-Libre by means of advance subscriptions meant that Antoine avoided having to pass through the Caudine Forks of the censorship, since the censors were concerned only with what was shown at theatres to which the general public had access by payment at a box-office. But although these subscriptions mounted up year after year (he had 26,000 subscribers in 1889, 42,700 in 1890, 53,600 in 1891), he was perpetually short of cash; lamentations to this effect recur constantly in his diary. 'Subscriptions cannot be increased and costs increase inexorably', he wrote on 6 March 1891; 'the deficit yawns ever wider, I have a firm presentiment, though I keep it to myself, that we are heading for an abyss into which the Théâtre-Libre will one day tumble'. By 1893, in spite of efforts to raise extra money by taking his company on tour in the provinces and abroad, Antoine realized that the end was near. On 10 November he put on Björnson's *The Bankrupt*, 'a title', he noted, 'of which I alone can fully savour the applicability in the present state of my finances'.[36] The following year he signed an agreement for a take-over and left with his company for a six-month tour of Europe beginning in September.

On his return he accepted the directorship of the Théâtre des Menus-Plaisirs which, renamed the Théâtre-Antoine, played with considerable success over a number of years, though his repertoire was never as adventurous as it had been; his most impressive achievement was a production of *King Lear* in an uncut version (5 December 1904). In 1906 Antoine, by now an establishment figure, was offered the directorship of the Odéon, which he succeeded at last in transforming into a truly popular theatre: box-office receipts rose from 725,000 francs in 1908 to 904,000 francs in 1913. But the profits were constantly swallowed up in expensive sets for plays that were taken off prematurely in favour of some other that he was dying to produce. His secret ambition in accepting the post was summed up in a phrase in his diary: 'I shall introduce surreptitiously the old Théâtre-Libre into the very heart of the official Odéon.'[37] But precisely because the Odéon was an official, that is, state-sponsored institution, he could never feel for it the same affection as he did for 'the old Théâtre-Libre' which had been his personal creation. As Christophe Charle has observed, 'the avant-garde cannot become institutionalized without contradicting itself. In accepting the Odéon, Antoine exchanged total freedom for freedom under supervision.'[38] He who pays the piper calls the tune and in the last resort it was the state here that called the tune.

For all that, Antoine's experiment paved the way for later ventures, notably that of Aurélien Lugné-Poë, founder of the Théâtre de l'Œuvre – another delocalized amateur theatre, which opened with a striking production of Maeterlinck's *Pelléas et Mélisande* on 17 May 1893, and then continued Antoine's work in acclimatizing the Scandinavians in France. But it may well be that Antoine's principal claim to distinction was that he was the first *entrepreneur-directeur* in France to be less *entrepreneur* than *directeur*. All his predecessors, whether in the state-supported or commercial sectors, had been primarily interested in making a living, if not in making a fortune; to achieve this end, they needed to fill their theatres night after night, which meant leaving it to the public to have the last word in choosing the kind of dramatic entertainment they wanted. Since the public, on the whole, tended to be conservative in its tastes, this led them to prefer well-tried playwrights and to treat new names with suspicion; Antoine concentrated on providing *inédits*, in both senses of the French word, that is, what has not been seen before, and what is out of the common ruck. The great directors who succeeded him in the following century were all men of this kidney, adventurers and innovators rather than businessmen, which is to a large extent why the French theatre, though widely regarded, even by contemporaries, as being in a state of decadence in the latter part of the nineteenth century, enjoyed a timely renaissance in the earlier part of the twentieth century.

Notes

1 THE ROYAL THEATRES OF THE *ANCIEN RÉGIME*

1 Young, *Travels in France*, pp. 82, 86.
2 Bachaumont, *Mémoires secrets*, I, 38 (30 January 1762).
3 Reproduced in Des Essarts, *Les Trois Théâtres de Paris*, pp. 50–1.
4 The word came to be applied to any actor or actress in the employ of a theatre director.
5 Collé, *Journal*, II, 338.
6 His full title was: Intendant-Contrôleur de l'Argenterie et des Menus Plaisirs de la Chambre du Roi.
7 Papillon de la Ferté, *L'Administration des Menus, journal*, pp. 324–6, 347–8.
8 See Aghion, *Le Théâtre à Paris au XVIIIᵉ siècle*, p. 124. In 1777 Papillon got them to agree to a further division of responsibilities, Duras being placed in sole charge of the Comédie-Française, while Richelieu, conjointly with his son the Duc de Fronsac, was given responsibility for the Comédie-Italienne: see Papillon de la Ferté, *L'Administration des Menus, journal*, p. 409.
9 Funck-Brentano, *La Bastille des comédiens*, pp. 200–3.
10 Papillon de la Ferté, *L'Administration des Menus, journal*, p. 164.
11 Quoted by Funck-Brentano, *La Bastille des comédiens*, p. 215. The letter was in all probability leaked to the public: cf. Bachaumont, *Mémoires secrets*, II, 198.
12 Métra, *Correspondance secrète*, V, 31–2.
13 Malliot, *La Musique au théâtre*, p. 57.
14 Bachaumont, *Mémoires secrets*, VII, 360.
15 Grimm, *Correspondance littéraire*, part 2, IV, 365.
16 Bachaumont, *Mémoires secrets*, XII, 243.
17 La Harpe, *Correspondance littéraire*, II, 337.
18 From 11 November until Advent, and from Epiphany until Shrove Tuesday, according to Demuth, *French Opera: Its Development to the Revolution*, p. 303. The wearing of masks preserved anonymity up to a point, though the identity of high-born participants was occasionally guessed none the less.
19 Related by Campardon in his introduction to *Les Comédiens du Roi de la troupe italienne*, pp. xx–xxi.

20 'La police intérieure des Comédiens-Italiens est presque conforme à celle des Français' (Des Essarts, *Les Trois Théâtres*, p. 195).
21 See below, p. 26.
22 Favart, *Mémoires et correspondance*, I, 234. Cf. Bachaumont, *Mémoires secrets*, I, 40.
23 Bachaumont, *Mémoires secrets*, XXII, 135 (3 March 1783).
24 'At the first glance you can see immediately / That the new theatre is in truth Italian, / For it is so disposed / That it is made to present its posterior to the passers-by': quoted by Métra, *Correspondance secrète*, XIV, 255.

2 THE RISE OF THE COMMERCIAL THEATRE

1 See Vulpian and Gauthier, *Code des théâtres*, p. 9.
2 See above, p. 21.
3 The Foire Saint-Germain ceased operating in 1786, the Foire Saint-Laurent in 1789.
4 Boulevard is, etymologically, the same word as our bulwark. Today's Boulevard du Temple represents only a small fraction (about 400m) of the original promenade.
5 Goldoni, *Mémoires*, p. 345.
6 Thrale, *The French Journals*, p. 110. Sadler's Wells, at the time, was a place of amusement in Islington, where a theatre had been built of stone shortly before.
7 This *tour de force* was mentioned by a number of contemporary writers, but the most detailed account is to be found in Métra, *Correspondance secrète*, II, 113–15.
8 Changed again, for understandable reasons, on 22 September 1792, when it was renamed the Théâtre de la Gaîté, and continued to be so called throughout the following century.
9 Bachaumont, *Mémoires secrets*, VII, 91.
10 Mayeur de Saint-Paul, *Le Chroniqueur désœuvré*, pp. 62, 72.
11 Cf. the proverbial expression: 'Toujours de plus en plus fort, comme chez Nicolet.'
13 The term *ambigu* was used by certain boulevard authors who shunned the words comedies, comic operas, since if used they might draw down the wrath of the royal theatres who claimed the monopoly for such pieces. 'The designation was not inappropriate, justified as it was by the composite, diverse and invariably merry character of such plays, in which there were spoken passages, singing, miming, dancing' (Goizet and Burtal, *Dictionnaire universel du théâtre*, p. 102).
14 See Bernardin, *La Comédie-Italienne*, p. 228. An even earlier attempt to start up a theatre with a company of child actors called Les Petits Comédiens Français had been quashed in 1688 by Louis XIV, anxious to uphold the monopoly of the recently founded Comédie-Française.
15 Thiéry, *uide des amateurs*, I, 609.
16 The names and ages of the two dozen or so child actors employed by

Audinot in 1773 are given in Laplace's study, 'Des théâtres d'enfants au XVIIIe siècle', *Revue d'Histoire du Théâtre* (1980), p. 23.

17 By Rahill, *The World of Melodrama*, p. 24.

18 The Opera was not given ownership of the theatres considered as structures, but of the all-important *privilège*, the right to operate, without which of course the theatres were useless.

19 Described by Valpy ('A Short Sketch of . . . Paris in 1788', *The Pamphleteer* (1814), p. 537) as 'a set of the most miserable wretches that ever trod the creaking boards of a village barn'.

20 See Brazier, *Chroniques des petits théâtres*, I, 92.

21 Lécluse's debts were settled, happily, and he was allowed a pension of 6,000 *livres* on which he lived quietly until his death in 1792.

22 Oberkirch, *Mémoires*, I, 266.

23 The full text of the contract is given in Lecomte, *Histoire des . . . Variétés-Amusantes*, pp. 104–5.

24 The official title given to the troupe was: Petits Comédiens de Son Altesse Sérénissime Monseigneur le Comte de Beaujolais. Beaujolais was the name customarily borne by the sons of the House of Orléans before they reached their majority.

25 Valpy, 'A Short Sketch', p. 539. An unsuccessful attempt to renew the experiment was made by Lugné-Poë more than a hundred years later in his production of Régnier's *La Gardienne* on 21 June 1894: see Knapp, *The Reign of the Theatrical Director*, pp. 107–8.

26 Millin de Grandmaison, *Sur la liberté des théâtres* (1790), quoted in Hérissay, *Le Monde des théâtres pendant la Révolution*, p. 21.

27 Mercier, *Tableau de Paris*, II, 171.

28 Albert, *Les Théâtres de la Foire*, p. 283.

29 Manne and Ménétrier, *Galerie . . . des scènes secondaires*, p. 14.

30 See Métra, *Correspondance secrète*, XIII, 195 (7 August 1782).

31 Analysed in some detail by Root-Bernstein, *Boulevard Theater*, pp. 25–7.

32 Grimm, *Correspondance littéraire*, part 3, III, 79.

33 Quoted (from *Paris en miniature*) by Péricaud, *Théâtre des . . . Beaujolais*, p. 7.

34 Quoted in Root-Bernstein, *Boulevard Theater*, p. 62.

35 Métra, *Correspondance secrète*, XVII, 68–9.

36 Bonnassies, *Les Spectacles forains*, p. 57. Cf. also Fuchs, *La Vie théâtrale*, pp. 47–8.

3 DRAMATIC CENSORSHIP DOWN TO ITS ABOLITION

1 Article VIII of the 1757 constitution of the Comédie-Française: 'Quand une pièce aura été reçue et qu'elle sera venue à son tour d'être jouée, l'auteur aura soin de se munir de l'autorisation de la police; ensuite il enverra les rôles aux acteurs.'

2 Grimm, *Correspondance littéraire*, part 3, II, 178–9.
3 Ibid., part I, IV, 11 (January 1765).
4 Letter quoted in Nisard, *Mémoires et correspondances*, p. 175.
5 Grimm, *Correspondance littéraire*, part I, V, 546.
6 The Comédie-Italienne 'had remarkably few difficulties with the censor. The only play they accepted that they were not allowed to produce was *Jeannette* (1782), on the grounds that it reflected unfavourably on the reputation of a member of the Academy (La Harpe)' (Brenner, *The Théâtre-Italien*, p. 28).
7 These two proclamations have been reproduced in Hamiche, *Le Théâtre et la Révolution*, pp. 41–2.
8 This account follows Grimm, *Correspondance littéraire*, part 3, V, 239–40.
9 Bailly, *Mémoires*, II, 286.
10 Quoted in Hamiche, *Le Théâtre et la Révolution*, p. 46.
11 Full text given in Bureau, *Le Théâtre et sa législation*, p. 240.
12 The word *sauf* in 'sauf la responsabilité des auteurs et des comédiens' is to be understood in the sense, listed as archaic in Robert's dictionary: 'sans qu'il soit porté atteinte à', i.e. 'without prejudice to the responsibility of the authors and actors'.
13 Quoted in Goncourt, *Histoire de la société française pendant la Révolution*, p. 153.

4 THE LIBERATION OF THE THEATRES

1 The span of five years was subsequently extended to ten by a law enacted 24 July 1793; to twenty years by another law of 3 August 1844; and finally to fifty years on 14 July 1866: see Lacan and Paulmier, *Traité de la législation ... des théâtres*, II, 240–1.
2 *Mémoires de Mlle Flore*, p. 84.
3 Grimm, *Correspondance littéraire*, part I, VI, 236–7.
4 See above, pp. 33–4.
5 Mercier, *Du théâtre*, pp. 364–5.
6 Grimm, *Correspondance littéraire*, part 2, II, 510.
7 *Il est temps de parler et il est temps de se taire*: passage quoted in Albert, *Les Théâtres de la Foire*, p. 294.
8 Lagrave, 'La Comédie-Française au XVIIIe siècle', *Revue d'Histoire du Théâtre* (1980), p. 136.
9 Root-Bernstein, *Boulevard Theater*, pp. 209–10.
10 According to Brazier, (*Chroniques des petits théâtres*, II, 24–5) who, having been born in 1783, was just – though only just – of an age to have witnessed such scenes.
11 Quoted in Bossuet, *Histoire des théâtres nationaux*, p. 73.
12 See above, p. 36.
13 Biré, *Journal d'un bourgeois de Paris*, III, 89. Amanda Binns's estimate that by the end of 1791 'forty theatres were open' ('Popular Theatre and

Politics in the French Revolution', *Theatre Quarterly*, 16 (1974–5), p. 21) appears based on faulty arithmetic.

14 Quoted in Pougin, *Acteurs et actrices d'autrefois*, p. 81.
15 See below, p. 67.
16 Goncourt, *Histoire de la société française pendant le Directoire*, p. 59.

5 THE ROYAL THEATRES UNDER THE REVOLUTION

1 Halem, *Blicke auf einen Teil ... Frankreichs*, II, 36.
2 Before the Revolution, it had been customary for performances at the Opera to take place only on Sundays, Tuesdays and Fridays.
3 Quoted in Pougin, *Un directeur d'opéra*, p. 75.
4 La Harpe, *Correspondance littéraire*, III, 297–8; Métra, *Correspondance secrète*, XII, 142, 164.
5 See above, p. 38.
6 Quoted by Lecomte, *Histoire des théâtres de Paris: le Théâtre National*, p. 40.
7 Quoted in Pougin, *Un directeur d'opéra*, p. 98.
8 The terms of this resolution were reported in *Le Moniteur* of 19 September 1793 and are quoted in Biré, *Journal d'un bourgeois de Paris*, III, 326–7.
9 Details in Gourret, *Histoire de l'Opéra-Comique*, p. 85.
10 Péricaud, *Théâtre de Monsieur*, p. 135.
11 Reichardt, *Vertraute Briefe*, I, 161; Carr, *The Stranger in France*, p. 252.
12 *Mémoires de Fleury*, I, 219.
13 Quoted in Hamiche, *Le Théâtre et la Révolution*, p. 87.
14 The words are those that Fleury himself recorded in his memoirs (*Mémoires*, II, 66), but are textually identical with the report given in the *Chronique de Paris* and reproduced in Pougin, *La Comédie-Française et la Révolution*, p. 25.
15 Reproduced in Etienne and Martainville, *Histoire du Théâtre-Français*, I, 160–2.
16 Bailly was referring to a decision taken on 12 October 1789, by which the Gentlemen of the Bedchamber were relieved of the functions they had discharged relative to the Comédies Française and Italienne, and 'le Théâtre-Français est prévenu qu'à l'avenir il doit s'adresser au Maire de Paris pour toutes les affaires qui concernent la Comédie' (Laugier, *Documents historiques*, p. 26).
17 The only account so far discoverable of this crucial confrontation is that given by Fleury, *Mémoires*, 70–7. It may not be textually accurate, but it does have the ring of truth.
18 Quoted in Hamiche, *Le Théâtre et la Révolution*, p. 114.
19 The text of the letter is given in Dussane, *La Célimène de Thermidor*, pp. 75–7.
20 Goncourt, *Histoire de la société française pendant la Révolution*. pp. 101–2; based on contemporary reports in the *Chronique de Paris* and the *Journal*

de la cour. Naudet had fought a pistol duel with Talma after the latter had publicly given him the lie by declaring that it would be possible to stage a performance of *Charles IX* for the *fédérés.*

21 Figures given in Alasseur, *La Comédie-Française au XVIIIᵉ siècle*, p. 142.

22 'Dès 1790, une loi des 11–20–21 septembre rejeta du compte du Trésor public la dépense relative aux pensions des Comédiens Français et Italiens, à la garde militaire des spectacles et aux pompes d'incendie' (Bureau, *Le Théâtre et sa législation*, p. 161).

23 See above, pp. 59–60.

24 The affair caused great scandal at the time: see Bachaumont, *Mémoires secrets*, XVII, 268, 274; Grimm, *Correspondance littéraire*, part 2, V, 303–4; Métra, *Correspondance secrète*, XI, 327–8.

25 *Les Spectacles de Paris*, 1794: quoted in Goncourt, *Histoire de la société française pendant la Révolution*, p. 302.

26 The broader message of *L'Ami des Lois* was encapsulated in a couplet spoken by Forlis, act III, sc. 3:

> Royalistes tyrans, tyrans républicains,
> Tombez devant les lois: voilà vos souverains!

(Tyrants, whether royalist or republican, bow ye the knee to the laws: these are your sovereign masters!)

27 Quoted by Hallays-Dabot, *Histoire de la censure théâtrale*, p. 175.

28 This version of events is that given the same evening (4 February) to the Jacobin Club by one of those present at the interview; see Liéby, 'La Presse révolutionnaire', *Révolution Française* (1903), pp. 315–16.

29 A fact noted in one of the earliest reviews of the play, that published in *La azette nationale* of 14 August 1793; see Welschinger, *Le Théâtre de la Révolution*, p. 56.

30 Letter quoted by Biré, *Journal d'un bourgeois de Paris*, III, 288.

31 As quoted in Liéby, 'La Presse révolutionnaire', pp. 334–7.

32 It must have been difficult for the actors to be word-perfect in a speech which had been modified in the middle of a run. Did Fleury make an honest mistake here, or a deliberate one? It seems impossible to say.

33 Arnault, *Souvenirs d'un sexagénaire*, II, 49.

34 Cf. Lemazurier, *alerie historique des acteurs*, II, 260, and Etienne and Martainville, *Histoire du Théâtre-Français*, III, 135.

35 They numbered thirteen (according to Tisseau, *Une comédienne sous la Révolution*, p. 102 n.), and included Dazincourt, La Rive, Fleury, Mlles Raucourt and Louise and Emilie Contat.

36 The full text of their petition to the authorities is given in Etienne and Martainville, *Histoire du Théâtre-Français*, IV, 185–9.

37 Legouvé, *Soixante ans de souvenirs*, IV, 58.

38 The list of names, in order of seniority, is given in Copin, *Talma et la Révolution*, pp. 286–7.

6 THE THEATRE IN THE SERVICE OF THE REPUBLIC

1 See above, p. 39.
2 Quoted in Hérissay, *Le Monde des théâtres pendant la Révolution*, p. 36.
3 Quoted in Hamiche, *Le Théâtre et la Révolution*, p. 76. Talma never delivered this address (a more anodyne one, spoken by Naudet, was substituted for it), but Chénier's elucubration was printed in time to be distributed to the audience: see Liéby, *Etude sur le théâtre de M. J. Chénier*, pp. 61–2.
4 Quoted in Hérissay, *Le Monde des théâtres pendant la Révolution*, p. 138.
5 See Krakovitch, *Hugo censuré*, p. 79: 'la censure répressive … s'exerce non pas sur les manuscrits, mais sur les représentations'.
6 Quoted in Hallays-Dabot, *Histoire de la censure théâtrale*, p. 174.
7 Ibid., p. 189.
8 Figures given by Cahuet, *La Liberté du théâtre*, p. 135.
9 Janin analyses it at length in his *Histoire de la littérature dramatique*, IV, 274–82. Cf. also Biré, *Journal d'un bourgeois de Paris*, IV, 222.
10 Quoted in Liéby, 'La Presse révolutionnaire', *Révolution Française* (1903), pp. 348–50.
11 See the Marquis de Ximénès's account, related by Jouslin de la Salle, *Souvenirs*, p. 29.
12 By Lumière, *Le Théâtre-Français pendant la Révolution*, pp. 115–16.
13 Quoted by Hérissay, *Le Monde des théâtres pendant la Révolution*, pp. 340–1.
14 See Alméras, *La Vie parisienne sous … le Directoire*, pp. 108–14.
15 Pujoulx, *Paris à la fin du XVIIIᵉ siècle*, pp. 242–3.
16 As adduced by Welschinger, *Le Théâtre de la Révolution*, pp. 122ff.
17 See Estrée, *Le Théâtre sous la Terreur*, p. 296.

7 RE-ESTABLISHMENT OF THE STATE THEATRES

1 Quoted in Maurice, *Le Théâtre-Français*, pp. 174–5. Conversely, in a letter to Mahérault dated 29 ventôse an XI (19 March 1803), Chaptal advised him that he was taking steps to restore to the Théâtre-Français its former monopoly in 'la tragédie et la haute comédie', by forbidding all theatre managers in Paris to stage such pieces: see Lang, *L'Etat et le théâtre*, pp. 91–2.
2 There is reference to these loans in Fleury, *Mémoires*, II, 118.
3 The complete texts of the *acte de dotation* of 1802 and the *acte de société* of 1804 are given in Laugier, *Documents historiques*, pp. 64–6 and 29–44.
4 Text given in Bureau, *Le Théâtre et sa législation*, pp. 174–6.
5 Rémusat, *Lettres de Mme de Rémusat*, I, 315.
6 Tolstoy describes her reciting a speech from *Phèdre* at one of Countess Bezukhov's receptions in *War and Peace*, book 2, part 5, ch. 13.
7 See above, p. 71.
8 See above, p. 89. There being no obvious reason why the building

should have caught fire nor why the fire should have raged unchecked until everything was consumed, the disaster was thought by many at the time to have been started by arsonists. The actor Naudet, seeing the flames from afar, is said to have exclaimed: 'Ah! pour nous forcer à déménager, voilà une assignation bien chaude!' (Maurice, *Histoire anecdotique du théâtre*, I, 56).

9 Lanzac de Laborie, *Paris sous Napoléon*, VII, 324.

10 See above, p. 67.

11 Abrantès, *Mémoires*, III, 374.

12 Blagdon, *Paris As It Was and As It Is*, II, 49.

13 A *bon mot* attributed to Audiffret, quoted in Bossuet, *Histoire des théâtres nationaux*, p. 157. For murdering their husbands on their wedding night, the Danaides were condemned in the afterlife to use sieves to try and fill a leaky barrel; the Garden of the Hesperides was a fabulous orchard where the trees bore apples of pure gold.

14 Lasalle, Albert de, *Les Treize Salles de l'Opéra*, p. 202.

15 Brifaut, *Souvenirs d'un académicien*, I, 108–9.

16 Reproduced *in toto* by Laugier, *Documents historiques sur la Comédie-Française*, pp. 45–59.

17 Claretie, Jules, *Profils de théâtre*, p. 176; cf. also ibid., p. 147.

18 Dussane, *La Comédie-Française*, pp. 123–39.

8 CURBS ON THE COMMERCIAL SECTOR

1 Quoted in Hérissay, *Le Monde des théâtres pendant la Révolution*, p. 367.

2 Pujoulx, *Paris à la fin du XVIIIe siècle*, pp. 104–6.

3 Quoted by Bossuet, *Histoire des théâtres nationaux*, p. 96.

4 Chabaud-Latour, quoted in Bossuet, ibid., p. 98.

5 Quoted by Lecomte, *Napoléon et le monde dramatique*, p. 36.

6 Blagdon, *Paris As It Was and As It Is*, I, 223; Reichardt, *Vertraute Briefe*, I, 263.

7 Geoffroy, *Cours de littérature dramatique*, VI, 106.

8 *Lettres de Mme de Rémusat*, I, 224–5, 314.

9 These clauses are discussed below, in chapter 10. The text of the decree of 8 June 1806 is given in Véron, *Paris en 1860*, pp. 92–5.

10 The terms of this decree, and of the preceding *arrêté* of the Minister of the Interior, are reproduced as an appendix to the first volume of Muret's *L'Histoire par le théâtre*. The formula 'Our fair city of Paris' ('notre bonne ville de Paris') was that used by the Bourbon monarchs before the Revolution.

11 What purports to be a complete list is given in Muret, ibid., I, 227–8.

12 Reproduced in Lecomte, *Histoire des ... Jeux ymniques*, p. 2.

13 The anecdote has been pieced together from references in Brazier, *Chroniques des petits théâtres*, II, 166; Manne and Ménétrier, *alerie ... des scènes secondaires*, p. 151; and Copin, *Talma et l'Empire*, p. 134.

14 Halévy, *Notes et souvenirs*, pp. 117–18.
15 Scott, *A Visit to Paris*, p. 166.
16 Cf. Lanzac de Laborie, *Paris sous Napoléon*, VIII, 174. The enforced move of the Variétés to a less central location must have accounted, in some degree, for this drop in income.

9 POLITICS AND THE PIT

1 Moore, *A View of Society and Manners in France*, I, 90.
2 Collé, *Journal*, II, 312. The author was referring to a play he had just completed, *L'Amour d'autrefois*, which he foresaw would be suitable only for private performances.
3 Bachaumont, *Mémoires secrets*, XVII, 205.
4 Grimm, *Correspondance littéraire*, part 2, V, 298–9.
5 Hallays-Dabot, *Histoire de la censure théâtrale*, p. 140.
6 Reichardt, *Vertraute Briefe*, II, 291.
7 Ferrières, *Correspondance inédite*, p. 269.
8 Etienne and Martainville, *Histoire du Théâtre-Français*, I, 196–7. This report is broadly confirmed by the accounts of two other eye-witnesses, the future King Louis-Philippe, then only a youth of 17, as quoted in Desnoiresterres, *La Comédie satirique au XVIII*e *siècle*, pp. 317–18, and G. A. von Halem, *Blicke auf einen Theil ... Frankreichs*, II, 195–6.
9 *Lettres de Madame de Rémusat*, I, 398–401 (letter dated 29 December 1805).
10 Instances quoted in Lanzac de Laborie, *Paris sous Napoléon*, VIII, 164.
11 Halévy, *Notes et souvenirs*, pp. 125–6. The arietta in question occurs in scene 5 of *Le Tableau parlant*.
12 *Mémoires de Paul de Kock*, pp. 150–2.
13 Hallays-Dabot, *Histoire de la censure*, p. 259.
14 Bouffé gives his account of the incident in *Mes souvenirs*, pp. 60–5. The play in question was almost certainly *Le Veuvage de Manon*, which had its first performance at the Panorama-Dramatique on 9 February 1823, only eighteen days before the celebrated scene in the Chamber.
15 A police report dated 3 March 1842 on audience interventions at the Odéon during performances of Félix Pyat's *Cédric le Norvégien* mentioned that the drama 'abondait en allusions politiques ... avidement saisies par le parterre turbulent du théâtre' (quoted by Krakovitch, *Hugo censuré*, p. 93)

10 THE THEATRE IN THE PROVINCES

1 Boncompain, *Auteurs et comédiens au XVIII*e *siècle*, p. 77.
2 When a Théâtre de l'Ambigu-Comique was established; see Lamothe, *Les Théâtres de Bordeaux*, p. 12.
3 Figures given by Lagrave, 'Les Structures du théâtre dans la province ...', *Studies on Voltaire ...*, CXCII, 1429.

4 Quoted in Detcheverry, *Histoire des théâtres de Bordeaux*, p. 94.

5 For the sake of comparison, the new theatres at Marseilles cost 1,278,000 *livres*, at Nantes 450,000 *livres*, at Montpellier 200,000 *livres*, at Besançon 160,000 *livres*. The new Théâtre-Français on the left bank of the Seine, built for the Comédie-Française in 1782, cost the Crown 3,156,000 *livres*.

6 Fuchs, *La Vie théâtrale*, pp. 50–3.

7 Moore, *A View of Society and Manners in France*, I, 143–4.

8 Cf. the terms of a royal *ordonnance*, issued 1 March 1768, quoted in Fuchs, *La Vie théâtrale*, p. 46 (n.).

9 Quoted ibid., p. 46.

10 In 1751 the uniformed element in the audience brought in little short of 20,000 *livres*, all other spectators a mere 6,000; see Deck, *Histoire du théâtre français à Strasbourg*, p. 49.

11 'The talk of Paris, the desire of the provinces, the favourite amusement of our princes, the delight of the plebs and the pleasure of the nobility': Alcandre, in *L'Illusion comique*, act v, sc.5.

12 Quoted in Vingtrinier, *Le Théâtre à Lyon*, pp. 92–3.

13 Mercier, *Du théâtre*, p. 368.

14 See Courteault, *La Révolution et les théâtres de Bordeaux*.

15 Quoted by Bossuet, *Histoire des théâtres nationaux*, p. 476.

16 *Marseille: notice historique sur ses théâtres privilégiés*, pp. 18–19, 27.

17 Detcheverry, *Histoire des théâtres de Bordeaux*, p. 212.

18 The municipal revenues of Marseilles were estimated in 1866 at 10.5 million francs, those of Lyons at 9 million, whereas Bordeaux had to manage on a budget of 4 million.

19 Monval, 'Les Théâtres subventionnés', *Revue Générale d'Administration*, 1878, p. 514.

20 Quoted in Bossuet, *Histoire des théâtres nationaux*, p. 458.

21 Alhoy, *Grande Biographie dramatique*, p. 248.

22 Quoted in Destranges, *Le Théâtre à Nantes*, pp. 225–6.

23 Ibid., p. 493.

24 Baret, *Le Théâtre en province*, p. 263.

25 Quoted in Sorin, *Du rôle de l'état en matière d'art scénique*, pp. 152–3.

26 Lhomme, *Etudes sur le théâtre contemporain*, p. 101.

27 Auger, 'Mémoires inédits', *Revue rétrospective*, 1891, p. 195.

28 Combarnous, *Histoire du Grand-Théâtre de Marseille*, p. 231.

29 According to Laval, *La Liberté des théâtres au point de vue de la province*, p. 29.

30 *Journal de Mme Cradock*, p. 186.

31 See Bouteiller, *Histoire ... des théâtres de Rouen*, I, 99–100.

32 The witness's account is given both in Grimm, *Correspondance littéraire*, part 3, III, 318–21, and in Bachaumont, *Mémoires secrets*, XXIX, 223–5.

33 Details in Lefebvre, *Histoire du théâtre de Lille*, II, 362–4.

34 Jouy, *L'Hermite en province*, II, 104–5.

35 As quoted in Longuemare, *Le Théâtre à Caen*, pp. 301–2.
36 Bouchard, *La Langue théâtrale*, p. 276. Cf. Marie Dorval's disconcerting experiences at Sète some time in the late 1830s, as recounted by Pollitzer, *Trois reines de théâtre*, p. 65.
37 Got had used a month's leave in August 1860 to give eight performances at the Célestins in Lyons, but found he was acting below his own standards and resolved never to be tempted into the provinces again: see his *Journal*, II, 12.
38 The tour is recorded in Heylli, *Journal intime de la Comédie-Française*, and in greater detail in the preface to the same author's *La Comédie-Française à Londres*.
39 Cf. Alphonse Daudet, 'Tournées de province', in *Entre les frises et la rampe*; also Ginisty, *La Vie d'un théâtre*, p. 245; Eugène Lassalle, *Comédiens et amateurs*, pp. 127–8; Weiss, *A propos de théâtre*, pp. 52–5.
40 Baret, *Le Théâtre en province*, p. 136.
41 Jouy, *L'Hermite en province*, VIII, 275–7.
42 Longuemare, *Le Théâtre à Caen*, p. 161. The play in question was performed at Caen on 25 December 1805.

11 THE LICENSING SYSTEM, 1814–1864

1 See above, p. 116.
2 The word commonly used was *privilège*; in legal parlance, *autorisation*, for which 'licence' seems to be the ordinary English equivalent.
3 See Agnel, *Code-manuel des artistes dramatiques*, p. 13.
4 According to the terms of a royal *ordonnance* of 8 December 1824.
5 Malliot, *La Musique au théâtre*, pp. 157–8.
6 Lacan and Paulmier, *Traité de la législation ... des théâtres*, I, 72.
7 See Astruc, *Le Droit privé du théâtre*, pp. 13–14.
8 Krakovitch, *Hugo censuré*, p. 96.
9 See Géréon, *La Rampe et les coulisses*, p. 286.
10 The particulars that follow are derived from Lecomte, *Histoire des ... Jeux Gymniques*, *passim*.
11 See above, p. 109.
12 See Vulpian and Gauthier, *Code des théâtres*, p. 78. In his *Illusions perdues* Balzac portrayed, in Matifat, 'riche droguiste de la rue des Lombards', and his friend Camusot, a silk-merchant, typical specimens of such sugar-daddies of the Restoration period; each enjoys the favours of one of the actresses at the Panorama-Dramatique.
13 Figures given in Lecomte, *Histoire des théâtres de Paris: la Renaissance*, pp. 92–3.
14 Nerval, *La Vie au théâtre*, pp. 396–7.
15 Mme de Girardin, *Lettres parisiennes*, II, 53.
16 Dumas *fils*, *Nouveaux entr'actes*, p. 218.
17 This is why the composer was always mentioned, along with the

librettist, as co-author of a comic opera, while it was only the writer or writers of the words of the songs and the dialogue who were listed as authors of a vaudeville.

18 Plus or minus 960, according to Corinne Pré, 'La Parodie dramatique en vaudevilles', in *Burlesque et formes parodiques*, p. 265.

19 Lecomte, *Histoire des théâtres de Paris: la Renaissance*, pp. 6–7.

20 Gautier, *Histoire de l'art dramatique*, IV, 225.

21 Dumas *père* summarized his own views and those of some of his fellow playwrights in his *Souvenirs dramatiques*, II, 181–206.

22 Simonet, *Traité de la police administrative*, p. 2.

23 Fiorentino, *Comédies et comédiens*, I, 314–15.

24 'En fixant le nombre des théâtres, les conditions dans lesquelles ils devaient fonctionner, l'Etat se rendait en quelques sorte garant, au moins en équité, de leur prospérité' (Sorin, *Du rôle de l'Etat en matière d'art scénique*, p. 88). This was held to justify their appeal to the state for funds to tide them over the difficult years of 1848 and 1849.

25 Text in Bureau, *Le Théâtre et sa législation*, pp. 137–8.

26 Got, *Journal*, II, 35.

12 THE STATE-SUPPORTED THEATRES IN THE NINETEENTH CENTURY

1 Micheline Boudet relates the pert retort made to him by Mlle Mars, when Papillon de la Ferté asked her pettishly when she was going to stop wearing violets: 'Quand les papillons seront des aigles' (*Mademoiselle Mars l'inimitable*, p. 186).

2 According to Sanderson, *The American in Paris*, II, 178.

3 See above, p. 67.

4 For an account of his colourful career, see Ernest Lebègue, *Boursault-Malherbe, comédien, conventionnel, spéculateur*.

5 Quoted in Bossuet, *Histoire des théâtres nationaux*, pp. 329–30.

6 Quoted by Fouque, *Histoire du Théâtre Ventadour*, p. 55.

7 See above, p. 170.

8 Harel, *et al.*, *Dictionnaire théâtral*, p. 180.

9 Quoted in Porel and Monval, *L'Odéon, histoire administrative*, II, 11 (n.).

10 Ibid., p. 118.

11 Alhoy, *Grande Biographie dramatique*, p. 102. David was eventually (1825) welcomed back to the Comédie-Française where, after 1830 and until the arrival of Rachel, he was one of the few actors who continued to uphold the time-honoured traditions of the classical tragedy.

12 Notably in the prologue entitled 'L'Esprit chagrin', written in 1845 for the reopening of the Odéon under Bocage's management.

13 Gautier, *Histoire de l'art dramatique*, IV, 95.

14 Lewald, *Album aus Paris*, II, 33.

15 Descotes, *L'Acteur Joanny*, p. 59.

16 See above, p. 169. La Rochefoucauld's letter is reproduced *in extenso* by Lecomte, *Histoire des théâtres de Paris: Les Nouveautés*, pp. 2–4.

17 Descotes, *L'Acteur Joanny*, p. 59. *Les Vêpres siciliennes*, a five-act verse tragedy by Casimir Delavigne, had had a notable success at the Odéon in 1819.

18 Cited in Descotes, *Le Drame romantique*, p. 49.

19 Figures given in Lyonnet, *Les Premières de Victor Hugo*, p. 32.

20 Plunkett, *Fantômes et souvenirs de la Porte-Saint-Martin*, p. 162.

21 That is, the Ministry of the Interior, replacing (by an ordinance dated 25 January 1831) the Royal Household as the embodiment of the state in matters concerning the royal theatres.

22 *Mémoires de Samson*, p. 272.

23 Letter reproduced in Bouteiller, *Histoire . . . des théâtres de Rouen*, III, 306–7.

24 Loliée, *La Comédie-Française*, p. 214 (n.).

25 Frances Trollope, *Paris and the Parisians in 1836*, I, 19.

26 Got, *Journal*, I, 212.

27 Reproduced *in extenso* in Lacan, *Traité de la législation . . . des théâtres*, II, 332–7.

28 The text of these two decrees will be found in Lacan, ibid., II, 340–7.

29 Matthews, *The Theatres of Paris*, p. 76.

30 Sarcey, *Comédiens et comédiennes: la Comédie-Française*, chapter 'La Maison de Molière', p. 7.

13 THE THEATRE IN CRISIS: COMPETITION FROM THE *CAFÉ-CONCERT*

1 Weiss, *Le Théatre et les mœurs*, pp. 47–8.

2 Plunkett, *Fantômes et souvenirs de la Porte-Saint-Martin*, p. 135. His figure is, if anything, an underestimate; Wicks lists, in vol. III of *The Parisian Stage*, 280 new works produced in 1832; this rose to a top figure (for the July Monarchy) of 369 in 1839.

3 Charle, *La Crise littéraire à l'époque du naturalisme*, p. 37.

4 Dubois, *La Crise théâtrale*, p. 25.

5 Quoted in Aderer, *Le Théâtre à côté*, pp. 195–6. Aderer, who had a theatre column in *Le Temps* in the 1890s, conducted an inquiry on the question and reprinted the replies sent to him by a number of leading dramatists and theatre directors.

6 Ibid., pp. 218, 221.

7 According to Charle, *La Crise littéraire à l'époque du naturalisme*, p. 39.

8 Quoted by Pougin, *Dictionnaire . . . du théâtre*, p. 130.

9 Mayeur, *Le Chroniqueur désœuvré*, p. 47.

10 Métra, *Correspondance secrète*, VIII, 68–9: 5 June 1779.

11 Schulz, *Ueber Paris und die Pariser*, pp. 308–9.

12 *Almanach général des spectacles de Paris, 1791*: quoted in Beaulieu, *Les Théâtres du Boulevard du Crime*, p. 170.

13 Alméras, *La Vie parisienne sous ... le Directoire*, pp. 68–9.
14 Hostein, *Historiettes et souvenirs*, p. 256.
15 Brazier, *Chroniques des petits théâtres*, I, 100.
16 See above, p. 120.
17 Manne and Ménétrier, alerie historique des comédiens de la troupe de *Nicolet*, p. 40.
18 Hervey, *The Theatres of Paris*, p. 173.
19 Banville, *Souvenirs*, p. 109.
20 Audebrand, *Petits mémoires d'une stalle d'orchestre*, pp. 151–2.
21 See Echinard, 'Louis Rouffe et l'école marseillaise de pantomime', in *Théâtres et spectacles hier et aujourd'hui*, p. 550.
22 Matthews, *The Theatres of Paris*, pp. 192–3
23 Lavedan, *Avant l'oubli*, II, 110.
24 Goncourt, *Journal*, VII, 41.
25 According to figures given by Hostein, *La Liberté des théâtres*, p. 167, and by Bonnassies, *Les Spectacles forains*, p. 203.
26 Cf. Ouvrard, *La Vie au café-concert*, pp. 241–2.

14 DRAMATIC CENSORSHIP IN THE NINETEENTH CENTURY

1 Letter dated 5 December 1799, from the Bureau des mœurs et opinions publiques; quoted in Cahuet, *La Liberté du théâtre*, pp. 160–1.
2 Letter of 4 April 1800, quoted in Lecomte, *Napoléon et le monde dramatique*, pp. 35–6.
3 *Mémoires de Mme de Rémusat*, II, 131.
4 *Mémoires de Mme de Chastenay*, II, 45.
5 Hugo, *Actes et paroles*, I, 50.
6 Audibert, *Indiscrétions et confidences*, pp. 160–2.
7 Brifaut, *Souvenirs d'un académicien*, I, 282.
8 Audibert, *Indiscrétions et confidences*, p. 164.
9 According to Krakovitch, *Les Pièces de théâtre soumises à la censure*, p. 21.
10 An additional reason for the ban, as Michèle Jones points out, was that 'un sujet montrant la France tiraillée entre les partis et livrée aux Anglais par les grands du royaume rappelait trop aux Français de 1820 que les Bourbons avaient reconquis leur trône avec l'aide de la perfide Albion' (*Le Théâtre national en France*, p. 71).
11 Quoted by Thomasseau, 'Le Mélodrame et la censure', *Revue des Sciences Humaines* (1976), p. 180.
12 Cf. Bailey, *Hamlet in France*, p. 37.
13 Quoted by Krakovitch, *Les Pièces de théâtre soumises à la censure*, p. 35.
14 Dumas, *Souvenirs dramatiques*, I, 240.
15 Krakovitch, 'Les Romantiques et la censure au théâtre', *Revue d'Histoire du Théâtre*, 36 (1984), p. 58.
16 As happened to Victor in 1829: see Péricaud, *Le Théâtre des Funambules*, p. 88.

17 Heine, 'Ueber die französische Bühne', in *Sämtliche Werke* (Munich: Winkler), III, 720.
18 See above, p. 94.
19 According to Krakovitch, *Hugo censuré*, pp. 201–4; cf. also Allard, *Esquisses parisiennes*, pp. 256–8.
20 See above, p. 46.
21 Hervey, *The Theatres of Paris*, p. 206. *Les Gamins de Paris* had its first performance at the Théâtre du Vaudeville on 13 February 1844.
22 Hostein, *La Liberté des théâtres*, p. 139.
23 Muret, in *L'Histoire par le théâtre*, III, 385–6.
24 Hugo, *Actes et paroles*, I, 155–6.
25 Krakovitch, *Hugo censuré*, p. 224.
26 This was certainly true of Nogaret, the first censor under the Consulate who, according to Brazier (*Chroniques des petits théâtres*, I, 248–9), 'disait aux auteurs qui bataillaient pour obtenir un mot ou un couplet: "Messieurs, ça vous est bien facile à dire; mais quand le ministre m'aura donné un coup de pied dans le derrière, me le rendrez-vous?"'
27 Lemonnier, *Les Mille et un souvenirs d'un homme de théâtre*, p. 87.
28 Cf. Poulet-Malassis, *Papiers secrets*, p. 209.
29 Hostein, *La Liberté des théâtres*, p. 137.
30 A ministerial circular dated 24 April 1858 (quoted in Cahuet, *La Liberté du théâtre*, p. 230) warned theatre directors about 'l'usage des locutions vulgaires et brutales et de certains termes grossiers empruntés à l'argot' which were beginning to creep into the language of the theatre.
31 Claretie, *La Vie moderne au théâtre*, I, 105.
32 Instances quoted in Ginisty, *La Vie d'un théâtre*, pp. 171–3, and based on censors' reports published after the fall of the Second Empire.
33 See Soubies, *Le Théâtre à Paris du 1er octobre 1870 au 31 décembre 1871*, p. 4.
34 Benjamin and Buguet, *Coulisses de bourse et de théâtre*, pp. 140, 237.
35 Carruthers, 'Theatrical censorship in Paris from 1850 to 1905', *New Zealand Journal of French Studies* (1982), p. 38.
36 In a letter published in *Le Gaulois*, 10 December 1901, quoted in Cahuet, *La Liberté du théâtre*, pp. 280–1.
37 Zola, 'La Censure', *Le Figaro*, 7 November 1885; reprinted in 'Mélanges critiques', p. 638.
38 According to Antoine, *Mes souvenirs sur le Théâtre Antoine*, p. 186.

15 THE PRIVATE SECTOR

1 *Mémoires de la baronne d'Oberkirch*, II, 70.
2 Bachaumont, *Mémoires secrets*, VI, 195 (23 July 1768).
3 Cf. above, pp. 72–3.
4 *Mémoires de Fleury*, I, 211–12.
5 Prince de Ligne, *Lettres à Eugénie*, p. 120.
6 Mercier, *Tableau de Paris, nouvelle édition* III, 18–19.

7 160 according to Du Bled, *La Comédie de société*, p. 2; 200 according to Pougin, *Dictionnaire ... du théâtre*, p. 727.

8 Bachaumont, *Mémoires secrets*, XIX, 281: 17 November 1770.

9 Young, *Travels in France*, p. 58.

10 See Coindreau, *La Farce est jouée*, p. 11.

11 A technical description will be found in Moynet, *L'Envers du théâtre*, pp. 273–4.

12 Maurice, *Épaves*, p. 24.

13 Brazier, *Chroniques des petits théâtres*, II, 300–2.

14 Geoffroy, *Cours de littérature dramatique*, VI, 55.

15 Bouffé, *Mes souvenirs*, p. 16.

16 Details of the two cases are given respectively in Vulpian and Gauthier, *Code des théâtres*, pp. 46–7, and in Vivien and Blanc, *Traité de la législation des théâtres*, p. 14.

17 Péricaud, *Le Panthéon des comédiens*, p. 200.

18 Bernier de Maligny, *Nouveau manuel théâtral*, p. 254.

19 Jouy, *L'Hermite en province*, II, 269–70.

20 Kock, *Mémoires de ... Paul de Kock*, p. 354.

21 Simonet, *Traité de la police administrative*, p. 6.

22 See Baradal, 'Le Théâtre dans le Haut-Rhin au XIXe siècle', and Rochat Hollard, 'L'Administration, partenaire de la vie théâtrale en province au XIXe siècle', pp. 219–34 and 313–30 in *Théâtre et spectacles hier et aujourd'hui: époque moderne et contemporaine*.

23 Sand, *Souvenirs et idées*, pp. 156–7; fuller details are given in a letter written by her in December 1846 to Pierre-Jules Hetzel and published in vol. VII of her *Correspondance*, ed. Georges Lubin.

24 Houssaye, *Les Confessions*, III, 193.

25 See Leveaux, *Le Théâtre de cour à Compiègne*.

26 Quoted in Léo Claretie, *Histoire des théâtres de société*, p. 126.

27 E. and J. de Goncourt, *Journal*, V, 163–4.

28 It was in 1798 that Pierre Léger composed the vaudeville entitled *Il faut un état, ou la Revue de l'an VI*. This was followed in due course by a *Revue de l'an VIII*, concerned particularly with the consequences of the new divorce law, and a *Revue de l'an IX*. See Dreyfus, *Petite histoire de la Revue de fin d'année*, pp. 41–8.

29 Mortier, *Les Soirées parisiennes*, IX, 231.

30 Quoted in Aderer, *Le Théâtre à côté*, p. 49. Gautier's article was not included in his collected dramatic criticism.

31 Lemaître, *Impressions de théâtre*, VII, 363.

32 Quoted in Henderson, *The First Avant-Garde*, p. 137.

33 Antoine, *Mes souvenirs sur le Théâtre-Libre*, pp. 42–3.

34 Figures given by Henderson, *The First Avant-Garde*, p. 55.

35 Bernheim, *Trente ans de théâtre*, I, 22–3.

36 Antoine, *Mes souvenirs sur le Théâtre-Libre*, pp. 288, 295.

37 Quoted in Touchard, *Grandes Heures de théâtre*, p. 254.

38 Charle, *La Crise littéraire à l'époque du naturalisme*, p. 141.

Bibliography

This bibliography is confined to providing full details of the abridged references made in the footnotes. It is not intended as an exhaustive list of all printed sources consulted.

Abrantès, Laure Junot d'. *Mémoires de madame la duchesse d'Abrantès*. Paris: Garnier. 10 vols. 1900–23.

Aderer, Adolphe. *Le Théâtre à côté*. Paris: Librairies-Imprimeries Réunies. 1894.

Aghion, Max. *Le Théâtre à Paris au XVIIIᵉ siècle*. Paris: Librairie de France. 1926.

Agnel, Emile. *Code-Manuel des artistes dramatiques et des artistes musiciens*. Paris: Mansut. 1851.

Alasseur, Claude. *La Comédie-Française au XVIIIᵉ siècle: étude économique*. The Hague & Paris: Mouton. 1967.

Albert, Maurice. *Les Théâtres de la foire (1660–1789)*. Paris: Hachette. 1900.

Alhoy, Maurice. *rande Biographie dramatique, ou Silhouette des acteurs, actrices, chanteurs, cantatrices, danseurs, danseuses, etc., de Paris et des départements*. Paris: chez les marchands de nouveautés. 1824.

Allard, Louis. *Esquisses parisiennes en des temps heureux, 1830–1848*. Montreal: Editions Variétés. 1943.

Alméras, Henri d'. *La Vie parisienne sous la Révolution et le Directoire*. Paris: Albin Michel. 1909.

Ambard, Robert. *La Comédie en Provence au XVIIIᵉ siècle*. Aix-en-Provence: La Pensée Universitaire. 1956.

Antoine, André. *Mes souvenirs sur le Théâtre Antoine et sur l'Odéon (première direction)*. Paris: Les Œuvres Représentatives. 1928.

Mes souvenirs sur le Théâtre-Libre. Paris: Fayard. 1921.

Le Théâtre. Paris: Les Editions de France. 2 vols. 1932.

Arnault, Antoine-Vincent. *Souvenirs d'un sexagénaire*, ed. Auguste Dietrich. Paris: Garnier. 3 vols. 1908.

Astruc, Joseph. *Le Droit privé du théâtre ou Rapports des directeurs avec les auteurs, les artistes et le public*. Macon: Protat frères. 1897.

Audebrand, Philibert. *Petits mémoires d'une stalle d'orchestre*. Paris: Jules Lévy. 1885.

Audibert, Hilarion. *Indiscrétions et confidences: souvenirs du théâtre et de la littérature*. Paris: Dentu. 1858.

Auger, Hippolyte. 'Mémoires inédits d'Hippolyte Auger (1810–1869)', *Revue rétrospective*, vol. XIII (1890), pp. 1–48, 73–120, 145–288, 313–60, 385–432; vol. XIV (1891), pp. 49–72, 97–144, 169–216, 241–88, 385–432; vol. XV (1891), pp. 25–72, 169–216, 265–88.

Bachaumont, Louis-Petit de. *Mémoires secrets pour servir à l'histoire de la République des Lettres en France*. London: John Adamson. 36 vols. 1763–89. (Continued after Bachaumont's death in 1771 by Mathieu-François Pidansat de Mairobert and Moufle d'Augerville.)

Bailey, Helen Phelps. *Hamlet in France from Voltaire to Laforgue*. Geneva: Droz. 1964.

Bailly, Jean-Sylvain. *Mémoires de Bailly*. Paris: Baudouin. 3 vols. 1821–3.

Banville, Théodore de. *Mes souvenirs*. Paris: Charpentier. 1883.

Baradel, Yvette. 'Le Théâtre dans le Haut-Rhin au XIXe siècle, 1800–1870', pp. 219–34 in *Théâtre et spectacles hier et aujourd'hui. Epoque moderne et contemporaine*. Paris: Editions du Comité de Travaux historiques et scientifiques. 1991.

Baret, Charles. *Le Théâtre en province: propos d'avant-guerre*. Paris: La Renaissance du Livre. 1918.

Beaulieu, Henri. *Les Théâtres du Boulevard du Crime*. Paris: Daragon. 1905.

Benjamin, Edmond and Henry Buguet. *Coulisses de bourse et de théâtre*. Paris: Ollendorff. 1882.

Bernardin, N.-M. *La Comédie-Italienne en France et les théâtres de la Foire et du Boulevard, 1570–1791*. Paris: Editions de la Revue Bleue. 1902.

Bernheim, Adrien. *Trente ans de théâtre*. Paris: Fasquelle/Rueffe/Lemerre. 4 vols. 1903–8.

Bernier de Maligny, Aristippe. *Nouveau manuel théâtral théorique et pratique nécessaire à tous les acteurs; aux directeurs, régisseurs et employés des théâtres; aux auteurs et aux critiques*. Paris: Librairie encyclopédique de Roret. 1854.

Binns, Amanda. 'Popular Theatre and Politics in the French Revolution', *Theatre Quarterly*, 16 (1974–5), pp. 18–34.

Biré, Edmond. *Journal d'un bourgeois de Paris pendant la Terreur*. Paris: Perrin. 5 vols. 1898.

Blagdon, Francis. *Paris As It Was and As It Is; or a Sketch of the French Capital Illustrative of the Effects of the Revolution*. London: Baldwin. 2 vols. 1803.

Boncampain, Jacques. *Auteurs et comédiens au XVIIIe siècle*. Paris: Perrin. 1976.

Bonnassies, Jules. *Les Spectacles forains et la Comédie-Française. Le droit des pauvres avant et après 1789. Les Auteurs dramatiques et la Comédie-Française au XIXe siècle*. Paris: Dentu. 1875.

Bossuet, Pierre. *Histoire des théâtres nationaux*. Paris: Jorel. 1909.

Bouchard, Alfred. *La Langue théâtrale, vocabulaire historique, descriptif et anecdotique des termes et des choses du théâtre*. Paris: Arnaud & Lebat. 1878.

Boudet, Micheline. *Mademoiselle Mars l'inimitable*. Paris: Perrin. 1987.

Bouffé, Désiré-Marie. *Mes souvenirs, 1800–1880*. Paris: Dentu. 1880.

Bouteiller, Jules-Edouard. *Histoire complète et méthodique des théâtres de Rouen*. Rouen: Giroux & Renaux. 4 vols. 1860–80.

Brazier, Nicolas. *Chroniques des petits théâtres de Paris*, edited by Georges d'Heylli. Paris: Rouveyre & Blond. 2 vols. 1883.

Brenner, Clarence D. *The Théâtre Italien, Its Repertory, 1716–1793; with a Historical Introduction*. Berkeley & Los Angeles: University of California Press. 1961.

Brifaut, Charles. *Souvenirs d'un académicien sur la Révolution, le Premier Empire et la Restauration*. Paris: Albin Michel. 2 vols. 1921.

Bureau, Georges. *Le Théâtre et sa législation*. Paris: Ollendorff. 1898.

Cahuet, Albéric. *La Liberté du théâtre en France et à l'étranger: histoire, fonctionnement et discussion de la censure dramatique*. Paris: Dujarric. 1902.

Campardon, Emile. *Les Comédiens du Roi de la troupe italienne pendant les deux derniers siècles*. Paris: Berger-Levrault. 2 vols. 1880.

Carr, John. *The Stranger in France; or, A Tour from Devonshire to Paris*. London: J. Johnson. 1807.

Carruthers, Neil. 'Theatrical Censorship in Paris from 1850 to 1905'. *New Zealand Journal of French Studies*, 3 (1982), pp. 21–41.

Charle, Christophe. *La Crise littéraire à l'époque du naturalisme: roman, théâtre et politique*. Paris: Presses de l'Ecole Normale Supérieure. 1979.

Chastenay de Lanty, Louise-Marie-Victorine de. *Mémoires de Madame de Chastenay, 1771–1815*, ed. Alphonse Roserot. Paris: Plon-Nourrit. 2 vols. 1896–7.

Claretie, Jules. *Profils de théâtre*. Paris: Fasquelle. 1904.

La Vie moderne au théâtre: causeries sur l'art dramatique. Paris: Barba. 2 vols. 1869, 1875.

Claretie, Léo. *Histoire des théâtres de société*. Paris: Librairie Molière. 1906.

Coindreau, Maurice Edgar. *La Farce est jouée: vingt-cinq ans de théâtre français, 1900–1925*. New York: Editions de la Maison Française. 1942.

Collé, Charles. *Journal et mémoires de Charles Collé sur les hommes de lettres, les ouvrages dramatiques et les événements les plus mémorables du règne de Louis XV*, ed. Honoré Bonhomme. Paris: Firmin-Didot. 3 vols. 1868.

Combarnous, Victor. *L'Histoire du Grand-Théâtre de Marseille, 31 octobre 1787 – 13 novembre 1919*. Marseille: Imp. Méridionale. 1927.

Copin, Alfred. *Etudes dramatiques. Talma et la Révolution*. Paris: Perrin. 1888.

Etudes dramatiques. Talma et l'Empire. Paris: Frinzine. 1887.

Courteault, Paul. *La Révolution et les théâtres à Bordeaux*. Paris: Perrin. 1926.

Cradock, Anna Francesca. *Journal de Madame Cradock. Voyage en France 1783–1786, traduit d'après le manuscrit original et inédit par Mme O. Delphin-Baileyguier*. Paris: Perrin. 1896.

Daudet, Alphonse. *Entre les frises et la rampe. Petites études de la vie théâtrale*. Paris: Dentu. 1894

Deck, Pantaléon. *Histoire du théâtre français à Strasbourg, 1681–1830.* Strasbourg & Paris: Le Roux. 1948.

Demuth, Norman. *French Opera: Its Development to the Revolution.* Horsham, Sussex: Artemis Press. 1963.

Descotes, Maurice. *L'Acteur Joanny et son journal inédit.* Paris: Presses Universitaires de France. 1956.

   Le Drame romantique et ses grands créateurs. Paris: Presses Universitaires de France. 1955.

Des Essarts (Nicolas-Toussaint Lemoyne). *Les Trois Théâtres de Paris, ou Abrégé historique de l'établissement de la Comédie-Française, de la Comédie-Italienne et de l'Opéra; avec un précis des loix, arrêts, règlements et usages qui concernent chacun de ces spectacles.* Paris: Lacombe. 1777.

Desnoiresterres, Gustave. *La Comédie satirique au XVIIIᵉ siècle. Histoire de la société française par l'allusion, la personnalité et la satire au théâtre: Louis XV, Louis XVI, la Révolution.* Paris: Perrin. 1885.

Destranges, Etienne. *Le Théâtre à Nantes depuis ses origines jusqu'à nos jours.* Paris: Fischbacher. 1893.

Detcheverry, Armand. *Histoire des théâtres de Bordeaux depuis leur origine dans cette ville jusqu'à nos jours.* Bordeaux: Delmas. 1860.

Dreyfus, Robert. *Petite histoire de la Revue de fin d'année.* Paris: Charpentier-Fasquelle. 1909.

Du Bled, Victor. *La Comédie de société au XVIIIᵉ siècle.* Paris: Calmann-Lévy. 1893.

Dubois, Jean. *La Crise théâtrale.* Paris: Imprimerie de l'Art. 1895.

Dumas, Alexandre. *Souvenirs dramatiques.* Paris: Calmann-Lévy. 2 vols. 1868.

Dumas *fils,* Alexandre. *Nouveaux entr'actes.* Paris: Calmann-Lévy. 1890.

Dussane, Béatrix. *La Célimène de Thermidor. Louise Contat, 1760–1813.* Paris: Charpentier-Fasquelle. 1929.

   La Comédie-Française. Paris: La Renaissance du Livre. n.d. [1923].

Echinard, Pierre. 'Louis Rouffe et l'école marseillaise de pantomime dans la deuxième moitié du XIXᵉ siècle', pp. 547–60 in *Théâtre et spectacles hier et aujourd'hui. Epoque moderne et contemporaine.* Paris: Editions du Comité de Travaux historiques et scientifiques. 1991.

Estrée, Paul d'. *Le Théâtre sous la Terreur (théâtre de la peur) 1793–1794.* Paris: Emile-Paul. 1913.

Etienne, C. G. and A. Martainville. *Histoire du Théâtre-Français depuis le commencement de la Révolution jusqu'à la réunion générale.* Paris: Barba. 4 vols. 1802.

Favart, Charles-Simon. *Mémoires et correspondance littéraires, dramatiques et anecdotiques.* Paris: Collin. 3 vols. 1808.

Ferrières, Charles-Elie de. *Correspondance inédite (1789, 1790, 1791) publiée et annotée par Henri Carré.* Paris: Armand Carré. 1932.

Fiorentino, Pier Angelo. *Comédies et comédiens, feuilletons.* Paris: Michel Lévy. 2 vols. 1866.

Fleury (Abraham-Joseph Bénard). *Mémoires de Fleury, de la Comédie-Française*, ed. J. B. P. Lafitte. Paris: Delahays. 2 vols. 1847.

Flore, Mlle (Flore Corvée). *Mémoires de Mlle Flore, actrice des Variétés*, ed. Henri d'Alméras. Paris: Société parisienne d'édition. 1903.

Fouque, Octave. *Histoire du Théâtre Ventadour, 1829–1879. Opéra-Comique, Théâtre de la Renaissance, Théâtre-Italien*. Paris: Fischbacher. 1881.

Fuchs, Max. *La Vie théâtrale en province au XVIIIe siècle*. Paris: Droz. 1933.

Funck-Brentano, Frantz. *La Bastille des comédiens, le For-l'Evêque*. Paris: Hachette. 1910.

Gautier, Théophile. *Histoire de l'art dramatique en France depuis vingt-cinq ans*. Paris: Hetzel. 6 vols. 1858–9.

Geoffroy, Julien-Louis. *Cours de littérature dramatique, ou Recueil par ordre de matières des feuilletons de Geoffroy*. Paris: Blanchard. 6 vols. 1825.

Géréon, Léonard. *La Rampe et les coulisses: esquisses biographiques des directeurs, acteurs et actrices de tous les théâtres*. Paris: chez les marchands de nouveautés. 1832.

Giffard, Pierre. *Nos mœurs. La Vie au théâtre*. Paris: Librairie Illustrée. 1888.

Ginisty, Paul. *La Vie d'un théâtre*. Paris: Delagrave. 1906.

Girardin, Delphine de. *Lettres parisiennes, 1836–1848*. Reprinted as vols. IV and V of *Œuvres complètes de Madame Emile de Girardin, née Delphine Gay*. Paris: Plon. 1860.

Goizet, J. and A. Burtal. *Dictionnaire universel du théâtre en France et du théâtre français à l'étranger, alphabétique, biographique et bibliographique, depuis l'origine du théâtre jusqu'à nos jours*. Paris: Siège de l'Administration des arts internationaux. 1867.

Goldoni, Carlo. *Mémoires de M. Goldoni pour servir à l'histoire de sa vie et à celle de son théâtre*, ed. Paul de Roux. Paris: Mercure de France, 1965. (First published 1787.)

Goncourt, Edmond and Jules de. *Histoire de la société française pendant la Révolution*. Paris: Fasquelle. 1914. (First published 1854.)

Histoire de la société française pendant le Directoire. Paris: Fasquelle. 1914. (First published 1855.)

Journal. Mémoires de la vie littéraire. Monaco: Imprimerie Nationale. 22 vols. 1956–8.

Got, Edmond. *Journal de Edmond Got, sociétaire de la Comédie-Française, 1822–1901*, ed. Médéric Got. Paris: Plon-Nourrit. 2 vols. 1910.

Gourret, Jean. *Histoire de l'Opéra-Comique*. Paris: Publications Universitaires. 1978.

Grimm, Frédéric-Melchior de. *Correspondance littéraire, philosophique et critique, adressée à un souverain d'Allemagne*. (Part 1, 1753–69, 6 vols.; part 2, 1770–82, 5 vols.; part 3, 1782–90, 5 vols.) Paris: Buisson. 1812–13.

Halem, Gerhard Anton von. *Blicke auf einen Theil Deutschlands, der Schweiz und Frankreichs bey einer Reise vom Jahre 1790*. Hamburg: Bohn. 2 vols. 1791.

Halévy, Ludovic. *Notes et souvenirs, 1871–1872*. Paris: Calmann-Lévy. 1889.

Hallays-Dabot, Victor. *Histoire de la censure théâtrale en France*. Paris: Dentu. 1862.

Hamiche, Daniel. *Le Théâtre et la Révolution. La lutte des classes au théâtre en 1789 et en 1793*. Paris: Union Générale d'Editions. 1973.

Harel, F. A., P. M. Alhoy and A. Jal. *Dictionnaire théâtral ou Douze cent trente-trois vérités sur les directeurs, régisseurs, acteurs, actrices et employés des divers théâtres* ... Paris. Barba. 1824.

Heine, Heinrich. *Ueber die französische Bühne: vertraute Briefe an August Lewald (1837)*. Reprinted in vol. III of Heine, *Sämtliche Werke*. Munich: Winkler Verlag. 1972.

Henderson, John A. *The First Avant-Garde, 1887–1894: Sources of the Modern French Theatre*. London: Harrap. 1971.

Hérissay, Jacques. *Le Monde des théâtres pendant la Révolution, 1789–1800*. Paris: Perrin. 1922.

Hervey, Charles. *The Theatres of Paris*. London: John Mitchell. 1846.

Heylli, Georges d'. *La Comédie-Française à Londres (1871–1879). Journal inédit de E. Got. Journal de F. Sarcey*. Paris: Ollendorff. 1880.

Journal intime de la Comédie-Française, 1852–1871. Paris: Dentu. 1879.

Hostein, Hippolyte. *Historiettes et souvenirs d'un homme de théâtre*. Paris: Dentu. 1878.

La Liberté des théâtres. Paris: Librairie des Auteurs. 1867.

Houssaye, Arsène. *Les Confessions. Souvenirs d'un demi-siècle*. Paris: Dentu. 6 vols. 1885–91.

Hugo, Victor. *Actes et paroles*. Paris: Albin Michel. 2 vols. 1937.

Janin, Jules. *Histoire de la littérature dramatique*. Paris: Michel Lévy. 6 vols. 1855–8.

Jones, Michèle H. *Le Théâtre national en France de 1800 à 1830*. Paris: Klincksieck. 1975.

Jouslin de la Salle, Armand. *Souvenirs sur le Théâtre-Français (1833–1837)*, edited by M. G. Monval and the Comte Fleury. Paris: Emile-Paul. 1900.

Jouy, Etienne de. *L'Hermite en province, ou Observations sur les mœurs et usages français au commencement du XIXᵉ siècle*. Paris: Pillet. 14 vols. 1818–27.

Knapp, Bettina L. *The Reign of the Theatrical Director: French Theatre, 1887–1924*. Troy, N.Y.: The Whitston Publishing Co. 1988.

Kock, Charles-Paul de. *Mémoires de Ch. Paul de Kock écrits par lui-même*. Paris: Dentu. 1873.

Krakovitch, Odile. *Hugo censuré. La Liberté au théâtre au XIXᵉ siècle*. Paris: Calmann-Lévy. 1985.

Les Pièces de théâtre soumises à la censure (1800–1830). Paris: Archives Nationales. 1982.

'Les Romantiques et la censure au théâtre'. *Revue d'Histoire du Théâtre*, 36 (1984), pp. 56–68.

Lacan, Adolphe and Charles Paulmier. *Traité de la législation et de la jurisprudence des théâtres*. Paris: Durand. 2 vols. 1853.

Lagrave, Henri. 'La Comédie-Française au XVIIIe siècle ou les contradictions d'un privilège'. *Revue d'Histoire du Théâtre*, 32 (1980), pp. 127–41.
'Les Structures du théâtre dans la province française: le cas exemplaire de Bordeaux'. *Studies on Voltaire and the Eighteenth Century*, CXCII (1980), pp. 1425–31.

La Harpe, Jean-François. *Correspondance littéraire ... depuis 1774 jusqu'à 1791*. Paris: Dupont. 6 vols. 1801.

Lamothe, L. *Les Théâtres de Bordeaux, suivis de quelques vues de réforme théâtrale*. Bordeaux: Chaumas. 1853.

Lang, Jack. *L'Etat et le théâtre*. Paris: Librairie Générale de Droit et de Jurisprudence. 1968.

Lanzac de Laborie, Léon de. *Paris sous Napoléon*. Vol. VII. *Le Théâtre-Français*. Paris: Plon Nourrit. 1911. Vol. VIII. *Spectacles et musées*. Paris: Plon-Nourrit. 1913.

Laplace, Roselyne. 'Des théâtres d'enfants au XVIIIe siècle'. *Revue d'Histoire du Théâtre*, 32 (1980), pp. 21–31.

Lasalle, Albert de. *Les Treize Salles de l'Opéra*. Paris: Sartorius. 1875.

Lassalle, Eugène. *Comédiens et amateurs: le théâtre et ses dessous*. Montreal: Imprimerie du Devoir. 1919.

Laugier, Eugène. *Documents historiques sur la Comédie-Française pendant le règne de S. M. l'Empereur Napoléon Ier*. Paris: Firmin-Didot. 1853.

Laval, Charles. *La Liberté des théâtres au point de vue de la province*. Paris: Librairie Théâtrale. 1864.

Lavedan, Henri. *Avant l'oubli*. Paris: Plon. 4 vols. 1933–40.

Lebègue, Ernest. *Boursault-Malherbe, comédien, conventionnel, spéculateur*. Paris: Alcan. 1935.

Lecomte, Louis-Henry. *Histoire des théâtres de Paris: la Renaissance*. Paris: Daragon. 1905.
Histoire des théâtres de Paris: Les Jeux- ymniques; le Panorama-Dramatique. Paris: Daragon. 1908.
Histoire des théâtres de Paris: les Nouveautés. Paris: Daragon. 1907.
Histoire des théâtres de Paris: le Théâtre National; le Théâtre de l'Egalité. Paris: Daragon. 1907.
Histoire des théâtres de Paris: les Variétés-Amusantes. Paris: Daragon. 1908.
Napoléon et le monde dramatique. Paris: Daragon. 1912.

Lefebvre, Léon. *Histoire du théâtre de Lille de ses origines à nos jours*. Lille: Imprimerie Lefebvre-Ducrocq. 5 vols. 1901–7.

Legouvé, Ernest. *Soixante ans de souvenirs*. Paris: Hetzel. 4 vols. 1888.

Lemaître, Jules. *Impressions de théâtre*. Paris: Boivin. 11 vols. 1888–1918.

Lemazurier, Pierre D. *alerie historique des acteurs du Théâtre-Français, depuis 1600 jusqu'à nos jours*. Paris: Chaumerot. 2 vols. 1810.

Lemonnier, Alphonse. *Les Mille et un souvenirs d'un homme de théâtre*. Paris: Librairie Molière. 1902.

Le Senne, Charles. *Code du théâtre: lois, règlements, jurisprudence, usages*. Paris: Tresse. 1878.

Leveaux, Alphonse. *Le Théâtre de la cour à Compiègne pendant le règne de Napoléon III*. Paris: Tresse. 1882.

Lewald, August. *Album aus Paris*. Hamburg: Hoffmann & Campe. 2 vols. 1832.

Lhomme, F. *Etudes sur le théâtre contemporain*. Paris: Dupret. 1887.

Liéby, Adolphe. *Etude sur le théâtre de Marie-Joseph Chénier*. Paris: Société française d'imprimerie et de librairie. 1901.

'La Presse révolutionnaire et la censure théâtrale sous la Terreur'. *Révolution Française*, 45 (1903), pp. 306–53, 447–70, 502–29; 46 (1904), pp. 13–28, 97–128.

Ligne, Charles-Joseph, prince de. *Lettres à Eugénie sur les spectacles*, ed. Gustave Charlier. Brussels & Paris: Champion. 1922.

Loliée, Frédéric. *La Comédie-Française. Histoire de la Maison de Molière de 1658 à 1907*. Paris: Laveur. 1907.

Longuemare, Paul de. *Le Théâtre à Caen, 1628–1830*. Paris: Picard. 1895.

Lumière, Henry. *Le Théâtre-Français pendant la Révolution, 1789–1799*. Paris: Dentu. 1894.

Lyonnet, Henry. *Les Premières de Victor Hugo*. Paris: Delagrave. 1930.

Malliot, A. L. *La Musique au théâtre*. Paris: Amyot. 1863.

Manne, Edmond-Denis de, and C. Ménétrier. *alerie historique des acteurs français ... des scènes secondaires depuis 1760 jusqu'à nos jours*. Lyon: Scheuring. 1877.

alerie historique des comédiens de la troupe de Nicolet. Lyon: Scheuring. 1869.

Marseille. Notice historique sur ses théâtres privilégiés, par un ancien amateur. Marseilles: Camoin frères. 1863.

Matthews, James Brander. *The Theatres of Paris*. New York: Scribner. 1880.

Maurice, Charles. *Epaves. Théâtre – histoire – anecdotes – mots*. Paris: chez les principaux libraires. 1865.

Histoire anecdotique du théâtre, de la littérature et de diverses impressions contemporaines. Paris: Plon. 2 vols. 1856.

Le Théâtre-Français, monument et dépendances. Second edition, revised and enlarged. Paris: Garnier. 1860.

Mayeur de Saint-Paul, François-Marie. *Le Chroniqueur désœuvré ou l'Espion du Boulevard du Temple*. London. 1782.

Mercier, Louis-Sébastien. *Du théâtre, ou Nouvel essai sur l'art dramatique*. Amsterdam: Van Harrevelt. 1773.

Tableau de Paris. London. 2 vols. 1781.

Tableau de Paris, nouvelle édition. Amsterdam. 8 vols. 1782–3.

Métra, François. *Correspondance secrète, politique et littéraire, ou Mémoires pour servir à l'histoire des cours, des sociétés et de la littérature en France, depuis la mort de Louis XV*. London: John Adamson. 18 vols. 1787–90.

Monval, Georges. 'Les Théâtres subventionnés'. *Revue énérale d'Administration*, 3 (1878), pp. 496–516.

Moore, John. *A View of Society and Manners in France, Switzerland and ermany*. London: Strahan & Cadell. 2 vols. 1780.

Mortier, Arnold. *Les Soirées parisiennes, par un Monsieur de l'orchestre*. Paris: Dentu. 10 vols. 1875–84.

Moynet, J. *L'Envers du théâtre; machines et décorations*. Third edition. Paris: Hachette. 1888. (First edition: 1873.)

Muret, Théodore. *L'Histoire par le théâtre, 1789–1851*. Paris: Amyot. 3 vols. 1865.

Nerval, Gérard de. *La Vie du théâtre*. Edited by Jean Richer. Paris: Lettres modernes. 1961.

Nisard, Charles. *Mémoires et correspondances historiques et littéraires inédits, 1726–1816*. Paris: Michel Lévy. 1858.

Oberkirch, Henriette Louise d'. *Mémoires de la baronne d'Oberkirch*, ed. Léonce de Montbrison. Paris: Charpentier. 2 vols. 1869.

Ouvrard, Eloi. *La Vie au café-concert. Etudes de mœurs*. Paris: Imprimerie Paul Schmidt. 1894.

Papillon de la Ferté, Denis-Pierre-Jean. *L'Administration des Menus, journal de Papillon de la Ferté*, ed. Ernest Boysse. Paris: Ollendorff. 1887.

Péricaud, Louis. *Le Panthéon des comédiens, de Molière à Coquelin aîné. Notices biographiques*. Paris: Fasquelle. 1922.

Théâtre de Monsieur. Paris: Jorel. 1908.

Le Théâtre des Funambules: ses mimes, ses acteurs et ses pantomimes, depuis sa fondation jusqu'à sa démolition. Paris: Sapin. 1897.

Théâtre des Petits Comédiens de S. A. S. Monseigneur le comte de Beaujolais. Paris: Jorel. 1909.

Plunkett, Jacques de. *Cent soixante ans de théâtre. Fantômes et souvenirs de la Porte-St-Martin*. Paris: Ariane. 1946.

Pollitzer, Marcel. *Trois reines de théâtre: Mademoiselle Mars, Marie Dorval, Rachel*. Paris: La Colombe. 1958.

Porel, Paul and Georges Monval. *L'Odéon. Histoire administrative, anecdotique et littéraire du Second Théâtre-Français*. Paris: Lemerre. 2 vols. 1876, 1882.

Pougin, Arthur. *Acteurs et actrices d'autrefois: histoire anecdotique des théâtres de Paris depuis trois cents ans*. Paris: Juven. 1896.

La Comédie-Française et la Révolution. Paris: Gaultier. 1902.

Dictionnaire historique et pittoresque du théâtre et des arts qui s'y rattachent. Paris: Firmin-Didot. 1885.

Un directeur d'opéra au XVIIIe siècle: l'opéra sous l'ancien régime, l'opéra sous la Révolution. Paris: Fischbacher. 1914.

Poulet-Malassis, Auguste. *Papiers secrets et correspondance du Second Empire*. Paris: Auguste Ghio. 1873.

Pré, Corinne. 'La Parodie dramatique en vaudevilles de 1715 à 1789', pp. 265–81 in *Burlesque et formes parodiques*. Paris, Seattle & Tübingen. Papers in French Seventeenth-Century Literature. 1987.

Pujoulx, Jean-Baptiste. *Paris à la fin du XVIIIᵉ siècle, ou Esquisse historique et morale des monuments et des ruines de cette capitale*. Paris: Mathé, 1801.

Rahill, Frank. *The World of Melodrama*. Pennsylvania State University Press. 1967.

Reichardt, Johann Friedrich. *Vertraute Briefe aus Paris geschrieben in den Jahren 1802 und 1803*. Hamburg: Hoffmann. 3 vols. 1804.

Rémusat, Claire-Elisabeth de. *Lettres de Madame de Rémusat, 1804–1814*, ed. Paul de Rémusat. Paris: Calmann-Lévy. 2 vols. 1881.

Mémoires de Madame de Rémusat, 1802–1808, ed. Paul de Rémusat. Paris: Calmann-Lévy. 3 vols. 1880.

Rochat Hollard, Claude-France. 'L'Administration, partenaire de la vie théâtrale en province au XIXe siècle: l'exemple du département de Vaucluse', pp. 313–30 in *Théâtre et spectacles hier et aujourd'hui: époque moderne et contemporaine*. Paris: Editions du Comité de Travaux historiques et scientifiques. 1991.

Root-Bernstein, Michèle. *Boulevard Theater and Revolution in Eighteenth-Century Paris*. Ann Arbor: UMI Research Press. 1984.

Sala, George Augustus. *Paris Herself Again in 1878–9*. Sixth edition. London: Vizetelly; New York: Scribner. 1882. (First published 1880.)

Samson, Joseph-Isidore. *Mémoires de Samson, de la Comédie-Française*. Paris: Ollendorff. 1882.

Sand, Georges. *Souvenirs et idées*. Paris: Calmann-Lévy. n.d.

Sanderson, John. *The American in Paris*. London: Colburn. 2 vols. 1838.

Sarcey, Francisque. *Comédiens et comédiennes: la Comédie-Française*. Paris: Librairie des Bibliophiles. 1877.

Schulz, Friedrich, *Ueber Paris und die Pariser*. Berlin: Vieweg. 1791.

Scott, John. *A Visit to Paris in 1814, Being a Review of the Moral, Political, Intellectual and Social Conditions of the French Capital*. London: Longman. 1815.

Sélis, Nicolas-Joseph. *Lettre à un père de famille sur les petits spectacles de Paris, par un honnête homme*. Paris: Garnéry. 1789.

Simonet, Claude-Hubert. *Traité de la police administrative des théâtres de la ville de Paris*. Paris: Thorel. 1850.

Sorin, Paul. *Du rôle de l'Etat en matière d'art scénique*. Paris: Arthur Rousseau. 1902.

Soubies, Albert. *Le Théâtre à Paris du 1er octobre 1870 au 31 décembre 1871*. Paris: Marpon et Flammarion. 1892.

and Charles Malherbe. *Histoire de l'Opéra-Comique: la seconde salle Favart*. Paris: Marpon et Flammarion. 2 vols. 1892–3.

Thiéry, Luc-Vincent. *Guide des amateurs et des étrangers voyageurs à Paris, ou description raisonnée de cette ville, de sa banlieue, et de tout ce qu'elles contiennent de remarquable*. Paris: Hardouin. 2 vols. 1787.

Thomasseau, Jean-Marie. 'Le Mélodrame et la censure sous le Premier Empire et la Restauration.' *Revue des Sciences Humaines*, 162 (1976), pp. 171–82.

Thrale, Hester Lynch. *The French Journals of Mrs Thrale and Dr Johnson*, ed. Moses Tyson and Henry Guppy. Manchester University Press. 1932.

Tisseau, Paul. *Une comédienne sous la Révolution: Marie-Elisabeth Joly, sociétaire de la Comédie-Française*. Paris: Editions de la Bonne Idée. 1928.

Touchard, Pierre-Aimé. *Grandes Heures de théâtre à Paris.* Paris: Perrin. 1965.

Trollope, Frances. *Paris and the Parisians in 1835.* London: Roger Bentley. 2 vols. 1836.

Valpy, Richard. 'A Short Sketch of a Short Trip to Paris in 1788'. *The Pamphleteer*, 3 (1814), pp. 490–552.

Véron, Louis-Désiré. *Mémoires d'un bourgeois de Paris.* Paris: Gabriel de Gonet. 6 vols. 1853–5.

Paris en 1860. Les théâtres de Paris depuis 1806 jusqu'en 1860. Paris: Librairie Nouvelle. 1860.

Vingtrinier, Emmanuel. *Le Théâtre à Lyon au XVIIIᵉ siècle.* Lyon: Meton. 1879.

Vivien, Auguste and Edmond Blanc. *Traité de la législation des théâtres ou exposé complet et méthodique des lois et de la jurisprudence relativement aux théâtres et spectacles publics.* Paris: Brissot-Thivars. 1830.

Vulpian, Alphonse, and Gauthier. *Code des théâtres ou Manuel à l'usage des directeurs, entrepreneurs et actionnaires de spectacles, des auteurs et artistes dramatiques, etc., etc.* Paris: Warrée. 1829.

Weiss, Jean-Jacques. *A propos de théâtre.* Paris: Michel Lévy. 1893.

Le Théâtre et les mœurs. Paris: Calmann-Lévy. 1889.

Welschinger, Henri. *Le Théâtre de la Révolution, 1789–1799.* Paris: Charavay. 1880.

Wicks, Charles Beaumont. *The Parisian Stage: Alphabetical Indexes of Plays and Authors (1800–1900).* University of Alabama Press. 5 vols. 1950–79.

Young, Arthur. *Travels in France During the Years 1787, 1788, and 1789,* ed. Constantia Maxwell. Cambridge University Press. 1950. (First published, Bury St Edmunds, 1792.)

Zola, Emile. 'Mélanges critiques', pp. 529–770 in Zola, *Œuvres complètes,* ed. Henri Mitterand, vol. XII. Paris: Cercle du Livre Précieux. 1969.

Guide to further reading

GENERAL HISTORIES

Jomaron, Jacqueline (ed.). *Le Théâtre en France*. Paris: Armand Colin, 2 vols., 1988–9. The most recent standard history. The first volume covers the period before the Revolution, the second continues the story down to present times. Copiously illustrated.

[various]. *Théâtre et spectacles hier et aujourd'hui: époque moderne et contemporaine*. Paris: Editions du CTHS, 1991. A collection of some forty papers on different aspects of the theatre, from the seventeenth century down to the twentieth. The second part, entitled 'Les pouvoirs et les spectacles', has particular bearing on the subject of the present work.

THE EIGHTEENTH CENTURY

Larthomas, Pierre. *Le Théâtre en France au XVIIIᵉ siècle*. Paris: PUF, 1980.

Rougemont, Martine de. *La Vie théâtrale en France au XVIIIᵉ siècle*. Paris: Champion, 1988.

Fuchs, Max. *La Vie théâtrale en province au XVIIIᵉ siècle*. Paris: Droz, 1933.

Lough, John. *Paris Theatre Audiences in the Seventeenth and Eighteenth Centuries*. Oxford University Press, 1957.

Goodden, Angelica. *'Actio' and Persuasion. Dramatic Performance in Eighteenth-Century France*. Oxford: Clarendon Press, 1986.

Boncompain, Jacques. *Acteurs et comédiens au XVIIIᵉ siècle*. Paris: Perrin, 1976.

Howe, Alan and Richard Waller. *En marge du classicisme: Essays on the French Theatre from the Renaissance to the Enlightenment*. Liverpool University Press, 1987.

Isherwood, Robert M. *Farce and Fantasy: Popular Entertainment in Eighteenth-Century Paris*. Oxford University Press, 1986.

Root-Bernstein, Michèle. *Boulevard Theater and Revolution in Eighteenth-Century Paris*. Ann Arbor: UMI Research Press. 1984.

STATE-SUPPORTED THEATRES IN THE *ANCIEN RÉGIME*

Chevalley, Sylvie. *La Comédie-Française hier et aujourd'hui*. Paris: Didier, 1979.

Alasseur, Claude. *La Comédie-Française au XVIIIe siècle: étude économique*. The Hague and Paris: Mouton, 1967.

Demuth, Norman. *French Opera: Its Development down to the Revolution*. Horsham, Sussex: Artemis Press, 1963.

Brenner, Clarence D. *The Théâtre-Italien, Its Repertory, 1716–1793*. Berkeley and Los Angeles: University of California Press, 1961.

Gourret, Jean. *Histoire de l'Opéra-Comique*. Paris: Publications Universitaires, 1978.

Genty, Christian. *Histoire du Théâtre-National de l'Odéon, 1782–1982*. Paris: Fischbacher, 1982.

THE FRENCH REVOLUTION

Carlson, Marvin. *The Theatre of the French Revolution*. Ithaca, NY: Cornell University Press, 1966.

Guibert, Noëlle, and Jacqueline Razgonnikov. *La Comédie aux trois couleurs: le Journal de la Comédie-Française, 1787–1799*. Paris: SEDES, 1989.

Hamiche, Daniel. *Le Théâtre et la Révolution: la lutte des classes au théâtre en 1789 et 1793*. Paris: UGE, 1973.

Brown, Frederick. *Theater and Revolution: the Culture of the French Stage*. New York: Viking Press, 1980.

Rodmell, Graham E. *French Drama of the Revolutionary Years*. London: Routledge, 1990.

Convegno di studi sul teatro e la Rivoluzione francese. Vicenza: Accademia Olimpica, 1991. A collection of some twenty papers on aspects of the theatre and the French Revolution.

Tissier, André. *Les Spectacles à Paris pendant la Révolution. Répertoire analytique, chronologique et bibliographique*. Geneva: Droz, 1992.

THE NINETEENTH CENTURY

Berthier, Patrick. *Le Théâtre au XIXe siècle*. Paris: PUF, 1986.

Carlson, Marvin. *The French Stage in the Nineteenth Century*. Metuchen, NJ: Scarecrow Press, 1972.

Jones, Michèle H. *Le Théâtre national en France de 1800 à 1830*. Paris: Klincksieck, 1975.

Howarth, W. D. *Sublime and Grotesque: a Study of French Romantic Drama*. London: Harrap, 1975.

Krakovitch, Odile. *Hugo censuré. La Liberté au théâtre au XIXe siècle*. Paris: Calmann-Lévy, 1985.

Jones, Louisa E. *Sad Clowns and Pale Pierrots: Literature and the Popular Comic Arts in Nineteenth-Century France*. Lexington, Ky: French Forum, 1984.

McCormick, John. *Popular Theatres of Nineteenth-Century France*. London: Routledge, 1993.

Hobson, Harold. *French Theatre since 1830*. London: Calder, 1978.

Charle, Christophe. *La Crise littéraire à l'époque du naturalisme: roman, théâtre et politique*. Paris: Presses de l'ENS, 1979.

Henderson, John A. *The First Avant-Garde, 1887–1894: Sources of the Modern French Theatre*. London: Harrap, 1971.

Gontard, Denis. *La Décentralisation théâtrale en France, 1895–1952*. Paris: CDU/SEDES, 1973. See also Jack Lang, *L'Etat et le théâtre*. Paris: Librairie Générale de Droit et de Jurisprudence, 1968, an account of the 'decentralization' policy under the Fifth Republic by its main architect.

Index

In this index the names of writers using pseudonyms, and the stage-names of actors and actresses, are followed by their real names in square brackets.

Abbeville, 141
Abrantès, Laure Junot, duchesse d', 107
Académie de Musique, *see* Opera
Académie Française, 22, 217
Adam, Adolphe, 170, 180
Adrien (Méhul and Hoffmann), 94
Agamemnon (Lemercier), 205
Aida (Verdi), 151
Aix-en-Provence, 153
Alaux (director of the
    Panorama-Dramatique), 164–5, 167
Albert of Saxe-Coburg Gotha, Prince, 216
Alcazar (*café-concert*), 200
Alembert, Jean le Rond d', 92
Alhoy, Maurice, 147
Almanach forain, 29, 196
amateur theatricals, under *ancien régime*,
    72–3, 226–9; during the nineteenth
    century, 122, 146, 231–40
Amaury-Duval [Duval, Amaury Pineu], 114
Ambassadeurs (*café-concert*), 202
Ambigu-Comique, 2, 31–3, 36, 38, 63,
    99–100, 116, 118, 132, 150, 167, 193,
    195, 210, 221
Amelot de Chaillou, Antoine-Jean, 19
Ami des Lois, L' (Laya), 79–82, 92
Amiens, 155; Peace of, 71, 108
Amour quêteur, L' (Robineau), 28
Anaïs [Pauline Aubert], 183
Ancelot, Jacques-Arsène, 184
Ancey, Georges, 223
Andromaque (Racine), 135, 186
Anseaume, Louis, 131
Antigone (Doigny du Ponceau), 126
Antoine, André, 5, 195, 224, 239–43
Antony (Dumas), 186
applications (made by audiences of lines in
    plays), 123–36

Arnault, Alphonse, 134
Arnault, Antoine-Vincent, 84, 90, 134, 209
Arnault, Lucien, 184
Arnould-Mussot, *see* Mussot, Jean-François
Arras, 141
Artaxerce (Delrieu), 105
Artois, Comte d' (future Charles X), 70, 72,
    227
Asgill, Capt. Charles, 46–7
Assemblées primaires, Les (Martainville), 100
Athalie (Racine), 202
Athénée-Comique, 224
Auber, Daniel, 152, 170, 180, 210
Audebrand, Philibert, 199
Audinot, Nicolas, 30–3, 36–9, 55, 62–3, 97,
    118
Auger, Hippolyte, 151
Augier, Emile, 157, 183
Aumont, Louis-Marie-Céleste, duc d', 169
Austen, Jane, 229
Autié, Léonard, 69–70
Avare, L' (Molière), 106, 174
Avariés, Les (Brieux), 224

Bachaumont, Louis Petit de, 7, 17, 22,
    28–9, 229
Bailly, Jean-Sylvain, 51–3, 75–7, 112
Balzac, Honoré de, 141, 177
Bankrupt, The (Björnson), 242
bankruptcy (of theatre directors), 161,
    174–5, 179
Banville, Théodore de, 199, 202
Barba, Jean-Nicolas, 100
Barbier de Séville, Le (Beaumarchais), 72
Baret, Charles, 150
Barnevald (Lemierre), 46
Baroche, Pierre-Jules, 220
Barras, Jean-Nicolas-Paul, 90–1

274

Barré, Pierre-Yon, 62, 101, 117, 129, 162
Barrière, Théodore, 198, 220
Barry, Mme du [Jeanne Bécu], 32
Basset, André-Alexandre, 161
Battus paient l'amende, Les (Dorvigny), 34–5
Baudelaire, Charles, 202
Baudrais, Jean-Baptiste, 95
Bayonne, 139, 141, 156
Beauharnais, Joséphine, *see* Joséphine (Bonaparte)
Beaujolais, Théâtre des, 37–8, 66, 87
Beaulieu [François Brémond de la Rochenard], 121
Beaumarchais, Pierre-Augustin Caron de, 40, 46, 49, 56, 62, 72, 90, 127, 226
Beaumont, Christophe de, 48–9
Beaunoir, *see* Robineau, abbé
Beauvais, 62
Beauvallet, Pierre-François, 231
Beauvau (theatre at Marseilles), 149
Beffroy de Reigny, Louis-Abel, 61
Belhomme, Dr, 85
Bellemont [J.-B. Colbert de Beaulieu], 84
Bellini, Vincenzo, 181
Belloy [Pierre-Laurent Buirette], 12, 130
Béranger, Pierre-Jean, 211
Béranger, René, 224
Bérard (director of the Nouveautés), 169, 185
Bergerat, Emile, 240
Berlioz, Hector, 170
Bernard (civil servant), 110
Bernhardt, Sarah, 162
Bernheim, Adrien, 241
Bernier de Maligny, Aristippe, 233
Berry, Charles-Ferdinand, duc de, 67, 177
Bertin d'Antilly, Louis-Auguste, 53
Bibliothèque Nationale, 62, 66–7
Björnson, Björnstjerne, 252
Blagdon, Francis, 108, 115
Blangini (composer), 169
Bluettes-Comiques, 55, 63
Bocage [Pierre-François Touzé-Bocage], 168, 183, 191, 231
Bonaparte, Lucien, 115, 204
Bonaparte, Napoleon, *see* Napoleon I
Bonneval [Jean-Jacques Gimat], 12
Bordeaux, 36, 49, 78, 137–9, 143–4, 146–7, 150, 152, 155–7, 159
Bouffé, Désiré-Marie, 135, 156, 232
Bouffes, Les, *see* Théâtre-Italien
Boule-Rouge, 230
Boulevard du Temple, 2, 27, 31, 33, 36, 62–3, 97, 117, 164, 168, 196, 202
Bourgeois gentilhomme, Le (Molière), 106

Bourgogne, Hôtel de, 7, 21–2
Bourgoin, Marie-Thérèse-Etienne, 90
Boursault-Malherbe [Jean-François Boursault], 118, 122, 178–9
Brazier, Nicolas, 197, 231
Brême, La (Méténier), 224
Brest, 141, 144
Brieux, Eugène, 224
Brisebarre, Edouard, 220
Britannicus (Racine), 95, 131
Brizard [Jean-Baptiste Britard], 11
Brohan, Suzanne, 183, 231
Brouette du vinaigrier, La (Mercier), 41
Brussels, 149
Brutus (Voltaire), 128
Buloz, François, 190

Caen, 137, 155, 161
Café d'Apollon, 122, 197–8
Café de la Paix, 198
Café des Aveugles, 197
Café Goddet, 197
Café Montansier, 198
Café Vivaux, 200
Café Yon, 196
cafés-concerts, 4, 195–8, 200–3; pre-revolutionary origins, 196–7; suppressed, 1807–15, 197; noisiness of, 196, 201; compared to music halls, 200–1; increase in numbers after 1864, 201–2
cafés-spectacles, 198–9
cafés in competition with theatres, 146
cahier des charges, 167, 171
Caillavet Maurois, Simone de, 229
Caillet (of the Comédie-Italienne), 227
Calendrier historique et chronologique des théâtres (periodical), 29
Caligula (Roman emperor), 214
Calonne, Charles-Alexandre de, 125–6
Cambacérès, Jean-Jacques Régis de, 120
Campan [Pierre-Dominique-François Berthollet], 18
cancan, 217
Candeille, Amélie-Julie, 97
Candide (Voltaire), 221
Carcassonne, 157
Carmouche, Pierre-Frédéric-Adolphe, 210
Carnot, Lazare-Nicolas, 67
Carr, John, 71
Castagnettes, Les (Cercle des arts intimes), 239
Castellane, Jules de, 235
Castries, Charles de La Croix, marquis de, 141

Catherine ou la Belle Fermière (Candeille), 97
Catherine the Great (of Russia), 46
Caussidière, Louis-Marc, 218
caution-money (required of theatre
 directors), 160-1
Cavé, Hygen-Auguste, 217-18
Céard, Henry, 240
Célestins, Théâtre des, 145, 152
Cellérier (director of the Opera), 68
censeurs de la police, 44-5, 48
censorship, of plays in Paris before the
 Revolution, 44-9, 124, 126; of plays in
 the provinces, 49; campaign for
 abolition of, 49-53; officially abolished
 (1791), 3, 53-4; censorship of plays
 during the Revolution, 93-100;
 reorganized by Napoleon, 3, 204;
 retained during Restoration, 134,
 208-11; suspended at July revolution,
 3, 136, 211; reintroduced (1835), 4,
 215; suspended (1848), 172, 218;
 reintroduced (1850), 220; suspended
 (1870-4), 221; finally abolished (1905),
 4, 224-5; staffing of censorship bureau,
 216-18; relations between censors and
 playwrights, 220-1; private theatricals
 not subject to censorship 226-7
censors' rehearsal, 222
Cercle Gaulois, 239-40
Cercle Pigalle, 237-9
Ces Messieurs (Ancey), 223
Chambon (de Montaux), Nicolas, 80-1
Champigny (Minister of the Interior),
 117-18, 144, 154
Changarnier, Gen. Nicolas, 219
Chapelier, *see* Le Chapelier
Chaptal, Jean-Antoine-Claude, 101
Charivari, Le (satirical paper), 201, 236
Charle, Christophe, 194, 243
Charlemagne (Lemercier), 206
Charles I (of England), 207
Charles II (of England), 57
Charles VI, 60, 208
Charles IX, 52
Charles IX (Chénier), 50-3, 73-5, 77
Charles X, 67, 177, 185, 187, 209-11, 235
Chartres, Louis-Philippe-Joseph, duc de,
 37-8, 227
Chaste Suzanne, La (Barré), 129, 199
Chaste Suzanne, La (Carmouche and
 Courcy), 171
Châtelet, Théâtre du, 175
Chatterton (Vigny), 189
Chaumette, Pierre-Gaspard, 65, 67-8
Chénier, André, 70-1

Chénier, Marie-Joseph, 50, 53, 56, 73, 75,
 78, 92, 114, 127
Chérier, Claude, abbé, 44
Chérubini, Salvador, 69, 170
child actors, 31-2, 37-8
Christophe Colomb (Lemercier), 206
Chronique de Paris (newspaper), 76
Cid, Le (Corneille), 78
Ciguë, La (Augier), 183
Cimarosa, Domenico, 69, 107
Cinna (Corneille), 135
Cirque Olympique, 209
civil list subsidies to theatres, 177, 185
Clairon, Mlle [Claire-Josèphe-Hippolyte
 Léris], 13-15, 103
claque, 136
Claretie, Jules, 110-11, 191, 221
Claudius (Roman emperor), 215
Clermont, 233
Clootz, Anacharsis, 113
Cogniard brothers (Hippolyte and
 Théodore), 237
Collé, Charles, 9-10, 49, 73, 124-5, 226-7
Collot d'Herbois, Jean-Marie, 50, 56, 67
Combes, Emile, 223
Comédie bourgeoise, La (L. F. Faur), 232
Comédie-Française, 2, 6-7, 10-16, 21-3, 28,
 33-5, 38-42, 44, 46, 48-52, 54, 56-9,
 61-2, 64, 69-79, 84, 87-90, 92, 101-6,
 110, 116-17, 122, 124, 126, 129-30,
 134, 147, 153, 156-7, 174, 176, 182-8,
 190-2, 195, 202, 206-7, 213, 221,
 226-8, 230-1, 235; origins, 7;
 subvention under *ancien régime*, 7-8;
 constitution of 1757, 8, 10; shares in,
 under *ancien régime*, 8; committees of,
 9-11; reserved repertoire ('the
 monopoly'), 6-7, 21, 33-4, 57, 59, 106,
 117; financial situation (1791-2), 77;
 political divisions within, 73; leading to
 its break up (1791-2), 78; arrest of the
 actors (1793), 84-6; reconstitution
 (1799), 90-1; *acte de dotation* and *acte de
 société* (1802-4), 103; financial crisis
 (1831-3), 186-8; on tour in the
 provinces (1868), 157
Comédie-Italienne, 10, 20-3, 26, 30, 35, 38,
 41, 53, 58-9, 62, 64, 68-70, 72-3, 105,
 153, 168, 180-1, 184-92, 227; origins,
 21; expulsion (1697) and return
 (1716), 21, 26; new theatre erected in
 Rue Favart, 23, 69, 107
Comédiens de bois, Les (Audinot), 31
comic (light) opera, 70, 150, 168-71, 180
Committee of Public Safety, 67, 83-4, 94-5

Commune (of Paris, 1792–4), 67–8, 80–3, 94

Conciliateur, Le (Demoustier), 80

Confiance trahie, La (Bret), 47

Conservatoire de musique, 170

Constituent Assembly, 94, 173

Consulate, 129, 133

Contagion, La (Augier), 157

Contat, Emilie, 85

Contat, Louise, 73–4, 77, 79, 85–6, 90

Convention (1792–5), 81–3, 113, 129

Coppée, François, 202

copyright in plays, 55, 59, 173–4

Corbière, Jacques-Joseph-Guillaume, 169

Corneille, Pierre, 57, 78, 142, 205

Cornélie, Antoinette, 202

costs of theatre-going, 195

Coudray, Alexandre-Jacques du, 58

Coupe et les lèvres, La (Musset), 239

Coureur de veuves, Le (Brisset and Blangini), 169

court performances, 10

Courteline [Georges Moineaux], 222

Couvent des Anglaises (prison), 85

Covent Garden theatre, 57

Cradock, Francesca, 140, 153

Crébillon, Claude-Prosper Jolyot de, 45

Crébillon, Prosper Jolyot de, 45

Crosnier, Louis-François, 161, 171

Cuisot, Henriette, 120

Curtius (waxwork showman), 35

Dame aux camélias, La (Dumas *fils*), 168

Danger des liaisons, Le (Robineau), 40

Danton, Georges-Jacques, 50–1, 81

Darcier [Joseph Lemaire], 200

Dauberval (dancer at the Opera), 19

Daudet, Alphonse, 202, 240

Daumier, Honoré, 236

David, Jacques-Louis, 93

David, Joseph-Narcisse, 183

Dazincourt [Joseph Albouy], 72–3, 79, 88, 90, 101, 227

Deburau, Jean-Gaspard, 193

Décadence (Guinon), 222

decrees and ordinances affecting the theatres: 13 January 1791, 55, 113–14, 117, 143, 173; 8 June 1806, 116, 121–2, 144, 160; 29 July 1807, 118, 122, 154, 231; 14 December 1816, 176–7; 21 July 1819, 182; 8 December 1824, 145, 162; 29 August 1847, 190; 6 January 1864, 162, 173–4; *see also* Moscow Decree

Dehesse, Jean-François, 38

Déjazet, Virginie, 162

Délassements-Comiques, 55–6, 60, 63, 122

Delaunay, Louis-Arsène, 191

Delavigne, Casimir, 187, 210, 232

Delrieu, Etienne, 105

Demoustier, Charles-Albert, 80

Dépit amoureux, Le (Molière), 174

Dernier jour de Tibère, Le (Arnault), 184

Déserteur, Le (Monsigny), 22

Des Essarts [Nicolas-Toussaint Lemoyne], 23–4, 76, 85

Desèze, Raymond, 129

Desgarcins, Louise, 73

Desmoulins, Camille, 50

Destranges, Etienne, 148

Devin de village, Le (Rousseau), 174

Diderot, Denis, 92

Didon (Lefranc de Pompignan), 128

Dieppe, 156

Dijon, 157

Directory, 67, 87–9, 98, 100, 108, 115–16, 119

Disraeli, Benjamin, 199

Doigny du Ponceau, 126

Don Carlos, Infant von Spanien (Schiller), 46

Don iovanni (Mozart), 181

Don Juan (Molière), 116, 183

Donizetti, Gaetano, 152, 171, 181

Dorat, Claude-Joseph, 45

Dorfeuille [Pierre Poupart], 36, 38, 60, 62–3, 78, 102, 144

Dorfeuille, Mme, 144

Dorval, Marie, 168, 184, 189

Dorvigny, Louis, 35, 41, 87

Douai, 141

Doucet, Camille, 202

Doyen (impresario), 230–3

Dreyfus Affair, 223

Drouin, Mlle [Françoise-Jeanne-Elisabeth Gaultier], 71

Drury Lane theatre, 57

Dubois, Jean, 194

Dubois [Louis Blouin], 12–14

Dubois, Marie [Marie-Madeleine Blouin], 12–13

Dubois-Crancé, Edmond-Louis-Alexis, 81

Duchâtel, Charles, 190

Ducis, Jean-François, 90, 178

Ducis, Paul-Auguste, 178–9

Dugazon [Jean-Baptiste Gourgaud], 73, 88, 90, 116

Dugazon, Mme (*née* Louise-Rosalie Lefèvre), 153

Dumas, Alexandre, 163, 172, 185–6, 211

Dumas *fils*, Alexandre, 168

Dumesnil, Mlle [Marie-Françoise Marchand], 71, 103
Dumouriez, Charles-François, 94
Dunkirk, 141, 144
Dupin, Henri, 121
Duplay (actor), 237
Dupré, Mme (theatre manager), 62
Duras, Emmanuel-Félicité de Durfort, duc de, 11
Duret, Théodore, 240
Dussane, Béatrix, 111
Duvernois, Henri, 238

Ecole des vieillards, L' (Delavigne), 187
Ecosseuses, Les (Taconet), 28
Egarements du cœur et de l'esprit, Les (Crébillon), 45
Eldorado (*café-concert*), 200–2
Elisabeth de France et Don Carlos (Le Fèvre), 46, 216
Emile (Rousseau), 48
Empis, Adolphe-Joseph-Simonis, 191
En famille (Méténier), 240
Enghien, Louis-Antoine-Henri de Bourbon-Condé, duc d', 133
English theatres, compared with French, 6
entertainment tax, 194
Eric-Bernard (director of the Odéon), 164
Ericie (Fontanelle), 48–9
Escholiers, Les, 239
Esménard, Joseph-Alphonse, 205
Estaminet-Lyrique, 199–200
Etats de Blois, Les (Raynouard), 207

Fabre, Paul, 237
Fabre d'Eglantine, Philippe, 50, 56
Fagan, Christophe, 31
fairground theatres, 26, 29
Fanfan et Colas (Robineau), 41
Faust (Nodier), 169, 184
Favart, Charles-Simon, 22
Favre, Jules, 219
fédérés, 65, 73–4
Fenouillet de Falbaire, Charles-Georges, 49
Ferdinand VII (of Spain), 134
Ferrières, Charles-Elie de, 127
Fête de la Fédération, 65, 73
Feuille du jour, La (newspaper), 61
Feuille du Salut public, La (newspaper), 83, 85
Feydeau, Georges, 229
Fieschi, Giuseppe, 4, 215
Figaro (newspaper), 170
Filles de marbre, Les (Barrière), 220
Fiorentino, Pier, 147, 173

fire, destruction of theatres by, 55, 66, 89, 105, 142, 177, 181–2
Flers, Robert de, 229
Fleury [Abraham-Joseph Bénard], 51, 72–5, 79–80, 83, 87–8, 104, 116, 228, 230
Foire aux idées, La (Leuven, Lhérie and Alhoy), 218
Fontanelle, Jean-Gaspard de, 48–9
Fontanes, Louis de, 206–7
For-l'Evêque, le (prison), 15, 19, 21, 85
Fort, Paul, 239
Foucauld, Vicomte de (army officer), 134
Fouché, Joseph, 129–30, 205–7
Francœur, François, 17, 68, 162
Francœur, Louis-Joseph, 68
François I, 213
Froidure (dramatic censor), 95
Fronsac, Louis-Antoine du Plessis, duc de, 13, 226
Fuchs, Max, 139
Funambules, Théâtre des, 193

Gaillard (theatre director), 36, 38, 60, 62–3, 78, 102, 144
Gaîté, Théâtre de la, 2, 60, 97, 117–18, 157, 167, 175, 184, 193
gambling-houses (taxed to support state theatres), 177
amins de Paris, Les (Clairville), 217
Gardénia (club), 237
Gardeur, Jean-Nicolas, 37
Garibaldi, Giuseppe, 219
Garnier, Charles, 238
Garrick, David, 118
aston et Bayard (Belloy), 130
âteau des Rois, Le (Gozlan), 221
Gautier, Théophile, 172, 184, 236, 238, 240
Gentlemen of the Bedchamber, 9–12, 15–17, 21, 31, 51–2, 72–3, 75–6, 104, 111, 115, 176, 235
Geoffroy, Julien-Louis, abbé, 115, 232
George, Mlle [Marguerite-Joséphine Weimer], 105, 183
eorges Dandin (Molière), 60
erminal (Zola), 223
hosts (Ibsen), 241
Giffard, Pierre, 1
Girardin, Emile de, 168
Girardin, Mme de (*née* Delphine Gay), 168
Girondins, 79, 82–3
Gobelins (tapestry manufactory), 177
Goethe, Johann Wolfgang, 184
Goldoni, Carlo, 27, 69, 83, 118
Goncourt brothers, 63, 201, 236

Goncourt, Edmond de, 202
Gondinet, Edmond, 198
Gossec, François, 65
Got, Edmond, 157, 174, 190–1
Goubaux, Prosper, 215
Gozlan, Léon, 216, 220
Grammont [Jean-Baptiste Nourry], 74
Gramont, duc de, 30
grand opera, 151, 180
Grand-Guignol, Théâtre du, 224, 240
Grand-Théâtre (Bordeaux), 138, 143–4, 147, 155, 157
Grand-Théâtre (Lyons), 145, 150, 152
Grand-Théâtre (Marseilles), 151
Grandmaison, Millin de, 60
Grandmesnil [Jean-Baptiste Fauchard], 73
Grands Danseurs du Roi, Les, 29, 33
Grenoble, 139
Grétry, André-Ernest-Modeste, 22, 131
Grimm, Frédéric-Melchior, baron de, 46–8, 56, 58, 124
Grimod de la Reynière, Balthazar, 142
Grisi, Giulia, 181
Gromer (machinist), 232
Guénégaud, Théâtre, 7
Guernsey, 156
Guéroult, François, 138
Guilbert, Yvette, 202
uillaume Tell (Lemierre), 97
Guimard, Marie-Madeleine, 18–19, 72, 226–7, 235
Guinon, Albert, 222–3
Guiraud, Alexandre, 184
Guizot, François, 163
Gustavus III (of Sweden), 78
Guyenne, 138
Gymnase (theatre at Marseilles), 149
Gymnase-Dramatique, Théâtre du, 2, 156, 160, 167–8, 174, 186, 193, 236

Hadrian (Roman emperor), 93
Halévy, Ludovic, 121, 131, 180, 198
Hallays-Dabot, Victor, 95
Hamlet (Shakespeare), 178, 209
Hapdé, Augustin, 119–20
Harel, François-Antoine, 214
Haymarket theatre, 57
Hébert, Jacques-René, 65, 67, 80
Heine, Heinrich, 212
Hennique, Léon, 240
Henri III et sa cour (Dumas), 185–6
Henri IV, 124, 130
Héraclius (Corneille), 205
Hernani (Hugo), 186, 213
Hérold, Ferdinand, 179

Hervey, Charles, 217
Hoffmann, François-Benoît, 93–4
Homme à l'oreille coupée, L', (Wiener), 224
Homme dangereux, L' (Palissot), 47
Honnête Criminel, L' (Fenouillot de Falbaire), 49
Horace (Corneille), 135
Hostcin, Hippolyte, 171, 218, 221
Hôtel de Bourgogne (housing Comédie-Italienne), 7, 21–2
Houssaye, Arsène, 191, 235
Hugo, Victor, 135, 163, 170, 172, 186, 206, 210, 213, 219

Ibsen, Henrik, 239, 241
Il était une fois un roi et une reine (Gozlan), 216
Imprimerie Nationale, 177
imprisonment of actors, 12–16, 54, 83–6, 144, 211
inspector of plays (attached to censorship bureau), 222
Institut de France, 206
intendant des Menus, 10, 111
Intrigues de cour (Jouy), 210
Iphigénie (Racine), 130
Isaure (Cornu, Antier, and Nézel), 170
Italian opera, 107, 181
itinerant theatre companies, 25

Jacobins, 54, 62, 70, 79–80, 82–3, 85, 89, 98, 129
Jacques Damour (Hennique), 240
Janin, Jules, 95
Jardin Biron, 98
Jenny (Saint-Georges), 170
Jérôme Pointu (Beaunoir), 35
Jersey, 156
Jesuits, plays performed at their schools, 228
Jeux-Forains, Les, 121
Joanny [Jean-Bernard Brissebarre], 183–4, 186
Joly, Anténor, 163, 166, 170–1
Joly, Marie-Elisabeth, 86
Joséphine (Bonaparte), 131
Journal de la Montagne (newspaper), 96
Journal de l'Empire (newspaper), 205
Journée d'élection, Une (La Ville de Mirmont), 210
Jouslin de la Salle, Armand, 189–90
Jouy, Etienne de, 134, 158, 209–10, 233
Jugement dernier des rois, Le (Maréchal), 97
Julien dans les aules (Jouy), 209–10
July Monarchy, 136, 163

Kemble, John Philip, 6
King Lear (Shakespeare), 178, 221, 242
Kock, Paul de, 132, 234
Kotzebue, August von, 118
Krakovitch, Odile, 220
Krauss (ex-army officer), 240–1

Labiche, Eugène, 198
Lablache, Luigi, 181
Laclos, Pierre Choderlos de, 40
Lacombe, Jean-Baptiste, 144
Lacretelle, Jean de, 217
Lady from the Sea (Ibsen), 239
Lady Melvil (Saint-Georges and Leuven), 171
La Fort, J. de, 88
Lagrave, Henri, 58
La Harpe, Jean-François de, 19, 46, 58–9, 66
Laloue, Ferdinand, 135, 219–20
Lange, Elisabeth, 74, 85
Langlois (manager of the Nouveautés), 212–13
La Rive [Jean Mauduit], 77, 153
La Rochefoucauld, Sosthène de, 178, 185
La Rochelle, 141
Lasalle, Albert de, 109
La Ville de Mirmont,
    Alexandre-Jean-Joseph de, 210
Laya, Jean-Louis, 79–82, 90, 92
Lazzari, Théâtre de, 63
Lebrun, Pierre, 133
Le Chapelier, Isaac-René-Gui, 92
Lécluse de Thilloy, Louis, 33–4, 61
Lefèvre (dramatist), 216
Lefranc de Pompignan, *see* Pompignan
Legouvé, Gabriel-Marie-Jean-Baptiste, 90, 130
Legrand, Marc-Antoine, 12
Legras, Capt., 198–9
Legs, Le (Marivaux), 187
Le Havre, 141
Lekain [Henri-Louis Caïn], 11, 13–15, 34, 153, 230
Lemaître, Frédérick [Antoine-Louis-Prosper Lemaître], 156, 174, 183, 191
Lemaître, Jules, 239
Lemercier, Népomucène, 205–6, 208
Lemercier (coal-merchant), 34
Lemierre, Antoine-Marin, 46, 97
Lenoir, Jean-Charles-Pierre, 29
Lenoir, Samson-Nicolas, 66, 120–1
Lesage, Alain-René, 228
Le Senne, Charles, 223
Lhomme, F., 150

L'Hospital, comte de, 139
Liaisons dangereuses, Les, 40
licensing system, 3–4, 160–73
Ligne, Charles-Joseph, prince de, 228
Lille, 144–5, 149, 155, 159
Limodin (secretary of central police bureau), 100
Lirieux, Auguste, 183
Lohengrin (Wagner), 151
Lornaizon, Clément de, 55–6
Louis XIII, 37, 210
Louis XIV, 1–2, 7–8, 21, 37, 43, 57, 59, 69, 110–11, 116, 177, 208, 235
Louis XV, 8, 21, 32, 35, 45, 49, 71, 73, 111, 124
Louis XVI, 19–20, 38, 60, 79, 128–9, 134, 176, 227
'Louis XVII', 176
Louis XVIII, 67, 69, 160, 176–7, 182, 208
Louis-Philippe, 187, 212, 214–15
Louis, Victor, 138
Lubbert, Emile-Timothée, 179
Lucia di Lammermoor (Donizetti), 171
Lucrèce (Ponsard), 183
Lugné-Poë, Aurélien-François, 243
Lully, Jean-Baptiste, 16–17
Lycée-Dramatique, 60
Lyons, 49, 50, 137–8, 142, 144–5, 147, 150, 152–3, 157, 159

Macbeth (Shakespeare), 178
Madame de Valois (Kock), 132
Madelonnettes (prison), 85
Maeterlinck, Maurice, 243
Mahérault, Jean-François-Régis, 90, 103, 110
Mahomet (Voltaire), 45
Maillard, Mlle (ballet dancer), 65
Maintenon, Françoise d'Aubigné, marquise de, 21
Maison du baigneur, La (Maquet), 151
Malesherbes, Chrétien-Guillaume de Lamoignon de, 18
Mallet, Compagnie, 178, 180
Malliot, A. L., 161
managers of provincial theatres, 145–6
Mansfield Park (Austen), 229
Manuel, Jacques-Antoine, 134
Maquet, Auguste, 151
Marais, Théâtre du, 232
Marat, Jean-Paul, 80
Marchand d'amour, Le (Carmouche), 210
Maréchal, Sylvain, 97
Mariage de Figaro, Le (Beaumarchais), 35, 46, 49, 53, 73, 127, 186, 226

Marie-Antoinette, Queen, 4, 67, 69, 72, 96, 128, 227
Marie-Louise (of Austria), 131
Marin, Louis, 45, 48
Marino Falieri (Delavigne), 210
Marion de Lorme (Hugo), 186, 210
Marivaux, Pierre Carlet de, 22, 58, 97, 187
Mars, Mlle [Anne-Françoise Hippolyte Boutet], 90, 188
Marseillaise, La, 65
Marseilles, 144, 146–7, 149 54, 156–7, 200
Martainville, Alphonse, 100
Martignac, Jean-Baptiste Gay, vicomte de, 210
masked balls, theatres used for, 20, 141, 166
Matrimonio segreto, Il (Cimarosa), 107
Matthews, Brander, 191, 200
Maurice, Charles, 230
Maury, abbé Jean-Suffrein, 54
Mayeur de Saint-Paul, François-Marie, 30, 144, 196–7
Mazzini, Giuseppe, 219
Mécontents, Les (Mérimée), 239
Médecin malgré lui, Le (Molière), 60
Méhul, Etienne-Nicolas, 93
Meister, Jacques-Henri, 35, 41, 58, 124
Mélingue [Etienne Marin], 191
melodrama, 150, 167–8, 185, 193
Menzicoff (La Harpe), 46
Mercier, Louis-Sébastien, 39, 41, 56–7, 92, 142–3, 158, 229
Mère coupable, La (Beaumarchais), 62
Mérimée, Prosper, 239
Merlin (de Douai), Philippe-Antoine, 88–9
Mérope (Voltaire), 96, 133
Méténier, Oscar, 224, 240
Métra, François, 16, 40, 42, 196
Métromanie, La (Piron), 6
Metz, 141, 156
Meyerbeer, Giacomo, 152, 170
Mézeray, Joséphine, 85
Michelot, Théodore, 188, 235
Michu, Louis, 72
Millin de Grandmaison, Aubin-Louis, 60
Mirabeau, Honoré-Gabriel Riquietti, comte de, 74, 92
Mirlitons, Club des, 237
Misanthrope, Le (Molière), 95, 189
Miss Julie (Strindberg), 241
Molé, François-René, 13–14, 28, 79, 84, 95, 230
Molière [Jean-Baptiste Poquelin], 6, 8, 14, 21, 56–8, 60, 69, 91, 95–7, 106, 111, 116, 174, 183, 187, 228
Moniteur, Le (newspaper), 83

Monnet, Jean, 22
Monrose, Louis, 191
Monsigny, Pierre-Alexandre, 22
Montalivet, Camille, 170–1, 215
Montansier, Mlle [Marguerite Brunet], 60–2, 66–7, 86–7, 96, 107, 117, 119–20, 150, 162
Montesquiou-Fezensac, abbé François-Xavier, duc de, 160
Montesson, Charlotte-Jeanne Béraud de la Haie de Riou, marquise de, 71, 227, 235
Montpellier, 137, 144, 156
Monvel, Jacques-Marie Boutet de, 78, 90
Moore, John, 123, 140
Morel (director of the Théâtre des Arts, Rouen), 188
Mort de César, La (Voltaire), 97, 128
Mort de Socrate, La (Sauvigny), 48
Moscow Decree, 110–11, 176
Mozart, Wolfgang Amadeus, 151, 181
Muette de Portici, La (Auber), 210
Muret, Théodore, 219
Musard, Philippe, 166
Musset, Alfred de, 219, 221, 239
Mussot, Jean-François, 31–2
Mystères des théâtres (Goncourt and Holff), 201

Nancy, 156
Nanine (Voltaire), 58
Nantes, 138, 142, 144, 147–8, 152, 159
Napoleon I, 3, 102–12, 115–16, 119–22, 129–34, 153, 160, 166, 171, 176–7, 197, 204–12, 217
Napoleon III, 3, 173
Naudet, Jean-Baptiste, 73–4, 77
Navigation, La (Esménard), 205
Necker, Jacques, 123–5
Neerwinden, battle of, 94
Nerval, Gérard de [Gérard Labrunie], 168
Neufchâteau, François de, 54, 83
Ney, Marshal Michel, 212
Nice, 144, 157
Nicodème dans la Lune (Beffroy de Reigny), 61
Nicolet, François-Paul, 27
Nicolet, Jean-Baptiste, 2, 27–31, 35–6, 38–9, 55, 60, 63, 70, 97, 117, 144
Nièce vengée, La (Fagan), 31
Noces houzardes, Les (Dorvigny), 41
Nodier, Charles, 167, 184
Nœuville [Honoré Bourdon], 67
Nogaret, Félix, 204
Notables, Assembly of, 125–6

Nouveautés, Théâtre des, 169–70, 173, 180, 185, 212–13
Nouveaux-Troubadours, Théâtre des, 122
Nuit bergamasque, La (Bergerat), 240

Oberkirch, Henriette-Louise d', 35, 227
Observations sur les spectacles (Amaury-Duval), 114
Odéon, Théâtre de l', 6, 88–9, 104–7, 135, 157, 161, 177, 182–4, 206, 208–9, 214, 242–3; rebuilt (1807–8) after earlier destruction by fire, 106; subventions under Restoration, 182; remoteness from main theatre complex, 182–3
Offrande à la Liberté (Gossec), 65
Olympia (*café-concert*), 195
On ne badine pas avec l'amour (Musset), 221
Opera, 10, 16–21, 23, 29, 32, 34, 36, 38, 42, 64, 73, 86, 93, 105, 107–10, 117, 122, 147, 160, 162, 165, 170–1, 173, 179–81; internal organization of, under *ancien régime*, 17–21; new building at Porte-Saint-Martin (1781), 66, 119; move to Théâtre National (1794), 67, 119; rehoused after 1820, 177; fees exacted from minor theatres, 33, obtains monopoly of theatre licences (1784), 36; subventions granted under Directory, 68, and under Consulate and Empire, 108–9; partly supported (after 1811) by tax on places of entertainment, 109–10.
Opéra-Comique, 27–8, 30–1, 70–1, 104–5, 117, 122, 131, 147, 161, 169–71, 173, 176–81; taken over (1762) by Comédie-Italienne, 22, 26; reconstituted (1800) by merger of the Favart and Feydeau theatres, 71, 105; subventions allocated by Napoleon, 105; repertoire disputes with the Nouveautés, 169–70, and with the Renaissance, 170–1; subvention during Restoration and July Monarchy, 178–80
operetta, 117
Ophis (Lemercier), 205
Orléans, Louis-Philippe d', 37, 46, 102
Orléans, Louis-Philippe-Joseph d' (Philippe-Egalité), 102
Orléans, Philippe d', 37, 72
Othello (Shakespeare), 178

Paesiello, Giovanni, 69, 125
Palais du Luxembourg, 106
Palais-Royal, 2, 36–7, 60–1, 66, 120–1, 197

Palais-Royal, Théâtre du, 167, 188, 191, 193, 198
Palissot de Montenoy, Charles, 47
Paméla (Neufchâteau), 83–4
Pamela (Richardson), 83
Pamela nubile (Goldoni), 83
Panama Canal Company, 194
Panorama-Dramatique, Théâtre du, 135, 164, 167
Panthéon, Théâtre du, 164
pantomime, 32, 193
pantomimes dialoguées, 32
pantomimes nationales, 28
Papillon de la Ferté, Denis-Pierre-Jean, 10–14, 39, 42, 72, 176
Partie de chasse de Henri IV, La (Collé), 49, 73, 124–5, 226
Paulus [Jean-Paul Hubens], 200, 202
Peau d'âne (Hapdé), 157
Peau de chagrin, La (Balzac), 177
Pélagie (prison), 85
Pelléas et Mélisande (Maeterlinck), 243
pensionnaires (at state theatres), 9, 30, 156, 188, 191
Père Duchesne, Le (newspaper), 67
Perpignan, 156
Perrier, Antoine, 183, 188
Perrin, Emile, 191
Perrin, Pierre, 16
Pétion, Jérôme, 81, 94
Petit-Bourbon, Théâtre du, 7, 21
Petit-Lazari, Théâtre du, 193
Petits-Beaujolais, 61
Phèdre (Racine), 186
Philippe-Egalité, *see* Orléans, Louis-Philippe-Joseph d'
Philippe le Bel, 27, 206
Philosophe sans le savoir, Le (Sedaine), 45
Picard, Louis-Benoît, 108
Piedmont, 144
Piis, Pierre-Antoine-Augustin, 62, 101, 117, 162
Piron, Alexis, 6
Pius IX, Pope, 218
Plancher-Valcour, Philippe-Alexandre, 55, 96, 122
Plunkett, Jacques de, 193
police supervision of fairground theatres, 26
Pompadour, Mme de [Jeanne-Antoinette Poisson], 17, 71
Pompignan, Jean-Jacques Lefranc, marquis de, 128
Ponsard, François, 183
Pontons anglais, Les (Sue and Goubaux), 215

Porte-Saint-Martin, Théâtre de la, 117, 119–20, 122, 160, 167, 174–5, 184, 186, 193–4, 199, 219
Potier [Gabriel Potier de Cailletières], 56
Powers of Darkness, The (Tolstoy), 241
Presse, La (newspaper), 168
Préville [Pierre-Louis Dubus], 34, 38
Prévost, Augustin, 122
privileged (protected) repertoires, 106, 117, 119
Procès d'un maréchal de France, Le (Fontan and Dupeuty), 212–13, 218
Propriété, c'est le vol, La (Clairville and Vaulabelle), 218
Proudhon, Pierre-Joseph, 218
Proust, Antonin, 223
Proust, Marcel, 229
Provence, Comte de, *see* Louis XVIII
provincial theatre directors, 148–9, 152
provincial tours (by Paris actors), 153–8
Provost, Jean-Baptiste-François, 183, 191
Pujoulx, Jean-Baptiste, 113
puppet shows, 31, 37
Puvis de Chavannes, Pierre, 236
Pyat, Félix, 214

Quatremère de Quincy [Antoine Chrysostome Quatremère], 216

Rabouilleuse, La (Balzac), 141
Rachel [Elisabeth Félix], 135, 156, 190–1
Racine, Jean, 57, 78, 95, 116, 130–1, 134, 186, 202, 205
railways (affecting theatre audiences), 136, 149, 156–8
Raucourt, Mlle [Françoise Saucerotte], 73–4, 77, 87–8, 130
Raynouard, François, 206–7
Re Teodoro, Il (Paesiello), 125
Rebel, François, 17, 162
Réclamations contre l'emprunt, Les (Dorvigny), 87
Regent, during Louis XIII's minority (Philip II of Orleans), 21, 23, 37
Regnard, Jean-François, 21, 57
Régulus (Arnault), 134
Reichardt, Johann Friedrich, 71, 115, 126
Réjane [Gabrielle Réju], 162
Religieuses danoises, Les (Bertin d'Antilly), 53
Rémusat, Auguste-Laurent de, 104, 110, 116, 131
Rémusat, Claire-Elisabeth de, 116–17, 129, 205
Renaissance, Théâtre de la, 162, 166, 170–1, 173, 216

repertoires of minor theatres, 39–40; supervised by major theatres, 38–41
Restoration (period), 133, 176
retirement pensions (payable to *sociétaires* at the Comédie-Française), 103
Révolution d'autrefois, Une (Pyat), 214
Révolutions de Paris (newspaper), 53
revue, 236–7, 239
Ribié, Louis-François, 63
Richardson, Samuel, 83
Richelieu, Jean-Armand du Plessis, cardinal-duc de, 36
Richelieu, Louis-François du Plessis, duc de, 11, 13–14, 73, 137–9
Rigoletto (Verdi), 181
Robespierre, Maximilien de, 67–8, 80, 84, 86, 94–5, 98, 144
Robineau, Alexandre-Louis-Bertrand, abbé, 28–9, 35, 39, 41
Roi s'amuse, Le (Hugo), 213
Rome (Laloue), 219–20
Rome sauvée (Voltaire), 35
Root-Bernstein, Michèle, 60
Rosalba (*café-concert* singer), 197
Rose et Colas (Monsigny), 22
Rouen, 49, 138, 140, 144–5, 150, 153–4, 157, 159, 188
Roujon, Henry, 224
Rousseau, Jean-Jacques, 48, 174
Rouvière, Philibert, 191
Rubini, Giovanni-Battista, 181
Ruy Blas (Hugo), 163

Sageret (impresario), 88–9
Saint-Germain (fair), 26, 62, 70
Saint-Huberty, Mme de [Antoinette-Cécile Clavel], 153
Saint-Laurent (fair), 26, 30
Saint-Ovide (fair), 26, 39
St Petersburg, 7, 85, 105
Saint-Prix [Jean-Amable Foucault], 74
Saint-Quentin, 139
Saint-Saëns, Camille, 151
Sainval aînée [Marie-Pauline-Christine d'Alziari de Roquefort], 103
Sainval cadette [Marie-Blanche d'Alziari de Roquefort], 231
Sallé, Louis-Gabriel, 33–4, 63
Salle des Machines, 70
Salle Favart, 181
Salle Feydeau, 177
Salle Olympique, 107
Salle Ventadour, 178–81
Samson, Joseph-Isidore, 183, 188, 231
Samson et Dalila (Saint-Saëns), 151

Sand, George [Lucile-Aurore Dupin], 234–5
Santerre, Antoine-Joseph, 82
Saqui, Mme [Marguerite Lalanne], 197
Sarcey, Francisque, 192, 240
Sardou, Victorien, 195, 221
Sartine, Gabriel de, 45
Saurin, Bernard-Joseph, 75
Sauvigny, Louis-Edmé Billardin de, 45–6, 48
Scala (*café-concert*), 203
Schiller, Friedrich, 46, 184
Schulz, Friedrich, 197
Scott, John, 121
Scribe, Eugène, 168, 172, 187
second national theatre, agitation for, 57–9, 106
Sedaine, Michel-Jean, 45, 56, 92
Sémiramis (Voltaire), 130
Seveste, Edmond, 191
Sèvres (porcelain manufactory), 35, 129, 177
Shakespeare, William, 57, 178, 184, 209
Sheridan, Richard Brinsley, 118
Siddons, Sarah, 6
Siège de Calais, Le (Belloy), 12–14
Sieyès, Emmanuel-Joseph, abbé, 24
Smollett, Tobias, 123
sociétaires (at state theatres), 8–9, 12, 20, 30, 72, 74, 76, 90, 103, 154, 187–91, 228, 231
sociétés bourgeoises (amateur drama clubs), 230–1, 237
Sophocles, 126
Soubise, Charles de Rohan, prince de, 73
Souvestre, Emile, 172
Spartacus (Saurin), 75
Spectacles de Paris (journal), 65
Stendhal [Henri Beyle], 107, 210
Stockholm, 78
Strasbourg, 141–2, 144, 153
Strindberg, August, 241
strolling players, 25–6, 137
Suard, Jean-Baptiste-Antoine, 45, 47, 52
subventions (granted to provincial theatre directors), 145–50
Sue, Eugène, 215
Sully, Maximilien de Béthune, duc de, 124–5
summer excursions (by Parisian actors to the provinces), 157–8
surintendant général des spectacles, 104, 111
Surprise de l'amour, La (Marivaux), 58
Sybil (Disraeli), 199
Sylla (Jouy), 134

Tableau parlant, Le (Grétry and Anseaume), 22, 131
Taconet, Toussaint-Gaspard, 28, 39
Talleyrand-Périgord, Charles-Maurice de, 216
Talma, François-Joseph, 73–8, 87–9, 92, 116, 131, 133–4, 155–6, 184, 230–1
Tamburini, Antonio, 181
Tarare (Beaumarchais), 127
Tartuffe (Molière), 86, 95, 174, 189
Taylor, Isidore-Séverin-Justin, baron, 164, 167
Templiers, Les (Raynouard), 206–7
Théagène et Chariclée (Dorat), 45
theatre licences, duration of, 161; transmission of, 161; holders nominated by state, 162–3; required for *café-concerts*, 198
Théâtre-Antoine, 224, 242
Théâtre-Beaumarchais, 222
Théâtre Carlotti, 233
Théâtre d'Art, 239
Théâtre de la Cité, 120–1
Théâtre de la Concorde, 61
Théâtre de la Liberté, 61
Théâtre de la Montagne (Bordeaux), 144
Théâtre de la Nation, 44, 64, 75, 78–81, 83–4, 86, 94, 105, 128
Théâtre de la République (Bordeaux), 144
Théâtre de la République (Paris), 62, 78, 86–90, 97
Théâtre de la rue Feydeau, *see* Théâtre Feydeau
Théâtre de l'Egalité, 86–8
Théâtre de l'Impératrice, 106
Théâtre de l'Œuvre, 243
Théâtre de l'Opéra-Comique National, 64
Théâtre de Monsieur, 60, 69–70, 105
Théâtre de société (Collé), 227
Théâtre d'Emulation, 61, 231
Théâtre des Arts (Paris Opera), 64, 93
Théâtre des Arts (Rouen), 138, 150–1, 188
Théâtre des Associés, 33, 41, 55, 63
Théâtre des Jeunes-Artistes, 100, 116, 122
Théâtre des Menus-Plaisirs, 241–2
Théâtre du Capitole (Toulouse), 151
Théâtre du Marais, 62, 96
Théâtre du Mont-Parnasse, 61
Théâtre du Palais-Variétés, 121
Théâtre Favart, 71, 107
Théâtre Feydeau, 70–1, 87–9, 105, 129, 178
Théâtre-Français (Bordeaux), 144
Théâtre-Français (Paris), 44, 60, 72, 90, 106, 120, 122, 123–6, 128, 133, 184–91, 206, 210, 228, 236

Théâtre-Français Comique et Lyrique, 61, 63
Théâtre Graslin, 138, 148
Théâtre-Historique, 218
Théâtre-Italien, 27, 35, 108, 181
Théâtre Jean-Jacques Rousseau, 61
Théâtre-Libre, 5, 240–2
Théâtre Louvois, 87–8, 105
Théâtre Lyrique, 175
Théâtre Mareux, 232
Théâtre Molière (Bordeaux), 143
Théâtre Molière (Paris), 60, 118
Théâtre-Montparnasse, 241
Théâtre National (de la Rue de la Loi), 66, 86–7, 96, 107
Théâtre-Patriotique, 60, 63
Théâtre sans Prétention, 122, 197
Théâtre-Saqui, 198
théâtres bourgeois, 232
théâtres d'application (drama schools), 230–1
théâtres de salon, 229
théâtres de société, 232–3
théâtres forains, 2, 24
Thérésa [Thérèse Valadon], 200
Thierry, Edouard, 191
Thierry (theatre proprietor), 232
Thiers, Adolphe, 189
Thrale, Mrs Hester Lynch, 27
Tivoli, 98
Tolstoy, L. N., 241
Tonnelier, Le (Audinot), 30
Toulon, 141, 152, 157
Toulouse, 137, 144, 151, 153, 155–6
Toulouse-Lautrec, Henri de, 202
Triomphe du temps, Le (Legrand), 12
Trois Frères rivaux, Les (La Fort), 88
Trois théâtres de Paris, Les (Des Essarts), 23
Trollope, Frances, 189
Trovatore, Il (Verdi), 181
Turco (monkey at Nicolet's theatre), 28
Turin, 144

Valcour, Aristide, *see* Plancher-Valcour
Valérie (Scribe), 187
Valmy, battle of, 65
Vanhove, Caroline (Mme Petit-Vanhove), 86, 89
Vanhove, Charles-Joseph, 86, 230
Variétés-Amusantes, 2, 33, 35–6, 38–9, 41, 56, 61, 121, 167–8, 186, 237

Variétés Comiques et Lyriques, 62
Variétés-Etrangères, 117–18, 122
Variétés-Palais-Royal (Variétés Montansier), 38, 62, 90, 117–18, 120–2, 198
vaudeville, 101, 167–71, 185
Vaudeville, Théâtre du, 2, 62, 117–18, 129, 162, 167–8, 193, 217–18
Védel, A. L. P., 190
Vénitiens, Les (Arnault), 209
Ventadour, *see* Salle Ventadour
Vêpres siciliennes, Les (Delavigne), 186, 232
Verdi, Giuseppe, 151–2, 181
Verrières sisters (Marie and Geneviève Rinteau), 235
Versailles, Théâtre de, 31, 49, 61, 66, 125
Verteuil, Armand, 146
Vert-Vert (newspaper), 163
Vestris, Gaetano, 19
Vestris, Mlle [Françoise-Rose Gourgaud], 73–4
Victoria, Queen, 32, 216
Vienne, Nicolas, 33
Vigny, Alfred de, 189
Villemot (journalist), 236
Villeneuve, Ferdinand de, 170
Viotti, Giovanni Battista, 69–70
Virginie (Guiraud), 184
Vismes, Jacques de, 18–20
Vitu, Auguste, 240
Volange [Maurice-François Rochet], 35
Voltaire [François-Marie Arouet], 15, 33, 35, 45, 56–8, 96–7, 128–30, 133, 153, 205, 221

Wagner, Richard, 151
Walter (theatre manager at Rouen), 145
Weiss, Jean-Jacques, 193
Wiener [F. de Croisset], 225
wigs (worn on stage), 10–11
Wild Duck, The (Ibsen), 241
women forbidden to manage theatres, 162–3

Young, Arthur, 6, 229

Zaïre (Voltaire), 33
Zampa (Hérold), 179
Zémire et Azor (Grétry), 22
Zola, Emile, 223, 240